THE CHRONIC MENTALLY ILL

THE CHRONIC MENTALLY ILL
Treatment, Programs, Systems

Edited by

John A. Talbott, M.D.

Professor of Psychiatry
Cornell University Medical College
New York City, N.Y.

Associate Medical Director
The Payne Whitney Psychiatric Clinic
The New York Hospital
New York City, N.Y.

HUMAN SCIENCES PRESS
72 Fifth Avenue   3 Henrietta Street
NEW YORK, NY 10011 ● LONDON, WC2E 8LU

Copyright © 1981 by Human Sciences Press, Inc.
72 Fifth Avenue, New York, New York 10011

Printed in the United States of America
123456789 987654321

Library of Congress Cataloging in Publication Data

Main entry under title:

The Chronic mentally ill.

Includes index.
1. Mentally ill-Care and treatment—United
States.   2. Mentally ill—Care and treatment.
I. Talbott, John A. [DNLM: 1. Chronic disease. 2. Mental disorders.
3.Mental health services—United States.   WM30 C557]
RC443.C5   362.2'0973   LC 80-24874
ISBN 0-87705-086-4

CONTENTS

CONTRIBUTORS

ARTHUR L. ARNOLD, M.D., is Chief, Psychiatry Service, Veterans Administration Medical Center, Tacoma, Washington, and was formerly Deputy Commissioner for Planning and Program Development, New York State Department of Mental Hygiene, Albany, New York.

LEONA L. BACHRACH, Ph.D., is Research Sociologist, Maryland Psychiatric Research Center, Catonsville, Maryland, and Associate Professor, Department of Psychiatry, University of Maryland School of Medicine, Baltimore, Maryland.

DOUGLAS R. BEY, JR., M.D., F.A.P.A., is in the private practice of psychiatry in Normal, Illinois, and a Clinical Associate, University of Illinois College of Medicine, Champaign, Illinois.

CLARENCE BOYD, M.S.W., is Director of Clinical Management Services, Dorothea Dix Hospital, and in private practice, and was formerly Regional Social Work Consultant, North Carolina Department of Mental Health, Raleigh, North Carolina.

GEORGE W. BROOKS, M.D., is Professor of Clinical Psychiatry, University of Vermont, College of Medicine, Burlington, and Superintendent, Vermont State Hospital, Waterbury, Vermont.

RICHARD D. BUDSON, M.D., is Assistant Professor of Psychiatry, Harvard Medical School; Director, Community Residential Services; and Associate Psychiatrist, McLean Hospital, Belmont, Massachusetts.

ROBERT E. CHAPMAN, M.D., is in the private practice of psychiatry in Normal, Illinois, and a Clinical Associate, University of Illinois College of Medicine, Champaign, Illinois.

JOHN E. CROWDER, M.D., is Deputy Director, Orange County Mental Health Services, and Associate Adjunct Professor, Department of Psychiatry and Human Behavior, University of California at Irvine, California.

JERRY DINCIN, Ph.D., is Executive Director, Thresholds, Chicago, Illinois.

GLADYS EGRI, M.D., is Associate Director for Rehabilitation Services, Department of Psychiatry, Harlem Hospital Center, and Assistant Clinical Professor of Psychiatry, College of Physicians and Surgeons, Columbia University, New York, New York.

CHARLES M. GAITZ, M.D., is Head, Patient Care Division and Department of Applied Research, Texas Research Institute of Mental Sciences, and Clinical Professor of Psychiatry, Baylor College of Medicine, Houston, Texas.

JACK GREENSPAN, M.D., is Director of Quality Assurance Program and President of the Medical Staff, The Institute of Pennsylvania Hospital, and Associate Clinical Professor of Psychiatry, University of Pennsylvania School of Medicine, Philadelphia, Pennsylvania.

SAMUEL GROB, Ph.D., is Executive Director, The Center House, Inc., and Associate Clinical Professor, Department of Psychiatry, Tufts University School of Medicine, Boston, Massachusetts.

NORRIS HANSELL, M.D., is Professor of Psychiatry, Northwestern University Medical School, Chicago, Illinois, and Attending Physician, Mercy Hospital, Urbana, and Veterans Administration Hospital, Danville, Illinois.

MARY J. HONAKER, R.N., is Administrator, Alternative Services Division, South Central Montana Regional Mental Health Center, Billings, Montana.

BRYCE G. HUGHETT, M.D., is Director, South Central Montana Regional Mental Health Center, Billings, Montana.

CYNTHIA JOHANSEN is Chief of Clinical Pharmacy for five Kings View community mental health centers (located in Tulare and Kings counties), Tulare County Substance Program, and Kings View Hospital in Reedley, California.

ERNEST W. KLATTE, M.D., is Chief of Professional Education and Clinical Professor of Psychiatry, Department of Psychiatry and Human Behavior, University of California at Irvine, California.

ROBERT A. KOOKER, M.D., is in the private practice of psychiatry in Normal, Illinois, and a Clinical Associate, University of Illinois College of Medicine, Champaign, Illinois.

SYDNEY KORET, Ph.D., is Director, Convalescent Hospital for Children, and Clinical Associate Professor (Psychiatry), University of Rochester, School of Medicine and Dentistry, Rochester, New York.

ALAN M. KRAFT, M.D., is Professor and Chairman, Department of Psychiatry, Albany Medical College, Albany, New York.

R. T. KRAUS is Chairman, Statewide Conference of Private Mental Health Facilities, California Association of Health Facilities, and Administrator, Crestwood Manor–Sacramento and Crestwood Manor–Carmichael, skilled nursing facilities for the mentally disordered, California.

H. RICHARD LAMB, M.D., is Associate Professor of Psychiatry and Director, Division of Community Psychiatric Services, Department of Psychiatry, University of Southern California, School of Medicine, Los Angeles, California.

LINDA G. MUSHKATEL, M.A., is Program Coordinator for the HUD-funded system of residential settings for the chronically disabled at Southwest Denver Community Mental Health Services, Inc., Denver, Colorado.

ROBERT L. OKIN, M.D., is Commissioner, Department of Mental Health, Commonwealth of Massachusetts, Boston, Massachusetts.

PAUL R. POLAK, M.D., is Executive Director, Southwest Denver Community Mental Health Services, Inc., Denver, Colorado.

ETHAN S. ROFMAN, M.D., is Associate Professor of Psychiatry, Boston University School of Medicine, and Medical Director of Charles River Hospital, Wellesley, Massachusetts.

JOHN J. SCHETZ, M.D., is in the private practice of psychiatry in Normal, Illinois, and a Clinical Associate, University of Illinois College of Medicine, Champaign, Illinois.

LEONARD I. STEIN, M.D., is Professor of Psychiatry, University of Wisconsin Medical School, and Medical Director, Dane County Mental Health Center, Madison, Wisconsin.

NICHOLAS E. STRATAS, M.D., is in the private practice of psychiatry and Associate Clinical Professor of Psychiatry, Duke University Medical Center, Durham, North Carolina, and was formerly Deputy Commissioner, North Carolina Department of Mental Health, Raleigh, North Carolina.

JOHN P. SULLIVAN, M.S.W., is Area Director, Brockton Multi-Service Center, Department of Mental Health, State of Massachusetts, and Consultant, Joint Commission on Accreditation of Hospitals—Community Mental Health Center Division, Chicago, Illinois.

PAUL L. TAYLOR, Ph.D., is in the private practice of clinical psychology in Normal, Illinois.

MARY ANN TEST, Ph.D., is Associate Professor, University of Wisconsin School of Social Work, Madison, Wisconsin.

NANCY L. WILSON, M.A., is Supervisor, Senior Information and Outreach Service, Texas Research Institute of Mental Sciences, and Lecturer in Social Work, University of Houston Graduate School of Social Work, Houston, Texas.

Chapter 1

SUCCESSFUL TREATMENT OF THE CHRONIC MENTALLY ILL

John A. Talbott

Successful treatment and care of the chronic mentally ill is an issue of increasing importance to psychiatry today. While chronic mental illness has been with us since the founding of this nation, it has only been in the past few years that there has been widespread interest in solving some of the problems posed by this patient population. In this chapter, I will summarize the history of treatment efforts in the United States, elucidate the question of what constitutes successful treatment for the chronically ill, review the literature on the subject, and enumerate several critical issues that need to be addressed if we are to come to grips with the problem and provide effective care for this long-neglected group.

HISTORICAL BACKGROUND

In the earliest days of colonial America, the mentally ill were cared for by and in their families, unless they became so disorganized and deteriorated that they wandered about the countryside. Some were incarcerated in makeshift cells near their family abodes, and some were annoying enough to the community that they were unceremoniously dumped over town or county lines in the middle of the night *(1, 2)*.

✓As American society developed, society's misfits were housed in jails, clearly intended for criminals, rogues, and vagabonds; workhouses, intended for the idle and disorderly; and almshouses, for the town's worthy but needy souls *(3)*. However this distinction was intended, many of the era's chronic mentally ill also were housed and "cared for" in these settings, with no intent to treat or minister to their special needs.

✓In the late eighteenth century, the first mental hospitals were founded. While their earliest days were characterized by a lack of what today we would consider even humane custodial care, a movement called "moral treatment" followed Pinel's lead in striking off the chains and established an encouraging and supportive familial atmosphere for the mentally ill in the early nineteenth century *(4)*.

Dorothea Dix, a crusading layperson, impressed with the results of moral treatment and horrified by the conditions of county almshouses and workhouses, argued for the states to assume responsibility for the care of the seriously and chronically mentally ill, and a new era, that of the state hospital, was born *(5)*. The results of her campaign were impressive. By 1860, 28 of the then 33 states had at least one public mental hospital.

However, translating the concept of moral treatment from small, well-run, private institutions to large, variably managed, public facilities was another matter. Since most mental illness is chronic, patients do not come in, receive care, and leave—as in the surgical model—they come, are cared for, and need continuing care for long periods. Thus, patients "silted up," and new institutions had to be built. They were chronically underfunded, and with the influx of tens of thousands of European immigrants, high at risk for mental illness, the crowded conditions in state hospitals soon approximated the horrible settings they were designed to replace *(6)*.

Scandals began to be reported soon after the introduction of the state hospital *(7)* and continued with the publication of Clifford Beer's firsthand account of treatment in a mental hospital *(8)* and Albert Deutsch's exposé of the scandalous conditions in state facilities *(9)*. These scandals and exposés, however, while heightening public awareness of the problems in treatment and care of the seriously and chronically mentally ill, produced little substantive change for the better.

During the twentieth century, American psychiatry was growing up and moving in several new and exciting directions. Alternatives to state mental hospitals were developed including: child guidance clinics, psychopathic hospitals, outpatient and aftercare clinics, and general hospital psychiatric services *(4)*. In addition, new treatment modalities were introduced, including group therapy, psychoanalysis, and crisis intervention.

Following World War II, the unprecedented interest in the mentally ill, coupled with the surge of work in social psychiatry and the initiation in 1955 of a Joint Commission on Mental Health and Illness, set the stage for the era of community mental health. A vast national network of community mental health centers was proposed by President John F. Kennedy, which would replace the obsolete state hospital and have a primary task of caring for the severely and chronically mentally ill in a far better, more humane way in the community than their discredited predecessor *(10)*.

The community mental health movement was coincident with several other developments during this time. These were the introduction of effective psychopharmacological agents for psychotic conditions; the legal and legislative forces calling for treatment in the least restrictive setting and a move from medical to legal conditions for commitment to a hospital; and the establishment of new federal funding mechanisms (Medicaid, Medicare, and Supplementary Security Income) that enabled discharged mental patients to move from total state to total federal financing *(4)*.

State mental hospital populations, which had climbed steadily and relentlessly since the introduction of state hospitals in the mid-nineteenth century, saw a drop for the first time in 1955. From a peak of 560,000 then, they have plummeted to their present low of 170,000 *(11)*. This mass migration of severely and chronically mentally ill persons was euphemistically called deinstitutionalization, but it is more correct to term it transinstitutionalization *(12)*. For as Kramer has shown *(13)*, the percentage of Americans housed in institutions has remained constant over the past several decades; it is their presence in individual institutions that has changed (e.g., the numbers in jails, nursing homes, and board and care homes have risen as the percentage of the population of state hospitals has fallen). In addition, huge numbers of chronic mentally ill persons are now highly visible in America's neighborhoods and receive highly variable and in most cases deplorable care in these communities. Again, there has been no reduction in admission of mental patients to hospitals, rather the locus of treatment has shifted—with a 35% reduction in admissions to state mental hospitals almost offset by a 32% increase in additions to general hospitals *(14)*.

The backlash against the deinstitutionalization policies of public psychiatric facilities took 20 years to develop, but when it came, it came with extreme force. Within two years, the federal government launched and published a major study of deinstitutionalization *(15)*; the "psychiatric think-tank" called the Group for the Advancement of Psychiatry issued a comprehensive report *(16)*; and the American Psychiatric Association (APA) established a committee at the national level, held an invitational conference of over 80 experts, and published the first comprehensive study of the problems and recommendations for a public policy to remedy these problems *(17)*.

In addition, the President's Commission on Mental Health, which cosponsored the Conference on the Chronic Mental Patient, along with the APA, issued its final report in 1978, which strongly advocated for a change in policy regarding the chronically mentally ill *(18)*. The subsequent federal legislation, the Mental Health System's Act, has as its first title the chronically ill *(19)*.

WHAT CONSTITUTES SUCCESSFUL TREATMENT OF THE CHRONICALLY ILL?

Despite the unprecedented interest in altering the nation's policies toward the severely and chronically mentally ill, questions abound, and central to most of them are the questions: what constitutes successful treatment and care of the chronically mentally ill and how do we provide that care to everyone in need of it? As part of the APA study of the chronic patient, a survey of American psychiatrists was conducted to ascertain their opinions on what the problems posed by and facing the chronic mentally ill were *(20)*. Fourth among the list of replies was the need for a model service system, with "flexible options so that it may be applied throughout the country, varying with regional needs and resources"; tenth was the need for a description of effective programs for the chronically ill; and following these was the request for more information on treatment modalities for chronic patients. The individual responses are illustrative of the problems we face. Respondents repeatedly asked for information that would enable them to solve their everyday problems dealing with the severely and chronically mentally ill. These included such questions as:

- What patients should be treated in which services?
- What programs are most effective in dealing with the chronically ill?
- How can we compare such programs?

- How can we combat resistance to treatment — on the part of patients, families, and professionals?
- How do we implement comprehensive aftercare services?
- And provide aggressive follow-up of discharged mental patients?
- How do we provide acute and emergency services for exacerbations in chronically ill persons?
- What is the role of long-term medication, including its effects and complications, in the treatment of chronic patients?
- What are adequate medication regimens?
- What modifications in psychotherapy will assist in their treatment?
- What is the role of inpatient hospitalization in the long-term course of treatment of the chronically ill?
- What is the role and efficacy of group psychotherapy? Behavior modification? Remotivation therapy?
- And how do we emphasize more the necessity of training in the skills of everyday living?

In addition, the respondants were skeptical that any treatment, no matter how effective, could do the job alone, without the necessary care, rehabilitation, and supportive services. These included the provision and role of:

Housing
Socialization
Social rehabilitation
Vocational rehabilitation
Low-level employment opportunities
Educational services
Income maintenance
Social services
Medical care
Nursing care
Transportation
Homemaking services

The respondents also asked for a description of the range of community services necessary to carry out a comprehensive program for chronic patients, including:

Domiciliary care

Inpatient units
Partial hospital facilities
Halfway and quarterway houses
Chronic care facilities
Foster care arrangements
Group homes
Self-care living
Outpatient clinics

The respondants also noted, however, the need to bind these programmatic elements together with some form of human glue, such as a case management system. They noted the present lack of a designated person or agency to be responsible for the coordination, continuity, implementation, monitoring, and evaluation of care and for the interagency communication necessary to ensure comprehensive care. And many called attention to the necessity of performing aggressive outreach, not only to "civilian" community abodes, but to nursing homes, prisons, and mental retardation facilities, where so many chronic mental patients reside.

If we summarize all these responses, we come up with three basic questions regarding successful treatment of the chronic mentally ill patient:

1. What treatment(s) is effective for the chronic mentally ill?
2. What programs, utilizing what treatment elements, are effective for the chronic mentally ill?
3. What systems, incorporating what program elements, are effective in treating the chronic mentally ill?

SELECTIVE REVIEW OF THE LITERATURE

Although chronic mental patients constitute the greatest single patient grouping and the largest problem for psychiatry, there has been proportionately little research and scholarly writing to attempt to answer these questions. While there are a tremendous number of anecdotal reports and program descriptions, there is an apparent lack of specificity regarding patient populations, comparability of treatment, and treatment outcome. While the authors that follow me have each summarized the literature pertaining to their area of expertise, I will give a selective overview of the major work to date in answering these three questions.

What Treatment Is Effective?

In 1968, the Joint Information Service published a review of the existing treatment of long-term mental patients in state mental hospitals (21). Even though the authors focused on the problems of treatment and care of inpatients, their survey of the comprehensive programming necessary (e.g., housing, vocational rehabilitation, socialization, activities therapies), as well as their emphasis on individual innovative program elements, presaged the existing awareness of the need for comprehensive, innovative, reality-based treatment and care.

The earliest attempt to provide a comprehensive description of treatment approaches for the chronic mentally ill was that provided at a conference celebrating the thirteenth anniversary of the famous thirteenth arrondissement mental health center, held in Paris in 1971 (22). While overemphasizing one modality (psychoanalytic psychotherapy), the contributors also discussed psychopharmacology, behavior therapy, and therapeutic communities.

May, in a review of treatment methods of schizophrenia, states that "there is impressive evidence that ongoing, aggressive, outpatient aftercare programs, combined with drug treatment, are effective in maintaining patients in the community and warding off deterioration." However, regarding the remainder of treatment approaches, of which he has written extensively, there is no specific research dealing with ambulatory treatment results for chronic schizophrenics, and most of the research cited concentrates on inpatients and is nonspecific as to chronicity (23).

Finally, Lamb and associates bring us closer to the current state of the art in the treatment of the chronic mentally ill with their description of treatment services that are effective for the chronic patient (24). The authors discuss a realistic psychotherapeutic approach, housing, socialization, and vocational rehabilitation.

What Programs Are Effective?

Another Joint Information Service publication, published in 1970, provided the first comprehensive appraisal of psychosocial rehabilitation programs functioning in various communities (25). In this publication, it became apparent how necessary it was to conceptualize the community treatment and care of the chronically disabled as a compendium of services (e.g., housing, socialization, vocational rehabilitation), bound together by a single program.

In the 1970s, two innovative programs were initiated to deal with the overwhelming problem posed by deinstitutionalization. The first, conducted by Paul and Lentz *(26)*, had a state hospital base; the second, administered by Stein and Test *(27)*, moved from the state hospital into a community-based operation. Both demonstrated the need to emphasize the skills of everyday living, and the latter skillfully highlighted the need to blend medical-psychiatric care (e.g., medication and psychotherapy) with a social support system (e.g., housing, social and vocational rehabilitation).

In their assessments of what programs worked and what programs did not work in dealing with the chronic mentally ill, Glasscote *(28)* and Barter *(29)* support the current sentiment that, while a variety of treatment modalities and supportive services need to be available to each chronic patient, more important is the program itself which weaves together availability, accessibility, advocacy, support, staff, and patients into a system which can truly provide to each according to his or her needs. Barter's closing statement describing the elements common to successful programs is worth repeating:

> Community programs that have been successful in helping the chronic patient a) have adequate funds from stable sources, b) possess an administrative structure that provides for leadership as well as cooperation and coordination, c) emphasize continuity of care between state institutions and the community and within community programs themselves, d) offer services that are tailored to individual needs and comprise a continuum of residential/treatment programs ranging from dependent through independent levels of care, e) feature crisis responsiveness to prevent regression and to promote easy entrance into treatment at any level of appropriate care, f) provide sophisticated and appropriate medication services, g) support the family in understanding and caring for the CMP [chronic mental patient], h) offer appropriate prevocational and vocational programs, i) assist patients in securing services through aggressive outreach and case management services, j) protect patient civil rights, and k) maintain educational programs designed to facilitate community acceptance and integration of the CMP.

What Systems are Effective?

It has been only recently that we have realized that the care and treatment of the chronically mentally ill is a systems problem. As of the late 1970s, most areas of the country have attempted to cope with deinstitutionalization by innovative programming and expansion of existing resources.

Individual states and counties have attempted a system's approach to mental health, and descriptions of such efforts in North Carolina *(30)*; Pima County, Arizona *(31)*; Columbia County, New York *(32)*; and Sacramento *(33)* and Orange *(34)* Counties, California, have been published.

However, these attempts to rationalize the mental health system have not been directed at the chronic patient. Glenn, in a background paper prepared for the APA's Conference on the Chronic Mental Patient, however, did spell out the beginnings of a systematic approach at all governmental levels to the care and treatment of the chronic mentally ill *(35)*.

WHAT QUESTIONS REMAIN ABOUT SUCCESSFUL PROGRAMMING?

Despite the good start we have made toward answering many of the questions posed, we are left with a number still unanswered. Too little of what has been written has addressed the chronic population specifically; too little has presented hypotheses that can be tested or research that has comparability or controls; and too little deals with programs outside of the traditional hospital or publicly funded program.

We still need to know what treatment works for which chronic mentally ill person. And we need to know how to fit these elements together in a successful program, which can emanate from a number of community or institutional bases. But in addition, we need to see how programs can fit together in a comprehensive mental health system to deliver the very highest quality and broadest ranging treatment and care for the chronically ill.

PREVIEW OF THIS BOOK

To further answer the three questions posed earlier, this book has been organized into three parts.

Part I presents the ingredients essential to the successful treatment of the chronic mentally ill patient: medication, drug monitoring, individual psychotherapy, socialization, vocational rehabilitation, community residential care, and case management.

Part II presents several models of successful programs that deal with the chronically ill—all from separate bases. The order in which they appear represents the importance they have hierarchically in terms of total expenditures of the mental health dollar. Thus, nursing homes lead off the list. It is important to recognize that these are not traditional programs, and while initiated from a particular base (e.g., the state hospital), their viability and success frequently comes from their modifications and growth away from that base. In addition, several programs are described which are not usually thought of as chronic patient programs—specifically, those representing private practice, private hospitals, and the Veterans Administration system. Part III presents several programs which are more specialized, dealing with rural, child, and geriatric populations.

Part IV presents three examples of state and county attempts to formulate a systems approach to the care and treatment of the chronic mentally ill patient.

A caveat is in order. These treatment elements, programs, and systems are described not as ideal models but as state of the art approximations of the best we are doing today. They should not be looked upon as finished products; their proposers would be the first to acknowledge this. They are all still growing and learning. But it is hoped that the publication of these descriptions will allow others to initiate and shape their own programs, given the wealth of ideas and programmatic bases presented. If this book stimulates others to act, promotes further research to answer the yet unanswered questions, and fosters better care and treatment of the most neglected group in mental health—the severely and chronically mentally ill— it will have succeeded admirably.

NOTES

1. Dain N: From colonial America to bicentennial America: Two centuries of vicissitudes in the institutional care of mental patients. Bull NY Acad Med 52:1179–1196, 1976

2. Deutsch A: The Mentally Ill in America: A History of Their Care and Treatment from Colonial Times (ed 2). New York, Columbia University Press, 1949

3. Maxmen J, Tucker GJ, LeBow M: Rational Hospital Psychiatry: The Reactive Environment. New York, Brunner/Mazel, 1974

4. Talbott JA: The history of the state mental hospital. In Talbott JA: The Death of the Asylum. New York, Grune and Stratton, 1978

5. Rothman DJ: The Discovery of the Asylum: Social Order and Disorder in the New Republic. Boston, Little Brown, 1971

6. Caplan RB: Psychiatry and the Community in Nineteenth-Century America. New York, Basic Books, 1969

7. Quen JM: Learning from history. Psychiatr Ann 5:15–31, 1975

8. Beers CW: A Mind that Found Itself (ed 5). Garden City, NY, Doubleday, 1960 (originally published in 1908)

9. Deutsch A: The Shame of the States. New York, Harcourt, Brace and Company, 1948

10. Kennedy JF: Message from the President of the United States relative to mental illness and mental retardation. Am J Psychiatry 120:729–737, 1964

11. Meyer NG: Provisional patient movement and administrative data state and county psychiatric inpatient services, 1 July 1974–30 June 1975. Mental Health Statistical Note No. 132. Rockville, Md., U.S. Department of Health, Education and Welfare, 1976

12. Michels R: Personal communication, February, 1979

13. Kramer M: Psychiatric Services and the Changing Institutional Scene. Bethesda, Md., National Institute of Mental Health, 1975

14. Bachrach L: Feedback: general hospitals taking greater role in providing services for chronic patients. Hosp and Comm Psychiatry, 30:488:79

15. Returning the Mentally Disabled to the Community: Government Needs to Do More. Washington, D.C., U.S. General Accounting Office, 1977

16. The Chronic Mental Patient in the Community. New York, Group for the Advancement of Psychiatry, 1978

17. Talbott JA (ed): The Chronic Mental Patient—Problems, Solutions and Recommendations for a Public Policy. Washington, D.C., The American Psychiatric Association, 1978

18. The President's Commission on Mental Health: Superintendent of Documents, U.S. Government Printing Office, Washington, D.C. 1978

19. U.S. Department of Health, Education and Welfare: Mental Health Systems Act, 15 May 1979

20. Talbott JA: What are the problems of the chronic mental patient—A report of a survey of psychiatrists' concerns. In Talbott, JA (ed): The Chronic Mental Patient: Problems, Solutions and Recommendations for a Public Policy. Washington, D.C., The American Psychiatric Association, 1978

21. Padula H, Glasscote RM, Cumming E: Approaches to the Care of Long-Term Mental Patients. Washington, D.C., JIS, 1968

22. Chiland C: Long Term Treatment of Psychotic States. New York, Human Sciences Press, 1977

23. May PRA. Schizophrenia: Evaluation of treatment methods. In Freedman AM, Kaplan HI, Sadock BJ: Comprehensive Textbook of Psychiatry, Baltimore, Md., Williams and Wilkins, 1975

24. Lamb HR and Associates: Community Survival for Long-Term Patients, San Francisco, Jossey-Bass, 1976

25. Glasscote RA, Cumming E, Rutman I, Sussex JN, Glassman SM: Rehabilitating the Mentally Ill in the Community: A Study of Psychosocial Rehabilitation Centers, Washington, D.C., JIS, 1971

26. Paul GL, Lentz RJ: Psychosocial Treatment of Chronic Mental Patients: Milieu Versus Social-Learning Programs. Cambridge, Mass., Harvard University Press, 1977

27. Stein L, Test MA: An Alternative to Mental Hospital Treatment: I. Conceptual Model, Treatment Program, and Clinical Evaluation, Arch Gen Psychiatry 37:392–397, 1980

28. Glasscote RA: What programs work and what programs do not work to meet the needs of chronic mental patients. In Talbott JA: The Chronic Mental Patient: Problems, Solutions and Recommendations for a Public Policy. Washington, D.C., The American Psychiatric Association, 1978

29. Barter JT: Successful community programming for the chronic mental patient: Principles and practices. In Talbott JA: The Chronic Mental Patient: Problems, Solutions and Recommendations for a Public Policy. Washington, D.C., The American Psychiatric Association, 1978

30. Osberg JW: Unifying state hospital and community systems through area programs. Hosp and Comm Psychiatry 23:105–108, 1972

31. Beigel A, Bower WH, Levenson AI: A unified system of care: Blueprint for the future. Am J Psychiatr 130:554–558, 1973

32. Snow HB, Blackburn OP: Unifying state hospital and local services to present a shorter hospitalization. Hosp and Comm Psychiatry 24:487–489, 1973

33. Barter JT: Sacramento County's experience with community care. Hosp and Comm Psychiatry 26:587–589, 1975

34. Elpers JR: Orange County's alternative to state hospital treatment. Hosp and Comm Psychiatry 26:589–592, 1975

35. Glenn T: Exploring responsibility for chronic mental patients in the community. In Talbott JA: The Chronic Mental Patient: Problems, Solutions and Recommendations for a Public Policy. Washington, D.C., The American Psychiatric Association, 1978

Part I

ELEMENTS IN THE SUCCESSFUL TREATMENT OF THE CHRONIC MENTAL PATIENT

Chapter 2

MEDICATION
Norris Hansell

Recent years have seen an expanding interest in the clinical problems of persons with prolonged psychiatric conditions. Major illnesses, such as schizophrenia, manic-depressive and repeating unipolar depression, alcoholism and substance abuse, and brain syndromes with emotional components, show features of prolonged duration, some lasting throughout life. The treatment needs of such persons contrast sharply with those of brief and single-episode users of services. The treatment plan does not organize around the problem of discharge but around that of continuity. Medications such as neuroleptics, tricyclics, and lithium often are required, and clinical planning centers on the consequent long-term hazards—dyskinesias, dysphorias, over-dosing, renal damage. Diagnostic precision is increasingly pursued because of its linkage with psychopharmaceutical specificity *(1)*. The didactic component of clinical service is growing because patients need to acquire a body of information about their illness, its treatment, and life practices affecting it in order to obtain the best results. A prolonged therapeutic relationship is beneficial in assisting patients to use their full potential within the constraints of a chronic condition.

The major scale of the opportunity for productive use of psychopharmaceuticals in chronic conditions is worth noting. Repeating and prolonged users of service constitute a large fraction of psychiatric patients. For example, 65% of persons admitted to public mental hospitals are readmissions, reflecting a chronic condition *(2)*. Most heavy and repeating users at any time in recent years are more likely to be in outpatient service than in–hospital service, a fact reflected in the tenfold expansion in the volume of outpatient services since 1950 *(3)*. A significant portion, one-third to one-half, and growing, of medication service to chronic mental patients is conducted by physicians who do not limit their practices to psychiatry *(4)*. A large number of persons who might benefit from prolonged psychopharmaceutical service are in nursing homes. The number of individuals with psychiatric illness in nursing homes has more than doubled in the past two decades *(3)*, and more than one-tenth of those in nursing homes are disabled younger persons, many in the earlier stages of prolonged psychiatric conditions *(5)*. In large measure, the diagnostic groups comprising chronic mental conditions are ones wherein psychopharmaceuticals are useful, even essential. About one-quarter are schizophrenics, using public hospital admissions as an index *(6)*, and such individuals are in need of service for many years, since the peak age of entrance to service is age 25 years and the peak age of termination from service is close to the end of life expectancy *(7)*. About one-quarter are bipolar and unipolar affective disorders, using estimates which reflect the fact that outpatient care by primary care physicians is the principle pattern for this group *(6, 8)*. About one-quarter are alcoholics *(6, 9, 10)*. About one-tenth are various brain syndromes, mental retardation with emotional reaction, and ictal disorders with emotional reactions *(6)*. Some observers would say there is an additional one-seventh showing character and personality disorders, conditions ordinarily not benefiting from medication. The relative size of the portion of this latter group which uses hospital or prolonged services has been declining in recent years *(11)*, probably reflecting a change in diagnostic practices.

CHRONIC SCHIZOPHRENIA

We can divide the problem of drug treatment of chronic schizophrenia into five parts. There must be demonstrated a substantial reduction of symptoms by the use of the medication. There must be a return of symptoms if medication is lowered past a threshold level or discontinued. There must be continuing medical observation of the patient. The patient must learn to participate in a sustained program of dose adjustment and vigilance for early warning observations regarding dyskinesias, dysphorias, and other hazards. There must be a continuing therapeutic relationship, including access to counseling and crisis management. Stated concisely these are the problems of efficacy, necessity, surveillance, cooperation, and emergency.

Neuroleptic medications have a demonstrated value in the management of acute and chronic schizophrenia *(12–16)*. However, not all chronic schizophrenics benefit, and the hazards of tardive dyskinesia and neuroleptic-induced dysphorias are serious *(17)*. Because the advantages of neuroleptics for controlling symptoms, prevention of job loss, school failure, and suicide can be dramatic, we have the classic clinical situation resulting from a high-gain, high-risk decision. The risks of overinclusion include unnecessary exposure to the possibility of tardive dyskinesia and the risks of underinclusion represent major degrees of missed therapeutic opportunity *(18)*.

The clinical indications for placing a presumed schizophrenic individual into a program of continuous or semicontinuous neuroleptic use are narrow. The diagnosis of schizophrenia must be reasonably secure, using criteria such as those of Taylor and Abrams *(19)* —thought disorder, affect reduction, delusions, and hallucinations, all in the absence of gross brain or toxic disease and intoxicated state or broad affect, and showing a duration of more than six months. It is particularly important to distinguish between single-episode forms of schizophrenia and chronic remitting or chronic unremitting forms. In the case of a young individual with no previous episodes, the neuroleptic should be gradually reduced and an attempt made to discontinue it after one year without symptoms while under observation for at least one additional year. Most physicians would not consider prophylactic neuroleptics in the absence of two or more hospitalizations or serious episodes in which neuroleptic treatment was successful. There must be a reduction of symptoms which is dose related and influential in the quality of life. Because chronic schizophrenia may comprise a heterogeneous group of biologic aberrations, some of which may not require nor benefit from neuroleptics, it is essential that the clinical impact of use and nonuse be assessed for each patient and during a prolonged interval of outpatient observation. If an individual does not appear to require neuroleptics but is otherwise presumed to show chronic schizophrenia, an extended program of service and surveillance should proceed with continuing openness to the later necessity of neuroleptics.

The selection of a neuroleptic for long-term use is a cooperative venture between patient and physician. Side effects tolerable in a short program will impede a long one. Individuals react varyingly to different neuroleptics, and probably no neuroleptic has across-the-board advantages regarding the balance of antipsychotic, extrapyramidal, dysphoric, metabolic, and endocrine effects nor for overall safety. Many patients experience major dysphorias with one neuroleptic but not with another, and such shifts should be attempted because of the pain, noncompliance, and suicidal acts associated with these dysphorias. When the dysphoria is associated with akinesia or other parkinson signs, it is often responsive to antiparkinson medication. Once-a-day oral administration of the neuroleptic offers advantages in cost and reliability. Intramuscular depot fluphenazine is useful for patients showing low reliability by the oral route and for a few patients who do not seem to absorb phenothiazines by the oral route *(20)*. The depot dose and interval should be lowered and stretched in a pattern analogous to that typically used with the oral route. Every attempt should be made to manage the tremors, dysphorias, akathisia, akinesias, and dyskinesias associated with neuroleptics. The patient should be instructed concerning the importance of reporting any extrapyramidal effects, because when unmanaged they create enough discomfort that patients nearly always stop the medication. Akathisia can appear in subtle forms, some of which simulate the motor and visceral experiences of anxiety or panic *(21)*. In most cases, extrapyramidal effects can be controlled by lowering the dose of neuroleptic and by continuous or intermittent antiparkinson medication. Occasionally, it is helpful to use a benzodiazepine to control akathisia when not relieved by an atropinic, and typically such usage is brief. A few persons abuse atropinic antiparkinson medications to achieve a euphoric, intoxicated state. Some of these persons can be managed by using amantadine, an antiparkinson material with a somewhat different mechanism, or by using antihistamines. Most physicians periodically redetermine whether antiparkinson medication is necessary by observing the effects of withdrawing it. However, the positive overall effects on comfort and compliance often result in continuous prophylactic use *(22)*.

The safety and reliability of prolonged medication programs for schizophrenics have been improved in recent years by the use of a strategy which combines a low-dosage pattern of maintenance with rapid increases in dose at the time of any episodic reappearance of symptoms. This plan offers the prospect of lower side effects and a smaller cumulative lifetime dose but requires major degrees of patient cooperation and instruction. Not all schizophrenics can make use of such instruction, particularly when the history includes mental retardation or prolonged psychosis. Typical instruction focuses on analogies to such chronic metabolic diseases as diabetes. Patients should be counseled that their disease likely is lifelong and often substantially modifiable with chemical and psychotherapeutic regulation. The development of an attitude of personal responsibility for making changes from a baseline dose in relation to criterion observations underlies the successful use of the low-dose strategy. In order to avoid the low-dose pattern of episodic reappearance of symptoms, the patient is instructed to temporarily increase the usual dose for the duration of each episode, using as guidepost observations the reappearance of a sleeping disturbance, difficulty concentrating, preoccupation with a narrow range of topics, anhedonia, audible thoughts, and floating affects. The term *floating affects* comprises the experiences of sadness, panic, suspicion, anger, and perplexity when they rise to high levels and last for hours or days. These observations constitute an early warning system, because typically they appear in advance of psychotic symptoms and offer a signal to increase promptly the dose of medication. At the first appearance of such symptoms, patients double their daily maintenance dose, wait three days, then assess the effect. They may repeat this maneuver several times. The low-dose strategy employs as a baseline dose the least amount that will control the sleeping disorders and floating affects between episodes. The method for lowering the dose is similar. Patients are instructed that feeling slowed, sleepy, or separated from their experience indicates the dose is too high. At the first appearance of such signs, they reduce the dose by one-third and wait three days to assess the effect. They may repeat this maneuver several times.

Patients can assist in assessing whether neuroleptics are essential. Members of the patient's family often can assist in assessing the patient's condition and the effects of medication. A large group of patients desire to experience the effect of discontinuing medications and can do so more safely if taught a method for observing very early signs of trouble. Many patients become reliable users over prolonged intervals through such experiences. Some patients can learn conveniently about their disease and its control in a group format. The participants in such a group discuss and react to each other's emerging experience with use of medication. Sessions typically include reports by each on the state of control of target symptoms and on setting next objectives for improving the state of regulation. Snyder's book *Madness and the Brain* can serve as a practical text for such instructional meetings *(23)*.

The outpatient care of chronic schizophrenic patients presents a continuing need to be aware of the interaction of the disease and the medications used for its control with alcohol, sedatives, minor tranquilizers, caffeine, anorectics, and decongestants. Patients sometimes attempt to use alcohol to control schizophrenic symptoms, particularly the sleep disturbances and floating affects. Not only is alcohol ineffective in the control of these symptoms in schizophrenia, but time is lost and attention is diverted from more precise methods of regulation. Also alcohol increases the akathisias and dystonias associated with neuroleptics. Abstinence from alcohol should be routine instruction with chronic neuroleptic use *(24)*. The clinical problem arising from the use of minor tranquilizers, sedatives, and soporifics is similar. As a rule, these materials are less efficient than neuroleptics in regulating the sleeping-waking cycle and the floating affects of schizophrenia. In addition, the duration of action of minor tranquilizers can be measured in hours, in contrast to the much slower, enduring effects of neuroleptics. Many clinicians find the too brief duration of action of minor tranquilizers yields inherently destabilizing effects. Nevertheless, the benzodiazepines, in particular, may occasionally be useful, usually briefly, to reduce a neuroleptic-induced dysphoria enough to allow continued use of the neuroleptic.

Of a different nature are problems with amphetamines, ephedrine, and congeners. Amphetamine psychosis has long been known to mimic schizophrenia. Continuing use of small amounts of many sympathomimetics has a similar deregulating effect on chronic schizophrenia, yielding subtle or dramatic exacerbations in the course of the illness *(25)*. The bulk of this problem lies with over-the-counter pharmaceuticals, particularly diet pills and respiratory decongestants. For example, anorectics that contain phenyl propanolamine—namely Diet-Trim, Hungrex, and Slender-X— and decongestants containing phenylephrine, phenylpropanolamine, ephedrine, and congeners—such as Allerest, Benzedrex, Contac, Coricidin "D," Dristan, Mistol, Neo-Synephrine, Novahistine, Ornex, Romilar, Sinarest, Super-Anahist, Vicks-Sinex, and 4-Way Cold Tablets—should be avoided. Also, patients should be instructed not to exceed three cups of coffee daily because of the dysphorias and sleep disorders which may be accentuated by caffeine *(26)*. Patients should be instructed that cannibis even in small quantities carries a definite risk of exacerbating their illness and of precipitating episodes. They should be advised that even though they may notice little difficulty during an intoxicated state, they may experience delayed and prolonged effects they might not otherwise connect with cannibis use. Increases in suspicion, panic, perplexity, and euphoria, and disturbances in concentration and sleep commonly appear after a delay of hours or days with cannibis use by schizophrenics.

The central problem in long-term neuroleptic treatment of schizophrenia is tardive dyskinesia *(17, 27)*. The prevention of tardive dyskinesia is approached via the strategies of narrow indications, and low dosage, and by continuing vigilance for beginning signs of lingual-facial dyskinesias. Dyskinesias may appear early or late, and the patient should be instructed regarding their importance. Tongue-pushing and chewing movements frequently are not noticed in their early forms by patients, so continuing observation by the physician is necessary. Early notice is essential because tardive dyskinesia apparently shows a phase of reversibility. Neuroleptic drugs should be reevaluated at the first sign of abnormal oral movements or choreoathetoid movements of the trunk or limbs. Sometimes reserpine can control the schizophrenic symptoms without reintroducing dyskinesias. A trial of reserpine is warranted in the group of schizophrenics whose condition is distinctly improved by neuroleptics. There is no established treatment for tardive dyskinesia. Lecithin used as a dietary supplement appears promising but is not yet evaluated *(28, 29)*.

An attempt should be made to minimize the dose for pregnant women using neuroleptics, because, although the risks to the fetus and newborn appear small, the evidence is inconclusive and the risks are not zero *(30–32)*. Mothers using neuroleptics should be instructed to bottle feed infants.

The availability of continuing medical care throughout the career of service of a chronic schizophrenic offers the patient an ally in the struggle against disability and it allows the essential element of surveillance. Many patients will consider a prolonged program of medication only as an aspect of a treatment relationship they recognize as a caring one. Missed appointments must be investigated and rescheduled. The didactic component, so important in using the low-dose strategy and for achieving reliability over decades, typically seems to commence as part of the physician's general therapeutic relationship. Continuing access to crisis services is central to any condition marked by an episodic course. Activity during such crises includes counseling, placement into a pattern of closer supervision than pertains ordinarily, and possible entry into inpatient care. Counseling enables many schizophrenics to move through episodes in a more orderly fashion. They are most able to enter counseling promptly at the onset of an episode if the groundwork has been laid earlier.

Counseling can assist the patient's efforts to start, stop, pace, and focus the current adaptive work. Regulating the pace of efforts to get rest, food, water, and relaxation during the period of challenge reduces the risk of exhaustion. Schizophrenics should be encouraged to keep in regular reporting contact with their helpers throughout an episode. After an episode is resolved, counseling can shift to a less frequent, less intense pattern and be held in readiness for the future.

Schizophrenics often need help in increasing their social activity and connectedness. Services which improve affiliations are important clinically, because such affiliations yield a beneficial effect on the quality of coping. An individual's distress signaling and affect displays ordinarily have the effect of convening around him a temporary helping group *(33)*. The schizophrenic often shows a pattern of stress behavior which is chaotic and overly prolonged. His imprecise signaling and his proclivity under stress to move into a condition of social isolation may deprive him of the presence of such a group at the very time it might assist to regulate him. Many have regarded the schizophrenic's often solitary condition as central to the accumulating disability. Helpful assists to affiliational activity during episodes include the convening of fragmenting networks—families, friends, and work associates—and linking with mutual-help groups such as First Friends and Recovery Incorporated.* Nonresidential clubs and lodges sometimes can serve as practical affiliational options for otherwise isolated persons.

Some of the most reliable preventive work possible today pertains to what may be done in aborting school and job failure, hospitalization, and suicide in chronic schizophrenics who can remain functional with precise service. Such service may offer the most solid domain for preventive efforts since the time when preventions were recognized for neurosyphilis and pellagra. Management of the risks of prolonged medication use requires medically trained judgment and a tight protocol. When adequate medical investment is not present in a program, for whatever reason, the risks are notably larger and the benefits erratic. The hazards of neuroleptic use raise to a high level of salience the standard problems in any program of chronic medication use—namely efficacy, necessity, surveillance, co-

---

*First Friends and Recovery Incorporated are club-like groups of patients and ex-patients who assist one another in the life problems associated with chronic mental illness.

operation, and emergency—and make the contribution of the physician a broad and interesting one, one as rewarding as anything in medical life.

AFFECTIVE DISORDERS

The management of chronic medication use for prolonged or episodic affective disorders presents the same high-risk, high-gain strategic problem as does schizophrenia. The risks of school and job loss, family disruption, and suicide are substantial for persons with repeating affective disorders. A program of continuous or semicontinuous medication has a demonstrated value in reducing the frequency and severity of episodes and the degree of accumulating disability (34). Such a program has risks and does not benefit all persons with affective disorders. Again, the conditions of efficacy, necessity, surveillance, cooperation, and emergency need be met. The reader is referred to other sources for general discussions of the use of tricyclics, lithium, and monoamine oxidase inhibitors (35–37). The tricyclics and lithium in particular require a major concern with the patient's physical status, including laboratory monitoring.

The clinical indications for placing an individual with an affective disturbance into a program of continuous or semicontinuous use of a tricyclic, lithium, or monoamine oxidase inhibitor (MOAI) are narrow. There should be at least two hospitalizations or otherwise serious episodes benefited distinctly by medication. A suicide attempt or a strong family history of affective disorder are additional markers of severity. Efforts to diagnose the type of affective disorder are significant, because lithium typically is reserved for bipolar disorders with at least one serious manic episode. Tricyclics are more desirable when possible because, although they have a serious overdose hazard and several largely reversible side effects, they do not appear to possess a serious cumulative hazard other than weight gain. Lithium in prolonged use may carry a risk of renal changes which at present have an unknown clinical significance (38, 39). Atrophic fibrosis of renal tissue has been reported in patients also showing diminished ability of the kidneys to concentrate electrolytes. The frequency and consequences of these effects are under active evaluation. Until these evaluations appear, some clinicians are restricting their use of lithium to affective conditions where other medications are not successful. Because the definitive studies will need to include data reflecting prolonged contact with lithium, the needed observations may not appear quickly. For the interim, some clinicians will withhold lithium from any bipolar patients who can be managed with a combination of a tricyclic and neuroleptic. It is sometimes feasible to use tricyclics within a pattern of close regulation for bipolar patients so long as manic attacks are not provoked *(40)*. In this connection, the manic components of a bipolar illness can appear in several forms besides a typical hyperactive euphoria, including catatonic, paranoid, dysphoric, and episodic aggressive forms *(41, 42)*. An attempt should be made to lower the dose or withdraw the tricyclic periodically to redetermine the necessity. In the case of lithium, an attempt can be made to discontinue it after any several-year period without a recurrence of serious affective disorder. Individuals using lithium on a continuing basis should receive a periodic review of their health status with particular attention to the possibilities of hypothyroidism and reduced renal function. The appearance of thirst, or declining renal clearance, or reduced urinary concentration after a stable interval on lithium raises the question of reassessing continuance.

The safety and reliability of tricyclic antidepressant use can be increased by using a method similar to that described for neuroleptics. A low-dose strategy is combined with rapid increases from a baseline dose at the beginning of any episode. The low-dose strategy offers advantages in safety and reliability because the patient experiences fewer side effects and is less likely to discontinue the medication. The method requires the patient's active cooperation, which generally can be achieved. When such cooperation cannot be achieved, the low-dose strategy should not be continued. Naturally, this method does not apply to lithium treatment, where a constant-dose strategy yielding a blood level of 0.8–1.0 mEq/L is the typical plan in prophylaxis *(43)*. The program of instruction which is essential for the patient's cooperation with tricyclics emphasizes the likely lifelong duration of the process and the advantages of a low-dose approach with increases during episodes. In order to suppress an incipient depressive episode, the dose increase must be early and quick. Patients are instructed to watch for changes in the sleeping-waking cycle, loss of social interest, loss of pleasure, decreased work energy, and preoccupation with a few repeating topics of thought as early markers of a beginning depressive episode. Early hypomanic signs include feelings of speed and urgency and major deviations from a prior daily schedule. Typically, these markers appear days or weeks before the major signs of the episode and, with a medication response, allow its control. When the markers appear, depressed patients double the baseline dose, wait three days, and assess the effect. Manic patients halve the dose or reintroduce a baseline level of neuroleptic. They may repeat this maneuver several times. Markers indicating the tricyclic dose is too high include sleepiness, slowing, dry mouth, impairments in recall or fluency, and peculiar intervals of dysphoric hyperactivity. This pattern of increases and decreases can be accomplished at the physician's direction or by the patient's initiation under the physician's general instruction. The latter is preferable when possible, because it allows a quicker response for a situation in which timeliness is essential.

The instructional component for the drug treatment of chronic affective disorders has applications besides the low-dose strategy. Patients should be advised that alcohol and minor tranquilizers often worsen mood disorders and should be avoided altogether. In addition, minor tranquilizers can mask the sleeping disorder being used as an early warning sign for episodes. Patients should be advised not to use over-the-counter soporifics for the same reasons and because their atropinic effects are additive with those of tricyclics and can lead to confusional states. Caffeine use should be limited to the equivalent of three cups of coffee daily, about 300 mg of caffeine, because of an exacerbating effect on mood disorders (26). Patients receiving tricyclics should report any medications they take for other conditions and should be advised on the importance of coordinating any changes in such usage between their physicians. A few individuals on tricyclics experience impulsive aggression, probably a manic equivalent, and advice on reporting any such experience should be offered. Lithium patients need to learn about the importance of salt loss, signs of hypothyroidism, and polyuria. Bipolar patients should be instructed against being lulled into a careless attitude during the early stages of mania and, so, letting it get out of hand (44).

An attempt should be made to withdraw tricyclics from women during pregnancy. Lithium is teratogenic (45) and should not be used in fertile women in the absence of a program of contraception; otherwise, the patient should be converted to tricyclic prophylaxis. Mothers using lithium during the puerperium should be instructed to bottle feed the infant (46).

A continued therapeutic relationship with counseling, surveillance, and crisis components is essential for the management of chronic affective disorders. The prevention of suicide is closely linked with the availability of crisis contact and with measures to avoid accumulations of lethal supplies of tricyclics. Patients should be closely instructed on the mechanics for using the hospital emergency room and advised of the appropriateness of using it should self-destructive impulses become prominent. Unless a continuing medical therapeutic relationship is maintained, the overdose hazards of tricyclics and the toxic hazards of lithium are excessive and prophylaxis should not be attempted. Again, the elements of a high-gain, high-loss situation are present together with preventive opportunity which can be approached safely only within a rigorous design.

CHRONIC BRAIN SYNDROMES

Psychopharmaceuticals can make an important contribution to the quality of life for some individuals with chronic conditions involving reduced brain function. A wide variety of disorders can lead to degenerative or dysfunctional changes of a diffuse nature in brain tissue, including vascular, metabolic, toxic, traumatic, and heritable conditions. Also, early onset developmental problems, including various forms of mental retardation, can involve a component of reduced brain function. In addition to various degrees of impairment in orientation, memory, intellectual functions, judgment, and lability and shallowness of affect—the well-known clinical hallmarks of these conditions—most of the patients show the whole range of behavior and emotional problems seen in other psychiatric conditions. Panics, hostility, suspicion, hyperactivity, assaultiveness, withdrawal, depression, delusions, and hallucinations are common problems. Minor tranquilizers, neuroleptics, antidepressants, and anticonvulsants can offer major symptomatic relief, although they do not alter the course of the disease. The significant difficulties in adapting and maintaining social relations often seen in chronic brain disease generally are not reversed by medication but form the basis of the almost universal necessity for counseling and other management.

The differential diagnosis of dementia and brain syndromes is an increasingly rigorous clinical activity because of the fact that remediable conditions such as hypothyrodism, normal-pressure hydrocephalus, drug toxicity, and megaloblastic anemias comprise a significant fraction of persons appearing for symptomatic management *(47, 48)*. Any person with a brain syndrome presenting for symptomatic treatment should be considered as suffering from a fresh, unstudied dementia until the clinician is satisfied an etiologic investigation has been pursued. As with any program of prolonged medication use, demonstrations of efficacy, necessity, cooperation, surveillance, and emergency apply. Individuals with chronic brain syndromes often have such major problems with memory and judgment that the responsibility for patient cooperation with the program may be best assumed by a relative or by institutional staff, as in a nursing home.

The choice of medication for symptomatic relief in chronic brain syndromes involves an exploratory and observational attitude. If panic, anxiety, or mild hyperactivity are present, some clinicians would start with a trial of benzodiazepines in low doses, recognizing that in brain syndromes this group of pharmaceuticals can yield unwanted slowing or affect-releasing phenomena similar to what might be seen in intoxicated states. When not recognized as medication induced, these affect-releasing phenomena—for example, rage attacks and poorly controlled sexual behavior—are sometimes treated mistakenly by further increases in medication. Their hallmark is an association with often subtle reductions in dexterity and fluency. If benzodiazepines are not helpful, or if suspicion, withdrawal, bizarre behavior, delusions, or hallucinations form the main problem, neuroleptics in low doses should receive a trial. Persons with chronic brain syndromes typically show increased sensitivity to the sedative, hypotensive, parkinson, and central anticholinergic effects of neuroleptics. A full anticholinergic psychosis can include anything from confused agitation to delerium. In its milder forms, it can appear compatible with the symptoms expectable with the underlying chronic brain syndrome and thereby plausibly but incorrectly suggest dose increases which would exacerbate the situation. Vigilance for peripheral anticholinergic signs, including dry, red face and mydriasis, can help distinguish these problems (49). Depression in any of its forms appears in persons with chronic brain syndromes; tricyclic medications are often helpful, typically in lower doses, as are neuroleptics. Again, watchfulness for the sudden or insidious development of central anticholinergic effects is warranted in persons with brain syndromes. Pseudodementia, a form of depression often involving complaints of memory loss and confusion, can be mistaken for a brain syndrome but can also be added onto a mild brain syndrome. It is often dramatically improved by tricyclic medication. Many focal ictal disorders show an accompanying chronic brain syndrome in which combinations of anticonvulsant and psychotropic medications prove helpful. Some individuals with chronic brain syndromes showing episodic violence can be dramatically benefited by anticonvulsants or meprobamate (50). Because episodic

violence of ictal origin can lead to disastrous effects on the quality
of life, including child abuse and senseless assault, efforts to modify
it by medication are warranted. A rigorous workup for ictal neurologic disease is necessary both to discover remediable lesions and to
improve the precision of pharmacotherapy. Abstinence from alcohol
is routine advice for all persons with chronic brain syndromes and
particularly for those with episodic aggression or affect-releases.
Many such persons are particularly sensitive to atropinic soporifics
sold over the counter and should be so warned. The availability of
a continuing therapeutic relationship assists an individual to maintain an active struggle against the disability state and to learn to
control any environmental factors which interplay with the condition. Many find that sleep deprivation worsens their symptoms.
Some find that they can develop habits which partially compensate
for such problems as memory loss and affect discharges. Any program of prolonged medication use in a person with a chronic brain
syndrome must exist within controls rigorous enough to operate
when the patient may not be able to supply sound judgment on his
own.

CONSENT

The application of a prolonged program of medication use for
treatment of a mental condition contains the classic elements of a
high-risk, high-gain decision reviewed in the preceding discussion.
For the patient, the decision to use medications over an extended
interval is an important life choice in which he relies upon the
physician for information and advice. After the acute situation is
stabilized and the physician is considering a program of maintenance
or prophylaxis, he has a duty to seek consent before entering a
prolonged phase. The reader is referred to other sources for discussions of the mechanics for obtaining consent (51) and tests of competency to give consent (52). The basic concept of consent implies a
discussion between the physician and patient reviewing the hazards
of the treatment, the hazards of the untreated condition, and the
possible gains of the treatment. For example, most physicians would,
in the case of neuroleptic treatment, review the risks of tardive
dyskinesia, including its potential seriousness, unknown frequency,
and possibility of occurrence even with careful observation. The
useful scope of disclosure can be envisioned by the query, "Does the
physician know something significant about the balance of risks in
this situation that the patient does not know?" The physician has a

duty to seek a basis for believing the patient understands the discussion and is competent to consider such a decision. When delusions or defects of memory or mentation, or other aspects of reduced competency, might be present, the physician should ask the consent of family members or seek another basis through a court. Periodically throughout a prolonged program, the consent discussion should be reviewed, particularly in the face of changes in the patient's condition or with the appearance of new information material to the consideration of risks. Because many physicians believe the signing of a consent form does not document the whole transaction involved in the consent discussion, they place an additional note in the record reflecting the hazards reviewed and the patient's action. In some parts of the United States, civic discussion and legislative review are in process which might create a basis for a program of continuing medication in the absence of consent. Such discussion focuses on a narrow set of conditions where the patient does not give consent, does not use medications regularly, and repeatedly experiences a major hazard thereby. Various remedies are under consideration to balance civil and civic values in the context of the least restrictive environment. Some observers believe a mechanism for creating a partial guardianship will evolve.

DISCUSSION

The significant opportunity for service which programs of prolonged medication use would appear to offer in appropriate psychiatric conditions can only be approached safely within a rigorous design. The design includes narrow indications, close observation, and linkage with laboratory, emergency room, and hospital services. When such medical investment is not present, the risks are correspondingly larger and the benefits erratic.

ACKNOWLEDGMENTS

Orlando Cabrera, Harry Little, Daniel Pugh, Thomas Tourlentes, and Harold Visotsky provided critical comment on this paper. Ronald Fieve, Eugene Caffey, and Gerald Klerman provided reactions to problems present in relation to chronic lithium use. The author is responsible for all opinion expressed.

NOTES

1. Weissman MM, Klerman GL: Epidemiology of mental disorders. Emerging trends in the United States. Arch Gen Psychiat 35:705–712, 1978

2. Taube CA: Readmissions to inpatient services of state and county mental hospitals, 1972. Mental Health Statistical Note No. 110, DHEW Publication No. ADM–75–158. Rockville, Md., National Institute of Mental Health, 1974

3. Redlich F, Kellert SR: Trends in American mental health. Amer J Psychiat 135:22–28, 1978

4. Regier DA, Goldberg ID, Taube CA: The defacto US mental health services system. Arch Gen Psychiat 35:685–693, 1978

5. Ingram DK: Profile of chronic illness in nursing homes, 1974. Vital and Health Statistics Ser. 13, No. 29, DHEW Publication No. PHS–78–1780. Rockville, Md., National Center for Health Statistics, 1977

6. Meyer NG: Diagnostic distribution of admissions to inpatient services of state and county mental hospitals, 1975. Mental Health Statistical Note No. 138, DHEW Publication No. ADM–77–158. Rockville, Md., National Institute of Mental Health, 1977

7. Kramer M: Trends in the usage of psychiatric facilities. Public Health Service Publication No. 1434. Rockville, Md., National Institute of Mental Health, 1966

8. Helgason T: Epidemiology of mental disorders in Iceland. Acta Psychiat Scand 40:Suppl 173:1–257, 1964

9. Faden VB: Primary diagnosis of discharges from non-federal general hospital psychiatric units, US, 1975. Mental Health Statistical Note No. 137, DHEW Publication No. ADM–77–158. Rockville, Md., National Institute of Mental Health, 1977

10. Bachrach LL: Characteristics of diagnosed and missed alcoholic male admissions to state and county mental hospitals, 1972. Mental Health Statistical Note No. 124, DHEW Publication No. ADM–76–158. Rockville, Md., National Institute of Mental Health, 1976

11. Kramer M: Psychiatric services and the changing institutional scene, 1950–1985. NIMH Reports Ser. B, No. 12, DHEW Publication No. ADM–77–433. Rockville, Md., National Institute of Mental Health, 1977

12. Baldessarini RJ: Schizophrenia. N Eng J Med 297:988–995, 1977

13. Davis JM: Overview: Maintenance therapy in psychiatry: 1. Schizophrenia. Amer J Psychiat 132:1237–1245, 1975

14. Davis AE, Dinitz S, Pasamanick B. Schizophrenics in the New Custodial Community. Columbus: Ohio State Univ Press, 1974

15. Rifkin A, Quitkin F, Rabiner CJ, Klein DF: Fluphenazine decanoate, fluphenazine hydrochloride given orally, and placebo in remitted schizophrenics. 1. Relapse rates after one year. Arch Gen Psychiat 34:43–47, 1977

16. Hogarty GE, Ulrich RF: Temporal effects of drug and placebo in delaying relapse in schizophrenic outpatients. Arch Gen Psychiat 34:297–301, 1977

17. Neurologic symptoms associated with antipsychotic–drug use. N Engl J Med 289:20 –23, 1973

18. Gardos G, Cole JO: Maintenance antipsychotic therapy: Is the cure worse than the disease? Amer J Psychiat 133:32–36, 1976

19. Taylor AM, Abrams R: A critique of the St. Louis psychiatric research criteria for schizophrenia. Amer J Psychiat 132:1276–1280, 1975

20. Groves JE, Mandel MR: The long-acting phenothiazines. Arch Gen Psychiat 32:893–900, 1975

21. Van Putten T: Why do schizophrenia patients refuse to take their drugs? Arch Gen Psychiat 31:67–72, 1974

22. Rifkin A, Quitkin F, Kane J, Struve F, Klein DF: Are prophylactic antiparkinson drugs necessary? Arch Gen Psychiat 35:483– 489, 1978

23. Snyder SH: Madness and the Brain. New York, McGraw-Hill, 1974

24. Lutz EG: Neuroleptic-induced akathisia and dystonia triggered by alcohol. J Amer Med Assoc 236:2422–2423, 1976

25. Hansell N: Sympathomimetics and schizophrenia (letter). J Amer Med Assoc 234:1220, 1975

26. Greden JF, Fontaine P, Lubetsky M, Chamberlin K: Anxiety and derpression associated with caffeinism among psychiatric patients. Amer J Psychiat 135:963–966, 1978

27. Casey DE, Rabins P: Tardive dyskinesia as a life-threatening illness. Amer J Psychiat 135:486 – 488, 1978

28. Growden JH, Gelenberg AJ, Hirsch MJ: Lecithin can suppress tardive dyskinesia (letter). N Engl J Med 298:1029–1030, 1978

29. Barbeau A: Lecithin in neurologic disorders (letter). N Engl J Med 299:200, 1978

30. Rumeau-Rouquette C, Goujard J, Huel G. Possible terratogenic effect of phenothiazines in human beings. Terratol 15:57–64, 1977

31. Slone D, Siskind V, Heinonen OP: Antenatal exposure to the phenothiazines. Amer J Obstet Gynec 128:486 – 488, 1968

32. Lundborg P, Engle J: Learning deficits and selected biochemical brain changes in 4-week-old offspring of nursing rat mothers treated with neuroleptics. In G. Sedvall (ed): Antipsychotic Drugs, Pharmacodynamics and Pharmacokinetics. Oxford, Pergamon Press, 1975

33. Hansell N: Enhancing adaptational work during service. In AG Hirschowitz, B Levy (ed): The Changing Mental Health Scene. New York, Spectrum-Wiley, 1976

34. Davis JM: Overview: Maintenance therapy in psychiatry: II. Affective disorders. Amer J Psychiat 133:1–13, 1976

35. Baldessarini RJ: Chemotherapy in Psychiatry. Cambridge, Harvard University Press, 1977

36. Walker JI, Brodie HKH: Current concepts of lithium treatment and prophylaxis. J Cont Educ Psychiat 39:19–30, 1978

37. Robinson DS, Nies A, Ravaris L, Lamborn KR: The monoamine oxidose inhibitor, phenelzine, in the treatment of depressive-anxiety states. Arch Gen Psychiat 29:407–413, 1973

38. Ayd FJ: Chronic renal lesions: A hazard of long-term lithium treatment. Int Drug Therap 12:37–40, 1977

39. Bucht G, Wahlin A: Impairment of renal concentrating capacity by lithium. Lancet 1:778–779, 1978

40. Freyhan FA: On the controversy of prophylactic antidepressants. Compreh Psychiat 16:1–5, 1975

41. Lipkin KM, Dyrud J, Meyer GG: The many faces of mania. Arch Gen Psychiat 22:262–267, 1970

42. Tupin JP, Smith DB, Clanon TL, Kim LI, Nugent A, Groupe A: The long-term use of lithium in aggressive prisoners. Compreh Psychiat 14:311–317, 1973

43. Prien RF, Caffey EM: Relationship between dosage and response to lithium prophylaxis in recurrent depression. Amer J Psychiat 133:567–570, 1976

44. Van Putten T: Why do patients with manic-depressive illness stop their lithium? Compreh Psychiat 16:179–183, 1975

45. Weinstein MR, Goldfield MD: Cardiovascular malformations with lithium use during pregnancy. Amer J Psychiat 132:529–531, 1975

46. Ananth J: Side effects in the neonate from psychotropic agents excreted through breast-feeding. Amer J Psychiat 135:801–805, 1978

47. Wells CE: Chronic brain disease: An overview. Amer J Psychiat 135:1–12, 1978

48. Rice E, Gendelman S: Psychiatric aspects of normal pressure hydrocephalus. J Amer Med Assoc 223:409–412, 1973

49. Dysken MW, Merry W, Davis JM: Anticholinergic psychosis. Psychiat Ann 8:452–456, 1978

50. Elliott FA: Neurologic factors in violent behavior. Bull Amer Acad Psychiat and Law 4:297–315, 1976

51. Meisel A, Roth LH, Lidz CW: Toward a model of the legal doctrine of informed consent. Amer J Psychiat 134:285–289, 1977

52. Roth LH, Meisel A, Lidz CW: Tests of competency to consent to treatment. Amer J Psychiat 134:279–284, 1977

Chapter 3

DRUG MONITORING

Cynthia Johansen

Drug surveillance, or "drug monitoring," can be broadly defined as a process which is utilized to evaluate a patient's response to drug therapy with the primary objective of promoting rational therapeutics for optimal patient care. The physician, when initially prescribing a drug for a patient, reaches a therapeutic decision through a series of considerations, observations, evaluations, and reevaluations. Subsequent visits of the patient include reviewing the patient's response to the drug therapy—that is, drug monitoring. Pharmacists in hospitals and skilled-nursing facilities are monitoring drug therapy on an individual patient basis. The community pharmacist is also monitoring drug therapy when a prescription is filled.

QUALITY ASSURANCE

Emphasis by the federal government, Joint Commission on Accreditation of Hospitals, third-party payers, and consumer groups on high-quality health care has prompted all health professionals to engage in much introspection *(1)*. Formalized quality control systems are being mandated in hospitals and skilled-nursing facilities by Professional Standards Review Organizations *(2)*, the Social Security Administration, and other organizations actively concerned with the quality of health care. The message is very clear: the professions and institutions will be held responsible and accountable for assuring patients of high-quality care. Health care literature of the past several years abound with articles on medical audit, utilization review, peer review, patient care audit, drug utilization review, and medical care evaluation, all of which are variants of quality assurance programs. The purpose of such studies is primarily to identify trends: utilization review studies (3), with a primary cost-effective goal, are designed to promote the most effective and appropriate use of available health facilities and services by emphasizing identification and analysis of patterns of patient care and changes which might be necessary to maintain them. Drug utilization review (4) is the ongoing study of the frequency of use and cost of drugs, from which patterns of prescribing, dispensing, and patient use can be determined and analyzed. A review of the current drug-monitoring efforts to provide quality health care seemed appropriate to point out that these efforts are facility or institution oriented and generally retrospective in nature, rather than prospective or concurrent (5).

To provide optimum drug therapy, monitoring must be prospective, where drugs to be prescribed are evaluated in relation to a comprehensive social, medical, and drug history of the patient, and concurrent, where evaluation of the drug therapy is carried out while the patient is being treated. A formal comprehensive system to monitor the effects of drugs in either the inpatient or the ambulant patient currently does not exist.

As the principal authoritative figure in the medical setting, the physician, who believes in the value of what he has prescribed, should make efforts to insure and monitor patient compliance to drug therapy—thus improving the effectiveness of that therapy (6). Medical care is a team effort by physicians, pharmacists, nurses, and patients; in mental health, additional professionals, such as psychologists and social workers, are important members of the team. The better the team works together, the better the result.

DRUG THERAPY PROBLEMS

Some of the problems which are currently identified and indicate a need for improving the quality of drug therapy, particularly in the mental patient, are polypharmacy, noncompliance, inaccurate documentation by physicians of medication prescribed, inappropriate drug therapy, adverse drug reactions, inadequate knowledge pertaining to proper use and expectation of drug therapy, and lack of drug monitoring.

Polypharmacy

A 1976 study *(7)* conducted in 12 Veterans Administration hospitals surveyed polypharmacy in 1,276 elderly patients and found that one out of every six patients received two or more psychoactive drugs.

Another study *(8)* indicates that 40–50% of hospitalized patients receive more than one psychoactive drug and that it is not unusual to find patients receiving three or four at the same time. A survey by Schroeder, Caffey, and Lorei *(9)* in February and March of 1975, from data contributed by 42 VA hospitals on 3,184 long-term chronic schizophrenic patients, identified that 34% of those patients were receiving two or more antipsychotic drugs and 61% were receiving two or more psychotherapeutic drugs.

Noncompliance

Noncompliance remains a continuing problem in the psychiatric patient; as has been previously documented, drug defaulting by the ambulatory patient ranges from 11% to 87% *(10)*. The importance of medications for the mental patients who are being treated on the community level cannot be overemphasized. With patients who fail to take their medication correctly, it is not uncommon for the physician to either increase the dose or change drugs when finding no improvement or an inadequate response. Patient noncompliance *(11)* with medication regimens not only curtails therapeutic benefits but also results in additional costs.

Inaccurate Documentation of Outpatient Drug Therapy

The records of 355 patients in outpatient clinics at Madison Veterans Administration Hospital were reviewed and compared with pharmacy files of the same patients. The records were evaluated for completeness and accuracy, with regard to the names, dosage, and directions for drugs ordered by the clinic physician. Twenty-one percent of the charts omitted the name of one or more drugs prescribed by the physicians, and 62% of the charts contained inaccuracies regarding dosage or directions. Documentation of potentially toxic drugs was not significantly different from that of less toxic drugs.

This study tested the accuracy and completeness of outpatient records in documenting medications prescribed by physicians. Based on this study, certain trends are apparent: (1) The more visits a patient makes, the more drugs are prescribed. (2) The more drugs a patient receives, the less accurately medical record reflects this therapy. (3) The more visits a patient makes, the more duplication of prescriptions occurs. Not documented in the study, but reasonable to assume, is that the sickest patients come to the clinic most frequently and receive the most drugs. These are the patients in whom overdosage, interactions, or adverse reactions are most critical. *(12)*

Inappropriate Drug Therapy

Rational drug therapy is widely defined as prescribing the right drug for the right patient at the right time in the right amounts and with due consideration of relative costs. Rational drug therapy is usually assumed to be intelligent or informed drug therapy. In fact, the behavior of the physician in prescribing a certain drug in a certain situation may be completely rational, based on inadequate, erroneous, or equivocal information *(13)*. Awareness by the prescriber of the individual's current drug therapy, including over-the-counter drugs, herbal therapies, and drugs from other prescribers, as well as the individual's social habits such as smoking and drinking is vital before rational drug therapy can be anticipated. The higher incidence of drug abuse in the psychiatric patient suggests that an increased awareness in this area is vital.

What is the message the patient receives when given a prescription, or not given one? Gutheil *(14)*, discussing the psychodynamics of drug prescribing, suggests that for a physician practicing psychoanalysis, using a drug may represent the failure of talk and this feeling may be communicated to the patient; or giving a patient a prescription may signal the end of the appointment; or giving a prescription may reassure the patient that he or she is "sick." Van Camerik *(15)*, in the *Journal of Legal Aspects of Medical Practice,* identifies 10 types of patients who do not follow the physician's prescribed regimen. The reasons range from ignorance to masochism —and sometimes the doctor is at fault.

Adverse Drug Reactions

An adverse drug reaction *(16)* can be defined as any undesirable, or unintended response to medication that requires treatment or alteration of therapy. A number of causes of adverse drug reactions have been identified.

MULTIPLE PRESCRIBERS.   The number of physicans a patient sees correlates directly with the adverse drug reaction rate *(17)*. Fifty percent
of general medical patients receive medication from more than one
physician at a time *(18)*. This problem is intensified in the chronic
mental patient who probably is receiving psychotropic medication
from the psychiatrist and medication for treatment of general physical problems from at least one other physician at another location.

MULTIPLE PRESCRIPTIONS.   The number of prescriptions being taken by
a patient correlates directly with the drug interaction-adverse reaction rate, and the benefit-to-risk ratio for each drug decreases as
additional drugs are taken *(19)*.

Constant encouragement is offered the public regarding the
utilization of one pharmacy for their drug needs. Institution and use
of patient medication profiles by community pharmacists have
proven to be very beneficial in detecting potential therapeutic problems in the ambulatory patient *(20)*. Personal experience, however,
indicates that even when a consumer utilizes one pharmacy, and that
pharmacy has a patient profile system, information about drugs received from hospital emergency rooms, birth control pills from family planning services, or samples from the physician is not generally
conveyed to the pharmacist for inclusion on the profile.

NONPRESCRIPTION MEDICATIONS.   "Home remedies" or the use of over-
the-counter drugs is an accepted way of life. It is projected that 30-
50%   of the public takes one or more drugs in this class with some
regularity *(21)*.

LACK OF MONITORING PARAMETERS.   Adverse drug reactions are also
caused by the failure to establish therapeutic end points for drug
therapy and an unreasonable expectation of drug therapy *(22)*.

PHYSIOLOGICAL VARIABLES.   Important determinants of the effects of a
drug are the physiologic states of the patient and the pathophysi-
ology of the disease *(23)*. Although multiple drug therapy may be
unavoidable, for example, in the schizophrenic patient who is also a
diabetic, awareness is essential and dose and/or drug adjustment
should be anticipated.

Lack of Drug Education

The public appears unsophisticated, at the very least, concerning the proper use of prescription and nonprescription drugs *(24)*.

In general, nonprescription drugs are considered totally safe "or they wouldn't be on the market." Prescription drugs are considered safe, because "a physician would give nothing that would harm a patient." Additional problems peculiar to psychiatric patients who are uninformed may include rejection of drug therapy when the crisis is over, thinking they no longer need drugs, or resistance to medication because taking it would indicate a "mental problem." Many patients also take someone else's prescription and therefore compromise their therapy and health.

Physicians, are confronted constantly with a wide variety of new drugs on which they need responsible drug information. Lack of understanding of pharmacology and pharmacokinetics of these drugs may contribute to poor prescribing practices and drug-induced disease *(25)*. Downplaying of side effects and adverse reactions in promotional literature and by drug manufacturers' salespersons probably results in an inadequate overview of drug toxicity and iatrogenic disease by the physician.

Lack of Monitoring

A general lack of drug therapy monitoring is exemplified by studies both of drug use in the ambulatory patient and of drug-induced hospital admissions.

A large community survey *(26)* done in western Maryland has revealed what a Johns Hopkins team called a "startling finding." The percentage of people who had taken drugs (prescription and nonprescription) within the previous 48 hours was shockingly high: more than 60% of the 1,059 women and nearly 42% of the 771 men interviewed had taken one or more drugs. The other surprise to the surveyors in this study was the high number of people with symptoms of depression who were receiving inappropriate medication. Drug use increased with age in the survey.

In a current paper, Rosalyn King *(27)* evaluates pharmaceutical services in 11 community health centers funded by the Department of Health, Education, and Welfare which were designed to meet the comprehensive health needs of the ambulatory population each served. None of the programs were rated adequate with respect to drug therapy monitoring. She suggested that, although traditionally pharmaceutical services have been viewed by pharmacists and other health care team members as the part of ambulatory care responsible only for providing drugs and supplies, there is now a recognition that the provision of drug use information is a part of pharmaceutical services. However, organizational and professional mechanisms necessary to enable provision of even basic patient-oriented information must be identified and instituted.

Many studies have been published depicting the association between hospital admissions and drug-related problems. Frisk, Cooper, and Campbell *(28)*, in a study of 392 admissions from whom medication histories were obtained within a six-month period, identified a 20% incidence of drug-related problems contributing to hospitalization. Although the geriatric patients in this study had a higher incidence of drug-related problems (29.4%), they comprised only 30% of the admissions, indicating a serious problem exists regardless of age. The drug-related problems identified were:

1. Adverse response to prescribed therapy.
2. Misuse or noncompliance.
3. Interaction of drug therapy and diet.
4. Multiprescriber treatment.
5. Ineffective or inappropriate therapy.

McKenney and Harrison *(29)* point out a need for improvement in drug monitoring and educational services available in the outpatient setting in their review of 216 hospital admissions in a two-month study conducted in 1974. Fifty-nine patients (27.3%) were found to have a drug-related problem associated with hospital admission; the most significant being 17 patients (7.9%) due to adverse reactions and 23 patients (10.5%) due to noncompliance. This study found no apparent differences in patients experiencing drug-related admission problems when age, sex, and race were compared. However, most patients were receiving multiple drugs for multiple medical problems. The authors suggest that a significant portion of the 590 hospital days and the approximately $60,000 needed to care for the 59 patients could have been avoided.

THE PSYCHIATRIC CLINICAL PHARMACIST

The literature supports the increasing interest in psychotropic drug therapy by pharmacists who (1) serve as educators for psychiatric residents; (2) use pharmacokinetic principles in evaluating drug regimens; and (3) participate directly in drug therapy of psychiatric patients *(30–32)*.

California's Experimental Health Power Act *(33)* has established a five-year pilot project "permitting the prescription, dispensing and administering of drugs and devices, with specified exceptions" by several types of health care professionals, including pharmacists (under the general supervision of a licensed physician or surgeon). This legislation in California aligns itself with the role now being provided by some psychiatric pharmacists *(34)*—that of providing direct patient care in management of maintenance drug therapy of the psychiatric outpatient, including altering drug dosages or schedules and discontinuing or adding drugs.

Straker *(35)*, in a review of clinical psychiatry and psychopharmacology, describes the pharmacist as a person who can fulfill an important role to both health provider and patient by serving as reinforcer, observer, educator, advisor, and consultant. The pharmacist continues to occupy a key role among the mental health disciplines by reinforcing medication compliance, monitoring drug utilization by the patient, and counseling the physician prescriber. The special awareness of drug interactions and incompatibilities adds a crucial dimension to safe and effective drug use.

The psychiatric clinical pharmacist provides a unique contribution to the mental health team, not only because of an expertise in drugs and their effects, but also because of the pharmacist's training and responsibility to total patient care—there is less of a tendency to interpret observations and evaluations as extensions of psychiatric pathology.

In addition, the pharmacist is seen by patients as a person knowledgeable in total health care and occupies a position of public trust and confidence, with an ability to empathize with the patients, showing concern for their well-being, and yet maintaining a professional attitude. These qualities, plus putting the patient at ease and being a good listener, enable a pharmacist to obtain information regarding the patient's total health care attitude, relevant to treatment, that is not conveyed to other team members.

In my opinion, accepting the psychiatric pharmacist as an equal team member, rather than as a manager of maintenance drug therapy in the chronic patient under the supervision of a psychiatrist, enables a more comprehensive treatment program resulting in optimum benefit to all patients seeking care in a mental health facility, whether inpatient or ambulatory.

In a study *(36)* evaluating psychotropic drug therapy knowledge of eight types of health care practitioners, clinical pharmacists in psychiatric practice scored highest, followed by psychiatrists.

Hospital pharmacists in mental institutions and nonmental institutions ranked third and fourth; physicians (nonpsychiatrists) ranked fifth. Psychiatric nurses, community pharmacists, and nonpsychiatric nurses ranked sixth, seventh, and eighth, respectively. Psychiatric clinical pharmacists scored significantly higher in the area of drug selection than did all other practitioners. In the area of drug monitoring, psychiatrists and psychiatric clinical pharmacists rated superior, nearly 30% better than the hospital pharmacist and 60% above physicians (nonpsychiatrists).

RESOLUTION TO DRUG PROBLEMS: MONITORING

This review has identified significant drug therapy problems which must be resolved to assure that rational drug therapy is provided to the patient. Inclusion of a psychiatric, patient-oriented pharmacist on the mental health team to monitor drug therapy will benefit the provider as well as the patient by improving drug use and compliance, resulting in better patient care, often at a reduced cost.

Public Law 94–63 (Federal Community Mental Health Center Amendments of 1975), Title III, Section 201 (Quality Assurance) is essentially alluding to drug therapy monitoring by inclusion of the drug use profile outlined as follows.

Part of every medical record should be a drug use profile. This should be in a separate section of the medical record and easily identifiable. The drug use profile is begun at the time of admission and should be reviewed at least every two months but more frequently at times of change or adjustment (not less than once a week).

The drug use profile has, but is not limited to, the following purposes:

1. to provide a medication history on the patient;
2. to provide information regarding the patient's drug utilization;
3. to provide data to facilitate patient consultation and communication with other health professionals.

The drug use profile shall include, but is not limited to, the following information:

1. history of drugs, prescription and nonprescription, being

taken at time of admission and for previous six months;
2. drug allergies, idiosyncratic reactions, and/or other adverse drug effects;
3. ineffective therapy;
4. drugs prescribed following admission:
    a. date prescribed
    b. drug product name, dosage, strength, route, schedule
    c. dates medication discontinued or changed

The approach and procedures discussed in the following section will ensure compliance with the above guidelines, which were provided by the National Institute of Mental Health on 16 January 1976.

A Systematic Approach to Drug Therapy Monitoring

Monitoring drug therapy is concerned with the medication, as a therapeutic agent, which may elicit both beneficial and adverse effects, as well as with the patient's response to the drug, or drugs, and must take into consideration the total care being provided the patient. The goal of monitoring drug therapy is basically to ensure rational drug therapy and optimal patient care, but in addition, it should be utilized as a method of drug information communication between the pharmacist and the physician, as well as providing information to other disciplines in a concise, organized manner, enabling assistance from these disciplines in identifying and documenting changes.

An efficient procedure for monitoring drug therapy describes thought processes to be used in approaching rational therapeutics. These thought processes occur in a defined and orderly sequence and are followed by an appropriate action or behavior. My approach to drug therapy monitoring basically correlates with the seven steps identified by Sax, Cheung, and associates *(37)*. The following procedural guidelines are provided the reader as an outline of the process:

1. Identify the patient's health problems or disease state.
    a. From interviewing the patient
    b. From the medical record
    c. From therapeutic indications for the use of medications the patient is taking
2. Obtain comprehensive information on past and current drug use patterns and allergies.
    a. Information of drug allergies, idiosyncratic reactions,

and/or adverse drug effects as described by the patient or significant others, or from the medical record

   b. History of drugs—prescription, nonprescription, and "street" drugs—including doses, length of time drug taken, and patient's description of why they were taken

   c. Patient's vital statistics—sex, age, weight, blood pressure

3. Review appropriateness of drug therapy, indication for use, route of administration, therapeutic, physical or chemical incompatibilities, and interactions—drug-drug, drug-disease, and drug-food.

4. Evaluate data on the drug use pattern (from chart, progress notes, and prescription file, if available).

   a. Compliance to prescribed instructions
      (1) overutilization
      (2) underutilization

   b. Types of drugs being taken
      (1) inappropriate combinations
      (2) duplication

   c. Determine if signs and symptoms manifested by the patient are adverse effects of prescribed, over-the-counter, or "street" drugs.

5. Establish a record for drug use and drug therapy monitoring. Institute drug use profile. Begin with patient's drug use for at least six months prior to admission; then keeping it updated, follow on continuous basis thereafter. Included on the profile are allergies, adverse reaction experiences, and pharmacist's pertinent comments.

6. Stating the therapeutic objective of each drug prescribed, develop criteria or findings for monitoring responses to the drug therapy, both positive and adverse, according to a problem-oriented approach. Monitoring parameters can be divided basically into two areas for both therapeutic and toxic drug effects.

   a. Subjective criteria—manifestations mentioned voluntarily by the patient or in response to questions of the clinical pharmacist. Usually not quantitatively measurable and requiring value judgments including general appearance, complaints, state of mind, strength, and weakness.

   b. Objective criteria—drug effects which are referable to or measurable, such as vital signs, laboratory reports, observed side effects, and expected therapeutic effects observed.

7. Summarize and document all pertinent findings and information in a concise and objective manner for communication.

Problem-Oriented Drug Therapy Plan

A drug therapy plan can be defined as an organized approach to the problem(s) of the individual patient under consideration. The plan identifies the most appropriate drug therapy that is consistent with the diagnosis and desired goals (correction of the problem) based on the patient's data base. The drug plan can be integrated into an existing record system, or utilized independently by the pharmacist as follows:

1. In mental health settings utilizing the Problem-Oriented Medical Record System (POMR) introduced by Weed *(38)* or variations of this system, the integration of drug therapy in the patient's total treatment plan would already be occurring; this is the ideal system. The writer's intent is not to create a separate plan for drug therapy; in fact, this would not be beneficial, since drugs are only one facet of treatment and to be most effective, must be integrated with all other facets of treatment. It is not uncommon, however, that reference to drug therapy obtained by the patient from other sources are not included in the record; this can be a serious oversight. All drugs being taken by the patient, along with dose and frequency, must be included and regularly reviewed to enable identification of possible drug interactions, toxicities, and other potential problems, with concurrent recognition that these problems require a plan for resolution.

2. Where POMR is not utilized, the problem-oriented drug therapy plan would ideally be included in the chart and utilized by the physician, pharmacist, and nurse, replacing the traditional progress notes and physician's medication order form. Progress notes by these professionals regarding medication would be written in the POMR format relating directly to problem number. Problems can be active or resolved. This type of record system enables the nonmedical health professionals to follow the patient's progress regarding drug therapy.

3. In settings where inclusion of a drug therapy plan in the patient's chart is not accepted, the pharmacist can utilize a modified version of this system to insure efficient identification of problems and documentation of action taken, thus maintaining a record of recommendations. This is the least desirable, since the pharmacist's input is not readily available to others involved in the patient's treatment.

The procedures for establishing a drug therapy plan are as follows:

1. Establishment of data base
    a. Drug and allergy history. The pharmacist will interview the patient upon admission and complete a drug and allergy history (see Figure 3–1). If the patient is an adolescent, or incompetent, the responsible person can provide the information. During the interview, the pharmacist is able to acquire an understanding of the patient's feelings and fears regarding the disease state and also to gain insight into the patient's attitude toward drugs, drug therapy, and drug usage patterns, for documentation and input with other team members.

    The drug and allergy history form was designed so that designated mental health workers, who had completed training (provided by the pharmacist) in the technique of obtaining the information requested, could be utilized to interview the patient. Or, since it is written in the third person, the form could be completed independently by the patient or the responsible person. This third alternative is not recommended.

    My experience has been that when a pharmacist is not able to personally interview the patient the information obtained, although not as comprehensive, is adequate to alert one to problem areas and/or the problem patient. The pharmacist can then resolve the concern by coordinating with the psychiatrist's evaluation of the patient, or input from other team members. On occasion a follow-up patient interview by the pharmacist may be necessary.
    b. Drug profile. The drug profile is to be initiated at the time of admission. The example provided in Figure 3–2 is for ambulatory care. (The conventional type of drug profile is appropriate for the hospital settings. Essentially the same

KINGS VIEW

1. What prescription drugs, medicines or pills have you taken in the past six months?
Please underline those now being taken. If you don't know the name, describe the medicine.

NAME OF DRUG	HOW TAKEN	CONDITION DRUG TAKEN FOR
EXAMPLE: NPH INSULIN	30 U Injected Daily	DIABETES

2. Have you ever taken someone else's prescription medicine?_____ If yes, what drug and why?_____

3. What over-the-counter medicines (drugs that do not require a prescription) do you take regularly?
Laxatives_____Vitamins _____Headache, cramps, general pain medicine (aspirin,
bufferin, tylenol, etc.)_____
Cold medicines_____ Cough medicines_____
Antacids_____ Drugs for nerves_____
Drugs to stay awake_____ Drugs to sleep_____
Ointments, acne medicine, others applied to skin_____
Other medicines_____

4. Are you allergic to any drugs?_____ If yes, please list with type of reaction experienced_____

5. Are you allergic to any foods or plants?_____ If yes, please list with type of reaction experienced_____

6. Are you allergic to animals, insect bites or stings?_____ If yes, please list with type of reaction experienced

7. Have you ever had hay fever, asthma, eczema or hives?_____ If yes, please list with type of reaction experienced

8. Do you have any family members with allergies? (relationship and allergies):_____

9. Do you drink coffee or tea?_____1-2 cups_____2-6 cups_____6 · cups (per day).

10. Do you drink Coke, Pepsi, or Dr. Pepper regularly?_____ If yes, how many per day?_____

11. Do you drink alcoholic beverages?
    A. Wine or beer_____. Occasionally_____ Regularly_____. How much_____?
    B. Hard liquor_____. Occasionally_____ Regularly_____. How much_____?

12. Have you ever taken street narcotics, LSD, sniffed glue or paint?_____ If yes, type and frequency:_____

13. Do you smoke or use herbs?_____ If yes, explain what and how used:_____

14. Do you smoke cigarettes?_____1 pkg._____2 pkgs. _____#2 · pkgs. (per day).

15. Do you smoke Marijuana?_____ If yes, occasionally_____ Regularly_____How much_____?

16. Have you ever taken any drugs that made you sick?_____. Specify:_____

17. Have you ever experienced side effects or undesirable effects from drugs you have taken?_____If yes, please
describe:_____

Person acquiring history (name and position)	Signature of person providing information
Date	If other than patient, relationship

NAME: Last	First	Middle	Unit Number

Figure 3-1. Drug and Allergy History

information is documented, the difference being that drugs dispensed rather than drugs prescribed are identified.)

The following is the procedure for using the drug profile:

(1) In the top right-hand corner, identify all physicians prescribing for the patient—if more than three, add D, E, etc. The letters (A, B, C) will be utilized in the column identified at the top by "M.D.," to indicate the prescriber of the prescription.

(2) The date of the profile entry is to be indicated in the left-hand column.

Physician A. _____

B. _____

C. _____

Date	M.D.	Prescriptions				Dates Filled											Notes
		Drug	Dose	Freq.	Quant.												

Blood Pressure/Pulse

Date													
B.P.													
Pulse													
Nurse													

Medical Problems #1 _____ #2 _____ #3 _____ #4 _____

Psychiatric Diagnosis _____

Adverse Drug Reaction History _____

Allergies _____

Comments: _____

_____

Age _____ Sex _____ Weight _____

NAME

Last	First	Middle	Chart #	Date Initiated _____
				Profile # _____

Figure 3-2. Patient Drug Profile

(3)   Document all prescriptions being taken by the patient in the space provided. Initially, the data on the prescription drugs received from the patient on the drug and allergy history can be transferred to this form; however, I would write it in pencil and request that the patient bring in all current prescription bottles on the next clinic visit. (Information regarding prescriptions is often unreliable when provided by the patient from memory.) Drugs prescribed within the mental health system are to be included on the profile. Under dates filled, identify the month and year at the top and record the days the prescription is filled in the appropriate squares.

(4)   Under "Notes" include lithium levels, length of time drug was taken prior to initiating profile, reason drug discontinued, or any important fact about that particular prescription.

(5)   The blood pressure and pulse section is self-explanatory; if another record is utilized there would be no reason for duplication.

(6)   Identify medical problems. This information can be obtained either from the chart, if available, or as related by the patient, or by the therapeutic indication of drugs prescribed.

(7)   The psychiatric diagnosis should be included as soon as it is determined, but this may not be on the initial visit of the patient.

(8)   Allergies and adverse reactions will be transferred from the drug and allergy history. Any additional reactions which are recognized throughout the course of treatment are to be added, along with the date of the reaction.

(9)   Under "Comments," the pharmacist would include any factors which might influence the effectiveness of drug therapy, such as smoking, coffee drinking, or regular use by the patient of antacids, laxatives, and the like.

(10)   Complete the balance of the form as indicated.

The drug profile enables an evaluation of drug interactions and a review of drug use—underutilization or overutilization is easily determined by the dates recorded. This is an integral part of the evaluation, since compliance to the physician's orders can be quickly identified. The types of drugs a patient is taking is very important. Duplication or inappropriate combinations are often discovered, particularly when more than one physician is prescribing. For example, it is very common to find that a patient is taking Valium, Serax, and perhaps Dalmane—or even Artane and Akineton—at the same time.

    c. The physical examination, available laboratory data, social history, all previous treatment records available, and initial intake (admission summary) would all be reviewed by the pharmacist, and significant facts which may pertain to drug therapy would be included as part of the data base. Notations may be made on the profile sheet under "Notes," or if the pharmacist's review identifies a more serious problem or potential problem such as drug toxicity or a significant drug interaction this observation would be identified as a problem on POMR record and/or discussed directly with the physician.

2. Formulation of the plan

    a. Utilizing the data base, the pharmacist identifies problems, or possible problems, related to the patient's drug therapy. Unexplained symptoms, possible drug toxicities, abnormal laboratory findings, over- or underuse of medications, use of "street" drugs, previous adverse reactions, and educational needs of the patient are examples which would be included. The problem list would be continued throughout a patient's treatment. Some problems will be resolved, new ones added, or sometimes two or more may be combined.

    b. The second step is to develop a plan for each problem identified. A plan, to be successful, must be a coordinated effort by all the mental health professionals dealing with the patient, with appropriate inclusion of the patient. I believe cooperation of the patient is very important.

    c. Finally, follow-up should be conducted, to assure that the plan is followed; if it is not followed, the plan should be reevaluated and the proper adjustments made.

A drug therapy plan, with its organizational clarity and completeness, will reduce many of the problems usually encountered and will subsequently promote rational drug therapy.

NOTES

1. Besti DF, deLeon RF: Medication process: Who is responsible. Hospitals 48:97–100, 1974

2. United States Social Security Administration: Social Security Amendments of

1972. PL 92-603, U.S. Code Congressional and Administrative News, Laws, 92nd Congress, Second Session. St. Paul, Minn., West Publishing Co., 1972

3. United States Social Security Administration skilled nursing facility standards for certification and participation in medicare and medicaid programs. Federal Register 39:2238, 1974

4. Brodie D: Drug utilization review/planning. J Am Hosp Assoc 46, 1972

5. Stolar M: Conceptual framework for drug usage review, medical audit and other patient care review procedures. Am J Hosp Pharm 34:139–145, 1977

6. Barday WF: Improving the effectiveness of therapy. JAMA 237(12):1236, 1977

7. Prien RF, Klett J, Caffey E: Polypharmacy in the psychiatric treatment of elderly hospitalized patients: A survey of 12 Veterans Administration Hospital diseases of the nervous system: 1.37 333–335, (June) 1976

8. Prien RF, Caffey EM: Guidelines for antipsychotic drug use. Medical Times 104 No. 5 87–103, 1976

9. Schroeder NH, Caffey EM, Lorei TW: Antipsychotic drug use: Physician prescribing practices in relation to current recommendations. Diseases of the Nervous System 38:114–116, 1977

10. Boyd JR, Covington JTR, Stanaszek WF, Zehand, S, Coussons RT: Drug defaulting, Part 1, Determinants of compliance. J Am Hosp Pharm 31:362–367, 1974

11. Nelson AA, Gold BH, Hutchinson, R, Benezra E: Drug default among schizophrenic patients. Am J Hosp Pharm 32:1237–1242, 1975

12. Monson RA, Bond, CA: The accuracy of the medical record as an index of outpatient drug therapy. JAMA 240:2181–2184, 1978

13. Smith M: Social barriers to rational drug prescribing. Am J Hosp Pharm 29:121–127, 1972

14. Gutheil TG: Psychodynamics of drug prescribing. Drug Therapy 82–95, 1977

15. Van Camerik S: Why don't patients do what you tell them. Legal Aspects of Medical Practice 7(7):30–33, 1978

16. Hartshorn EA: Adverse drug reactions. Drug Interaction-Induced Adverse Drug Reactions, Vol. 1, No. 6. Miami, Symposia Specialists, 1977

17. Stanaszek WF, Franklin, CE: Survey of potential drug interaction incidence in an outpatient clinic population. Hosp Pharm 13:255–263, 1978

18. Parker WA: Drug induced disease. Guidelines to Prof Pharm 5(2):1, 1978

19. Spaulding G, Hefner D, Campbell RK: Paying the pharmacist a fee for detecting adverse drug reactions. JAPhA NS 16:86–89, 1976

20. Solomon D, Baumgartner P, Glascock LM, Glascock S, Briscoe M, Phillips N: Use of medication profiles to detect potential therapeutic problems in ambulatory patient. Am J Hosp Pharm 31:348–354, 1974

21. Stewart E, Holloway P: Non-prescription medications a need for information. On Continuing Practice 5(1):7–13, 1978

22. Knapp DA, Knapp D, Brandon BM, West S: Development and application of criteria in drug use review programs. Am J Hosp Pharm 31:651–652, 1974

23. Hurwitz N: Predisposing factors in adverse drug reactions. Brit Med J 1:536, 1969

24. Kalman S: Patient education: It's straightforward. Am Pharm NS 18(13):26–28, 1978

25. Hamm MN, Stanaszek WF, Sommers B: Survey of physician's drug information. Am J Pharm Assoc NS 13:349–352, 1973

26. Craig TJ, Van Natta P: Current medication use and symptoms of depression in a general population. Am J Psychiatry 135(9):1036–1039, 1978

27. King R: Evaluating pharmaceutical services in community health centers. Contemporary Practice 2(1):30–38, 1979

28. Frisk P, Cooper J, Campbell N: Community hospital pharamacist detection of drug related problems upon patient admission to small hospitals. Am J Hosp Pharm 34:738–742, 1977

29. McKenney JM, Harrison WL: Drug-related hospital admissions. Am J Hosp Pharm 33:792–795, 1976

30. Cardoni A, Cancro R: A course on psychotropic drug therapy for first year psychiatry residents. Drug Intell Clin Pharm 9:316, 1975

31. Schumacher GE, Weiner J: Practical pharmacokinetic techniques for drug consultation and evaluation. Am J Hosp Pharm 31:59, 1974

32. Kohan S, Chung S, Stone J: Expanding the pharmacists role in a psychiatric hospital. Hosp Comm Psych 24:164, 1973

33. Lamy P: Pharmacy—Today and tomorrow. Contemporary Pharmacy Practice 1(1): V, 1978

34. Coleman JH III, Evans L, Rosenbluth S: Extended clinical roles for the pharmacist in psychiatric care. Am J Hosp Pharm 30:1143–1146, 1973

35. Straker M: Clinical psychiatry and psychopharmacology—A review. J Am Pharm NS 16(10):557–567, 1976

36. Weiner J, Schumacher GE: Psychotropic drug therapy knowledge of health care practitioners. Am J Hosp Pharm 33:237–241, 1976

37. Sax MJ, Cheung A, Brinkman J, Brady E: A systematic approach to drug therapy monitoring. Hosp Pharm 12(4):155–162, 1977

38. Weed LL: Medical Records, Medical Education and Patient Care. Chicago, Case Western University Press, 1969

Chapter 4

INDIVIDUAL PSYCHOTHERAPY

H. Richard Lamb

This chapter describes psychotherapy in the community, not in the hospital. It has been shown that psychotherapy in hospitals can improve the patient's in-hospital behavior but does not affect post-hospital adjustment *(1, 2)*. As a matter of fact, extensive and intensive psychotherapy in the hospital is likely to prolong hospital stay and increase costs *(3)*. This is not to say that there should not be one-to-one contact between therapist and patient in the hospital. Such contact is essential in helping the patient to identify and then to modify and resolve the precipitating problems that caused the hospitalization and in working out a comprehensive and appropriate aftercare plan. But psychotherapy, as described here, is best utilized after hospitalization. It is what happens after hospitalization that is crucial in determining whether the patient is able to remain in the community and improve his level of functioning *(1, 3, 4)*.

Individual psychotherapy is often dismissed, if it is thought of at all, when mental health professionals plan community programs for long-term, severely disabled patients. Individual psychotherapy

Much of the material contained in this chapter appeared in Lamb, H.R., and asssociates, *Community Survival for Long Term Patients.* San Francisco: Jossey-Bass, 1976.

can, however, play a key role, but first there must be a clearly understood point of view and rationale so that potential therapists do not turn away from the task in confusion and dismay.

First and foremost, we should direct our efforts to giving the patient a sense of mastery *(5)*—the feeling that he can cope with his internal drives, his symptoms, and the demands of his environment. With the development of mastery, the patient achieves not only a better adaptation to his world but also a significant rise in his self-esteem and sense of self-worth. To attain our object, we need to work with the well part of the ego. Regardless of the amount of psychopathology in evidence, there is always an intact portion of the ego to which treatment and rehabilitation efforts can be directed *(6)*. The goal is to expand the remaining well part of the person and thus his functioning rather than to remove or cure pathology; the focus should be on the healthy part of the personality, the strengths of the person.

The trend in the psychotherapy of schizophrenia has generally been toward a decreasing interest in psychopathology and an increasing interest in practical issues of adaptation *(7)*. The point of view expressed in this chapter is consistent with this trend. It focuses on reality rather than fantasy, on the present and the future rather than the past. It does not exclude, however, using the past to understand the present and predict what might happen in the future. The psychotherapy described in this chapter focuses on the exploration of the nature of the patient's problems and the kinds of stresses that precipitate them, as well as on the psychotherapeutic relationship itself. Explorations of the problems and of the psychotherapeutic relationship are not seen here as conflicting approaches but as two aspects of therapy that complement each other.

The kind of psychotherapy used with long-term patients does make a difference. Just putting patient and therapist in a room together for an hour a week does not automatically result in improvement for the patient. Whitehorn and Betz *(8)* have shown that there is a very definite difference in the success rates of psychotherapy with schizophrenics depending on the style and techniques of the therapist; in this research, they found that successful therapists grasped the personal meaning and motivation of the patient's behavior, going beyond the mere clinical description and narrative biography. Likewise, these therapists more frequently selected goals aimed at helping the patient to modify his adjustment pattern in a specific manner and to use his assets more constructively instead of seeking merely to decrease symptoms or focusing on psychopathology. The therapists with the lowest success rates tended to be passively permissive as contrasted with the successful therapists, who more frequently expressed their opinions about problems being discussed, expressed honest disagreement at times, sometimes challenged the patient's self-deprecatory attitudes, set realistic limits, and generally were more active in the therapy. The successful therapists conveyed to the patient a belief that he had a potential for independent action and thus for mastery of his environment and of himself.

A more recent study *(9)* focused directly on clinically meaningful personality dimensions of both patients and therapists. This study showed that (1) composed therapists work especially well when matched with schizophrenic patients who are anxious; (2) therapists judged to be comfortable with aggression work well with hostile patients; (3) grandfatherly therapists do well with seductive schizophrenic patients; and (4) therapists considered to be comfortable with depression do well with depressed schizophrenic patients.

The effectiveness and relatively low costs of aftercare programs that center around social and chemotherapy should not blind us to the importance of one-to-one psychotherapy with long-term patients. Individual psychotherapy, particularly if it takes a here-and-now problem-solving approach, can be a potent therapeutic tool for which the social therapy aftercare setting cannot compensate. It gives the long-term patient the opportunity to develop the ability to better understand what kinds of situations are anxiety-provoking for him and to develop healthier ways of dealing with such situations. The patient-therapist relationship itself affords the patient an ego-corrective experience and an opportunity for growth by teaching him to trust and to tolerate closeness and by providing a testing ground where he may learn to express anger without losing control.

INSIGHT REDEFINED

Insight is not to be neglected as a goal for the long-term patient. However, insight must be defined so that the therapist and his patient understand what their objective is. For the patient, insight means that such symptoms as delusions, hallucinations, and feelings that he is "falling apart" are understandable: the symptoms mean that he is under stress and is reacting to it. He is no longer overwhelmed by mysterious, frightening, all-powerful forces beyond his control, because the symptoms make sense. After helping the patient to see this much, the therapist works toward the recognition that logical, purposeful actions can follow from such insight. The patient must not panic but must try to understand what the stress is that is producing the anxiety and hence generating his symptoms. Having identified the stress, therapist and patient next need to determine what actions need to be taken to resolve the problem. In the meantime, the patient must understand that increasing his medications will alleviate his symptoms and help maintain his problem-solving abilities. Insight is very meaningful in treating the long-term patient if the insight is here-and-now and reality-based—if, for example, the patient understands what kinds of situations are extremely anxiety-provoking for him and that there are certain ways to deal with or to avoid these situations, and if he considers how he interacts with family and friends and how these interactions need to be changed.

Case Illustration

A 46-year-old, married woman had had numerous state hospitalizations for psychotic episodes over the past 15 years. She had been out of the hospital for two and a half years, and although on fairly high doses of psychoactive drugs, she continued to have ideas of reference and, at times, paranoid delusions. When especially upset, she was certain that everyone was saying that she ate her own feces.

Many of her early weekly sessions with the therapist centered around helping her recognize these ideas of referrence and delusions as symptoms, indicators that she was anxious and under pressure. She was at first skeptical, but since she had a positive relationship with her therapist, she was willing to entertain the idea. After four or five sessions, she was able to say, "I must tell you that I understand this on an intellectual level, but I'm not sure that I really believe it down deep. But I trust you, so I'll operate as if I really believed it." By examining her symptoms each time they occurred, she was able, with the therapist's help, to identify the particular stress that had precipitated them and to formulate a course of action that would resolve the situation. By dealing with the symptoms this way, she found that her life was becoming less chaotic and more enjoyable. Further, the situation was not being allowed to deteriorate to a point where the symptoms progressed to fixed paranoid delusions. It was only after six months of this kind of work in therapy that she was able to talk about the delusion of people saying that she ate her feces and in turn get some perspective on the fact that at such times her anxiety was especially severe. She was much relieved by being able to understand the symptoms as indicators of anxiety instead of experiencing them as very frightening feelings that seemed very real, very incomprehensible, and beyond her control.

A therapist, seeing his patient begin to decompensate under stress, will, of course, take some immediate action to intervene. Sometimes he can manipulate, or compromise with, the patient's environment to prevent or reverse this decompensation. But it is all-important that the patient be aware of the rationale for the action being taken and be as much a participant in the action as possible. Eventually the patient can incorporate this active process of being aware of and dealing with stressful situations, based upon an identification with the therapist.

THE PSYCHOTHERAPEUTIC RELATIONSHIP

The frequency and intensity of one-to-one therapy should be adjusted to the tolerance of the patient; it can be one hour a week, one hour every other week, half an hour a week, half an hour once a month, or whatever seems appropriate. Except at times of crisis, therapists should be very hesitant to see a schizophrenic patient more than one hour a week, because of the very real danger of developing a transference which neither the therapist nor the patient can handle. Schizophrenics generally have difficulty handling the closeness and regression that develop in intensive psychotherapy. To ignore this is to invite a transference psychosis *(10)*.

Case Illustration

A 32-year-old, married woman began outpatient therapy following a psychotic episode that had required hospitalization. It soon became clear that she had had a thought disorder and paranoid ideas for a number of years. In the first interview, she became extremely anxious and insisted that her husband be called inside from the waiting room. She was unable to explain what had happened but did ask that her husband be with her in subsequent sessions, and the therapist agreed. There were numerous problems in the marriage that needed to be discussed, and the patient seemed to feel free to talk about other problems in her husband's presence. On one occasion several months later, she arrived before her husband, again became very anxious, and again could give no explanation. From then on, she and her husband always came together.

The therapy progressed well. After being seen weekly for several months, every other week for another six months, and monthly for a year, her visits were put on an as-needed basis. It was agreed that either she or her husband would call for an appointment if any problems arose that they could not handle together. This they did, coming in approximately once a year for a joint session. But about seven years after her first interview, the patient called and requested to come in alone. When she arrived, she reported that her life generally and her marriage were going well but that she had two special reasons for coming. First, she wanted to tell the therapist that her initial problem had been that she was afraid that she would lose control of herself and ask the therapist to have intercourse with her on the couch in the office. Second, she felt that she now had more control, and she wanted to be able to prove to herself that she could sit in the office with her therapist for an hour and maintain control, which in fact she did. Further discussion revealed that beneath the concern about sexual intimacy was a more basic fear of losing control generally and allowing herself to be dependent and "at the mercy" of another person in a close relationship. She had used her husband's presence to dilute the relationship with the therapist and, considering the amount of anxiety involved, had prevented what would very likely have become a transference psychosis.

Other techniques that keep the patient's anxiety at a manageable level can be employed where appropriate. Long silences should be avoided. Eruptions of unconscious material at a rapid pace should be discouraged.

Treatment of long-term patients is a long-term process. A frequent error is premature termination of therapy. This does not necessarily mean that the patient should be seen for an hour a week indefinitely. But with the long-term schizophrenic, there is no real ending *(11)*. The therapy may be reduced to once a month, or to twice a year, or to times of crisis only. For that matter, there may be a lifelong maintenance of the therapeutic relationship, even if there is only an occasional telephone call or perhaps no contact at all. But the memory of the therapy stays with the patient, who knows that the therapist is only a telephone call away.

STRENGTHENING EGO CONTROLS

There is a popular notion that if a therapist can help a patient to "express his anger," something very therapeutic has been accomplished. And indeed this if often true, especially with nonschizophrenic patients. But with long-term schizophrenics, a sudden explosion of anger may really be a psychotic loss of control that may lead to a further loosening of controls generally and quite possibly to a hospitalization. The amount of anger may be so intense and the amount of ego control so tenuous that one should tread with caution in this area. However, appropriate expression of anger over which the patient has control can be an important long-term treatment goal. On a short-term basis, one should be cautious, paying fully as much attention to the patient's ability to retain control as is paid to the underlying anger.

Case Illustration

A 41-year-old man, a long-term schizophrenic, had been able to function quite well in a minor executive position between his infrequent psychotic episodes. Each psychotic episode, however, had been characterized by extreme anger and paranoia. In remission, he was a pleasant, friendly man with little overt hostility. He was universally described as a "nice guy." In therapy, each time the therapist allowed the situation to reach the point where the patient was expressing any real degree of anger, the patient began to decompensate. So, early in therapy (during the first few years), the therapist began encouraging the patient to suppress his anger, and each time the patient reconstituted and continued to function well.

As the relationship progressed and the patient felt more confident that his therapist would support him if he began to lose control, he began to assert himself, at first in small ways and later in more significant ways. It was a slow process, but after four years the patient was able to become overtly angry at his wife and more aggressive at work without losing control, disrupting his marriage, losing his job, or requiring hospitalization. He now has a feeling of mastery over his angry impulses that is very gratifying to him. Certainly his ability to be appropriately aggressive and at times angry without losing control has been a very healthy thing for him in terms of his own mental health and his improved relationships with his wife, employer, coworkers, and others.

A similar snare awaits the unwary therapist who tries to change the character structure of a borderline psychotic who has a saccharine exterior covering what is clearly a tremendous amount of underlying hostility. In the short term, such a character structure is best left intact as a necessary defense against a psychotic loss of control over angry impulses. In some cases, changes can be effected over a long period of time. But often this character structure is so necessary to help a weak ego deal with an immense amount of anger that little or nothing can be done to change it even over a span of years. Therapists must content themselves with settling for what is possible. Not every person who walks into a therapist's office can leave a well-analyzed person in tune with all his impulses and a model of mental health. Even though a character defense may annoy the therapist, it is far better than having a patient give up his defense and then become overtly psychotic.

Another way to help patients develop ego control is by encouraging them to confine their thinking to reality and preventing them from drifting off into ruminations about normally unconscious, primary-process fantasy. For instance, a woman with weak ego strength begins talking about a dream in which she had intercourse with her father. There is a great temptation here to get into a discussion of oedipal feelings, incestuous tendencies, and all the dynamics that easily flow from such a dream. A fascinating hour? Possibly. But that evening or the next day, one is quite likely to have to deal with an overtly psychotic patient. One should not ignore such material but rather should help the patient to repress it. The therapist can say, "You love and miss your father, and sometimes it shows up in dreams like this. The sexual part of the dream disguises the feelings of closeness you had for him." If it seems desirable, patient and therapist can then discuss the father in reality terms. Or they can go on to some other pressing issue. As this procedure is repeated in therapy, the patient herself learns how to turn away from primary-process material, and, with her ego more intact, feels better equipped to grapple with the problems in her life.

The therapist can supplement ego control by setting limits on behavior: "Don't stop therapy." "Continue taking your medications." "Don't impulsively quit your job." Often, retaining the therapist's approval is in itself sufficient incentive for the patient to adhere to limits set by the therapist. Occasionally, the family can become involved in enforcing limits. At the outset, the patient is the passive recipient of the limits and passively complies. In successful therapy, however, by identification with the therapist, the limits are internalized, strengthening the patients' own inner controls and enhancing his ego functioning and his feeling that he can control his own destiny.

GIVING ADVICE

Many long-term patients lack the ability to cope with the routine stresses of life. If these stresses are discussed in individual therapy, the patient may be helped to resolve problems that he cannot cope with alone. Sometimes the procedure is the same as that used with more healthy patients: the therapist acts as a catalyst, enabling the patient to identify the alternatives and choose the ones right for him. In other cases, the therapist may give direct advice. This may not come easily to the therapist, but it may be crucial for the success of the therapy. Sometimes the same advice has to be given over and over again to a patient, each time his maladaptive pattern of reacting to a particular stress is repeated. But it is hoped that the patient learns from the therapist new ways of handling situations and at the time of the next crisis will be able to arrive at the solution himself.

Case Illustration

A 36-year-old, married woman had been hospitalized five times for acute psychotic episodes between the ages of 20 and 31. For the past five years, she had been doing well in outpatient psychotherapy, with no hospitalizations and no overt psychosis. Her therapy, which initially had been once a week, was now once monthly. She was on vacation, visiting her mother in a distant city, when she called the therapist, obviously disturbed and in the incipient stages of a psychotic episode. Unraveling the story over the phone, the therapist finally ascertained that she had been going through her mother's cedar chest, bringing out all kinds of mementos from the past. Finally, she had come across a birthday card that she had received from her now dead father on her eleventh birthday, on which he had written, "Happy birthday to a good little girl who is doing the dishes on her own birthday." She was being flooded with memories of the deprivation she had experienced as a child, of the unreasonable demands that had been placed upon her, and of the feelings of loss for her dead father, about whom she felt quite ambivalent. The therapist's response was, "Put all those things back and close that cedar chest." The patient complied, and when she called back an hour later, she was much less distraught; she now felt in control of the situation, and a psychotic decompensation had been averted. In succeeding visits over the years, she did not reopen the cedar chest either literally or figuratively.

Persons from the lower socioeconomic classes, in particular, expect a professional to give advice, and the therapy may fail if advice is not forthcoming (12). This is particularly true for the lowest class position, the one into which most long-term schizophrenics fall (13). But nothing is more difficult for many therapists than to give direct advice and to give it in simple language without jargon. Nevertheless, the following example again illustrates what can be accomplished if the therapist feels free to give advice based on an understanding of the patient's psychodynamics.

Case Illustration

A 42-year-old married schizophrenic woman had had an intensely ambivalent relationship with her alcoholic mother. Throughout her adolescence and on into her adult life, the patient continued to seek from her mother the love and nurturing she had missed as a child; repeatedly the mother disappointed her and the patient reexperienced over and over her childhood resentment.

The mother died suddenly, the patient became extremely anxious and guilt ridden, and her thinking became increasingly disorganized. She was brought immediately to her therapist by her husband. Both patient and husband were agreed that she could not attend the funeral, that she would become overwhelmed by her feelings and fall apart completely. The therapist, on the other hand, realizing the depth of the patient's preexisting guilt, felt that this guilt would be greatly intensified by not attending the funeral. Further, he felt that the ritual and structure of the Catholic mass and funeral service would help this woman begin to work through her mourning. He strongly advised the patient to go to the funeral service but not to go on to the grave site. Reluctantly the patient attended the mass as instructed and afterward was much relieved. Though the work of mourning continued for some months, the crisis had passed.

Frequently it is helpful to assist the patient to rationalize a situation and thus save face and self-esteem. Take, for example, a man for whom being in psychiatric treatment means that he is sick, an inferior person, and not really a man. Often these feelings can be dealt with in time, but for the moment, the important thing is to keep him in treatment and his illness in remission. The therapist might say, "You know how concerned your wife is about you and how fearful she is you will have another breakdown. The more worried she gets, the more she upsets you, and the more preoccupied you become with the problems at home, the less you can function at work. So it really is important for you to remain in treatment to allay your wife's anxiety, to make her life more comfortable, and in the process to make your own life more comfortable." Of course, this should only be said if in fact the wife does have this reaction. Still, it is only a part of the picture. But it is a rationalization that helps the patient remain in treatment while retaining the self-image that is necessary for his psychological well-being.

Or take a person whose vocational potential appears limited but whose vocational aspirations are high. Referral to a sheltered workshop is indicated, but how to do it without shattering the person's self-image and self-esteem? Again, assisting the person to rationalize the situation may be crucial. The therapist may say, "It's not that you are going there for life. Look at it as a period of transition leading to your ultimate goal." The therapist himself may have some doubts that the person can in fact go on to competitive employment, but the person has been helped to rationalize entry into the workshop. If the patient cannot in fact move on, a year later he may be encouraged to feel that the workshop is his regular job where he is needed for the smooth working of the facility and to help break in new clients

—an assessment of the situation which may or may not be embellished to help him rationalize his remaining there. Not facing reality? How many persons really do? And would not we all become depressed if we suddenly had to give up all or even most of our rationalizations?

DEALING WITH LIFE PROBLEMS

There is no substitute for the therapist's possessing maturity and an understanding of the very real problems of the life cycle (14). The long-term patient's lack of ego strength results in an impairment of his problem-solving ability. Thus, much of psychotherapy with the long-term patient has to do with helping him handle the problems specific to that phase of the life cycle in which he finds himself. The crises in the lives of long-term patients tend to arise at the same times as in the lives of anyone else, that is, during childbirth, adolescence, the involutional period, changes in work status, rejection by or death of loved ones, serious physical illness, and failure of the person's support system (15). For instance, with adolescent patients, the therapist needs to understand the stresses of adolescence: the struggle for emancipation from parents and the conflict and ambivalence about becoming independent, the problems of identity formation, the difficulties of choosing a vocation, the task of achieving an adequate sexual adjustment, and the necessity of preparing to assume the responsibilities of an adult. Another example is what Marmor (16) has called "the crisis of middle life." Marmor points out that in midlife such stresses arise as the physical signs of aging, that is, the loss of hair and skin tone and the battle against weight gain, intimations of one's own mortality, and the deaths of friends and relatives. During this period, one very powerful stress for most people is recognition that they may never achieve the high goals they had set for themselves. And all of these stresses come at a time when there is the greatest demand on one's earning capacity to meet the needs of the family, including school-age children. The therapist must also understand the problems of reaching maturity, of graduation and going out into the world, and the feelings of uselessness and depression of the empty nest syndrome, when the children are grown and have left the home.

Although dealing with these kinds of problems may seem mundane to some therapists, it is central to psychotherapy, at least with long-term patients, who lack the ego strength to cope with these problems alone.

Failure to take reality factors into account may make psychotherapy fruitless, whether the therapist is attempting to explore the patient's personality or simply sees himself as providing support.

Case Illustration

> A 29-year-old schizophrenic woman had been seen weekly for one and a half years, with a steady downhill course including several hospitalizations. She was the mother of four children and had become psychotic shortly after the birth of the second child. Finally, consultation with another psychiatrist suggested that this woman did not possess sufficient ego strength to parent and nurture four children and that she was being constantly overwhelmed by the task. Work with the family resulted in the patient's mother assuming most of the responsibility for the care of the children; the patient was worked with to rationalize giving up her maternal role without suffering a devastating loss of self-esteem. Then, and only then, could outpatient psychotherapy proceed in the direction of helping her to improve her relationship with her husband and her interpersonal relationships generally and to explore the possibility of vocational goals.

GETTING THE FAMILY INTO PERSPECTIVE

Many schools of thought implicate the patient's family in aggravating and even generating his illness. Thus, mental health professionals often blame and mistreat the family, through either open hostility or vague innuendo *(17)*. Badly treated families in turn retaliate in ways that are detrimental to the patient. They become less willing to tolerate the problems he causes, are less agreeable to changing their behavior toward him, and do not give information that would help the therapist understand him. We also must recognize that being the relative of a mentally ill person is traumatic and often overwhelming. Usually the family is already guilt ridden and has a sense of failure for having "produced a schizophrenic" *(18)*. Mental health professionals must learn to treat families with sympathy, understanding, and respect, in order to win their confidence and cooperation.

Pursuing a similar train of thought, Arieti *(19)* observes that the schizophrenic tends to attribute to his parents full responsibility for his illness and his despair. Unfortunately, many psychiatrists have accepted these perceptions as real insights and as accurate accounts of historical events. Arieti believes it is the therapist's job to help the patient get his parents into perspective, by pointing out how the patient distorts and exaggerates. "For instance, a white lie is transformed into the worst mendacity, tactlessness into falsity or perversion" *(19)*. Of course, the therapist must be careful, for in some cases the parents have really been what the patient has depicted. But usually when the patient comes to recognize that the parents have played a role in his psychological difficulties, he also exaggerates and distorts that role. He is not able to see his own distortions until the therapist points them out to him. Further, the patient must be helped to realize that negative traits of parents or other important people are not necessarily arrows or weapons used purposely to hurt him; they may simply be characteristics of these people rather than attitudes directed solely toward the patient. Arieti *(20)* hopes that in psychotherapy the patient will stop blaming others for all his troubles. He will recognize the role others played in his life, but he will assume some responsibility for what happened to him in the past and especially for the way he will direct his life in the future.

Taking Sides Against the Superego

Sometimes the best course of action is an attempt to modify the patient's superego, thereby decreasing his guilt and the self-destructive behavior prompted by this guilt. In other words, the therapist takes sides against the superego. The patient may react to certain situations in a self-destructive way because of lifelong, inappropriate feelings of guilt, and the therapist not only must point this out but must say, "That is self-destructive. Don't do it."

Case Illustration

A 31-year-old woman had received a constant message during her childhood from her parents and siblings that her role in life was to compensate for the failings of her alcoholic mother and take care of her father and her brothers. She had been made to feel that any gratification or enjoyment of life was wrong, that she should instead be devoting herself to the welfare of her family. As an adult, simply taking an enjoyable vacation was enough to overwhelm her with guilt and precipitate a psychotic break. One of the critical elements in the therapy of this schizophrenic woman was to encourage her to stop taking care of her parents and siblings and to assure her that taking an enjoyable vacation, buying and enjoying a new house, and enjoying intercourse were not evil but in fact important for her to do, important not only for her but for the welfare of her own husband and children. Such intervention has not only helped this woman increase her enjoyment of life but has prevented a number of psychotic episodes and hospitalizations. For instance, early in the therapy, her therapist's statement "It's not wrong to enjoy a vacation" reduced her guilt and helped her both to enjoy the vacation and not to become symptomatic. But, for her, it was an external and foreign way of viewing the situation. As therapy progressed, the reduction in guilt became internalized, her superego became modified, and the patient became less dependent on the therapist to deal with and master what had been disabling guilt.

This is not unlike the corrective emotional experience described by Franz Alexander in which the therapeutic benefit derives from the therapist reacting, in the more favorable circumstances of the transference relationship, in a way very different than had the parents in the patient's earlier life *(21)*.

Guilt reduction can be extremely useful in a variety of ways.

Case Illustration

A 52-year-old schizophrenic woman felt a tremendous amount of resentment about the way her husband was treating her. She felt, however, that she was exaggerating the husband's behavior and that in any case she had no right to feel resentment. Her therapist had known the patient and the family for over ten years and was in a good position to assess the situation. His response was, "You are not at all exaggerating the way he is treating you. And it is a normal, human response to feel resentment about such treatment. Part of the problem is that your parents made you feel that all angry feelings are wrong. It is normal, it is all right, to feel resentful about this." By pointing out to the patient that her resentment was appropriate and reducing her guilt about the anger she was feeling, the therapist was helping her to see the realities in her life more objectively and to allow herself to have appropriate feelings about them. The result was a lessening of her depression and her need to use psychotic defenses to deal with her feelings of guilt.

CONCLUSIONS

These examples illustrate still another crucial point that is too often neglected in community mental health—the importance of understanding the individual psychodynamics of long-term patients. Aftercare programs consisting primarily of medication and social therapy, even when the relationships between the patient and the staff are good and there is close staff involvement, are often superficial. One can find a happy medium between the formal psychoanalysis of the schizophrenic patient and a program consisting only of medications and social therapy. It is important to understand the psychodynamics of the patient's illness, have at least a modicum of information about his early life, and in particular understand what kinds of real life situations interact with his internal dynamics in such a way as to cause a psychotic episode, interfere with growth, or deprive him of gratification from life. Mental health professionals must be able to combine the techniques of medication, social therapy, and individual and group psychotherapy, based on a practical understanding of psychodynamics. They need not apologize if their work is not psychoanalytically oriented psychotherapy delving into the person's childhood, nor should they feel apologetic about delving into the patient's psychodynamics to deepen their understanding of what causes illness and unhappiness in him.

Several other themes have been dominant in this chapter. First of all, the patient's symptoms should make sense to him and be understood as his reaction to stress. From this understanding can come practical resolutions of his problems. Insofar as possible, this should be a joint process in which both patient and therapist participate. The patient begins to become master of his own destiny.

Probably no part of therapy of the long-term patient is as important as giving him a sense of mastery over his internal drives, his symptoms, and the demands of his environment. From the ability to master and cope with both his internal and external demands comes not only a better adaptation to the world in which he has to live but also a sharp rise in his self-esteem and feelings of self-worth. It is in this context that regression, especially in the form of continued psychotic experiences and ego disintegration, is seen as contraindicated. Such experiences undermine the person's self-confidence and sense of mastery and reinforce his conviction that he is living in a world where he will always be at the mercy of all-powerful forces, both internal and external, which are beyond his control.

It is hoped that this chapter also has underlined the importance of flexibility on the part of the therapist. He must work in the present but be able to delve into the past when necessary. He may at one time serve as a catalyst, while the patient performs the actual decision making, and then in the next hour be equally comfortable as a giver of direct advice or a setter of limits, or both. He must be able to assess when his task is to strengthen the ego and when it is to take sides against the superego. He needs to establish a warm, meaningful relationship without exceeding the patient's tolerance for closeness and intimacy.

In short, if the therapist will modify many of the techniques that he learned for working with patients who had quite different problems, he can accomplish a great deal in psychotherapy with long-term patients.

NOTES

1. Anthony WA: Efficacy of psychiatric rehabilitation. Psychological Bulletin 78:447–456, 1972

2. Messier M, Finnerty R, Botvin CS, Grinspoon L: A follow-up study of intensively treated chronic schizophrenic patients. Am J Psychiatry 125:1123–1127, 1969

3. May PRA: Modifying health-care services for schizophrenic patients. Hospital and Community Psychiatry 20:363–368, 1969

4. Stein LI, Test MA, Marx AJ: Alternative to the hospital: A controlled study. Am J Psychiatry 132:517–522, 1975

5. Fenichel O: The Psychoanalytic Theory of Neurosis. London: Routledge, 1946

6. Lamb HR (ed): Rehabilitation in community mental health. San Francisco, Jossey-Bass, 1971

7. Gunderson JG: Controversies about the psychotherapy of schizophrenia. Am J Psychiatry 130:677–681, 1973

8. Whitehorn JC, Betz BJ: Effective Psychotherapy with the Schizophrenic Patient. New York, Jason Aronson, 1975

9. Gunderson JG: Patient-therapist matching: A research evaluation. Am J Psychiatry 135:1193–1197, 1978

10. Fox RP: Therapeutic environments. Arch Gen Psychiatry 29:514–517, 1973

11. Mendel WM: Supportive Care. Los Angeles, Mara Books, 1975

12. Carlson DA, Coleman JV, Errera P, Harrison RW: Problems in treating the lower class psychotic. Arch Gen Psychiatry 13:269–274, 1965

13. Frank A, Eisenthal S, Lazare A: Are there social class differences in patients' treatment conceptions? Arch Gen Psychiatry 35:61–69, 1978

14. Lidz T: The Person: His Development Throughout the Life Cycle. New York, Basic Books, 1968

15. Mendel WM, Allen RE: Treating the Chronic Patient. In Masserman JH (ed): Current Psychiatric Therapies. New York, Grune & Stratton, 1977

16. Marmor J: The crisis of middle age. Psychiatry Digest 29:17–21, 1968

17. Appleton WS: Mistreatment of patients' families by psychiatrists. Am J Psychiatry 131:655–657, 1974

18. Lamb HR, Oliphant E: Schizophrenia through the eyes of families. Hospital & Community Psychiatry 29:803–806, 1978

19. Arieti S: Interpretation of Schizophrenia. New York, Basic Books, 1974

20. Arieti S. Psychiatric controversy: Man's ethical dimension. Am J Psychiatry 132:39–42, 1975

21. Alexander F, French T, Bacon C, Benedek T, Furst R, Gerard M, Grinker R, Grotjahn N, Johnson A, McLean H, Weiss E: Psychoanalytic Therapy. New York, Ronald Press, 1946

Chapter 5

SOCIALIZATION

Samuel Grob

The shift in public policy and practice since the 1960s to deinstitutionalization of the care and treatment of the mentally ill, now sanctioned by law, has served to return this long-neglected population to the mainstream of social and community concern. While impressive reductions in hospital census, 65% and better, are widely acclaimed, along with vastly increased community-based services, the net gains reported in the broader process of socialization are often equivocal and ambiguous *(1)*. In fact, periodic outbursts of criticism appearing in the mass media across the country temper any enthusiasm we may experience at this development. Necessary, though belated, attention to the problems of treating the mentally ill in community-based programs only mitigates the severity of the strain in hospital-community relations. The lag in properly instrumenting appropriate community programs designed to effectuate improved community care results less from lack of knowledge and expertise in implementation than from the economics and politics impacting self-interest of professional groups and vested interests threatened by change. Nevertheless, in spite of initial distortions of planning designs, programmatic development, and funding, enough progress is manifest to justify reaffirmation of public policy and continuation of effort with suitable adjustments *(2)*. The aspect of such adjustment I will examine in this chapter relates to the meaning and role of socialization as a necessary independent generic process in any substantive program for the chronic psychiatric patient.

INDIGENOUS ROOTS IN WESTERN EXPERIENCE

Community mental health as we know it is new only in name, modern dress, and context. A review of psychiatric history reveals the existence of prototypes since the Middle Ages. The classic example is the first family care system initiated in Geel (Belgium), neither by churchmen nor by physician, but by simple peasants residing on marginal farmland in the fifteenth century. They began a tradition, lasting to this day, of opening their homes to mentally ill pilgrims who came for the ritual of the novena at the shrine of Geel's locally canonized St. Dymphna. This unique phenomenon has been under study since 1966 by Leo Srole, a social anthropologist at Columbia University, and his team. He is presently preparing a final report of this study to be entitled, "Community Remarkable of the Western World: Geel, Belgium, 1475–1975." Mental patients have lived and worked with these simple farm families for generations, fully accepted and sharing in the culture and society of the home and community. These Geel care-givers have evolved over the centuries what may be described as a natural therapeutic community with all the features of normalization, socialization, destigmatizing, and parent-teacher roles we consider innovative in our day. Evaluation of patient progress in these homes revealed higher levels of social functioning across the board. Srole is very impressed, stating: "Having previously observed custodial patients on the wards of traditional American and Belgian hospitals, I saw Geel's patients (1) actively engaged in the business of normal family living, rather than apathetically disengaged, and (2) outer-directed in their public behaviors rather than inaccessibly withdrawn into their private worlds" (3).

Another significant prototype may be found in the early and middle periods of the nineteenth century in American psychiatry, characterized at that time as "moral treatment." Quite modern in other than name, this treatment was essentially social and humanitarian, calling for compassionate and understanding care through personal interest, friendship, interpersonal dialogue, and purposeful activities in both dyadic and group situations. Bockhoven observes in his survey of the moral treatment era that "mental disorders could

be understood and successfully treated on the basis of many conceptual approaches long before the modern era of scientific psychiatry"
(4). Pinel in France, Tuke in England, Chiarugi in Italy, Reil in
Germany, and Rush in America were leaders who exemplified this
spirit in the wake of eighteenth-century enlightenment.

As happens so often in the cyclical or spiral fortunes of history,
moral treatment was soon forgotten, despite its success, to be followed in the latter half of the nineteenth century by custodial care.
The cause of this decline appears to have been the attrition of leadership following the death of the innovators. The drop in recovery rate
from 45% to 4% reflected the decline. It is ironic that the zeal of a
Dorothea Dix for more mental hospitals at the midpoint of the
nineteenth century resulted in more custodial facilities where chronic
mental patients could languish rather than in continued reform of
abuse. The beginning of scientific psychiatry at the same time, with
its emphasis on physical cause and disease concepts, further stimulated this trend to custodialism and pessimism. The work of William
Graham Summer, Yale social scientist from 1872–1901, in espousing
social Darwinism, provided additional rationalization for isolating
and segregating the mentally ill from the community *(5)*. The forces
of immigration, financial crisis, and pseudoscience served effectively
to hasten this dehumanizing attitude toward the chronic mental
patient.

This grim turn of events was relieved somewhat by the painstak-
ing efforts of Adolph Meyer and others at the turn of the century and
into the twentieth century *(6)*. Meyer emphasized the importance of
seeing patients not only as physical organisms but also as social
beings, the products of an idiosyncratic cultural environment and life
experience. He believed in understanding patients within the context
of social ties and conflicts. Furthermore, his plans for prevention and
treatment required the participation of the entire community and its
institutions *(7)*. The broad social perceptions and thoughts of William James, John Dewey, and G. Stanley Hall combined with
Meyer's psychobiology, Freud's psychoanalysis, and Southard's social psychiatry to undermine the physical disease entity concept of
mental illness then so dominant. By World War I, the importance
of psychological and social factors in the etiology and treatment of
mental illness was revived in American psychiatry.

From this brief review of prescientific psychiatry and its after-
math, we arrive at the paradoxical conclusion that moral treatment,
which emerged out of eighteenth-century philosophy of human free-

dom and individual rights, was superior in its results to the later custodial nontreatment phase of institutional care which ensued upon early scientific medicine conditioned by a growing technological, industrial, urban society. Fortunately, we are witness to the persistent reassertion of voices of reason and humanity through the chaos of human suffering and despair.

SOCIALIZATION OF SCIENTIFIC PSYCHIATRY IN EARLY TWENTIETH CENTURY

Sigmund Freud pronounced *arbeiten* ('to work') and *lieben* ('to love') essential components of psychic health. However, while Freud emphasized the sexual aspect of sociality, Alfred Adler broadened the concept to social interest. For him, this concept subsumed three tasks of life confronting every individual (1) the attitude taken up toward our fellow human beings; (2) vocation; (3) love. In these terms, any person's fund of self-esteem derives from individual solution of these problems. "The worse the failure the more numerous are the complications that threaten the possessor of a faulty style of life" (8). The equivalent word in German to social interest is *Gemeinschaftsgefuhle,* which may be translated variously as social feeling, community feeling, fellow feeling, communal intuition, community interest, social sense, or sense of solidarity.

Early in the 1930s, Harry Stack Sullivan, the famous American psychiatrist, after ten years of intensive work with schizophrenic patients, concluded that his success resulted from his use of a socio-psychiatric approach. He saw his patients improve in *social* insight rather than personal insight into the roots of behavior, as Freud maintained. He came to strive for the path to social recovery through the mediation of a sympathetic environment. Intimations of both Adler and Skinner may be seen in his formulation:

> Given the correct situation, the "social" recovery goes far towards a "real" recovery and certainly includes much of a true reorganization of the disordered personality—The sympathetic environment to which I refer is a group of persons, some "psychotic" (patients), some relatively "sane" (personnel), in the latter of whom there is conscious formulation of *community* with the more disordered ones, and a deliberate, rather than a good-naturedly unconscious, purpose to enter into the life of the patient to a beneficial goal—the situation is one of education, broadly conceived, not by verbal teaching but by communal experience—good tutoring." (9)

Of parenthetical interest is his remarkable foresight in predicting an increase in the relapse rate without the intervention of "convalescent camps and communities for those on their way to mental health" *(9)*.

These few gleanings from the best of early social-psychiatric thought and practice reveal the beginnings of an emerging theoretical view which can comprehend both the success of the moral treatment era and the promise of community psychiatry. Fundamental concepts from sociological literature, one German and the other American, help to elucidate the nature of the socialization process from the standpoint of both the individual and society. Ferdinand Tonnies introduced the concepts of *Gemeinschaft* and *Gesellschaft* in 1887, to which Adler referred in his use of social interest. At the risk of oversimplification, Gemeinschaft may be likened to an organic embeddedness of the individual in the group, almost as a natural instinctual association, and Gesellschaft to a more rational, instrumental relation of the individual to a specific goal—that is, they represent the difference of undifferentiated to differentiated, the whole to the part. In Tonnies' view, the process by which Gemeinschaft-like societies are "freed" and become the subject of rational will, and consequently more Gesellschaft-like, is "healthy" and "normal" *(10)*. We may exercise some license here in utilizing these concepts in the interest of more systematic theorizing about Sullivan's empirical generalization. Thus, we see these two concepts in a relation analogous to Freud's use of a differentiated and an undifferentiated id, both descriptive of evolutionary and developmental process.

George Herbert Mead, the American sociologist, on a more intuitive though highly theoretical basis, cuts through socialization from another angle. He explains how integrated personalities individuate out of social processes without doing violence to either these processes or the institutions they represent. The organized community or social group which gives to the individual his unity of self is conceptualized "the generalized other." Through the generalized other, the individual may internalize expectation from cooperative participation in group life, evolve a self-concept, internalize the attitudes of others, and develop self-control out of social control *(11)*. Utilizing these theoretical constructs of sociology in conjunction with the empirical work of the aforementioned precursors of social psychiatry makes possible a coherent rationale on which to base a specific deliberate methodology of therapeutic socialization relevant to chronic psychiatric patients.

TOWARD A METHODOLOGY OF SOCIAL THERAPY IN
MID-TWENTIETH CENTURY

The Russian Revolution and spread of Marxist thought during the Bohemian 1920s and the depression of the 1930s gave a special fascination to the importance of social, economic, and cultural determinants of individual and social behavior. Alfred Adler was a psychoanalytic variant of this influence, an early disciple of Freud who broke away because of his belief in the overriding importance of the social factor. He may, therefore, justly lay claim to being the Father of Social Psychiatry. Joshua Bierer, an Adlerian and a refugee from Nazi Germany, started the first therapeutic social club, as we know it, in Great Britain shortly after he arrived there from Vienna in 1938. Perhaps because of the circumstances of his time, he adopted a simple social psychological model for his therapeutic practice. The key concept of this model was socialization, by which he meant that process in which the individual acquires behavior appropriate to constructive participation in his society. By contrast, psychoses involved the breakdown of the individual's basic socialization skills within one or more of the following areas: (1) the family; (2) the occupational environment; or (3) some aspect of general interpersonal relationship. Bierer came increasingly to center his efforts on the idea that treatment of the mentally ill should remain within the realm of community as much as possible. He was the first to suggest the use of social club therapy as a specific treatment modality for associability, although he acknowledged the crucial role of the personality and experience of the psychiatrist. He defined the aim of the club to prepare the patient to adapt himself to everyday social life and participate in normal social functions. Finally, he predicted that the next steps in psychiatry would be on organizational levels—for example, the introduction of the therapeutic group, the therapeutic club, the community clinic as the future milieu therapies replacing mental hospitals—as well as on levels of the analysis of relational process *(12)*.

In America, new social methods of treatment began to emerge during the 1930s and 1940s. A gradual shift in attitudes toward mental hospitals developed in reaction to the use of seclusion and restraint; the new attitudes advocated open-door policies and use of the therapeutic community model both within and outside the institution. Examples of these changing attitudes in Massachusetts were the pioneering work of Marsh at Worcester State Hospital in the early 1930s, known for his creed "By the group you have been broken, by the group you will be healed" and of Myerson with his "total push therapy" *(13, 14)*.

The term *therapeutic community* was coined by Main in 1946 in describing the work done at Northfield Hospital, Birmingham, England, during the latter part of World War II *(15)*. The primary developer of the concept was Maxwell Jones, who in 1946 took over a wing of Belmont Hospital in England as a treatment unit for semiderelict men. At first, it was called the Industrial Neurosis Unit, then the Social Rehabilitation Unit. Throughout the day, there was a pattern of meetings and discussions which included workshop groups, domestic groups, small psychotherapy groups, staff sensitivity groups, assessment sessions, all with the aim of increasing the individual's awareness and understanding of what he was doing to himself and to other people *(16)*.

Many of these ideas and practices have been widely accepted in America as part of good social therapy over a wide range of clinical psychopathology, including schizophrenia. Some variants of this trend in America are Alcoholics Anonymous, founded in 1935, and Recovery, Inc., founded in 1937, for former mental patients. These latter two programs, however, tended to offer a ritualized and limited form of group therapy compared with the more informal, broadly based socialization activities characteristic of the social therapeutic club. Slavson and Moreno began their work with group therapy in the 1930s and 1940s, which eventually merged with other developments during the war and postwar years to become a significant part of the socialization modality in community mental health. World War II, by its organized approach to group culture and structure, lent impetus to the use of social therapeutic modalities in psychiatric care systems. In addition, the induction of more varied professional disciplines and skills in psychiatric service served as a catalyst during both the war and the postwar years and fed fresh streams of thought and experience into the new psychosocial endeavor.

ASSUMPTIVE BASIS OF SOCIALIZATION AS A FOCUS OF THERAPY

Angyal once defined psychiatry as the application of a science which does not exist *(17)*. Many theoretical models exist today with respect to the etiology and treatment of schizophrenia, including genetic (sociobiology), biochemical (drugs), psychological (psychoanalysis), learning theory (behavior modification), family dynamics (family therapy), and sociocultural (sociotherapy). Like the elephant and the blind men, each exponent of a special school sees the phenomenon from his or her own point of view. While approaching a problem from a single point of view may have heuristic value for science, it does not do justice to the complexity of the psychiatric problem. Throughout the history of psychiatry, we have seen emphases fluctuate back and forth from one end of the continuum to the other. Having been exposed to all these models at one time or another, and having tested them in the crucible of experience, my associates and I find an eclectic attitude most conducive to a sound pragmatic approach at this stage of the art. We cut across all theoretical possibilities and adopt the following logic: until the specific cause(s) of schizophrenia is scientifically established, socialization whether curative or meliorative remains a common denominator, whatever the context of theory. The results of 30 years of systematic practice appear to justify this strategy.

BEHAVIORAL PROPERTIES OF POPULATION AT RISK

We have described our view of the therapeutic value of socialization as relevant to any possible theory of schizophrenia and exclusive to none. Having eschewed any one theoretical bias, we nevertheless expressed partiality for an integralist hypothesis consistent with historical experience and empirical data. Finally, we limited our application of socialization as a necessary, if not sufficient, condition of therapy to the care of the chronic psychiatric population.

In our lifetime, following World War II, we have seen a profound change take place, sometimes referred to as the third psychiatric revolution, embodied in the development of community mental health centers as a salutary replacement for outmoded, inhumane mental institutions. The Community Mental Health Center's Act of Congress in 1963, following the final report of the historic Joint Commission on Mental Illness and Health in 1961, was really addressed to the problem of the institutionalized mentally ill, the failure of institutions, and the need for alternatives. In the implementation of this act, however, for a variety of reasons we will not go into here, chronic patients were the least and last considered in the planning, staffing, and program construction of these centers. Many knowledgeable observers of the scene were critical of this major flaw, but it was not until the mid-1970s, after much unfavorable publicity and with the reports of the Senate Sub-Committee on Long-Term Care and the General Accounting Office study of deinstitutionalization in

1976, that correction of this error began to be taken seriously.

It is now generally agreed and accepted that the major problem in community mental health today is the orderly return of chronic patients to community life. Coleman has given the best nonschematic description of this group *(18)*.

> If they can be characterized in any way, one may think of them as people who are more vulnerable than others, more easily hurt, less resilient in the face of stress and rejection ... with a long history of severe characterological problems ... suffering from a chronic in-grained disturbance. There are many such people in communities, and they do not all become patients in mental hospitals. Their relation to others is often tenuous, lacking in closeness, and peripheral. Often, too, they are socially isolated, particularly in terms of their own feelings, and need an acceptance which does not impose pressures or demands for emotional response. By and large, these are the most neglected patients in our society, not only because it is so difficult for them to make known their distress, but also because, made known, it is often likely to arouse little response of sympathy or concern.

It is estimated that 10–15% of patients become chronic after an acute episode. Failure to provide social underpinning for these individuals in community life could well undermine the entire community mental health enterprise.

SOCIALIZATION IN LATE TWENTIETH CENTURY

Klerman has warned that "one of the unintended consequences of decarceration and deinstitutionalization may be new forms of anomie and isolation for the schizophrenic in the community" *(19)*. Research studies by Pasamanick, Zwerling, Gruenberg, Fair-weather, and others since the 1950s have provided considerable evidence in support of socialization as a crucial factor in the success of deinstitutionalization.

I wish to draw particular attention to those aspects of socialization in practice which have sprung, for the most part, out of traditions of humanism, cultural anthropology, sociology, psychology, and rehabilitation *(20)*. This movement, independent of medical-psychiatric authority and theory, had its origin when patients in Rockland State Hospital, New York, began meeting on the steps of the New York Public Library in 1948. They went under the name WANA, "We Are Not Alone," without any professional or financial backing other than the help of some volunteers. These informal meetings gradually assumed the form of a social club for mutual aid and emotional support. This is the foundation on which the Fountain House* model is built.

Horizon House in Philadelphia was begun in 1953 by a former mental patient and a group of interested citizens mostly from the Society of Friends, also with little psychiatric sponsorship and financial support, but responding to group self-help impulses of expatients in an alien society. Council House in Pittsburgh began in 1957 as an expatient social club sponsored by the local chapter of the National Council of Jewish Women, inspired by the example of Fountain House. Their ground plan was to establish a resocialization program that would serve as a bridge to the community. They followed a path of utilizing existing community resources as sites for program activities instead of their own center. Thresholds in Chicago was founded by their local chapter of the National Council of Jewish Women in 1958, aided by a grant from the National Institute of Mental Health (NIMH) to provide socialization experience to discharged mental patients.

In Massachusetts, the first social club was known as the 103 Club because of its address, right outside the Boston Psychopathic Hospital, now the Massachusetts Mental Health Center. This club grew out of a patient government program encouraged by a progressive staff in 1948. Discharged patients met weekly at the club quarters under indigenous leadership, with the help of volunteers and occasional access to hospital staff across the street; the club was not purely self-governing because of its proximity to the hospital. It enjoyed a surprisingly long life, as long as it maintained its charismatic leadership, but when this failed, the club began to disintegrate. When the Center Club was formed in 1959 by a group of expatients meeting with me and some volunteers under the sponsorship of the Massachusetts Association for Mental Health, the old 103 Club merged with us at the suggestion of Jack Ewalt, then superintendent of the Massachusetts Mental Health Center.

Similar programs have spread to other places, such as Friendship House, Prospect House, and The Club in New Jersey; Hill House in Cleveland; Portals House in Los Angeles; The Stairways in Erie, Pennsylvania; and Fellowship House in Miami. Though no two programs are exactly alike, and all show variations according to local circumstances, they are in essential respects comparable in

*The Fountain House was the first psychosocial rehabilitation center to be established in New York City in mid-1948.

origin, purpose, and program development. Furthermore, over the years, they have shown a vigorous growth rate in size and diversity of program, staff, and budget, reflecting social need, program effectiveness, and staff productivity. In 1975, leaders in the development of such programs decided to formalize their long association by organizing the International Association of Psychosocial Rehabilitation Services, the Fourth Annual Conference of which was held in Miami, November 1978.

New support from NIMH for the development of such community support systems for chronic psychiatric patients, reinforced by the 1978 report of the President's Commission on Mental Health, will provide further stimulus to this form of socialization as a therapeutic element in the network of community mental health. Though these programs represent the forward thrust and cutting edge of treating long-term emotionally disabled citizens in comprehensive, multiservice rehabilitation agencies allied to community mental health centers, their full potential will probably not be reached until the end of the century. Conditioning their continued progress, however, will be the continuing commitment to the basic premise and promise of socialization within a deeply resistive society.

PARAMETERS OF SOCIALIZATION: A DECALOGUE

In light of this somewhat discursive survey of past and recent work with the chronic mentally ill, I believe we can identify some major parameters and operational criteria that establish socialization as an independent, substantive agent in therapy:

1. Rooted in Judeo-Christian and democratic tradition
2. *Frees* mental patients from a segregated role in society
3. Maximizes utilization of *natural* community processes and modalities
4. Restores individualism, voluntarism, and free choice
5. Adapts *rehabilitation* theory as a conceptual and instrumental tool
6. Utilizes *group* situations as the principal vehicle of change
7. Emphasizes *competency* rather than status in staff, volunteer, and client roles
8. Oriented to *process* rather than product in program content
9. Prepares the soil for social and *self-governance*

10. Primary attention to *here and now* rather than past or future.

It is suggested that only to the extent we legitimate and incorporate these parameters in future community mental health systems will we be assured of success in providing effective community support to chronic mental patients. Concurrently, final documentation of results will rest upon the availability of research funds and capability for mounting definitive, controlled studies *(19, 22)*.

Notes

1. Klerman GL: New trends in hospitalization. Hosp & Comm Psych 30:119–123, 1979

2. Report of the President's Commission on Mental Health, Vols. 1 & 2. Washington, D.C., U.S. Government Printing Office, 1978

3. Srole L: Geel (Belgium), The natural therapeutic community: 1475–1975. Fourth International Symposium of Kittay Scientific Foundation, March 1976

4. Bockhoven JS: Moral Treatment in American Psychiatry. New York, Springer, 1963

5. Caplan RB: Psychiatry and the Community in 19th Century America. New York, Basic Books, 1969

6. Lief A: The Commonsense Psychiatry of Dr. Adolph Meyer. New York, McGraw-Hill, 1948

7. Zilboorg GW: A History of Medical Psychology. New York, Norton, 1941

8. Adler A: Social Interest: A Challenge to Mankind. Faber & Faber Ltd., London, 1938

9. Sullivan HS: Socio-psychiatric research: Its implications for the schizophrenic problem and for mental hygiene. Amer J Psych 87:977–991, 1930–1931

10. Tonnies F: Gemeinschaft und Gesellschaft. Leipzig, Fue's Vorlag (R. Reisland), 1887

11. Mead GH: Mind, Self, and Society. Chicago, Univ Chicago Press, 1934

12. Bierer J: A self-governed patients' social club in a public mental hospital. J Ment Sci 87:419–426, 1941

13. Marsh LC: An experiment in the group treatment of patients at the Worcester State Hospital. Mental Hygiene 17:396–416, 1933

14. Myerson A: Theory and principles of the 'total push' method in the treatment of chronic schizophrenia. Amer J Psych 95:1197–1204, 1939

15. Main TF: The hospital as a therapeutic institution. (Bull Menn Clinic, 1946, 10 p 66) In Barnes E (ed): Psychosocial Nursing, London, Tavistock, 1968

16. Jones M, The Therapeutic Community: Social Psychiatry: A Study of Therapeutic Communities. London, Tavistock, 1952

17. Angyal A: Foundations for a Science of Personality. New York, Commonwealth Fund, 1941

18. Coleman J: Adaptational problems characteristic of returning mental hospital patients. In Grob S (ed): The Community Social Club and the Returning Mental Patients. NIMH Conference, Boston, 1963

19. Klerman GL: Community Treatment of Schizophrenia. New England Conference on the Chronic Psychiatric Patient in the Community, Spectrum Publications Expected Publication Date Winter 1980 Barofsky IT, Budson RD, (eds.) Boston, 1976

20. Glasscote RM, Cumming E, Rutman ID, Sussex JN, Glassman SM: Rehabilitating the Mentally Ill in the Community: A Study of Psychosocial Rehabilitation Centers. Washington, D.C., Joint Information Service APA and NIMH, 1971

21. Hogarty GE: The plight of schizophrenics in modern treatment programs. Hosp. & Comm. Psych 22:197–203, 1971

22. Grob S: Psychiatric social clubs come of age. Mental Hygiene 54:129–136, 1970

Chapter 6

VOCATIONAL REHABILITATION
George W. Brooks

Work is a key factor in the care, treatment, and rehabilitation of the chronic mental patient. It has a history as old as the literature. In 1842, Kirkbride said, "The value of employment in treatment is now so universally conceded that no arguments are required in this favor. Its value cannot be estimated in dollars and cents . . . the object is to restore mental health and tranquilize the restlessness and mitigate the sorrows of disease" *(1)*. In 1939, Freud said, "Work has greater effect than any other technique of living in the direction of binding the individual more closely to reality; in his work at least, he is securely attached to a part of reality; the human community" *(2)*. Work has been, and remains, a major feature of treatment throughout Europe, as it was when Kalinowsky *(3)* reported in 1956. It at first seemed somewhat puzzling that studies cited by Zubin and Spring *(4)*, Serban *(5)*, Christensen *(6)*, Turner *(7)*, and Weiner et al. *(8)*, found that "occupational competence generally confers no immunity to schizophrenia" and "the highly vulnerable individual, even when ill, may be able to demonstrate satisfactory levels of work competence under suitable conditions."*(4)* This should not surprise us however, since we knew that our long-stay hospital population had retained work competence. Indeed, they were primarily responsible for the operation of our state mental hospitals. Only a little over two decades ago, two out of every three hours of labor in hospital were performed by unpaid patients. We said, and it was true, that if patients joined a union and went on strike, the hospital would have to close. We could not have operated the power house, the sewing room, the greenhouse, the storehouse, the food service, the housekeeping service, the farm and garden, the paint crew, and many other basic functions without this patient labor. Why, then, is work the key to rehabilitation and deinstitutionalization of this population? Because, this is the very essence of rehabilitation. In rehabilitation, as opposed to symptom control, we work with the strengths and assets of the individual, and work competence was the most obvious asset that the patient had. Through the world of work, these people were also able to gain readmission to the many other satisfactions of everyday living, including a place to stay, people to be with, and a social life to enjoy. The first order of business in deinstitutionalization is getting the institution out of the person. Only secondarily should we be involved in getting the person out of the institution. Simply controlling symptoms and putting the individual in "less restrictive" settings is a gross disservice to the principle of deinstitutionalization. Many, many such people remain in limbo on the fringes, or just outside the fringes, of society—unable to participate in or enjoy a quality life style and still, apparently, "institutionalized."

In 1961, Brooks and Deane (9) had the temerity to predict that with adequate research in vocational rehabilitation this work would "be more solidly based" and thus "help to reduce the shameful undulation between progression and regression, which has been characteristic of this field in the past." This prophesy is, to some extent, fulfilled. There is considerable recent research which solidly demonstrates the superiority of work experiences and vocational rehabilitation in the degree of independence achieved by chronic patients.

Such studies as those cited by Weiner et al. (8) indicate that maintaining high expectations and retaining links with the world of work can effectively prevent institutionalization. Studies such as those by Lamb and Goertzel (10) clearly show that high rehabilitation expectations increase vocational and social functioning of long-term patients. The experiences in ghetto psychiatry of Christmas (11) emphasize the high expectations and the potential for personal growth in successful rehabilitation programs. This principle has been demonstrated in many different ways in many different settings. For example, a high-expectation community rehabilitation program established by Koonce *(12)* at Mendota State Hospital in Madison, Wisconsin, clearly demonstrates the development of competence in a very disabled group when expectations are high; similar findings are indicated in the Netherne Study by Ekdawi *(13)*.

Despite these reported demonstrations, the situation has become somewhat confused since the 1973 decision enforcing the 1966 Fair Labor Standards Act prohibiting unpaid labor by mentally ill patients. However, this situation is beginning to sort itself out through paid patient labor *(14)*, Comprehensive Employment and Training Act (CETA) positions, and, perhaps most notably, the Innovation Diffusion Project; these are small group ward and lodge programs as an essential phase of any complete hospital treatment program. As part of the hospital's treatment program, the lodge provides an effective and less costly way to help ex-mental patients overcome their problems and find meaningful community roles. In addition, the lodge program makes economical use of available human resources. Since existing mental health workers can be trained to manage the lodges, no other personnel are needed. This project has succeeded in establishing a number of Fairweather Lodges throughout the country *(15)*.

We clearly have the knowledge, the techniques, the demonstrations, and the wherewithal to successfully rehabilitate most of our chronic mentally disabled population. However, the developments of the past several years have hampered progress in this field. The dilemma is perhaps most clearly stated in the background statement on the "Vocational Rehabilitation of the Mentally Ill," prepared by the Rehabiltation Service Administration:

> The person severely incapacitated by mental illness may benefit maximally from the treatment modalities available in an institution, and be transferred to the community; nevertheless, he has virtually no potential for gainful employment. Thus the individual is caught between the medical (therapeutic) and rehabilitation models or systems, with the result that he exchanges the dependency of institutional life for an equally dependent status in the community. *(16)*

This dilemma is, of course, largely due to the recent rush to get patients out into the community, whether properly prepared or not. It may take some judicial ruling on the right to rehabilitation to rectify this. There can be no doubt that a structured rehabilitation program characterized by high expectations is restrictive in the sense that any intensive training program is restrictive. One of my own patients perhaps stated the situation most succinctly. She said, with

some feeling, "You used to have camisoles*—now you have rehabilitation." Maxwell Jones once stated to the writer, "The progression
is from mechanical restraints to chemical restraints to social restraints." It is the social restraints which provide for all our lives the
stable base for the satisfactions of everyday living.

The impact of these recent developments is clear in the reports
of the number of rehabilitations of the psychotically disabled. They
are disappointingly very low compared to the potential need. Although rehabilitation of the mentally ill accounts for nearly 22% of
all rehabilitation nationwide, rehabilitation of psychotics accounts
for only 22% of these, or 4.8% of the total. The number of rehabilitated psychotics, which nationwide reaches about 13,500, seems to
me to be quite obviously far below the need represented by the
number of chronically disabled who have migrated into the community.

It is difficult to compare the rehabilitations of the psychotically
disabled with the magnitude of the need. It is unlikely that large
portions of the less than 5% of rehabilitations accounted for by the
psychotically disabled are of the chronically disabled. It is much
more likely that most of these are relatively short-term cases. It has
been estimated that over 800,000 chronically disabled psychotic individuals are now in the community *(17)*, so that a very few thousand
rehabilitated annually will make little impact on this huge need.

Until the right to rehabilitation is as firmly established as the
right to treatment and the right to least restrictive settings, we will
continue to have the national shame of chronic community custodial
care for our most needy citizens.

NOTES

1. Bond ED: Dr. Kirkbride and His Mental Hospital. Philadelphia, Pa., J. B.
    Lippincott Co., 1947

2. Freud S: Civilization and Its Discontents. London, Hogarth, 1939

3. Kalinowsky L: Advances in management and treatment in European mental
    hospitals. American Journal of Psychiatry 113(6):549–556, 1956

4. Zubin J, Spring B: Vulnerability—A new view of schizophrenia. Journal of
    Abnormal Psychology 86(2):103–126, 1977

5. Serban G: Stress in schizophrenics and normals. British Journal of Psychiatry
    126:397–407, 1975

*An old hospital word for straight jackets.

6. Christensen JK: A 5-year follow-up study of male schizophrenics: Evaluation of factors influencing success and failure in the community. Acta Psychiat Scand 50:60–72, 1974

7. Turner RJ: Jobs and Schizophrenia. Social Policy 8:32–40, 1977.

8. Weiner H, Akabas S, Somer J: Mental Health Care in the World of Work. New York, Associated Press, 1973

9. Brooks G, Deane W: Research in rehabilitation of the mentally ill. Rehabilitation Literature 22(6):166–170, 1961

10. Lamb HR, Goertzel V: High expectations of long-term ex-state patients. The American Journal of Psychiatry 129(4):471–475, 1972

11. Christmas J: Rehabilitation—General and special considerations. Psychiatric Annals 4(4):49–59, 1974

12. Koonce G: Social work with mental patients in the community. Social Work 18(3):30–34, 1973

13. Ekdawi M: The Netherne Resettlement Unit: Results of ten years. British Journal of Psychiatry 121(563):417–424, 1972

14. Safier D, Barnum R: Patient rehabilitation through hospital work under fair labor standards. Hospital & Community Psychiatry 26(5):299–303, 1975

15. MSU-NIMH Innovation Diffusion Project, Michigan State University, Department of Psychology, Olds Hall, East Lansing, Michigan

16. Selected pages from a statement on mental illness: Vocational Rehabilitation of the Mentally Ill, received from Thomas J. Skelley, Director, Division of Innovative Programs and Demonstrations, Office of Human Development Services, Rehabilitation Services Administration, Department of Health, Education, and Welfare, Office of the Secretary, Washington, D.C. 20201: 10–11, 1978

17. Minkoff K: A map of chronic mental patients. In Talbott JA (ed): The Chronic Mental Patient: Problems, Solutions, and Recommendations for a Public Policy. Washington, D.C., The American Psychiatric Association, 1978

Chapter 7

COMMUNITY RESIDENTIAL CARE
Richard D. Budson

Community residential care is an essential element of a comprehensive treatment program for the chronically mentally ill patient in the community. This is represented by a broad spectrum of residential opportunities. The best of these are carefully planned, staffed, and operated under professional supervision. Other housing to which many thousands of patients have been discharged is neither planned nor supervised. This has become an increasing concern to responsible mental health planners who are attempting to meet more adequately the housing needs of the chronic mental patient. The magnitude of unevenness in the field of housing for the chronically mentally ill is partly a result of the spontaneous and undefined manner in which these programs originated.

BACKGROUND—PHARMACOLOGICAL, SOCIOLOGICAL, AND LEGAL ISSUES

In the last three decades, pharmacological, sociological, and legal influences have contributed—often in contradictory ways—to the development and expansion of community living arrangements for the chronically mentally ill in the United States. In the 1950s, the advent of the psychotropic medications set the stage for this revolution in domiciliary care. They permitted once unruly and disorganized patients who were unable to effectively care for themselves to have clarity of mind and controlled affect sufficient to enable them to live in the community.

The disenchantment with large institutions in general in the 1960s had its effect on the care of the mentally ill as well. Just as there was criticism of such large institutions as the federal government with its Vietnam policy, the university with its arbitrary curriculum, and the big city with its bewildering bureaucracy, so too there was a growing abhorrence by many professionals of the abominable conditions of the large state hospital. The 1960s also saw, in the social experiment of the commune, a reaction against a unique smallness that was part of the American scene—the isolated nuclear family.

It was in this context of dissatisfaction with impersonal bigness and isolated smallness that small groups of mental health workers began, largely on their own, to develop in different parts of the country the first psychiatric halfway houses. Community residences thus began with a low profile, not as part of a directed, unified, official policy coming from above, but as offspring of antiestablishment experimentation. They were designed to alleviate four basic deficiencies of the traditional large state hospital. The overly large state hospital ward, using a universal medical model, functioned as a closed society, in isolation from the community. In contrast, the community residences were designed to be relatively small, family modeled, living arrangements, functioning as open social systems, integrated with rather than isolated from the community *(1, 2)*. These carefully and professionally conceived programs grew from only seven in the entire country in 1960 *(3)* to a reported 209 by 1973 *(4)*. There are surely more by now. This type of program has been described in the literature in a variety of volumes by Landy and Greenblatt *(5)*, Rothwell and Doniger *(6)*, Raush and Raush *(7)*, Glasscote et al. *(8)*, and Budson *(1)*.

The 1970s also brought a series of important court decisions, which have influenced the states, the institutions, and the local communities—often with the effect of forcing many patients into the community before adequate facilities were there to receive them.

Wyatt v. *Stickney,* (325F, Supp. 781 M.D. Ala. 1971), now known as *Wyatt* v. *Anderholt,* in 1971 "represented the first class-action suit brought against a state's entire mental health system." In this case, the court "affirmed the constitutional right to treatment for those mentally disordered persons who were involuntarily civilly committed" *(9)*. Since the court then dictated for the first time specific and very costly standards to the state, the states defensively began to discharge patients to avoid the threat of state fiscal chaos, a threat implicit in judicial orders defining, for example, staff/patient ratios. Fewer patients in the hospitals required fewer staff and fewer state appropriations. Dischargees could receive, instead, federal monies through Supplemental Security Income to support them. Tragically, however, formally organized community residential facilities were woefully inadequate. Thus, large numbers of discharged patients drifted into proprietary-run boarding homes and single-occupancy hotels. Daily programs also were lacking so that the deterioration that occurred in the hospital continued in the community. This led to pressures for more effective community care for the mentally ill. The inadequacy of this care, in turn, led to a community outcry against these discharges.

In the *O'Connor* v. *Donaldson* decision in 1975, the Supreme Court stated for the first time that a mentally ill person could not be held against his will in a state hospital if he was not dangerous to himself or others, he was not being offered treatment, and he was able to survive on his own in the community. This decision did not address itself to the possible alternative of release to a halfway house if the patient was not able to survive on his own in the community. This omission is ironic, because denying the plaintiff the right to move to a halfway house was a crucial precipitating factor in the case.

A decision that did importantly address itself to community treatment was the 1974 judgment of a district court case in Washington, D.C. *(Dixon* v. *Weinberger,* now *Dixon* v *Califano)*. In this class-action suit against the federally operated Saint Elizabeths Hospital, the court ruled that mental patients were guaranteed "suitable care and treatment *under the least restrictive conditions,* including placement of patients in community-based facilities." The impact of this decision was to move states' policies and legislation toward the requirement for the least restrictive alternative. However, the court did not in this instance explicitly identify what these community facilities would be, and there continues to be debate and litigation with regard to the criteria for community placement of these patients.

Most recently in Massachusetts (*Brewster* v. *Dukakis,* 1978), there was an explicit agreement by the state to develop the required community alternatives. The parties agreed that, as these carefully designed community residential facilities were developed and hospital patients placed in them, the hospital itself would proportionately diminish until over time the hospital would close.

Ultimately, the U.S. Congress in 1975 enacted Public Law 94 –63 which, for the first time, included the community residence as an essential component of the community mental health center.

Thus, there are strong medical, social, and legal currents within our society that have moved the locus of the treatment of the severely mentally ill from the state hospital to the community. However, major attempts at reform have resulted in a complex system of contradictory demands and requirements—that patients not be incarcerated without treatment; that patients not be released into the community before there are adequate community care programs; that large, expensive institutions not continue to drain dwindling state coffers; that unscrupulous private entrepreneurs not victimize again the vulnerable population of discharged patients. In general, destruction and reform of the old have outstripped creation of the new, and inadequate development of proper rehabilitative facilities in the community has had serious consequences for patients.

CURRENT CONTROVERSY—A BRIEF REVIEW

The unevenness of the community care resulting from this chaotic situation has been increasingly documented in the literature. Greenblatt and Budson *(10)* have recently summarized the work of Polak and Kirby, Stein and Test, Beigel et al., and Mosher and Menn. All of these investigators have reported generally favorable results using a variety of community-based treatment approaches. On the other hand, Kohen and Paul *(11)* have reviewed the work of other investigators in the field whose results have been unfavorable. For example, Chu and Trotter *(12)* are quoted as suggesting that the community treatment movement has simply resulted in "more of the same" being given in different locations. Koltuv and Neff *(13)* similarly warned that *without a new technology* the only accomplishment of community treatment will be to move "the locus in which the emotionally disturbed [individual] vegetates and experiences personal misery."

A closer examination of the literature reveals that there are some community programs that are rehabilitative and some that are not. The use of so-called boarding homes without bona fide rehabilitation programs and without a trained professional staff has generally been viewed as disastrous. Reporting on the problems in New

York, Reich and Siegel *(14)* described proprietary homes with as many as 285 beds that failed to provide any day programs, rehabilitative services, or systematic psychiatric care. Shadoan *(15)* addressed this problem and suggested improving the rehabilitative quality of such homes either "through individual consultation with administrators" or having "mental health professionals and the administrator jointly develop and conduct the facility's therapeutic program." Lamb and Goertzel *(16)* in 1971, comparing boarding homes to high-expectation halfway houses, concluded that boarding homes are characterized by an assumption that "guests" will "remain regressed and dependent indefinitely," whereas high-expectation halfway houses facilitate a "process of delabeling—the residents [being] less segregated, less likely to be labeled as deviate, and experiencing less stigmatization—with the individuals seeing themselves as functioning members of the community." Then again, in 1976 Lamb did not "really see halfway houses as being much of an answer to the problem of the long-term, severely ill mental patient." He complained that they "require around-the-clock staffing, are difficult to set up and maintain, and when they are professionally run, they somehow wind up frequently excluding the long-term severely ill, either by high expectations which are not realistic for these patients, or by the preferences of the staff who'd rather serve other kinds of people" *(17)*.

Steven P. Segal draws upon two sets of psychological assessments—"psychological disturbance" which is considered "gross symptoms or deviant behaviors such as motor retardation, hallucinating behavior, grandiosity, mannerisms, and posturing," and "psychological distress," meaning the ability to verbalize one's internal discomforts. He found that these two types of problems differed "importantly in terms of the characteristics of the population in need of sheltered care." He concluded that

the environments in which we find the psychologically distressed are more likely to be halfway houses. The psychologically disturbed are more likely to be found in board and care homes. The severely psychologically disturbed population constitutes approximately 19% of those living in community based sheltered-care facilities in California. However, half of the total sheltered-care population in California is showing serious psychological distress *(18)*.

From these conclusions there is clearly a need for adequate facilities for both types of populations. Budson *(19)* comparing cooperative apartments to halfway houses has documented such a division of facilities in Massachusetts serving these two different populations, stating that "the cooperative apartment has served a more chronic, older population with fewer vocational skills, and community ties. The community residence population, on the other hand, is more likely to be a younger, more vocationally able population, with retention of their ties to the community to which they return, usually within a year."

Rog and Raush *(20)* reviewed follow-up studies of 26 halfway houses. Although there was no uniformity of follow-up intervals or indices, a composite picture emerged of 20% rehospitalized, 58% living independently in the community, and 55% employed or in school. The finding in this review of only 20% recidivism ought to be considered a favorable result. Other comprehensive reviews of the community residence field are also available *(21, 22, 23)*.

We are clearly in the infancy of a new era of mental health care. The range of difficulties of the patients to be served is great. Their numbers are also great. The services required to sustain them with dignity in a rehabilitative program are numerous. It appears clear that a carefully designed range of residential rehabilitative services is required for the spectrum of disability to be served. These residential services should have the primary goal of maintaining a high rehabilitative level in regard to each resident's program. These programs should be "adequate to assure that the person's unmet needs are met" *(24)*.

Further, Budson and Jolley, in looking for the "crucial factor" which may lead to effective care have suggested that those programs which create an effective "extended psychosocial kinship system" for the residents may be the most successful *(25)*.

DIFFERENT MODALITIES IN USE

There are ten different types of community residential housing currently being employed in the United States: (1) transitional halfway houses; (2) long-term group residences; (3) cooperative apartments (satellite housing, landlord-supervised apartments, post–halfway house accommodations); (4) lodge programs; (5) total rural environments (work camps); (6) foster care (family care); (7) crisis centers; (8) nursing homes; (9) board and care homes; and (10) hotels.

Some of these are usually bona fide components of comprehensive mental health programs (nos. 1–7). Others are often not (nos.

8–10). Irrespective of the geographic locus of the residential care or the level of care for which the program was conceived, it would appear that, at best, one of the essential requirements to ensure an adequate rehabilitative focus is the sustained involvement of a mental health service agency.

The transitional halfway house has been defined by the National Institute of Mental Health as a "residential facility in operation seven days a week with round the clock supervision (often a staff member living on the premises) and providing room, board, and assistance in the activities of daily living." These facilities are usually operated by nonprofit, private corporations, in large old homes, with 15–20 residents, who spend a planned daily program outside the dwelling. Although such facilities are increasingly serving as an alternative to hospitalization, most usually the halfway house is used as a transitional facility from hospital to the community. In-house services include counseling, house meetings, and recreational activities, with an emphasis on mutual support and understanding among house residents. The transitional halfway house is more likely to have a younger population which has been sick a shorter duration of time and is more able to readily enter the community (1, 5, 6, 7, 8, 19, 26, 27, 28).

The long-term group residence is similar to the transitional halfway house in most respects except for the fact that residents not only need a group living arrangement but are behaviorally so lacking in living skills, or potentially symptomatic, that an increased on-site staff/resident ratio is required. In addition, the duration of tenure in this community residence may exceed one year, in contrast to the transitional facility, where the average stay may only be six to eight months. This facility, however, is designed to care for the most difficult patients who otherwise would be detained in a psychiatric hospital.

Cooperative apartments are unique in that they have no on-site staff and are usually made up by groups of four expatients, each group living in a separate unit, with regular visiting staff. An outside daily program is generally arranged and supervised for each resident by the sponsoring mental health agency (19, 29, 30, 31). Landlord-supervised apartments are similar to other cooperative apartments, except that the landlord is in a contiguous dwelling and sees that some of the programmatic goals of the sponsoring agency are being met—such as insuring the residents leave for their daily program in the morning, are properly dressed, prepare their meals adequately, sustain their physical health, and adequately maintain the premises. Both the landlord and the resident are assisted by visiting staff of the sponsoring agency.

Mannino, Ott, and Shore have succinctly described the nature of these apartments.

> Apartment programs frequently begin as an addition to another resi-dential program such as a halfway house or as an extension of a hospital or community program. The sponsor searches for willing landlords, leases and furnishes the apartments, selects and matches roommates, and is responsible for maintaining full occupancy. Some apartments have time limits after which the resident must leave to find independent living arrangements; others allow indefinite stays. Apartment programs usually provide for regular meetings between residents and a staff member; in most cases, residents take part in other aspects of the parent organization's activities such as day center programs (21).

Cooperative apartments may be developed not only to provide pro-grammatic scope but also to avoid various constraints, to minimize start-up costs, to lower operating costs, to avoid community opposi-tion, and to circumvent special restrictive building codes (19).

Lodge programs are based upon the model developed by George Fairweather. "They consist of a group of patients formed in the hospital who move together into the community. The group is an independent one, usually based on a business operated by the group. Preparation for the business and the living situation is made by the patients with the help and supervision of hospital staff. Patients function together as a cooperative communal society, running the household and working together to earn money" (21, 32, 33, 34).

Total rural environments have been pioneered by such facilities as Gould Farm in Massachusetts and Spring Lake Ranch in Ver-mont. These are nonhospital residential facilities for clients who are judged neither to need the hospital nor to be able to manage effec-tively on their own or in other types of residential facilities in the community. Thus, this program offers a total environment of super-vised living that includes on-premises regular daily farming chores. Since it is a total environment, the focus instead of being that of a medically oriented hospital is that of an operational farm. The atmos-phere often resembles that of a summer camp (35, 36).

Foster or family care refers to the placement of expatients in private homes. The patient is supervised by the caretaker or sponsor who is in turn supervised by a professional social worker. Programs are sponsored by hospitals, state mental health systems, and most prominently by the Veterans Administration, which has relied heavily upon foster care for placing former patients in the community. Often up to four residents are placed into one foster home. State systems formerly funded many such foster homes. However, states now tend "to carry former patients on foster care rolls only long enough to transfer financing arrangements to other sources of funding such as Supplemental Security Income. Long-term arrangements are seen as more and more falling within the welfare or housing sectors" (23). One continuing problem about foster home care is the concern that it serves primarily a custodial function. A significant study by Murphy et al. on foster homes in Canada showed that there was little improvement in social function or participation (37, 38, 39, 40).

Crisis centers are a new concept whereby residential care could be used as an alternative to the hospital in a crisis intervention mode prior to a full-blown relapse in a psychotic patient. This would reduce the potential need for a long-term hospitalization (45).

Nursing homes represent an important community residential site to which the elderly and physically handicapped, chronically mentally ill patients are discharged. The nursing home clearly represented one of the most readily available, existing, supervised residential facilities in the community in the early 1970s. Indeed, from 1964 to 1969, the number of nursing homes doubled from 10,000 to almost 20,000 facilities. Much of this growth was due to the 1965 and 1967 amendments to the Social Security Act, namely, the Medicare and Medicaid programs. These facilities continue to play a controversial role in the rehabilitation of the chronically ill in the community. Goldmeier has stated that "nursing homes appropriate for the patient's level of functioning have a definite role to play in a continuum of community mental health services." He felt that ideally these facilities "should serve those requiring a relatively high degree of personal, medically oriented attention." As part of the whole continuum of service, "nursing homes are probably the most closely supervised of residential facilities, i.e., they have a high staff/resident ratio" (23). At the same time, it must be noted that a variety of studies have suggested that more developed activity programs were needed in nursing homes in order to prevent physical and self-care decline (41, 42, 43, 44).

Board and care homes range from proprietary facilities which house hundreds of persons to private homes which house very few. Commercial buildings, such as hotels, are often used to house ex-mental patients as well. "The quality and kinds of services offered run the gamut from merely providing room and board in dingy surroundings to organized services in modern facilities" *(21)*. In general, boarding homes are custodial in nature and rarely have active rehabilitation programs. A number of authors and agencies have proposed methods of increasing standards of care in these facilities. This is a very important area, since such a large number of patients are involved *(14, 15, 16, 46, 47, 48, 49)*.

DEVELOPMENT AND CLINICAL OPERATION OF PROGRAMS

There is an increasing need for carefully planned community residences, which range from the transitional halfway house, through the long-term group residence, and to various apartment programs. These will, if creatively established, fulfill the need to provide just enough care to facilitate the resident's attainment of his highest adaptive capacity. Planning and starting such a facility is a complicated and demanding job. A proper beginning is more likely to bring about an effective result; thus, the steps broken down, task by task, should be known. These include (1) forming the operating organization; (2) establishing the type of client who clearly needs community residential services; (3) identifying the type and size of the facility that will meet the specific needs of this clientele; (4) planning the program components of the facility; (5) establishing the network of ancillary services to be made available to the client off the premises; (6) establishing staff requirements, job descriptions, staffing patterns, and hiring procedures; (7) finding a suitable location; (8) finding a suitable building; (9) planning and implementing a community entry strategy; (10) developing a budget (capital and seed money) in relation to the building, initial staffing, and operating expenses; (11) establishing sources of funds; (12) monitoring these tasks to keep them in compliance with relevant laws and regulations; (13) drafting a comprehensive program statement suitable for public education, describing effective completion of all these tasks. The reader can find a detailed description of each of these tasks elsewhere *(1)*. A few of the more critical issues will be explored here.

There must be a core of dedicated persons who conceive, back, and pilot the project from its initial conceptualization to functional maturity. Starting a community residence requires commitment and preparation. False starts by poorly prepared sponsors who drop the project at the first difficulty, or seriously blunder in their public relations, create ill will in the community and make entry all the more difficult for groups who try to follow them. Ideally, the core group should consist of skilled and influential members of the community in which the residence is to be located. The initiators, often members of an organization with a special interest in mental health, usually form a nonprofit corporation. A mental health professional should be on the corporate board to coordinate program planning and to maintain its clinical integrity in the face of a multitude of administrative decisions. Expertise is also required in the following areas: legal, to facilitate compliance with zoning and other regulations; fiscal, in the areas of accounting, to assist in preparing a sound budget, and banking, to help in obtaining a loan for start-up costs; architectural, to assist with building code compliance and structural renovations; and real estate, to inform the group of new properties available. Further, important community leaders, such as a clergyman, a local politician, or a respected businessman, can help with strategies for community entry by educating other community members, thus facilitating acceptance and support.

It is essential that the characteristics of the client type be carefully assessed so that there can be a planned rehabilitative programmatic component for each resident's deficiency. The specifics of each program will, therefore, be dictated by the spectrum of problems presented by the residents. Potential categories of the client population which should be considered include the diagnostic group, time in history of illness (acute or chronic), source of residents (from home, hospital, mental health center, etc.), age of residents, educational level, life skills development, and psychosocial network-community linkages.

Residents who have schizophrenia will generally need an environment which is very supportive and which fosters socialization. Special alertness should be maintained to those issues and situations injurious to the fragile self-esteem of such residents. These events can initiate such reactions as social withdrawal, activation of a delusional system, or a paranoid episode. Patients in this group who are on antipsychotic medication will usually need careful monitoring to ensure they are following their prescriptions. This is a crucial issue.

It must be emphasized that chronic patients frequently demonstrate a loss of socialization and life skills, the absence of a functional psychosocial kinship system, considerable dependence on the program, and slow progress. They often require a long-term group residence with staff who can maintain a therapeutic stance over the long haul. The program must be one which expects only gradual improvement—but nevertheless must sustain itself as rehabilitative rather than custodial. Interactions with the "real world" through shopping, entertainment, and work (even if sheltered) should be maximized. Once essential life skills are attained, and the patient is stable and can reliably travel to his daily program, a cooperative apartment arrangement should be considered.

The rehabilitative aim is enhanced if there is a major emphasis placed on the resident's participation in the definition of goals. Thus, goal definition coupled with the delineation of expectations of both the resident and the staff in meeting these goals should be pursued. A written program plan should be developed when each resident enters the program, and it should be reviewed at least monthly. The program should emphasize: *Life skills improvement,* including personal hygiene, cooking skills, ability to get around in the community, use of public transportation, ability to handle money, capacity to shop in local stores, and acquisition of knowledge in apartment selection. *Vocational planning* to ensure that each resident participates in a daily program at maximum potential, including the use of employment agencies and counseling when the resident is capable of competitive employment, sheltered workshops when the resident is deficient in work skills but is trainable, and a psychosocial rehabilitation center, day center, or social club if he is unsuited for work. *Education planning* for either elementary, high school, or college levels. An educational consultant may be used in planning goals. *Social programs* in the house, assisting the development of interpersonal relations that are free from such pathological patterns as isolation and withdrawal, grandiose hypomanic intrusiveness, or paranoid suspiciousness. *Avocational interests* in the house, such as developing a capacity to be aware of the world about and to engage in such social activities as card playing, ping pong, and other games. *House and staff milieu planning,* involving anticipatory consideration of requirements for staff and peer group to provide support, limit setting, reality testing, confrontation, and the like in individual cases as appropriate. *Family relations,* involving planning for crucial relationships with close family members, including parents, spouses, and children. *Physical health care management,* including general medical care, dental care, exercise, diet, and birth control. *Psychiatric care and therapy.* The client's needs, resources, and problems should determine the treatment plan. Relevant therapies may include chemotherapy; individual counseling; family, group, or couples therapy, day hospital behavior therapy; and availability of crisis inpatient care.

THE FUTURE CHALLENGE—LEGAL, FINANCIAL, AND COMMUNITY CONSTRAINTS

In order to facilitate the expansion of carefully designed, effective community residential programs, a variety of serious impediments must be addressed.

It is important to acknowledge that there are three legal areas which require careful resolution if community residential programs are to be enhanced. First is the problem of building codes. It is vital that building codes permit the use of existing buildings to allow true community integration, but at the same time, the occupants should be assured a safe situation. A successful resolution to this dilemma was achieved in Massachusetts, where a unique fire safety system was developed that emphasized preserving life rather than the building. This system was based on three essential elements: (1) a fire detection alarm system; (2) two independent means of egress from each sleeping quarter; and (3) the certification of the capability of self-preservation of each of the occupants assuring that egress was achievable within two and a half minutes of the alarm. This new system eliminated most of the structural changes required in stricter codes, which were not only expensive but also rendered homelike dwellings into institutionlike buildings. This system should be a model for the nation *(1, 50)*.

Second, licensing standards are essential if there is to be adequate quality control on a statewide basis. At the same time, it is vital that these programmatic standards set by governmental agencies not be so rigid as to render the program sterile. The critical issue is that the fear of potential provider abuse not be expressed by demanding more care than is required by the residence involved. For example, quality control that ignored the varying degrees of dependence of the residents could require excessive numbers of staff that not only would make the program unmanageably expensive to operate but would perpetuate the old system by relegating citizens to unnecessary dependency on professional helpers.

The third legal issue that is of vital importance to the development of community residential care is the potential exclusion of community residences through local zoning ordinances. The possibility of such exclusion has been made greater by the Supreme Court decision of *Belle Terre* v. *Boraas* in 1974. In this decision, Justice William O. Douglas wrote that a group of unrelated adults could be zoned out of a residential neighborhood restricted to one family dwellings, because the word *family* was defined to mean one or more persons related by blood, adoption, or marriage or not more than two unrelated persons living and cooking together in a single housekeeping unit. A group residence being more than two unrelated persons was thus put in jeopardy with regard to zoning decisions. This is still the case in spite of the fact that a subsequent decision suggested that a group home for dependent and neglected children was a special case *(City of White Plains* v. *Ferriaioli) (1, 50)*.

Another important goal for the future is the staffing of these programs with trained and effective workers. It is essential that community residential programs continue to be operated by people with a commitment to growth and rehabilitation. The spark of enthusiasm accompanying creativity and innovation should not be lost, for it fosters a lasting renewal of spirit that keeps the program vital and relevant to both the residents and the community. More and better staff will be needed in the future. Educational institutions must address this new field of community residential care in planning curricula in the human services. Staff from phased-out institutions as well as new students must be educated in the principles of community residential care outlined in this chapter.

Two other important roadblocks to these programs remain: inadequate funding and community opposition. We must pursue the slow process of educating the public and setting society's priorities to cope with the complex issues of caring for the chronically mentally ill. Community residential programs are caught in the funding intricacies of a mental health delivery system in evolution. Innovative programmatic concepts and court orders insuring the constitutional rights of mental patients have not been matched by legislative appropriations. There are a multitude of state and federal funding programs involving, among others, Title XX, the Social Security Act, the Community Mental Health Center Act, and Department of Housing and Urban Development allocations, which are confusing and, albeit, ultimately inadequate. All of this is in spite of the fact that a variety of investigators have shown that, from the view of cost effectiveness, there are distinct financial as well as clinical advantages to these community programs *(51, 52, 53, 54, 55)*.

Finally, the success of community residential programs will ultimately depend upon their true integration into the fabric of society. Even if community entry of these programs is supported by the courts, it is equally important that neighbors accept these patients without harrassment. True rehabilitation will only be achieved in an accepting, helpful atmosphere. Public education in the principles and aims of community mental health programs is essential to the fulfillment of this goal.

Notes

1. Budson RD: The Psychiatric Halfway House: A Handbook of Theory and Practice. Pittsburgh, Pa., University of Pittsburgh Press, 1978

2. Budson RD: The psychiatric halfway house. Psy Annals 3(6):64–83, 1973

3. Wechsler H: Halfway houses for former mental patients: A survey. Journal of Social Issues 16:20–26, 1960

4. National Institute of Mental Health: Reference Data on Halfway Houses for the Mentally Ill and Alcoholics, United States. Washington, D.C., Superintendent of Documents, U.S. Govt. Printing Office, 1973

5. Landy D, Greenblatt M: Halfway House. Washington, D.C., U.S. Department of Health, Education, and Welfare, Vocational Rehabilitation Administration, 1965

6. Rothwell ND, Doniger JM: The Psychiatric Halfway House: A Case Study. Springfield, Illinois, Charles C. Thomas, 1966

7. Raush HL, Raush CL: The Halfway House Movement: A Search for Sanity. New York, Appleton-Century-Crofts, 1968

8. Glasscote RM, Gudeman JE, Elpers JR: Halfway Houses for the Mentally Ill. Washington, D.C., Joint Information Service of the APA and the NAMH, 1971

9. Kopolow LE, Brands A, Burton J, Ochberg FM: Litigation and Mental Health Services. Rockville, Md., NIMH, DHEW Publication No. ADM 75–261, 1975

10. Greenblatt M, Budson RD: A symposium: Follow-up studies of community care. Am J of Psy 8:916–921, 1976

11. Kohen W, Paul G: Current trends and recommended changes in extended care placement of mental patients: The Illinois system as a case in point. Schiz Bul 2(4):575–594, 1976

12. Chu FD, Trotter S: The Madness Establishment. New York, Grossman, 1974

13. Koltuv M, Neff WS: The comprehensive rehabilitation center: Its role and realm in psychiatric rehabilitation. Community Mental Health J 4:251–259, 1968

14. Reich R, Siegel L: The chronically mentally ill shuffle to oblivion. Psy Ann 3:33–55, 1973

15. Shadoan RA: Making board and care homes therapeutic. In Lamb HR, et al. (eds): Community Survival for Long-Term Patients. San Francisco, Jossey-Bass Publishers, 1976

16. Lamb HR, Goertzel V: Discharged mental patients—Are they really in the community? Arch of Gen Psy 24:29–34, 1971

17. Lamb HR: What array of residential programs is required to meet the full range of special needs. In Community Living Arrangements for the Mentally Ill and Disabled: Issues and Options for Public Policy. Rockville Md., NIMH, 1976

18. Segal SP: Individual characteristics affecting the sheltered care needs of the mentally ill. Health Soc Work 4:41–58, 1979

19. Budson RD: Community residential care for the mentally ill in Massachusetts: Halfway houses and cooperative apartments. In Goldmeier J, Mannino FV, Shore MF (eds): New Directions in Mental Health Care: Cooperative Apartments. Adelphi, Md., Mental Health Study Center, Monograph, NIMH, DHEW Publication No. ADM 78–685, 1979

20. Rog DJ, Raush HL: The psychiatric halfway house: How is it measuring up? Comm Mental Health J 11:155–162, 1975

21. Mannino FV, Ott S, Shore MF: Community residential facilities for former mental patients: An annotated bibliography. Psychosoc Rehab J 1(2):1–43, 1977

22. Carpenter MD: Residential placement for the chronic psychiatric patient: A review and evaluation of the literature. Schiz Bul 4:384–398, 1978

23. Goldmeier J: Community residential facilities for former mental patients: A review. Psychosoc Rehab J 1(4):1–45, 1977

24. Test MA, Stein LI: Special living arrangements: A model for decision making. Hosp & Comm Psy 28:208–620, 1974

25. Budson RD, Jolley RE: A crucial factor in community program success: The extended psychosocial kinship system. Schiz Bul 4:609–621, 1978

26. Cannon MS: Halfway houses serving the mentally ill and alcoholics, United States, 1973. Mental Health Statistics, Ser. A, No. 16, Rockville, Md., NIMH, 1975

27. Cannon MD: Selected characteristics of residents in psychiatric halfway houses. HSMA, NIMH Statistical Note 93, Rockville, Md., NIMH, 1973

28. Beigel A, Hollenbach H, Gurgevich S, Scanlon J, Geffen J: Practical issues in developing and operating a halfway house program. Hosp & Comm Psy 28:601–607, 1977

29. Goldmeier J, Mannino FV, Shore MF (eds): New Directions in Mental Health Care: Cooperative Apartments. Adelphi, Md., Mental Health Study Center, Monograph, NIMH, DHEW Publication No. ADM 78–685, 1978

30. Sandall H, Hawley T, Gordon GL: The St. Louis community homes. Am J Psy 32:617–622, 1975

31. Chien C, Cole JO: Landlord supervised cooperative apartments: A new modality for community-based treatment. Am J Psy 130:156–159, 1973

32. Fairweather GW, Sanders, DH, Maynard H: Community Life for the Mentally Ill: An Alternative to Institutional Care. Chicago, Aldine, 1969

33. Anthony WA: Efficacy of psychiatric rehabilitation. Psychol Bul 78:447–456, 1972

34. McDonald L, Gregory GW: The Fort Logan Lodge: International Community

for Chronic Mental Patients. NIMH Final Report, Grant No. 1 R01 MH 15853-02, Rockville, Md., NIMH, 1971

35. Huessy HR: Spring Lake Ranch—The pioneer halfway house. In Huessy HR (ed): Mental Health With Limited Resources. New York, Grune & Stratton, 1966

36. Wechsler H: Transitional residences for former mental patients: A survey of halfway houses and rehabilitation facilities. Mental Hygiene 45:65–67, 1961

37. Murphy HBM, Engelsmann F, Tcheng-Laroche F: The influence of foster home care on psychiatric patients. Arch of Gen Psy 33:179–183, 1976.

38. Morrissey JR: The case for family care of the mentally ill. Comm Mental Health J, Monograph Series 2:1–64, 1967

39. Chouinard E: Family homes for adults. Soc and Rehab Record 2:10—15, 1975

40. Fields S: Asylum on the front porch: Foster communities for the mentally ill. Innovations 1:3–10, 1974

41. Dobson WR, Patterson TW: A behavioral evaluation of geriatric patients living in nursing homes as compared to a hospitalized group. Gerontologist 1:135–139, 1961

42. Epstein L, Simon A: Alternatives to state hospitalization for the geriatric mentally ill. Am J of Psy 124:955–961, 1968

43. Gaitz CM, Baer PE: Placement of elderly psychiatric patients. J of the Am Ger Soc 19:601–613, 1971

44. Goldstein SE, Rogers L: Community liaison with a mental hospital. J of the Am Ger Soc 21:538–545, 1973

45. Smith BJ: A hospital's support system for chronic patients living in the community. Hosp & Comm Psy 25:508–509, 1974

46. Tunakan B, Schaefer, I: The community boardinghouse as a transitional residence during aftercare. Cur Psy Ther 5:235–239, 1965

47. Fields S: Rethinking rehabilitation: 1. Breaking through the boarding homes blues; 2. A vocation in Vermont; 3. No bedlam in Bethlehem. Innovations 2:2–14, 1975

48. Murphy HBM, Pennee B, Luchins D: Foster homes: The new back wards? Canadian Mental Health, Supp. 71:1–17, 1972

49. Roberts PR: Human warehouses: A boarding home study. Am J of Pub Health 64:276–282, 1974

50. Budson RD: Legal dimensions of the psychiatric halfway house. Community Mental Health J 11:316–324, 1975

51. Gunderson J, Mosher L: The cost of schizophrenia. Am J of Psy 132:901–906, 1975

52. Murphy JG, Datel WE: A cost-benefit analysis of community versus institutional living. Hosp & Comm Psy 27:165–170, 1976

53. Sharfstein S, Nafziger JC: Community care: Costs and benefits for a chronic patient. Hosp & Comm Psy 27:170–173, 1976

54. Weisbrod BA, Test MA, Stein LI: An alternative to mental hospital treatment: III. Economic benefit-cost analysis. Arch of Gen Psy, in press

55. Beigel A: The politics of mental health funding: Two views, a look at the issues. Hosp & Comm Psy 28:194–195, 1977

Chapter 8

CASE MANAGEMENT
John P. Sullivan

Case management has been described by some as the process of linkings between a service system and the consumer *(1)*. Others describe it as a role that expedites the provision of services in such a manner that an overall good occurs *(2)*; while still other authors describe case management as the process of integrating discrete services for the purpose of achieving problem reduction *(3)*. Each view points out truths about case management, yet the variations among them leave doubt about its precise nature. This chapter will deal with these issues in a somewhat different manner. Each element of the process will be looked at in the hopes of gaining greater clarity, while pointing out the imprecise nature of this rather new service role.

To accomplish our task, we must begin by defining case management. One way to do this is to make a literal interpretation.

In the typical jargon of human service provision, individuals who have sought assistance have been traditionally referred to by such terms as patients, recipients, clients, or consumers. In each instance, however, once the individual is accepted for service, a record is kept of all the events that take place between the person and the provider. This record of events or transactions is commonly called a *case* and, as such, is unique. A case, then, represents the permanent record of events of a particular person (or a couple or family) and, therefore, is synonymous with the unique experiences of that person while obtaining help. Management is the process of planning, organizing, and controlling these unique experiences toward an effective outcome.

Case management then is the process of planning for individuals or families who require the organization of services to effect desired outcomes by assuring that all aspects of that outcome are controlled by reducing harmful effects. The process of case management is carried out by case managers, who in turn maintain a complete record of interactions by timely notations in the case record.

Our objective in this chapter is to review case management as it applies to the field of mental health, specifically with the population of severely disabled mentally ill. Since there are many terms which are used to describe this population, let it suffice to say that the severely disabled include both developmental as well as functional categories. Although to date case management has been generally associated with the latter group, this should not be viewed as a limitation of the role but more perhaps to do with the development of the role within both categories.

The severely disabled individual has been at times more commonly referred to as the "chronic mental patient" *(4)*. In the experience of the author the term *chronic* has had some limiting aspects which have led to attitudinal barriers regarding just how much can be done. By preference, then, the term *severely disabled* will be used to describe the same group. This should not be interpreted to mean that the degree of disability does not have a chronic element, it merely points out a problem in the misuse of the term. The population in question has the following characteristics:

1. Adult, aged 18 plus.
2. Primary disability is emotional rather than organic.
3. Twenty-four-hour nursing case is inappropriate.
4. Role functioning is severely impaired.
5. Psychiatric hospitalizations have been multiple and/or long term.
6. Psychosocial rehabilitation is generally long term.
7. Traditional approaches have generally failed.

With the above definitions and descriptions, it is hoped that the following will provide some small measure of understanding about the case management process and its emerging role as a significant factor in the mental health service delivery system.

As we look at the art of case management, it is important to recognize the limitations placed upon us both in terms of definition as well as by the paucity of acceptable research studies. Our intent is to add something to our knowledge about case management as a tool and, also, to encourage widespread interest in it as an exciting addition to the care and treatment of the severely disabled.

During the 1970s, the mental health field has been experiencing a number of agonizing throes. Each weakness of the system has been magnified to the point of questioning if there is any viability left. Civil rights issues have altered treatment for both consumers as well as providers. Criticisms about the lack of planning have raised significant questions about the ability of the mental health field to survive, and among the field's best efforts have been its worst accomplishments. The now famous General Accounting Office report pointed out the misuse and apparent lack of clear direction in the use of funds to serve the severely disabled (5). Likewise, the President's Commission on Mental Health reiterated that fact by pointing out our disregard for the "chronic mentally ill," and the lack of service to the urban poor and racial and ethnic minorities as well as to the migrant or seasonal worker.

Although there are problems, the mental health system, nevertheless, is a meaningful part of our care-giving structure and, as such, there is a need to look more closely at the elements of that structure which do not produce the expected results and make recommendations for corrective action. For the professional, the onslaughts are unnerving but must be dealt with. For the consumer, however, the confusion adds to the burdens they face as they attempt to seek resolution of problems. For instance, added to the criticisms of mental health service delivery are the variety of difficulties that have cropped up during the phenomenal growth period of the last two decades. Growth has meant a proliferation of specialists and a plethora of treatment modalities that provide a seemingly endless array of methods or answers which confuse even the most sophisticated. Among the general public, however, these conditions make it more difficult for the general public to feel confident about mental health services and their delivery. The problem becomes one of how to distinguish between the fruitful and the worthless, the competent and the incompetent, the reasons to accept and the facts of rejection.

One of the emerging responses has been the need for someone to clarify for the consumer the many choices; that someone is the case manager. The case manager can be called upon to assist and link the consumer with the various service providers and then to monitor those interactions during the period of care and treatment to see that they are all successfully completed. The case manager has the single point of accountability between the consumer, the provider, and successful resolution.

In the case of the severely disabled, there are many barriers as they attempt to resume normal lives following lengthy hospitalizations or extended periods of role dysfunction. Such factors as lack of social skills, lack of employment potential, damaged family relations, lack of any mutual support system, feelings of isolation, and, above all, rejection and ridicule by others add to the long list of things to overcome. In the face of these difficulties, a variety of existing as well as new services are needed. For instance, counseling, health care, housing, recreation, socialization, employment, and education or training already exist, while mutual support groups and host families need to be developed. Additionally, the individual has no membership—they are neither patients nor citizens with roots. As Bill Moyers pointed out, they are told, "Anywhere but here" (6) . All of this begins usually without the financial ability to obtain even the most essential of needs. The case manager can and has begun to help this group regain some of its dignity by increasing their capacity to overcome barriers while they search for a place to be.

Although the literature is not well developed in the area of case management and does not offer conclusive evidence for such functions as assessment, planning, linking monitoring, and advocacy, there are certain groups who are dealing with some of these aspects. Caragon (7) in Texas, Dorgan (8) in Illinois, and Berry (9) in Massachusetts are all working on the development of the literature bank and to date have begun to produce significant findings.

Authors have described the elements of the case manager role in various ways (2, 3, 10, 11). These roles or functions provide some insight into the essentials of case management as a process rather than as a distinctly different specialty. Some of the key functions which emerge are monitoring, linking, integrating, expediting, and managing. Each of the authors' views refer to a discrete function of a process which includes many of the above, but likewise leaves out others. Lawrence (3), for instance, feels that as specialization continues to grow and organizations require greater integration of effort there will be an increased need for individuals to carry out effective integration separate from the role of specialist. Hansell (2) agrees and believes that expediting a number of events and seeing that they happen in an overall good manner is an important role. Berry (9), on the other hand, points out that it is essential to monitor all aspects of the interchange which takes place between an individual seeking help and the helper. Each author points out an aspect of the case manager role which when taken in toto requires broader action than any one element alone. Dorgan *(8)* perhaps comes closest to describing a full range of functions by talking about the need to assess, plan, monitor, link, and advocate as basic functions of case management. It is becoming clearer that the role of case manager is emerging with multiple requirements which not only are administrative but, more importantly, include a variety of functions which will establish it as a service in and of itself.

More than five years ago, the Multi-Service Center (in Brockton, Massachusetts) developed a role called client monitor *(9, 12)*. The role became an integral part of a well–defined systems approach to service delivery. Client monitoring is the responsibility of one person who provides the interface between the system (all services delivered), the consumer (individual seeking assistance of the system), and the providers of service (agents of the system). The responsibility that must be carried out is similar to that described in our earlier definition of case management. That is, the client monitor has single-point accountability to see that each individual seeking assistance from the system is linked to all providers and is provided all services as defined by the individual's service plan. In addition, the client monitor must assure the manager of the total system (person responsible for managing all system resources) that the manager's system is responsive to the consumer and that the necessary resolutions are being achieved. This role is similar to what Hansell *(2)* calls the expediter. The functions carried out include planning, assessing, linking, monitoring, and advocacy, those cited by Dorgan *(8)*. An additional responsibility carried by the client monitor in the Brockton model, and not mentioned elsewhere, is that of contracting with each service provider on behalf of the consumer. Obviously, this role has considerable responsibility and power since the client monitor can also terminate a contractual agreement should the need arise. In all respects, the client monitor acts as the agent of the consumer whenever the consumer must seek the assistance of the system. This model has been in operation a little over three years and is still undergoing changes to refine its role for that particular system and model of design.

The design used to evaluate community mental health facilities and programs is largely based upon the concepts developed by Miles, Dorgan, and Gearhart *(13)*. They refer to their overall model as the Balanced Service System and to case management per se in describing the functions of planning, assessing, linking, monitoring, and advocacy. The consumer receives continuity of service through the case manager as each of these functions are carried out. The model describes three environments (protective, supportive, and natural) in which all services are carried out. As a model, the Balanced Service System is perhaps the most comprehensive in design as any reviewed by the author. Like the Brockton model, it requires the case manager to play a key role in managing the interplay between all providers, institutions, and the consumer in resolving the consumer's problems. It is recommended that for a more extensive review one should study this model.

Another model would have to be described more as a movement than any single design, and it produced a myriad of activities which began in the early 1970s and became known as the services integration effort. Although there are as many negatives as positives to be said about the movement, nevertheless, some tools emerged that were worthwhile. The movement flourished as a result of a concerted effort by the federal government to systematically reduce the rapid unplanned proliferation of human services in the 1960s. The effort was furthered by Elliot Richardson *(14)*, who personally believed in the need to integrate and coordinate the many human services. During the period this movement existed, the many suggestions that emerged called for such things as shared services, agency collaboration, single-point accountability, single or common intake, and reorganization of statewide public human services under a single umbrella. And yet, we saw the proposed Allied Services Act, which was to have provided the capacity to state human services secretariats to shift dollars from one category of service to another, defeated in Congress.

Although the services integration effort was never generally accepted, one commonly agreed upon view emerged, and that was the recognition of case management as a new role. Federal legislation required states to have case managers or at least the case management function in many of the federally funded social service programs. A companion piece to the need for case managers was a vigorous effort to train "generalists" rather than "specialists." The case manager was seen as the worker for the individual in need and, in this way, acted as the sole agent who had the "portfolio," so to speak, for the person. In this way a person "with skill and knowledge" would be able to overcome any barrier put in the way of seeking successful resolution of problems among the many categorical services.

In summary, the need to have a case manager as an integral role in the existing human services is well documented. The role emerges as an additional specialty, which provides a solution for the present problem of selecting appropriate services from among the variety of existing remedies.

As the field continues to utilize the services of the new role and as its functions become much clearer, there will be further documentation to substantiate the necessity of the role in the care and treatment of the mentally ill. Regardless of the progress, however, we are only beginning to understand the implications of case management for the severely disabled. For them, the problems are more complicated to contend with; they have been rejected by the field as too difficult to work with; they require greater energies and resources than society is willing to spend. Yet this group has hardly been worked with, let alone understood, by the very field making all the judgments.

By the 1970s, it was clear that a process called deinstitutionalization was failing. Many of the discharged expatients were ill-equipped to deal with the harsh realities of the rejecting community. The fearful community was not prepared to deal with their being released in its midst. The many needs of the severely disabled were overlooked or minimized at the time of discharge, and, therefore, no plan existed for them. The resultant human misery represented a massive failure at a time when mental health was struggling with its need to compete for shrinking resources.

The community mental health movement, although committed to the care and treatment of the mentally ill as a "bold new approach" (15) provided little, if any, service to the chronic mental patient (16). In fact, statistics reveal their needs have greatly exacerbated during this period (17). Although the needs among this group for housing, education, belonging, training, counseling, medical care, companionship, and other social services were greater than among other populations of the mentally ill, community mental health centers were ill-equipped to provide many of these, and, even today, they remain poorly motivated and unready to change traditional methods of care for the severely disabled.

The population of severely disabled has been so deemphasized by the mental health system that its needs have increased and the severity of the problems has worsened. Case mangement as a service cannot resolve these problems alone. However, it can begin to resolve the many questions of what needs are not being met, and how we can begin to build a reliable service system among the many service providers for this population of needy. Case managers will have to operate in a nontraditional manner, that is, looking at each client's specific circumstance in a more critical way. Thus, they will need to evaluate such basic needs as the ability to feed, clothe, survive, and perform daily tasks of living, as well as the more traditional mental health needs such as counseling, etc. Once assessments are made, there must be a linking of the individual to the unique service designed to care for individual needs. The variety of services will be somewhat different than traditionally provided in comprehensive community mental health centers and will include centers of daily living, mutual support groups, temporary employment, psychosocial rehabilitation centers as well as other programs not yet defined. A case manager must carefully orchestrate the link between the chronic patient and the community. The need is not for initial adjustment but lifelong membership. Transferring this responsibility will be a slow, carefully planned event, which must take into account the capacity of each individual to assimilate at his or her own pace. For many of the severely disabled, it has been a long time since they had expectations of independent functioning, and for some, it will be a wholly new experience. To overcome the causes of the dysfunctional state and the negative results of institutionalization will require careful planning, linking, monitoring, advocacy, and, above all, appropriate assessment.

Among the many tasks required of case managers will be to select on the basis of judgment appropriate solutions to the problems of the severely disabled. In order to do this, the case manager must be aware of the myriad of available services as well as each service's capacity to provide the necessary solutions to the patient's problems. In today's society, this is not easily done. The increase in human service providers has been unplanned and tremendous, with the unfortunate result of having as many poor providers as good providers. In the area of counseling or the verbal therapies, for instance, there are more disciplines that refer to their ability to provide a wider range of modalities than ever before. Selecting the right modality is part of the problem. There are a greater number of disciplines now involved in the area of counseling or the verbal therapies, reflecting the availability of a wider range of modalities. A case manager must possess the finely tuned skill to recognize the differences between potential success and failure. The implication here is that training of case managers cannot take place primarily in centers of higher learning, and, therefore, we must be willing to develop more experiential training sites and programs. The key to success appears to lie somewhere between the untried and the nontraditional approaches.

Effective case management will provide the much needed direction in determining which services need to be developed as well as which need to be altered or phased out regarding the severely disabled. The very functions performed will provide a basis of research to determine just what elements prove worthwhile and those that wane in the face of experience. Our interest must at least take us into exploring the five essentials, and as our knowledge increases, perhaps there will emerge clearer choices from among a wider variety of role functions.

At the very least, if it is to succeed in its intended mission, case management must embrace the following functions: assessment, planning, linking, monitoring, and advocacy.

ASSESSMENT

Determining the dysfunctional state of an individual requires more than knowing the individual's capacity to comprehend or perform certain roles in society. For the severely disabled, it includes much more. Replacing an individual's folk support system, or assuring the individual that trusting a distrustful world is better than remaining an isolate, is an extremely difficult and often misunderstood process. Often missed by well-intentioned workers is the need for constant reassurance regarding daily adjustment in a community that does not understand or, for that matter, does not want to understand. We must remember that rehospitalization often occurs because the assessment lacked the necessary care and detail required to succeed at establishing roots. For instance, once in the community severely disabled individuals require more than medication to stabilize their existence. More often than not, a mental health worker tends to think only about the psychological adjustment and either obscures or leaves out the personal, interpersonal, and environmental elements which have proven to be the most critical factors in securing the solid foundation necessary for the future of the severely disabled individual.

PLANNING

Once an accurate, detailed assessment is made, goals and the means of successfully achieving them must be well thought out.

While the goals and objectives must be measurable, that is, based on clearly delineated milestones, they must be flexible and, above all, realistic. To secure a placement in an acceptable residence is a genuine hope for each person, but for the severely disabled, it must be more than that—it must assure understanding, security, and acceptance of failure. Unless these objectives are planned for, these residences will not exist for the severely disabled.

LINKING

The severely disabled individual lacks the capacity to orchestrate complex combinations of services. The more services individuals are required to obtain to relieve their dysfunctional state, the greater the chance of failure. Secondly, linking provider and severely disabled is not accomplished by agreement but by repeated success and failure of establishing a meaningful relationship. Overcoming the sense of impending rejection is eased only slightly with massive doses of caring. Seldom in this age of specialization and duplication is the chance of success for many severely disabled accomplished without constant reassurance that the link is solidly supportive and interested in seeing the goal achieved.

Because resolution of problems or even maintenance of progress requires constant vigilance on the part of service providers, there is definitely a need to keep track of significant milestones of progress. One way of achieving this is through regular linking sessions between the various helpers, so that significant progress can be noted and charted. The significant points at which a linking between the many actors must take place are from outreach to intake; from intake to services provision; from provider to provider; from agency to agency; and in addition a timely check every 30 days.

MONITORING

Modern technology has increased our terminology significantly. Among the many new terms in the mental health field today that we hear more and more about is the need to *monitor* our performance. Larry Weed *(18)* of the University of Vermont, in presenting the justification for his problem-oriented record system, states that increased knowledge has produced increased information which makes it impossible for the human mind to maintain an updated, accurate information bank. Therefore, we must rely upon current technological tools such as computers to assist us. As such the case manager must rely more and more upon mechanisms such as computers for monitoring the many interactions that take place between the severely disabled and the service providers. The value of such monitoring lies in the fact that individuals do not get lost or "fall through the cracks" of the human service system. This is of particular significance for the severely disabled, who experience a high initial dropout rate in most endeavors. The objective of monitoring is to make it possible to take corrective action early enough that any necessary change is both effective and cost efficient.

ADVOCACY

Webster distinguishes two meanings of *advocacy:* (1) to plead the cause of another; and (2) to defend or espouse a cause by argument *(19)*. For the severely disabled, advocacy in both senses of the word is required. In case management, it is perhaps the first meaning that is more associated with the services, while the second applies to collective action on behalf of these individuals. Individuals who appear different or act different in our society are suspect, isolated, rejected, and, above all, misunderstood. The severely disabled is just such a group. Due to the chronicity of the dysfunctioning, certain manifestations become the basis of unacceptable performance by society. Therefore, the case manager has a constant role to plead for justice on behalf of these individuals before the courts and welfare, health, social, and other "helping" agencies. It is not easy to present their case when the tide of sentiment is to reject these "misfits" of society, but the case manager must persist. As time passes and case management becomes more accepted as a real service, it must take on a much larger role of advocacy and "defend or espouse" the cause of the severely disabled as a civil right much the same way that Martin Luther King advocated for the blacks a decade ago.

Case management is an old process that dates back to the actions of Dorothea Dix and others, yet it has become a renewed hope in the delivery of psychiatric care for the severely disabled. Although few would argue against the merits of case management, mental health programs do not generally provide assessment, planning, linking, monitoring, and advocacy in a systematic way. As such, fragmented functions are provided on a haphazard basis, which becomes as much a problem to the severely disabled as do other barriers to systematic care.

The future looks bright for case management and the road somewhat clearer; however, there remains much to be done in understanding how to develop a body of knowledge that will capture the service in theory and practice. There must also be vigorous efforts to develop educational programs that will provide a sound training ground in which to develop future case managers, whose role it will be to add to the growing knowledge base of how we can be more responsive to the severely disabled mentally ill *(20)*.

NOTES

1. Felton G, Wallach H, Gallo C: New roles for new professional mental health workers: Training the patient advocate, the integrator, and the therapist. Community Ment Health J 10:52–65, 1974

2. Hansell N, Wodarczyk M, Visotsky HM: The mental health expediter. Arch Gen Psychiat 18:392–399, 1968

3. Lawrence PR, Lorsch JW: New management job: The integrator. Harvard Business Review November–December:142–151, 1967

4. Colton SI: Integrative mental health programming. Psychosocial Rehab J 1:19–31, 1976

5. Returning the Mentally Disabled to the Community: Government Needs to do More. Comptroller General, Report to the Congress, January 1977

6. Moyers W: Anywhere but Here, CBS, November 1978 (film)

7. Caragon P: Bibliography on Service Integration Literature. Center for Social Work Research, University of Texas, Austin, 1977 (unpublished)

8. Dorgan R, Gerhard R. The Balanced Service System. Draft manuscript used in surveyor training by JCAH, New York, June 1977

9. Berry J: Client Monitor Manual. Brockton, Mass., BAHRG Publications, 1977

10. Organ DW: Linking pins between organizations and environment. Business Horizons, 13(4):73–80, December 1971

11. Washington RO: ECCHSC as a case management service delivery system. Second year evaluation report of the East Cleveland Comprehensive Human Services Center. Case Western Reserve University, 1974

12. Sullivan J: The Technology Report. Brockton, Mass., BAHRG Publications, 1977

13. Principles for Accreditation of Community Mental Health Service Systems. Chicago, Ill., Joint Commission on Accreditation of Hospitals, 1977

14. Richardson E: Changing Human Services. Speech given at ground breaking ceremony, Brockton Multi-Service Center, Brockton, Mass., 5 July 1963

15. Congressional Report (94–63), President's Commission on Mental Health, 1963

16. Report to the President. President's Commission on Mental Health, Vol. 1, Washington, D.C., Superintendent of Documents, 1978

17. Sullivan JP: Brockton Multi-Service Center, Statistical Report, Brockton, Mass., 1979 (unpublished)

18. Weed L: Problem Oriented Record System, Burlington, University of Vermont, 1973 (film)

19. Webster's New Collegiate Dictionary (ed 2). Springfield, Mass., Merriam Co. Pub., 1959

20. Granet RB, Talbott JA: The continuity agent: Creating a new role to bridge the gaps in the mental health system. Hosp Community Psychiatry 29:132–133, 2 February 1978

Chapter 9

DISCUSSION
Treatment of the Chronic Mental Patient
Arthur L. Arnold

The elements of successful treatment of chronic mental patients include the use and monitoring of psychotropic medications, psychotherapy, socialization, vocational rehabilitation, housing, and case management. The chapters in Part I provide valuable guidance for individual psychiatrists, psychologists, social workers, nurses, rehabilitation specialists, case managers, and others responsible for critical elements in individual treatment plans of chronic mental patients.

Dr. Hansell characterizes the use of psychopharmacological agents in the treatment of chronic mental patients as a "high gain, high risk" task which requires sophisticated, careful practice of medicine no less than does, for instance, the treatment of acute psychoses in a general hospital setting. This is borne out in his admonition to physicians that they assure careful medical monitoring of dyskinesias, dysphorias, and renal damage and have available the resources of laboratories, emergency rooms, and hospitals. It is worth emphasizing a point he makes almost in passing: the psychopharmacological specificity of today provides both reason and necessity for diagnostic precision. Because this is both a high gain and a high risk era because of the use of psychotropic medications, the psychiatrist can no longer act on the basis of diagnostic impressions without a differential diagnosis which gives special attention to patients with affective disorders who also manifest delusions or hallucinations and to patients with most of the essential symptoms of schizophrenia but also significant mood disturbances, as well as to patients with dementias which may be reversible or a misleading consequence of underlying depression or chronic schizophrenia. The consequences of missed therapeutic opportunities or chronically disabling drug effects make treatment of chronic mental patients a high-expectancy matter for physicians as well as for the patients themselves. It is also a time of greater scientific excitement, with more practical reasons to be aware of almost daily developments of neurophysiological research in mental illness stimulated by the specificity of psychopharmacological agents.

Dr. Hansell makes a major point of the patient as a partner with the physician in the use of psychopharmacological agents, stressing the problems of noncompliance and the opportunities for self-titration. He wisely urges the education of patients (using the apt analogy of diabetes, with which chronic mental illness has much in common in principles of management) in medication actions, side effects, indications for increase or decrease of dosage, incompatabilities with over-the-counter preparations, and effects of street drugs, alcohol, and xanthine-containing beverages. This approach is much to be preferred over the unilateral manipulation of medications to assure constant absorption, such as by substituting injections of long-acting drugs. This is far different from a "do as you are told—doctor knows best" attitude toward medication. Dr. Hansell describes the participation of the patient (and often of the family) in consenting to long-term medication as making a "life choice," as well as a matter of concern to the public at large.

In light of the high gain, high risk situation presented by psychopharmacological agents, the vagaries of their use reviewed by Ms. Johansen well support the exercise of stringent controls. Vigilance is required to identify patterns of polypharmacy prescribing, inconsistent medication data on medical records, and noncompliance in self-medication. This is made much more difficult when multiplicity of health practitioners are involved in a patient's treatment, which is the usual situation for chronic mental patients.

Ms. Johansen proposes that a combination of facility-wide drug utilization review and individual patient drug use profiling be the role of a new member of the mental health team—the psychiatric clinical pharmacist. Every effort should be made to assure acceptance and funding of this resource, which is especially feasible where a service system designates a single lead agency to take responsibility for all medications for chronic mental patients.

As Dr. Hansell does for psychopharmacological agents, Dr. Lamb does for psychotherapy, in setting forth applications of a nearly universally employed modality which are specific to chronic mental patients. Due at least in part to the limitations in transfer of learning, it is essential that psychotherapy be employed after patients are discharged from the hospital to the community if it is to be of practical benefit.

It is impossible to overemphasize the first principle: that the goal of psychotherapy for the chronic mental patient is to facilitate the development of a sense of mastery. Dr. Lamb describes a practical approach with a focus upon present reality which is successfully used by therapists who are unprovoked by hostility or seductiveness but are not passive and permissive. He stresses that for the chronic mental patient the development of insight is a means, not an end, and that symptoms may be understood as signals (as a urine test or symptoms of insulin reaction are to a diabetic) so that timely actions may be taken to master a stress situation.

The other important principles of psychotherapy for the chronic mental patient follow logically and include the appropriateness of environmental intervention and manipulation by the therapist with the understanding of the patient, careful limitation of the intensity and frequency of sessions but allowing for "no real ending," avoidance of catharsis and primary process thinking, and even the giving of direct practical advice when needed. In recognition of the common human dimension and the ways in which chronic mental patients are like all of us, Dr. Lamb notes that some rationalizations should be supported because we all need them at times and that life cycle stresses, which are part of the universal human experience, should be accommodated. In the same vein, he describes the reasonableness of accepting the validity of stress experiences of the chronic mental patient's family, not only of guilt and embarrassment but also of the cost and even danger, and of not accepting the validity of accusations by the superego (and, one assumes, by the family if applicable), to reduce the chronic mental patient's guilt, which can be disabling.

In his chapter on socialization, Dr. Grob provides a clear perspective on the disability of the chronic mental patient. It is social, and "social recovery is real recovery." He outlines the vicissitudes of professional, scientific respectability of socialization therapy since the Middle Ages, with special emphasis on the influence since the

1930s of Sullivan and Adler, up to the introduction in the late 1970s of the community support program by the National Institute of Mental Health *(1)* and the social support services for chronic mental patients recommended by the President's Commission on Mental Health.

It is noteworthy that the most successful of the psychosocial rehabilitation centers in the United States which are cited by Dr. Grob (including Fountain House, Horizon House, Thresholds, and The Center Club) were established through the initiative of expatients of mental hospitals with the assistance of private philanthropic organizations. They are not part of the mental health treatment establishment but operate in cooperation with treatment centers through, for example, the payment of membership fees. By implication, this is related to the most essential characteristic of such centers. They are freeing, natural, rehabilitating, group based, focused upon competency in the here-and-now, and self-governing, and emphasize particularly social activities and work placement for their members (not clients or patients). It appears certain that the most necessary experience for chronic mental patients is that of community, which is perhaps also the experience most difficult to obtain, considering the problems such individuals frequently face due to inexperience with unstructured social situations and hesitancy born of low self-esteem.

There may be no more potent enhancer of self-esteem than work, which provides an identity acquired in structured social situations within the context of the community. Dr. Brooks, also through a historical perspective, describes the role of work in the life of the chronic mental patient. It is well we are reminded that patient labor was necessary for the operation of public mental hospitals until the late 1960s, when federal law prohibited such unpaid labor. Only recently have mental health service systems begun to move from their earlier institutional exploitation of the chronic mental patient's basic work skills to a facilitation of their community roles through occupational roles. The paucity even now of rehabilitation for chronic mental patients demonstrates how far we have yet to go.

In his statement that "through the world of work, these people (are) also able to gain readmission to the many other satisfactions of everyday living, including a place to stay, people to be with, and a social life to enjoy," Dr. Brooks points out another area shared by the chronic mental patient with all people everywhere. Furthermore, he makes the point that structured rehabilitation programs are restrictive and that it is part of the natural round of life to find work both a social restraint and a means of acquiring life's satisfactions. Chronic mental patients have proportionately less access to vocational rehabilitation than people with physical disabilities, and since many of the same programs could be utilized, one must assume this is related to the relative powerlessness of chronic mental patients in the open community.

In fact, access to any generic service or resource in society is difficult for the chronic mental patient. Largely to address this problem, case management is now considered one of the essential staff roles in mental health services for chronic mental patients. Mr. Sullivan has drawn from his own experience in developing the new service role of case manager, which he refers to as an "art form." The usual terms applied to the tasks case managers perform are assessment, planning, linking, monitoring, and advocacy. Mr. Sullivan has made these managers the "single point of accountability between the consumer, the provider, and successful resolution," as they work at the interface between counseling, health care, housing, recreation, socialization, with the powerful role of contractor for such generic services.

As with any new service role, there are many issues yet to be resolved, especially such practical matters as overlap with existing mental health professions and the necessity for professional education. One fact with which no one takes issue is the need for case managers, especially by expatients of large public institutions which suppress individual initiative. To be allowed to remain physically idle and mentally in fantasy, or to be immobilized by medication or shepherded about in a monotonous routine, provides no opportunity for developing the ability to manage one's life.

The New York State program to fund local community support systems refers to case managers as "a new aftercare assurance mechanism" with this charge:

> A case manager cares that his clients make it. He knows whether they are up and dressed and ready to start the day's activities and how well they do. He knows whether they take needed medication. He knows whether they get to their jobs, whether in sheltered work or competitive employment. He helps them celebrate their accomplishments and responds when they are in trouble. Nevertheless, he is not a friend but a dedicated professional disciplined against taking advantage of his clients and applying his knowledge of life to supporting and enriching that of his clients. He assumes total responsibility to help them attain all of the services and satisfactions of their needs from the providers and resources according to an individual plan. He is an advocate and arranger, providing assistance in life management. *(2)*

This is a tall order that is being proven feasible. Next to a satisfying place to live, case management is probably the most critical need of the chronic mental patient.

Dr. Budson makes the point that the satisfying place to live for the chronic mental patient must be part of an "extended psychosocial kinship system," with rehabilitative capacity to be other than simply custodial, which fosters regression. While halfway houses with trained rehabilitation staff most nearly meet the need, he notes that most of them serve verbal, distressed people, rather than those with the disturbed behavior characteristic of the chronic mental patient. These patients are more often to be found in nursing homes (many inappropriately), board and care facilities, foster homes, and inexpensive residential hotels. The model followed by leading psychosocial rehabilitation centers is a short-term transitional halfway house for 15–20 residents and a number of subsidized shared apartments nearby. This allows progression in life-management skills without a fixed timetable, which may be long.

Two variations described by Dr. Budson—the commune-like "lodge" and the summer camplike farm—may work best for particular types of chronic mental patients or in particular situations. They deserve more widespread development and study of their self-contained mutual support systems.

The sequence of practical steps sponsors should take to establish community residences are outlined by Dr. Budson. They range from setting up an operating organization and deciding on kinds of clients and staff, to budgeting and funding. The barriers against residences which are neither family nor commercial are formidable and have stopped or long delayed many community residence projects. Building codes and zoning ordinances deny recognition of community residence groups, which are family in the sense of sharing common purposes and needs and commercial in the sense of having a distinct group of owners and staff. While local governments and neighborhoods may erect barriers through a lack of sympathy and knowledge, one must assume that there are other reasons for mental health service systems erecting barriers (which are often more frustrating) in the form of inappropriate licensure standards and inadequate funding. At least in the area of fire safety codes, Dr. Budson provides a working model for overcoming one of the most common obstacles.

The ideal program plan of a community residence outlined by Dr. Budson includes life skills improvement, vocational and educational planning, social and avocational programs, milieu planning, family relations improvement, and medical and psychiatric care. In range, this is similar to the community support program developed by New York State, which also, however, includes crisis intervention, home visits, transportation, and case management. The latter two have been found to be the most commonly inadequate components necessary for community support of chronic mental patients in urban, suburban, and rural areas alike. Transportation, whether by private car or public transit, is often effectively inaccessible to chronic mental patients because of expense or complexity. While money and training needed by chronic mental patients to use transportation are not usually considered elements of their treatment, like case management, they are clearly necessary or treatment may not be utilized at all.

The essential elements in the successful treatment of chronic mental patients includes special applications of the traditional clinical modalities of psychopharmacological agents and psychotherapy. Since the ultimate goal is the development of social competence, socialization and vocational rehabilitation programs should constitute most of the daily round of life for the chronic mental patient. Living arrangements which provide for social rehabilitation and serve as the focus for the entire program of each individual are needed by most chronic mental patients, especially during the transition to community living, but are still available to few. And finally, to assure actual use of these treatment elements and all the other benefits of citizenship chronic mental patients cannot obtain for themselves, case management is a necessary element. Recent improvements in federal and state funding for planning and implementing community support programs for chronic mental patients raise the possibility that for the first time it may be possible to organize these essential elements into comprehensive (3), financially viable systems which include but extend beyond clinical treatment, which is necessary but not sufficient to facilitate the social competence of chronic mental patients.

NOTES

1. Turner JC, TenHoor WJ: The NIMH Community Support Program: Pilot approach to a needed social reform. Schiz Bull 4:319–348, 1978

2. New York State Department of Mental Hygiene: Appropriate Community Placement and Support. Albany, N.Y., January 1978

3. Turner JC, Shifren I: Community support system: How comprehensive? In Stein LI (ed): Community Support Systems for the Long-Term Patient. New Directions for Mental Health Services, No. 2, 1979

Part II

SUCCESSFUL PROGRAMS FOR THE CHRONIC MENTAL PATIENT

Chapter 10

A NURSING HOME MODEL

R. T. Kraus

Since the passage of the California Community Mental Health Services Act in 1969, the state hospital population has declined from 30,000 mentally disordered persons to approximately 5,000 in 1979. Thousands of patients were relocated to so-called community facilities, leaving the illusion that some formal, planned network of appropriate programs existed. In reality, as we have come to learn, most of these people were "dumped" into whatever living arrangements were available—cheap hotels, board and care homes, nursing homes —and the cost savings to the California state government was pocketed back into the general fund.

Today, over a decade after initial efforts toward implementation of the community care philosophy, the California state government and the 58 county mental health programs are still trying to sort out the ensuing chaos known as the California Mental Health System. The scope of the problem can best be illustrated by the fact that no one really knows where all of the mentally disordered are, what they need, or what treatment they currently are receiving. Repeated legislative and executive branch studies have documented this sad state of affairs, but budgetary considerations have repeatedly thwarted any real attempt at resolution.

At the nursing home, or skilled nursing facility level of care, it is currently estimated that some 7,000 mentally disordered persons are being housed. Only 1,500 of these persons reside in facilities with a distinct designation of "skilled nursing facility—mentally disordered" and receive $5.68 per day of special psychiatric programming above the basic nursing home services. The remaining 5,500 persons reside in regular skilled nursing facilities and receive no mental health services.

In Sacramento County, James Barter, then director of the Department of Mental Health, foresaw the strain to local programs that this dramatic reduction of state hospital, beds would create. In early 1973, sensing the need for a local alternative to the state hospital, Dr. Barter approached the management of Crestwood Manor, a 130-bed locked nursing home, and suggested the creation of a program to provide enriched psychiatric rehabilitation services within that facility.

The concept that Dr. Barter proposed involved adding a "patch" funding mechanism to an existing nursing home. In doing so, he recognized that the basic Medi-Cal (Medicaid) reimbursement rate for nursing homes (then $15.52 per patient day) was woefully inadequate to allow the facilities to provide more than custodial care to a docile, well-institutionalized population of long-term patients. The shorter-term patients, that is, chronic schizophrenics who when in remission could function in less structured settings (boarding homes), desperately needed a facility at which they could receive intensive rehabilitative services during exacerbations of their illnesses. Such a facility would ideally provide an extension or an alternative to costly acute psychiatric hospitalization ($100 per patient day) and would also replace in large measure, Sacramento County's traditional dependence upon the state hospital system (approximately $65 per patient day).

Crestwood Manor was a logical choice for such a program, for several reasons. It had been constructed in 1971 as an "L" Facility, the designation then given to those California nursing homes which had locked-door security and cared for a population of behaviorally disordered geriatric patients whose bizarre behaviors prohibited their placement in regular, unlocked nursing homes. However, due to the timing of its opening concurrently with the massive depopulation of the state hospital system, Crestwood Manor's management found that the facility increasingly was being called upon to admit a younger, more volatile psychiatric population. Between 1971 and 1973, attempts at meeting this community need had yielded disastrous results. Their traditional nursing home staff, oriented to medical-model care and a custodial role, could not cope with the acting-out demands of this younger, more acute patient. Moreover, the Medi-Cal reimbursement rate paid to the facility was based upon the theoretical needs of a typical physically ill nursing home patient and therefore did not provide adequate funding for a psychiatric rehabilitation component.

Faced with these institutional limitations, the management of Crestwood Manor had decided that it could not admit the younger, more acute population. Simultaneously, the Sacramento County Department of Mental Health was feeling more economic and program pressures to minimize their state hospital population. The California Community Mental Health Services Act of 1969 emphasized community autonomy in the management of mental health programs, and the State Department of Mental Hygiene instituted a disincentive program to financially penalize those counties which "overutilized" state hospitals. As a result of these factors, it was clearly in the best interest of both Crestwood Manor and Sacramento County to create a treatment program at Crestwood Manor to meet this need.

The California Community Mental Health Services Act created a funding mechanism to finance local mental health programs. The Short–Doyle Program, as it is known, provides 90 cents of matching state funds for each 10 cents of county funds, and the intent of the act was to encourage counties to contract for services with local providers. Utilizing this mandate, Sacramento County and Crestwood Manor entered into a contract in May 1973, under which Crestwood Manor would provide a psychiatric rehabilitation program in addition to its basic nursing home service. The initial annual contract targeted $95,000 for the treatment of 40 patients, or $6.50 per patient, per day. By June 1973, the program was in full operation, with the following supplemental staff:

Day Shift
1   occupational therapist
1   occupational therapist assistant
5   licensed psychiatric technicians
1   recreation therapist
Evening Shift
2   licensed psychiatric technicians

POPULATION TREATED

In terms of the sources of referral for the treatment population, the majority of patients (60–65%) are admitted from acute psychiatric facilities, with the remaining 35–40% coming from board and care homes, private residences, nursing homes, state hospitals, and penal institutions. These statistics reveal several phenomena which characterize both the strengths and weaknesses of the total community mental health system and reflect the very chronic nature of the treatment group.

    a)   It appears that the "system,"[1] because of a lack of a patient tracking capability, virtually forces the mentally disordered person to reach a well-decompensated state before treatment is received. Thus, too often the entry or reentry point to the system becomes the costly acute psychiatric ward (studies have revealed that the most frequent cause for such exacerbations and rehospitalizations is the patients' failure to follow prescribed medication regimens). Despite this system failure, the other 40–45% of the Crestwood admissions represent an *avoidance* of costly acute hospital treatment. Moreover, the existence of the Crestwood program also allows a more economical and therapeutic *extension* of care for those mentally disordered persons who do not respond adequately to the average 10–14 days of acute psychiatric care received in one of the community's three acute psychiatric wards.

    b)   Studies for the six years of the program's existence revealed a 29.2% recidivism rate. Although this figure represents the patients' contacts with Crestwood Manor only, and not with other providers, it does manifest the "revolving door" syndrome characteristic of this very chronic population.

In essence, Crestwood Manor can be seen to be one part of the community continuum of psychiatric care that has developed in Sacramento. Visually depicted, that continuum is:

Acute psychiatric care wards

Crestwood Manor—state hospitals[2]

Residental care homes with a treatment program

[1]Ancillary mental health agencies within the community.

[2]State hospitals are equated with Crestwood Manor, since most of the state hospital beds are also licensed in the same "skilled nursing facility" category. However, a vast disparity in reimbursement rates ($40 per diem at Crestwood, approximately $100 per diem for the state hospital) creates obvious differences in treatment resources and capabilities.

Residental care homes
Independent living

However, the progression of the patient is not always sequential, nor do all persons achieve the most independent level of that continuum. At each level there is a certain "settling" process which occurs; that is, patients have optimized their functioning and can progress no further. At Crestwood Manor, that population, generally geriatric and organic in character, is transferred to a separate "maintenance" ward within the facility when it becomes apparent that they are not responsive to the more intensive treatment program. This policy insures that the very limited Short–Doyle funds provided are utilized on that target group with the best potential for rehabilitation and discharge to a less expensive and less structured setting. Moreover, it insures that the 57-bed Short–Doyle founded unit does not experience a "bottleneck" effect and can continue to meet the ongoing community demands for its services.

Thus, it can be seen that although Crestwood Manor occupies only one notch in the community mental health treatment continuum, it actually serves a multiple treatment role. Specifically, patients can be transferred to Crestwood under any of the following circumstances:

1. From acute psychiatric wards, for extended care.
2. From the state hospitals, for alternative, community-based treatment.
3. From independent living settings, for treatment of acute or subacute exacerbations; such care is in lieu of acute or state hospitalization.

In any of the three situations, Crestwood Manor is supplanting traditional state or acute care facilities at significant cost savings to the taxpayer. In 1977-78 those cost savings were $60 per diem as compared to the state hospital and from $80 to $200 per diem when compared to local acute facilities (Mental Health Plan, Sacramento County, 1979-80).

The following demographic statistics are from "Crestwood Manor Quarterly Progress Report to the Mental Health Director." These statistics compare the nature of the treatment population for the quarter ending 31 March 1974 and the quarter ending 31 December 1978.

	January– March 1974	October– December 1978
Average age:	46.6	42.2
Average number of psychothera- peutic needs per patient	2.25	1.3
Volunteer activity in facility (hours per week)	70	159
Number of discharges to the lower levels of care	6	17
Number of psychiatric crises re- quiring outside intervention	7	7
Average length of stay for dis- charged patients (months)	6	2.93

From 1 July 1978 through 31 December 1978, the treatment population was characterized by the following primary discharge diagnoses:

FINAL PRIMARY DIAGNOSIS

DSM*–II reporting diagnostic codes		Number	Percent
291	OBS**—alcoholic psychosis	1	1.49
309	OBS—nonpsychotic	3	4.48
295	Schizophrenia	26	38.81
296	Major affective disorders	15	22.38
297	Paranoid states	15	22.38
298–299	Other psychosis	2	2.99
301	Personality disorders	3	4.48
303	Alcoholism	2	2.99
Total		67	100.00

*DSM–Diagnostic and Statistical Manual II.
**OBS–Organic Brain Syndrome.
Final Primary Diagnosis is from the "California Department of Mental Health Statewide Evaluation Report."

A typical inhouse sampling of the behavioral deficits which characterize the treatment population reveals the following patient profiles (at admission):

Physical aggression	18.7%
Verbal aggression	20.6%
Suicidal behavior	3.7%
Bizarre, inappropriate behavior	17.8%
Hallucinations	7.5%
Delusions	14.0%
Depression, withdrawn behavior	17.7%

California law requires that any mentally disoriented person who is incapable of giving informed consent must first be adjudicated incompetent before being placed in a locked-door facility, such as Crestwood Manor. Thus, most of the treatment population (85%) is admitted to Crestwood Manor in an involuntary status.

Patient progress is measured by the application of the Spitzer Global Assessment Scale at admission and discharge. For the period 1 July 1978 through 31 December 1978, 75% of the discharged patients indicated decreased impairment as demonstrated by that change matrix.

Treatment Philosophy and Modalities

During its first year of operations, the enrichment program (Short–Doyle funded psychiatric care program) suffered the usual growing pains and identity crises characteristic of such fledgling efforts. These difficulties stemmed largely from two serious misjudgments by management in staffing and implementing the programs. The decision was made to hire only "experienced" personnel to staff the program and to pay them at rates in excess of those then being earned by the facility's existing nursing staff.

In reality, "experienced" proved to mean former state hospital employees. With these personnel came the same attitudes that had been characteristic of the state hospitals. Moreover, this staff's relatively high salaries quickly earned them the resentment of the traditional nursing staff, thus insuring a lack of integration and cooperation between nursing and enrichment programs.

Finally, the program lacked a philosophical patron, since no psychologist or psychiatrist was employed to design a specific format for the staff to implement. After seeking the services of several psychologists in an attempt to define an effective program format, it finally became apparent that our efforts had been misdirected. At this point, the bulk of "experienced" staff were terminated and a new consultant, Terry Sandbeck, was employed on a half-time basis to design an entirely new program.

Mr. Sandbeck, a Ph.D. candidate in psychology at the Fuller Graduate School of Psychology (Pasadena, CA), quickly saw that the chronic nature of the patient population and the limited program budget (about $110,000 annually) dictated that any program designed be characterized by pragmatic methods and goals. Previous efforts had centered on traditional psychotherapy modalities, with large doses of group and individual counseling sessions. These efforts were far too esoteric to affect the deeply embedded asocial behaviors exhibited by the majority of the chronic psychotic patients in the program. As a result, staff generally found most of their efforts being directed toward intervening in psychiatric crisis situations, with little time or resources left for constructive therapies. In short, Crestwood Manor's initial "program" differed little from the maintenance-oriented state hospital wards that it was ostensibly replacing.

Mr. Sandbeck researched psychiatric literature to discover what modalities had proved most successful with similar, chronic, institutionalized patients. In so doing, he synthesized a behavior modification program which dealt with psychotic behaviors in a most pragmatic way. Rather than attempt to intellectualize the illness, this treatment program identified those asocial behaviors which caused the patient to fail in less structured settings and then devised an individualized behavior modification program to bring those behaviors within socially accepted limits.

Documentation plays a very important role in the day-to-day functioning of a nursing home, and an effective means of communicating the treatment program methodologies was considered fundamental to the success of the new program. Thus, the problem-oriented medical record (POMR), then becoming popular in medical recordkeeping, was seen as a logical and compatible vehicle for implementing the new program. In essence, the program functioned in the following manner:

> *Problems* were identified specific to each individual patient. These problems were defined on a multidisciplinary basis, utilizing various sources of information derived from families, social workers, treating psychiatrists, and others who have close contact with the patient, but most of all from observing behaviors exhibited in the facility. All such prob-

lems identified had to be specific, observable, time limited, and quantifiable. Traditional types of statements, such as "the patient was very hostile today," were replaced by more descriptive and tangible phrases, such as "the patient struck out at other patients four times this week."

Objectives for each patient were then determined with the obvious goal of eliminating the listed problems or reducing them to acceptable levels at which the patient might return to a less structured, more normal living setting. As with the problems, the objectives must be stated in specific, observable, time-limited, and quantifiable terms. As an example, the previously listed problem might have as an objective: "reduce the incidence of striking out at others to one time per month."

Methods provide the specific tools required to achieve the objectives. In the institutional setting, the most effective behavior modification rewards appear to be coffee, cigarettes, money, and special privileges. Utilizing these reinforcers, the patients' positive behaviors are rewarded. Likewise, the negative behaviors are extinguished through the withholding of such reinforcers. However, it is the policy of the program that positive reinforcers will always be emphasized in modifying behavior.

This method of stating individualized treatment programs insures that (1) the patient and staff know specifically what is required of the patient to achieve discharge from the facility; and (2) negative, disruptive behavior is decreased rapidly, allowing the staff more time to concentrate on crisis prevention rather than on crisis intervention.

Having designed this effective program format, it was then necessary to recruit a new staff which could successfully implement its tenets. In considering the previous experiences, management decided that the new staff should be selected on the basis of their adaptability to the new program philosophy and their lack of ties to the state hospital treatment model. Moreover, the pay scales offered would be on a parity with those of the existing nursing staff. Finally, new titles and job descriptions would be defined which would insure better integration between nursing and program and would afford a career ladder for those nursing personnel wishing to become more skilled in psychiatric care. The practical application of these principles produced a new staff that was generally younger, less experienced, but more educated, and very motivated. The new job titles developed were (in the order of increasing competence and responsibility):

psychiatric aide; psychiatric assistant; licensed psychiatric techni-cian. In some instances, long-time nurse aides with no previous psychiatric experience were selected for the entry-level positions.

Having assembled a new staff and a viable treatment philoso-phy, it was necessary to create a succinct and effective training program in order to merge these two essential elements. Concur-rently, the State of California Medi-Cal program created a new psychiatric treatment program of its own for nursing homes. The new program came to be known as the Special Rehabilitation Pro-gram, and it provided participating facilities with an additional $3.19 per diem reimbursement per certified psychiatric patient. In turn, each facility had to have a detailed, written program approved before this supplemental program could be reimbursed. The requirements were quite compatible with the efforts already under way at Crest-wood Manor, so it was decided that the two programs would be consolidated.

Among the requirements in the new regulations was a 20-hour program orientation for all new staff. Thus, the following curriculum was devised to teach the behavior modification principles utilized:

I. Observing behavior (6 hours)

    You will learn how to observe human behavior in a way which will enable you to define problem situations clearly, objectively, and constructively.

    A. Pinpointing behavior
        You will learn how to describe behavior clearly, pre-cisely, and objectively.

    B. Counting behavior
        You will learn four different ways to count behavior, that is, to find out how often a particular behavior occurs during any given time period. You will also learn some techniques you can use to make counting as easy and efficient as possible.

    C. Charting behavior
        You will learn how to record your behavior counts in a form that is readable, useful, and permanent.

    D. Identifying the observable causes of behavior
        You will learn what types of environmental factors are most likely to contribute to or improve upon a problem behavior in any given situation.

II. Increasing desirable behavior (4 hours)

You will learn the principles, procedures, and skills you need to increase the frequency with which desirable behavior occurs in your environment.

A. Identifying reinforcers
You will learn to isolate particular consequences which are responsible for maintaining behavior.

B. Reinforcing behavior
You will learn various rules and procedures for changing the environment so that reinforcing consequences work to increase the frequency of desirable behavior.

C. Ensuring reinforcement effectiveness
You will learn procedures and trouble-shooting methods to apply when reinforcement may not work as swiftly or as effectively as you might like.

III. Decreasing problem behavior (4 hours)

You will learn procedures which can be used to reduce or eliminate the occurrence of disturbing, destructive, or other problem behavior.

A. Positive punishment
You will learn three specific procedures using positive consequences, which will decrease problem behavior.

B. Negative punishment
You will learn three specific procedures, using negative consequences, which will decrease problem behavior.

C. Ensuring the effectiveness of punishment procedures
You will learn procedures, and trouble-shooting methods to apply when decreasing problem behavior may not work as swiftly or as effectively as you might like.

IV. Creating new behavior (3 hours)

You will learn various ways of bringing about new behavior —behavior which has not previously occurred but which you would like to see occur.

A. Modeling, prompting, and fading
You will learn how to demonstrate and produce desirable behavior in situations where it had not been occurring before.

B. Shaping and changing behavior
You will learn how to produce more complex behavior from simple behavior, which is already occurring.

C. Efficient ways of using the above procedures
You will learn techniques for ensuring the effectiveness of modeling, prompting, fading, shaping, and changing.

V. Implementing the system (3 hours)
A. Using token systems to implement specific programs
B. Ensuring token system effectiveness
C. Ethical issues in behavior modification

Additionally, two hours per week of ongoing in-service training are also required, and that time is utilized to transmit a better understanding of mental illness and treatment techniques (e.g., psychopharmacology, diagnostic definitions). Further, it is utilized to "fine tune" individual patient programs which are not proving successful. Moreover, ancillary staff (housekeepers, nurses aides, etc.) are exposed to these courses, thus encouraging their critical support and consistency in dealing with the patient population. These in-service education methods have become the backbone of the entire program, and currently a part-time instructor is employed to provide them.

By the time the first Special Rehabilitation Program was submitted for approval to the State Department of Health (February 1976), it was obvious that Crestwood Manor had developed a program which actually effected improvement in mentally disordered persons deemed to be chronic and unsalvageable. Since the development of the initial program plan, only a minor evolution of its components has been necessary. Further, it is noteworthy that the same plan has been adopted by various other facilities in the state. The specific program modalities utilized are outlined below.

I. Counselor groups
A. Groups will not exceed ten residents to one staff member on the morning shift and 12 residents to one staff member on the afternoon shift.
B. All residents are assigned staff counselors upon admission, with the purpose being to provide support and continuity through the orientation, treatment, and discharge phases of their stay.

C. A staff counselor will be any member of the Special Rehabilitation Team who has completed the initial 20-hour behavior modification course under the supervision of the consulting psychologist and program director.

D. All counselors will evaluate individuals for appropriateness for other program groups (e.g., personal effectiveness, adult education, recreation, industrial therapy).

II. Daily-living skills training

This is considered the backbone of preparing the resident to cope with greater independence. The skills taught here are pragmatic, fundamental, and vitally important. This is accomplished under the supervision of the assistant program director, who is a licensed psychiatric technician.

A. Homemaking skills.
  1. Cooking, planning menus, shopping.
  2. Sewing.
  3. Housekeeping.
B. Personal care.
  1. Grooming.
  2. Hygiene.
C. Money management.
  1. Industrial therapy (IT)—a small renumeration is given and is the resident's to manage.
  2. Access to purchases—a lightly stocked, nonprofit commissary is provided for residents who wish to "stretch" their dollars. However, those with a leave of absence may go to local stores.
D. Other responsibilities.
  1. Time awareness.
  2. Attending activities and meals.
  3. Attitudes and behavior toward peers and staff.
  4. Being available for medications on time.
  5. Aiding other less physically abled residents.

III. Physical fitness
A. Objective: encourage active participation in order to maintain or improve physical health and mental alertness.

B. General exercise classes are held for 30 minutes, five times per week.

C. Recreational activities are provided for more active residents (e.g., intramural basketball, jogging, and weight lifting).

D. Outdoor activities (e.g., walks, trips to the park, games for those of less physical strength or stamina).

IV. Recreation therapy

Recreation therapy is an integral part of the treatment plan. It is used to enhance the mental and physical functioning of the resident and to provide a physical link to the community. It is used as a positive reinforcer and a motivation for social contact.

A. Arts and crafts.

B. Physical exercise.

C. Field trips, both educational and recreational.

D. Movies.

E. Social gatherings, parties, dances, etc.

F. Discussion groups.

G. Music.

H. Outside entertainment.

V. Resident government

VI. Psychotherapy

A. Behavior modification.
1. Resident is made aware of behavior to be modified.
2. Goals shall be determined from stated care plans.
3. Positive reinforcers will be the primary mode of treatment.
4. Aversive therapy will be used only as described in facility policy.

B. Relaxation therapy.
1. Reduces anxiety.
2. Assists in control of acting-out behavior.
3. Increases frustration tolerance.
4. Used discriminately to assist in weight reduction.

C. Remotivation therapy.
1. Provides a stimulus for involvement with peers.

      2. Provides opportunity for positive behavior.

      3. Decreases antisocial behavior.

  D. Reality orientation/reminiscence therapy.

      1. Facilitates the life review process.

      2. Determines past coping mechanisms.

      3. Encourages positive self-concept.

VII. Personal effectiveness group (PET)

  A. Held as regular group therapy once weekly for one hour.

  B. Develops social skills needed in relating to peers in positive manner.

  C. Two counselors are assigned to each group.

  D. Assignments are made on the basis of how residents perceive their needs.

  E. Out-of-class work is expected from each participant.

These modalities will be utilized extensively for correcting problems of behavior control, impulse control, frustration tolerance, and antisocial behavior, as well as for a stimulus to provide more positive, appropriate, and effective behavior for the resident.

All modes of therapy are conducted by trained personnel under the supervision of the consulting psychologist and program director.

VIII. Vocational adaptation

  A. The Sacramento City Unified School District Adult Education Program offers a full spectrum of prevocational and vocational services. These programs are tailored to complement the educational programs offered in-facility. The following services are available to residents, based upon their own individual capabilities.

      1. Prevocational.

        a) Adult Extension School.

        b) Purple Heart Program.

        c) Goodwill Program.

      2. Vocational.

        a) Vocational counseling (where appropriate) through (state) vocational rehabilitation center.

        b) Work activity—industrial therapy.

        c) Volunteer placement—when work or vocational

placement is an unrealistic expectation, volunteer placement may be coordinated through the Mental Health Association, Volunteer Bureau, etc.

    d)   Skills center.

IX. Evaluation procedures

A. All incoming persons will be evaluated by the MACC Behavioral Adjustment Scale (1971).

B. Problem lists will be reviewed by the attending physician and appropriate staff each month.

C. Objectives and treatment plans will be reviewed at least quarterly.

D. Program staff will chart progress of each resident at least weekly.

E. Quarterly reports to the director, County Mental Health Department.

F. Test batteries are given to those incoming residents for whom more data are needed. This need is determined by the program psychologist. Examples of tests utilized are Minnesota Multi-phasic Personality Inventory; 16 Personality Factors; Rorschach; Thematic Apperception Test; Weschler Adult Intelligence Scale.

THE PSYCHIATRIST'S ROLE

All of the above treatment modalities, as well as medication therapies, are prescribed or approved by the patient's attending psychiatrist. All patients are under the care of a psychiatrist; however, the Medi-Cal reimbursement structure for such care essentially limits the psychiatrist's involvement to one or two visits per month. As a result, the role of the facility's treatment staff is greatly magnified in comparison with the role of similar personnel in the acute or state hospital, where psychiatrists are in daily attendance.

SUMMARY AND CONCLUSIONS

The Crestwood Manor program developed in response to a specific community mental health need. Although only minimal statistics are available to document its success as an economical, human, and viable alternative to state hospitals and the local acute psychiatric wards, emulation of the concept at various other localities around California attests to its success.

The advantages that have derived from the Crestwood Manor concept are significant.

1. Community involvement creates a more human environment and greater staff accountability to the public. These factors tend to promote humane treatment, avoid institutionalization, and provide or retain the patients' involvement with the "real world." They are particularly important to the avoidance of the kinds of patient abuse experienced in some of California's state hospitals.

2. Program visibility has increased (as defined by the number of complaints received from neighboring residents and businesses) the level of community tolerance to the mentally disordered. This tolerance in turn provides a more receptive environment for those mentally ill persons able to reside in independent community settings.

3. Community involvement and program visibility generally create more awareness of patients' rights and thus result in shorter institutional stays. The old state hospital horror stories of patients being locked away for life as the result of one episode of deviant behavior are virtually impossible in such community-based facilities. Shorter, more appropriate stays in these facilities in turn insure better, more efficient utilization of their services.

4. Because of their smaller size, nursing homes are able to avoid much of the severe regimentation and institutionalization which inevitably occurs in large state hospitals.

5. Most importantly in these post-Proposition 13 days, facilities such as Crestwood Manor can provide good care for the chronically mentally disordered for less than half the cost of state hospitalization for the same patients.

At the same time, because the Crestwood Manor concept was a response to a specific problem in a single locale, it has suffered from many disadvantages deriving from the fact that it is a bureaucratic hybrid. To list a few of these bureaucratic obstacles:

1. The nursing home category of care, largely federally defined, emphasizes the provision of physical care in a medical model setting. No regulatory provision or category exists

for the care of the mentally ill in such facilities. As a result, many of the regulations under which the facility operates are counterproductive to a psychiatrically therapeutic program and discourage individuality. Further, salary levels in the nursing home industry tend toward the minimum wage, thus discouraging good staff and insuring high employee turnover rates.

2. Federal Medicaid law indicates that the provision of psychiatric services to those mentally disordered persons between the ages of 18 and 64 cannot be rendered as a Medicaid benefit in nursing homes. Thus, California and other states are in imminent danger of losing their federal matching funds for the nursing home care of such persons.

3. In too many cases, local mental health directors in California have not placed sufficient priority on the inpatient, long-term care of the chronically mentally ill. As a result, such programs are too few in number, and where they do occur, they are almost always underfunded. Further, such programs for the geropsychiatric patients are almost nonexistent.

4. As stated above, the lack of a coherent patient tracking system throughout the mental health continuum virtually condemns the chronic mentally ill to a "revolving door" recidivism rate.

Despite these system limitations, it is generally conceded that the Crestwood Manor concept is a viable alternative to the state hospital. There will always be a need for some state hospital beds in order to care for those few patients requiring high security for violence control. However, mental health policymakers would do well to examine this model more closely and attempt to build on its strengths, while minimizing bureaucratic obstacles through legislation and regulation.

The President's Commission on Mental Health recommended the creation of a Medicaid-funded "Intermediate Care–Mentally Disordered" category of care. The California legislature and the U.S. Congress were both considering legislation which would create such a category.* Such a move could substantially reduce the bureaucratic obstacles encountered by Crestwood Manor.

The Crestwood Manor experience proves that the concept of a psychiatric treatment component within a nursing home is a viable one, despite the limitations inherent in the current definitions of such facilities. Mental health professionals everywhere would do well to encourage such facilities, for the chronically mentally ill will always require them.

*The California Legislative bill was killed in January 1980. HR 2421 (Weiss, New York), the Federal bill, still languishes in the Health Subcommittee of the House Commerce Committee.

Chapter 11

A STATE HOSPITAL-INITIATED COMMUNITY PROGRAM*

Leonard I. Stein
Mary Ann Test

The treatment of the chronic psychiatric patient has changed dramatically since the 1950s. Rather than long years of custodial care in a state hospital, the chronic psychiatric patient is now treated with a relatively short hospital stay followed by community aftercare. One consequence of this change is the emergence of a new pattern of patient movement in which some patients rotate frequently between the community and the hospital. This pattern has been termed the "revolving door syndrome." Chronic patients, according to available data (1, 2), continue to spend considerable time in mental institutions, function poorly between admissions, and experience high readmission rates. A recent paper by Bachrach (3) comprehensively reviewed the historical antecedents and the current debate concerning deinstitutionalization. She concluded that limiting hospital treatment was a rational goal however, reaching that goal was markedly impaired by the woeful inadequacy of our present

*Some of the material for this chapter has been previously published in L.I. Stein and M.A. Test, *An Alternative to mental hospital treatment.* New York; Plenum Press, 1978.

This study was supported in part by Grant 05–R 000009 from the National Institute of Mental Health. The authors wish to acknowlege the skillfulness and diligence of their research staff: Rick Bowman, Carl Schwanz, Suzanne Senn, and Gene Jackson.

system of community care for the chronically disabled psychiatric patient. The revolving door syndrome, in large part, is a direct reflection of the inadequate and often inappropriate treatment provided the patient in the community *(4)*.

In the early 1970s, the authors of this chapter and Arnold J. Marx were staff members of a state hospital in Wisconsin. Disheartened by high readmission rates, we began experimenting with sending staff from our in-hospital unit into the community to help our discharged patients sustain their community tenure. Over time it became evident that the level of in-hospital adjustment attained was often a poor predictor of our ability to maintain the patient in the community. In fact, as we became more "experimental" in discharging relatively borderline patients, we were often surprised by the favorable response they appeared to show to our follow-up "treatment" in the community compared to their minimal response to in-hospital programs. It became increasingly clear to us that the crucial variable in producing postdischarge success was the amount and kind of support patients received in the community. This success in helping patients make a satisfactory community adjustment led to a controlled experiment in which we "prematurely" discharged patients whom ward staffs had deemed "not currently capable of sustained community living." These patients were provided intensive community treatment by hospital personnel who spent considerable time working with them in their homes, neighborhoods, and places of employment. The results of this study, reported in 1975, indicated that not only was it feasible to treat the experimental group in the community but following treatment these patients had attained more autonomous living and employment situations than the controls *(5)*. These results pointed to a successful alternative to institutional treatment, particularly in terms of enhancing patients' social adjustment.

The logical extension of the work was to test whether what we had learned could usefully be applied as a model to replace mental hospital treatment. In late 1971 and early 1972, the authors, with some contribution from Dr. Marx and Burton Weisbrod (an economist), wrote a hospital improvement project grant to evaluate the clinical efficacy of a model to replace the current mode for treating the chronic psychiatric patient, namely, short-term hospitalization coupled with the usual kinds of community aftercare. This new model, Training in Community Living (TCL), would provide treatment totally in the community, leaning heavily on the techniques learned in our earlier work. The present chapter describes the conceptual framework of the TCL model, summarizes its implementation, and presents its research evaluation and results.

CONCEPTUAL FRAMEWORK

It is our conclusion that the inadequacies of current models of community treatment are caused by the fact that they do not effectively address certain factors required by patients to achieve a satisfactory life in the community. Absence of one or more of these factors led to a tenuous community adjustment, keeping patients on the brink of rehospitalization. These requirements were derived from our clinical experience; similar ones were also clearly delineated in a paper by Mechanic *(6)*. They are as follows:

1. Material resources—food, shelter, clothing, medical care, recreation, and so forth. Community treatment programs must assume responsibility for helping the patient acquire these resources.
2. Skills to cope with the demands of community life. These are the kinds of skills we all take for granted, such as using public transportation, preparing simple but nutritious meals, budgeting money. We are convinced that the learning of these skills must take place in vivo, where the patient will be needing and using them.
3. Motivation to persevere and remain involved with life. Our patients experience a good deal of stress, and their motivation to remain in the community becomes easily eroded. A readily available system of support to encourage patients and to help them solve real life problems and to feel that they are not alone and that others are concerned about their welfare is crucial in keeping motivation intact.
4. Freedom from pathological dependent relationships. We define such a relationship as one which inhibits personal growth, reinforces maladaptive behavior, and generates feelings of panic when its loss is threatened. Many of our patients have been pathologically dependent on families or institutions all their lives. Unfortunately, hospitalization deepens pathological dependency, and upon discharge the patient is often returned to a highly conflictual family situation where the ingredients for another crisis and hospitali-

zation are omnipresent. Community programs must help the patient become free of pathological dependent relationships and in so doing must provide sufficient support to keep the patient involved in community life and encourage growth toward greater autonomy.

5. Support and education of community members who are involved with patients. An important factor influencing patient behavior and thus community tenure are the ways in which community members (family, law enforcement personnel, agency people, landlords, etc.) relate to them. Community programs must provide support and education to these community members to help them learn to relate to patients in a manner which is both beneficial for the patients and acceptable to the community members.

6. A supportive system which assertively helps the patient with the above five requirements. Chronically disabled patients are frequently passive, interpersonally anxious, and prone to develop severe psychiatric symptomatology. Such characteristics often lead these patients to fail to keep appointments and to drop out of treatment, particularly when they are becoming more symptomatic. Hence, a program designed for their care must be assertive in involving patients in a treatment program and be prepared to go to the patients to prevent drop out. Additionally, it must actively insure continuity of care among treatment agencies rather than assume that patients will successully negotiate the often difficult pathways from one agency to another on their own.

PROGRAM IMPLEMENTATION

The Training in Community Living program was designed to attend to the very requirements discussed above. Its base of operation is the community, and its goal is to help patients develop and maintain a satisfactory community adjustment. Use of the hospital is virtually eliminated. The implementation of the program will only be summarized here, since it has been described in considerable detail elsewhere (7). The program is implemented by a retrained mental hospital ward staff, transplanted to the community (8). The staff works in shifts so that coverage is available 24 hours per day, seven days a week. Patient programs are individually tailored, based primarily on an assessment of the patient's coping skill deficits and requirements for community living. Most of the "treatment" takes place in vivo—in patients' homes, neighborhoods, and places of work. More specifically, staff members, "on the spot" in patients' homes and neighborhoods, teach and assist them in such daily living activities as laundry upkeep, shopping, cooking, restaurant utilization, grooming, budgeting, and use of transportation. Additionally, patients are given sustained and intensive assistance in finding a job or sheltered workshop placement, and staff then continue daily contact with patients and their supervisors or employers to help with on-the-job problem solving. Furthermore, patients are aided in the constructive use of leisure time and the development of effective social skills by staff encouraging and supporting their involvement in relevant community recreation and social activities. An effort is made to take advantage of patients' strengths rather than focus on pathology. Providing support to patients, their families, and community members is an important function of the program. The program is assertive in carrying out the above functions; for example, if a patient does not show up for work, a staff member goes immediately to the patient's home to help with any problem that is interfering with the patient's functioning. The medical needs of patients are carefully attended to. Each patient's medical status is carefully monitored while in the program, and treatment is provided when indicated. Psychotropic medication is routinely used for schizophrenic and manic-depressive patients.

EVALUATION

The TCL model was rigorously evaluated by comparing patients in the program with a control group receiving progressive in-hospital treatment plus community aftercare. Subjects for the study consisted of all patients seeking admission to Mendota Mental Health Institute for inpatient care who met the following criteria: (1) residence in Dane County, Wisconsin (consisting of the city of Madison and surrounding area); (2) age 18–62; (3) any diagnosis other than severe organic brain syndrome or primary alcoholism.

Experiment Design

The subjects were randomly assigned to either the experimental (TCL) or control group by the admission office staff. Control subjects were treated in the hospital for as long as deemed necessary and were then linked with appropriate community agencies. Experimental subjects did not enter the hospital (except in rare instances) but instead received the "training in community living" approach for 14 months. After this time, they received no further input from the experimental unit staff. The last few months of the 14-month period was utilized to gradually wean the patients from the experimental program and to integrate them into existing programs the community made available to this population—in essence, the same programs treating the patients in the control group. Assessment data on all patients were gathered at baseline (time of admission) and every four months for 28 months through face-to-face interviews by a research staff which operated independently of both clinical teams. In cases where experimental subjects were hospitalized, these data are included and the results reported. Thus, no patients were excluded from the study on the basis of severity of symptomatology or for any reason other than failure to meet the three admission criteria specified above.

Control Treatment

Patients assigned to the control group were immediately screened by a member of the hospital's acute treatment unit serving Dane County. The patients were usually (though not necessarily) admitted to the hospital, where they received progressive treatment aimed at preparation for return to the community. The Dane County unit served as a stringent control for the experimental program, since it had a high staff to patient ratio and offered a wide variety of services: inpatient care, partial hospitalization, and outpatient follow-up. It was by no means a custodial unit; its median length of stay was only 17 days. In addition, the unit made liberal use of aftercare services available in Madison for the discharged patients.

Assessment Instruments

Measures taken at baseline were derived from the following: (1) Demographic Data Form, to collect standard demographic data on life situation and economic variables; (2) Short Clinical Rating Scale, to measure symptomatology (9); (3) Community Adjustment Form, to measure the patient's living situation, time spent in institutions, employment record, leisure time activities, social relationships, quality of environment, and subjective satisfaction with life; (4) Rosenburg Self-Esteem Scale, to measure the self-esteem reported by patients themselves *(10)*. Measures taken at the subsequent four-month intervals used the Short Clinical Rating Form, the Community Adjustment Form, and the Rosenburg Self-Esteem Scale.

RESULTS

The results reported here represent those on 65 experimental *(E)* and 65 control *(C)* subjects through their first year in the study. In the tables and discussion below, *n*'s of less than 65 are the result of missing data in cases where it was impossible to obtain the scheduled follow-up interview for reasons of patient nonavailability or lack of cooperation. Through assertive data collection, however, 89% of all possible interviews were completed. The results have been reported in detail earlier *(11)* and are therefore given in summary form below.

Characteristics of the Sample

There were no significant differences between groups on demographic characteristics: 73% of the patients were either single, separated, or divorced; 55% were male; the mean age was approximately 31; and the patients had accumulated a mean of 14.5 months in psychiatric institutions, with a mean of five hospitalizations per subject before presenting for the current admission. About 20% of the patients came to the hospital directly from another institution, and 14% came from sheltered living situations. Only 17% of the patients had no prior time in hospital. Patients covered a wide span of diagnoses; however, approximately 50% of the patients were schizophrenic. Additionally, the *E* and *C* groups did not differ significantly on any of the major measures given at the time of admission with the exception of self-esteem, which will be discussed later.

LIVING SITUATIONS. Results pertaining to living situation appear in Table 11–1. Throughout the first year, *E* subjects spent very little time in psychiatric institutions compared to controls. This avoidance of use of the mental hospital for the *E* patients did not lead to a greater utilization of medical or penal institutions, nor of supervised living situations in the community. In fact, the *E* group spent significantly more time than the *C* group in independent living situations in the community. Not indicated in the table is the additional

Table 11–1. Mean Percentage of the Data Collection Periods Spent in the Various Living Situations

		4 months			8 months			12 months		
		E (n = 62)		C (n = 60)	E (n = 62)		C (n = 60)	E (n = 62)		C (n = 59)
Institutions										
Psychiatric	$\overline{X}$	1.59	***	21.20	1.38	***	11.63	4.71	*	13.13
	SD	5.35		20.62	3.99		22.88	16.61		26.56
Medical	$\overline{X}$	.97		1.12	.11		.53	.77		.81
	SD	4.89		3.19	.44		1.85	3.83		2.17
Penal	$\overline{X}$	4.42		3.53	5.14		5.27	3.47		6.06
	SD	15.39		10.65	19.96		15.45	14.37		21.24
Total	$\overline{X}$	7.06	***	25.85	6.64	*	17.44	8.96	*	20.00
	SD	17.47		21.31	20.99		28.14	23.39		31.74
Noninstitutional										
Supervised	$\overline{X}$	7.83		10.73	6.37		12.02	8.95		12.27
	SD	20.49		21.58	22.39		24.69	26.38		26.90
Independent	$\overline{X}$	85.20		63.41	86.99	**	70.54	82.09	*	67.73
	SD	26.06		31.02	34.22		37.02	32.50		38.49
Total	$\overline{X}$	93.02	***	74.15	93.36	*	82.56	91.04	*	80.00
	SD	17.50		21.31	20.99		28.14	23.39		31.74

NOTE:: Differences between E and C groups within each of the data collection periods that are significantly different are indicated by an asterisk(s) between the two means:

* $p < .05$
** $p < .01$
*** $p < .001$
$\overline{X}$ = Mean percentage.
SD = Standard deviation.

fact that 34 of the 58 C patients hospitalized were readmitted at least once, for a readmission rate of 58% in the first year. Thus, many of the patients treated in the traditional manner were becoming involved in the familiar revolving door syndrome. On the other hand, only 6% of the E patients experienced a rehospitalization.

EMPLOYMENT STATUS.   As reflected in Table 11–2, E subjects spent significantly less time unemployed and significantly more time in sheltered employment than did C subjects. There was no significant difference between groups in percentage of time spent in competitive employment situations.

LEISURE TIME ACTIVITIES, SOCIAL RELATIONSHIPS, AND QUALITY OF ENVIRONMENT.   A measure of leisure time activities revealed no significant differences between the E and C groups. Likewise, several of the scales derived to measure social relationships revealed no significant difference. One scale, however, measuring "contact with trusted friends" revealed that E subjects had significantly more contact (p < .05) than did C subjects at the 12-month period. Additionally, on a scale measuring "social groups belonged to and attended in the last month," E subjects scored significantly higher than did C subjects. There was no significant difference between groups on quality of environment (meals, quality of living situations, etc.).

SATISFACTION WITH LIFE AND SELF-ESTEEM. E subjects were significantly more satisfied with their life situations than C subjects at the 12-month data collection point. The E group revealed significantly higher self-esteem than the C group at baseline (p < .05).[1]

SYMPTOMATOLOGY. E subjects revealed less symptomatology, postbaseline, than C subjects, indeed revealing better functioning on 7 of the 13 scales by the 12-month period (see Table 11–3).

[1]While the two groups may have actually represented different populations on this variable, this would seem unlikely in view of the fact that E and C groups differed significantly on no other variable at baseline. An alternative explanation is that, since this measure was taken a few days after the patient's admission to the study, a lower self-esteem in the C group may be related to the fact that almost all C patients were initially hospitalized while almost all E patients were kept in the community. Both t-tests and analyses of covariance of self-esteem scores to all the subsequent data collection periods revealed no significant differences between E and C groups.

Table 11–2. Time Spent Employed and Income Earned in Competitive Employment

	4 months		8 months		12 months	
	E (n = 61)	C (n = 60)	E (n = 61)	C (n = 60)	E (n = 57)	C (n = 59)

Mean Percentage of the Data Collection Period Spent in the Various Employment Situations

	E (n = 61)	C (n = 60)	E (n = 61)	C (n = 60)	E (n = 57)	C (n = 59)
Unemployed						
X̄	33.76 ***	61.74	22.97 ***	53.97	30.31	56.76
SD	36.48	37.04	36.23	42.93	41.34	43.31
Sheltered						
X̄	26.68 ***	5.06	22.50 ***	2.00	22.39 ***	1.10
SD	38.33	13.53	37.69	9.79	38.64	8.24
Competitive Employment						
X̄	39.63	33.20	54.52	44.03	47.30	42.14
SD	42.29	36.03	46.27	43.07	45.86	42.69

Mean Amount of Competitive Income ($) Earned by Subjects in Both Groups During the Data Collection Periods

	E (n = 61)	C (n = 59)	E (n = 61)	C (n = 59)	E (n = 57)	C (n = 59)
X̄	610.00	308.80	872.30 *	436.00	759.8 *	418.90
SD	1053.40	622.80	1260.00	834.00	1063.5	711.60

NOTE: Differences between E and C groups within each of the data collection periods that are significantly different are indicated by an asterisk(s) between the two means:

*** p < .001
** p < .01
* p < .05

X̄ = Mean percentage.
SD = Standard deviation.

Table 11-3. Significant Differences Between E and C Group
Means on Items of the Short Clinical Rating Scale

Items	Baseline	4 months	8 months	12 months
Depressed Mood	—	—	—	.01
Suicidal Trends	—	—	—	.001
Anxiety or Fear	—	.001	.01	.01
Expression of Anger	—	—	—	—
Social Withdrawal	—	—	—	—
Motor Agitation	—	.05	.01	—
Motor Retardation	—	—	—	—
Paranoid Behavior	—	—	—	.001
Hallucinations	—	—	—	—
Thought Disorder	—	—	.01	.001
Hyperactivity-Elation	—	.05	—	.01
Physical Complaints	—	—	—	—
Global Illness	.05*	.05	.001	.01

NOTE: Items on which the means of E and C groups differed significantly are indicated by the above figures, which represent the level (p) of statistical significance. In *all* cases of significant differences, except where asterisked, C subjects were *more symptomatic* than E subjects.

MEDICATION AND COMPLIANCE. No significant difference was found between groups on numbers of persons for whom the various types of psychotropic medications were prescribed. The only significant differences found between groups on compliance were at the 8- and 12-month data collection periods for antipsychotic medication, with the E group being more compliant than the C group.

DISCUSSION

The TCL program is an effective alternative to mental hospital treatment for a large majority of the chronic psychiatric patients now being admitted to our public mental hospitals. Specifically, virtually without use of the hospital it was possible to treat in the community an unselected group of patients presenting for admission to a state mental hospital. While most of the control subjects were admitted to the hospital and many subsequently readmitted, almost all experimental patients experienced a sustained community tenure while in TCL without suffering the disruption to life and reinforcement of symptomatic behavior frequently incurred through hospitalization. Additionally, and most important, the data indicate that the patients' sustained community living was not gained at the expense of their quality of life, level of adjustment, self-esteem, or personal satisfaction with life. Instead, relative to control patients, the experimental patients showed enhanced functioning in several significant areas and experienced less subjective distress and greater satisfaction with their lives. Further, a comparative economic cost-benefit analysis found the TCL program to be economically feasible (12), and a comparative study of social cost (13) found that treating patients in the TCL program rather than the hospital did not increase burdens to families or the community.

It is not unusual for hospitals to run outpatient clinics for its discharge patients. Hospitals, however, have been reluctant to permit staff, especially nursing and aide personnel, to leave the hospital grounds to work with patients in the community. Limiting hospital staff to intramural activities has led to problems for both patients and staff and to public expense. In this era of decreased hospital populations, hospital staffs have understandably become concerned about job security. This has resulted in organized efforts to block the closing and consolidation of hospitals that are operating well under 50% capacity. In addition, this legitimate concern about job security is often reflected in a reluctance to discharge patients as early as might be optimal. These problems would be markedly reduced if hospitals broadened their boundaries to include the community and utilized their personnel in programs similar to the one described in this chapter. As we have noted in a paper on training hospital personnel to work in the community (8), much of what they have learned by working with patients in the hospital is directly transferable to working with patients in the community.

We are aware that having teams of state or county hospital staff working with patients in the community will further feed the problem of squabbles over territoriality that already exists among community-based agencies. This preciousness of territoriality has protected the domains of agencies, kept hospital personnel within their walls, inhibited creative interagency cooperation, and predictably contributed to fragmentation of services. Although we are cognizant of the dynamics that lead organizations to protecting boundaries, the sad fact remains that for the chronic psychiatric population, there is more work that needs to be done than there are resources to do it. We are increasingly recognizing that, for the chronic psychiatric patient, surviving in the community requires a comprehensive community support system made up of many elements working together. The model of care this chapter described is but one element in a complete community support system. We believe this element to be a crucial one, and we recommend it to state hospitals both as a means to develop much needed services and as a way to effectively utilize the skills of hospital personnel. Although the model was initiated from a state hospital, we would like to stress that similar programs could be started by a wide variety of nonhospital organizations, such as mental health centers, psychosocial rehabilitation centers, day treatment centers, and day hospitals.

This model for providing care, however, has in addition to the problems of territoriality other barriers to becoming widely implemented. The major one is financing, even though the model is economically feasible in terms of total costs and benefits (12). The kinds of services it provides are largely not reimbursable by third-party payers. Less effective modes of treatment for this population are reimbursable, and this has a profound influence on shaping the types of services provided. As Mechanic (14) points out, it is relatively easy to determine what one must pay for a day in the hospital. It is much more difficult to determine how to pay for a total pattern of services including medical care, social support, and recreational and activity programs. One possible solution is payment on a capitation basis. There may be other solutions as well, but the point is clear, if funding mechanisms for programs such as TCL are not developed, these programs will not be widely implemented. Other barriers to widespread implementation are the difficulties inherent in disseminating programs requiring social technologies which call for considerable coordinative ability and which fall outside of the usual organizational patterns of the medical sector (14).

We believe our study is useful in helping define what the role of inpatient treatment can optimally be. Although the TCL program was designed as an alternative to hospitalization and every effort was made to minimize its use, 18% of the patients were hospitalized, albeit for very brief periods. First and foremost, it must be understood that the role of inpatient care, for any community, must be seen in the context of what kinds of programming are available in the community for the chronically disabled psychiatric patient. Although hospitalization may have undesirable effects on patients, there may be greater patient harm and certainly greater burden to the community if use of the hospital is denied on "principle" without providing adequate community programming in its place. The more comprehensive the community program, the less the need to use the hospital. With a program such as TCL available, we believe the hospital need be used only for the following cases:

1. For protection of the individual or others when patients are imminently suicidal or homocidal. Care must be taken not

to hospitalize patients who utilize self-destructive behavior as a means of getting help. This presents a very burdensome clinical judgment, but one that can be learned and made if the clinician is willing to do so. In our experience, if the patient is provided with the support needed, the danger is minimal.

2. For patients whose psychiatric illness is complicated by significant medical problems requiring the special diagnostic and treatment facilities only available in a hospital.

3. For patients whose psychosis is so severe that they require the structure and good nursing care only a hospital can provide. The goal here is to medicate the patient and interrupt the psychotic process as quickly as possible. We have used the hospital for this purpose with patients in the midst of a very manic episode or highly disruptive schizophrenic episode where we were unable to insure that the patient was being adequately medicated. The length of hospitalization in these cases was rarely over two weeks and often a matter of days.

Importantly, we found that psychosis per se was not necessarily an indication to hospitalize. We were able to treat successfully many patients presenting as acutely psychotic without use of the hospital. In short, given adequate community programming, we recommend use of psychiatric hospitalization only in the specific instances described above.

Finally, it is our conclusion that until we are able to prevent or cure chronic psychiatric disease we should change our treatment strategy from *preparing* patients *for* community life to *maintaining* patients *in* community living.

NOTES

1. Stein LI, Test MA: The revolving door syndrome—An empirical view. Presented at the annual meeting of the American Psychiatric Association, Miami, Florida, 1976

2. Mosher LR, Feinsilver D: Special report on schizophrenia. Bethesda, Md., National Institute of Mental Health, April 1971

3. Bachrach LL: National Institute of Mental Health Deinstitutionalization: An Analytical Review and Sociological Perspective. Department of Health, Edu-

cation, and Welfare Publication No. ADM 76–351. Washington, D.C.: U.S. Government Printing Office, 1976

4. The discharged chronic mental patient. Medical World News, 47–58, 12 April 1974

5. Marx AJ, Test MA, Stein LI: Extrohospital management of severe mental illness. Archives of General Psychiatry 29:505–511, 1973

6. Mechanic D: Alternatives to mental hospital treatment: A sociological perspective. In Stein LI, Test MA (eds): Alternatives to Mental Hospital Treatment. New York, Plenum Publishing Corp., 1978

7. Stein LI, Test MA: An alternative to mental hospital treatment. In Stein LI, Test MA (eds): Alternative to Mental Hospital Treatment. New York, Plenum Publishing Corp., 1978

8. Stein LI, Test MA: Retraining a hospital staff for work in a community program in Wisconsin. Hosp Community Psychiatry 27:266–268, 1976

9. French MH, Heninger GR: A short clinical rating scale for use by nursing personnel, I. Development and design. Arch Gen Psychiatry 23:233–240, 1970

10. Rosenburg M: Society and the Adolescent Self-Image. Princeton, N.J., Princeton University Press, 1965

11. Test MA, Stein LI: Training in community living: Research design and results. In Stein LI, Test MA (eds): Alternatives to Mental Hospital Treatment. New York, Plenum Publishing Corp., 1978

12 Weisbrod BA, Test MA, Stein LI: An Alternative to Mental Hospital Treatment. II. Economic Benefit-Cost Analysis. Archives of General Psychiatry 37: 400–405, 1980

13. Test MA, Stein LI: An Alternative to Mental Hospital Treatment. III. Social Cost. Archives of General Psychiatry 37: 409–412, 1980

14. Mechanic D: Consideration in the design of mental health benefits under national health insurance. American Journal of Public Health 68:482–488, 1978

Chapter 12

A GENERAL HOSPITAL MODEL

Gladys Egri

Harlem Rehabilitation Center (HRC) is a division of the Department of Psychiatry of Harlem Hospital Center,* physically separated from the hospital by seven street blocks. The very fact of separation enhances its perception as a community facility by patients, diminishing their sense of "patienthood" and dependence, thus reinforcing the passage to independence and autonomy so essential to successful rehabilitation. In the neighborhood, the Center is known as "the school."

The Center's program of psychiatric rehabilitation is guided by a philosophy which considers health not merely an absence of symptoms, but rather the actualization of the individual's highest potential. The emphasis is on remission of symptoms and the development of positive mental health, for example, mastery, autonomy. The Center operates on the hypothesis that the resultant decrease in vulnerability to stress increases chances of satisfactory life adjustment and minimizes the occurrence of acute psychotic episodes that require hospitalization. The ultimate goal is improvement of the

*Harlem Hospital Center, located in New York City, is a municipal general hospital, affiliated with Columbia University. It is one of the teaching facilities of the College of Physicians and Surgeons and other professional schools of the university and is fully accredited for all specialty health service delivery and teaching.

quality of life, that is, the development of functioning in basic roles: member of society, parent, homemaker, wage earner.

All studies and recommendations concerning treatment of the chronic psychiatrically disabled call for comprehensiveness, coordination, and continuity. Harlem Rehabilitation Center was founded and functions on this basis. Treatment begun at the time of discharge from intensive psychiatric care and containing the elements necessary to address all difficulties of patients in an explicit, goal-oriented manner enhances the chances of success. Patients require the active effort of the mental health worker to engage them in their own treatment process. Likelihood of cooperation increases when patients are presented with a treatment plan that they understand as relevant to their lives, and whose goals are consonant with their interests, and take into account their abilities and disabilities. The realization that support as well as opportunity for personal growth are available mobilizes the motivation necessary to remain in treatment and achieve improvement and can help avoid the hopeless cycle of rehospitalization. As Bennett *(1)* points out:

> Psychiatric rehabilitation aims to help the disabled to make the best of their abilities and to play the most normal role possible in society. If they are to meet these demands they must be helped to work and earn as well as to cope with their emotional conflicts. They must be able to manage stress and be motivated to do so. These aspects of rehabilitation are complementary. Recovery of the ability to work increases confidence and diminishes anxiety and depression, just as recovery from depression and anxiety increases ability to work.

Harlem Rehabilitation Center is unique in its origins, identity, and orientation. It was initiated, developed, and administered by psychiatrists, and it is an integral part of a department of psychiatry in a general hospital. Established in 1964 by Dr. June J. Christmas with the strong support of Dr. Elizabeth B. Davis, then director of the department, it was initially funded by a combination of state and federal grants. Since then, it has addressed itself to the psychiatric, social, and vocational needs of the residents of the community in which it is situated. The sociopsychiatric services were designed to help two groups *(2)*. Community residents who were under-or unemployed due to social reasons were to be recruited, trained, and employed as paraprofessionals. Patients who were disabled due to mental illness and institutionalization were to be provided with two major types of service—a psychiatric rehabilitation program, and, later, a vocational rehabilitation program. Such patients were to be resocialized and helped to function outside the institutional setting. The vocational program provided a range of services geared to patients' eventual entry into the world of work. The unique staffing pattern at HRC, which included a new category of health worker, was to provide potential for growth not only for the patients, but for the staff as well. In this manner, social health workers, activity therapy workers, vocational evaluators, rehabilitation counselor aides, and teaching aides were educated to work directly with patients, and many are at present members of the therapeutic teams.

In 1972, the emphasis of HRC shifted and the service aspect was intensified. Although paraprofessionals continued to learn as they functioned as team members, no new candidates for formal training were recruited since formal instruction was no longer conducted. From the time of this altered direction, concentration has been on expanding services for patients, while educational activities consist of psychiatric rehabilitation in-service training for professionals and paraprofessionals.

Over the years, the general characteristics of the patient population underwent a gradual change. In contrast to the early years of the program, the patients now are younger, are more psychiatrically symptomatic, have undergone fewer hospitalizations, are increasingly urban born, and are somewhat more highly educated. Still, all patients are supported by some form of public assistance. Very few patients have a history of ever having developed work habits and having sustained a job for any extensive period of time. The large majority never worked or worked only for short periods in odd jobs. Several of the women have lost custody of their children due to the inability to care for them appropriately. Health problems are prevalent. At least one-half of the population suffers from one or more physical illnesses, such as hypertension, diabetes, TB, obesity, chronic kidney and liver disease, orthopedic problems. Most require dental and ophthalmologic evaluation and treatment. Most of these problems were undetected until enrollment in the program. The environment in which these people live is Harlem—an inner-city community afflicted with poor housing, poor quality education, high unemployment, high occurrence of physical illnesses, high rate of drug and alcohol abuse, high rate of psychiatric hospital admission. Thus, HRC responds to the needs of a multihandicapped population, impaired due to a combination of factors: severe mental illness, institutionalization, discrimination, and poverty.

The services of HRC were designed to be and continue to be appropriate for and meaningful to this particular group of patients.

The rehabilitative process addresses many specific deficits that created the disability with the resultant inability to cope with environmental demands and to fulfill societal roles. Such deficits are universal and in the psychiatrically disabled exist regardless of social class. Whether a patient cannot deal with the problem of an incorrect or missing welfare check or whether a patient needs to challenge an item on a charge account, the coping deficit is the same. Whether a patient has lost skill and confidence at the typewriter or whether a patient has lost skill and confidence at the surgical operating table, the deficit is the same. However, for patients from lower socioeconomic groups, environmental conditions aggravate the disability. Therefore, although the components of rehabilitation described in this chapter apply to a psychiatric unit of a general hospital located in a disadvantaged area, the same principles apply and these services can be provided in a general hospital in a more privileged area.

The change in emphasis on service provision evolved as the patient population changed and as experience taught that each patient's pattern of deficits and ultimate potential is individual and, therefore, that each patient's treatment requires an individual "prescription" for matching the program's services to the patient's particular disabilities and abilities. It was found that enrolling patients in a specific type of program, such as vocational or social, as broadly indicated, was not truly accomplishing the goal. The patient's disability emerged as a result of a complex and subtle interaction of varying levels of deficits. The current approach of matching the components of the program to individual needs better suits each patient, and by giving the patient pieces of all of the available programs, the total disability can be treated.

HRC is equipped to treat 120 patients in its day program, which operates Monday through Friday, 9:00 A.M. to 3:00 P.M. The setting is a therapeutic milieu. Patients are referred from the other divisions of the department, other departments of the hospital (mainly rehabilitation medicine), other hospitals, clinics, and social agencies. Some of the applicants walk in without referral.

Criteria for admission are: being between the ages of 16 and 55 and having a severe impairment in the performance of a social and/or vocational role due to a psychiatric illness. Contraindications for admission are: active substance abuse, behavior violent or bizarre enough to disrupt communal activities, active suicidal or homicidal ideation, or intelligence that is lower than mild retardation.

Two paraprofessionals, specifically trained for the assignment, act as intake staff for all applicants referred to the program. They collect all relevant information, for example, discharge summaries, the individual's current social and medical circumstances; apply criteria for admission or exclusion; do outreach to other psychiatric facilities; function as liaison by personally escorting or arranging for such escorting of patients from the referring agency to the Center (this has drastically reduced no-shows and initial drop outs); when indicated, conduct group discussions at referring facilities to motivate potential applicants to follow through on their referral to the Center. These activities are conducted under the supervision of a social worker and in consultation with psychiatrists from HRC staff.

Patients are accepted for a two-week trial period. All applicants are informed during their first interview that these two weeks will be used for exploration and that at the end of the period a coactive contract will be arrived at between staff and patient to work toward a mutually agreed goal. Patients are asked to commit themselves to attend regularly and punctually, and assurance of support in handling problems is given by the staff. The two-week period is utilized by patients for exploration and by staff for evaluation: patients can decide whether they want to work toward their rehabilitation in this milieu, and staff evaluate the patients comprehensively.

The initial evaluation is conducted by the psychiatrist, or psychiatric resident supervised by an attending psychiatrist, who makes the mental status evaluation, establishes an initial diagnosis, assesses the individual's psychological assets and deficits (HRC has worked out a form to assist in this process), and, if indicated, prescribes a course of psychotropic medication. The social worker assesses the socio-environmental assets and liabilities, such as quality of housing, income, and family and other community support systems. The nurse assesses the individual's health* by taking a complete history of past illnesses, investigates dietary habits and special needs, arranges for complete medical examination and all indicated laboratory work-up—in this, the spectrum of services available in a general hospital are drawn on. The occupational therapist evaluates manual dexterity, attention span, and such daily living skills as ability to carry out household chores. The teacher evaluates functional reading

---

*At HRC, even the individual's dental problems and foot problems are considered and dealt with as important parts of the total rehabilitative process. Experience has shown that deficits in these areas are strong barriers to development of self-esteem, which is the ultimate goal of the program. For instance, if your teeth are bad or your feet hurt you have a general feeling of malaise and then cannot smile and, consequently, are less able to relate to others and will continue the pattern of isolation.

levels and mathematical ability. The vocational rehabilitation counselor determines a history of work experience, occupational skills, and work attitudes. The vocational evaluator measures work capacity, interests, and abilities in special areas through use of a variety of assessment tools such as simulated work tasks. These professionals from seven disciplines together with appropriately trained paraprofessionals, constitute the therapeutic team that forms the basis of the treatment modality. Paraprofessionals trained at the Center work with the social workers, occupational therapists, vocational rehabilitation counselors, vocational evaluators, and teachers.

When the evaluation procedures have been completed, these evaluators meet to share their findings and recommend and agree on specific goals, both short-term and long-term, to determine the patient's course through the program. Although the goals are set at this staff meeting, the flexible nature of HRC's program permits and usually entails changes as the patient progresses through the course of treatment. In this way, the evaluation procedure allows staff to arrive at the individual "prescription" and reinforces the patient's motivation to follow the "prescription." The patient and staff are now ready to enter into the contract.

When a patient enters the program, a staff member, usually a paraprofessional, is assigned as case manager to the patient. The case manager is responsible for coordination and continuity of services for the patient both within the Center and in the community. He discusses and concludes the contract and assumes a number of responsibilities vis-à-vis the patient. He checks on the patient's daily attendance and reasons for nonattendance when necessary; makes home visits; seeks out contact with family or significant others; accompanies the patient to welfare office, court, and other outside agencies; schedules and conducts individual and group sessions. The case manager is the specific focal point for the individual patient. It is the case manager to whom the patient applies for help with problems, to whom incidents are reported by other staff, and by whom all information about the patient's progress and problems is brought to the regularly scheduled team meetings for discussion and decision.

In the program, the patient's day consists mainly of participation in group activities geared to development of social, cognitive, and vocational skills. The characteristics of these group activities are those generally found in psychosocial rehabilitation programs. Group interaction is constant during all activities and in discussion periods. Each patient participates in the group activities most indicated for dealing with his individual deficits. All patients progress step by step to higher levels of functioning through exposure to increasing stress and incremental social, educational, and vocational skill mastery. All patients also take part in discussion groups, which range from general rap sessions to group therapy and special problem groups. Examples of problem groups are: mothers group, which provides a forum for problems related to children; alcoholism prevention group, which helps problem drinkers; the "world of work" group, which addresses common anxieties and deals with information related to employment.

During his stay in the program, the patient has an opportunity to receive academic instruction, which ranges from basic literacy skills to college brush-up, though the largest number of patients enroll in high school equivalency courses. Opportunity is provided for acquiring such daily living skills as food shopping, cooking, care of clothing, sewing, household management, use of public transport; and for learning good work habits and appropriate work attitudes and some vocational skills. Work habits, attitudes, and skills are assimilated through participation in the Center's building maintenance program and the patient-operated Unique Boutique (a small thrift shop so named by the patients).

The last step of the rehabilitation process is the Transitional Employment Program, pioneered by Fountain House. Patients in this program are placed for three to six months in part-time jobs where they are trained and periodically supervised by a staff member. They spend the other half day in the Center involved in therapeutic activities, education, or training. This method has proved to be extremely successful for patients with no work history. It provides them with a real job with real pay, with support while in and out of the job, and with job references—crucial for future employment. For employers there is a chance to learn about the value of the handicapped worker.

One evening per month at HRC, four hours are devoted to follow-up of patients who have reached their maximum level of achievement in the program, who are able to function outside of the day program, and who are in training, pursuing higher education, employed, or taking care of the home. The aims of the follow-up program are to retain the clinical gains, to provide support during the critical period of reintegration into the community full time, and to detect early signs of decompensation and provide the indicated crisis intervention. For psychiatric, vocational, social, and nursing services, discharged patients can call on the follow-up staff, who also serve the day program, and are thus available to follow-up patients on an as-needed basis at all times when the Center is open. Approximately 80–100 patients are served in this manner at any one time over periods of one to five years or more after discharge from the day treatment program.

Some years ago, follow-up patients expressed their positive attitude toward this service component by forming a social club, which they named the Rainbow Social Club. The club is governed by elected officers and organizes dances, outings, and other social events to which day patients are invited. These events serve as socialization opportunities that also give day patients exposure to a new kind of role model: the functioning ex-patient. The interaction of the day program and follow-up program, involving both patients and staff, results in continuity of care and continuity in time.

The continuity that is achieved at HRC is made possible by the outreach practiced in enrolling and assuring attendance of patients, maintenance of contact while the patient is absent from the Center for physical or psychiatric hospitalization, and encouragement of participation in the follow-up program. The coordinated interdisciplinary program of HRC and the continuity that is achieved is possible because the members of the therapeutic teams meet frequently for case discussions, staff role clarification, and patient goal reorientation. The two hours from 3:00 P.M. to 5:00 P.M. each day, after day patients have left the Center, are set aside for staff activities such as administrative decision making and program planning, therapeutic team meetings, in-service training, twice-a-week sitting rounds and case conferences, and monthly meetings of the entire staff. These meetings serve two important functions. They assure appropriate service delivery and maintain staff morale. Maintenance of staff morale cannot be stressed too strongly for staff who must deal daily with chronicity. The slow progress, frequent setbacks, and absence of dramatic improvement often cause apathy, hopelessness, disinterest, and feelings of inadequacy. An opportunity to be heard, appreciated, supported, and stimulated to contribute new ideas by peers and supervisors recharges the energies constantly drained by demands of a very needy patient population.

Harlem Rehabilitation Center conducts a comprehensive treatment program where the psychiatrist is integral to the treatment modality and where fragmentation is avoided, giving HRC its special character. A wide range of psychiatric treatment methods, such as group and individual psychotherapy and psychopharmacology, are provided. The full-time presence of psychiatric staff and nursing staff is a distinct advantage. It makes possible daily contact with the patient, while the patient encounters stress-provoking situations, and immediate intervention, if needed, with appropriate therapy, including types and dosages of medication. Paradoxically, it also makes possible less use of medication. Should the patient decompensate, early signs can be detected immediately and dealt with. Resistance to medication because of patients' fears of side-effects can also be diminished since the patient has access to immediate intervention. Should a psychiatric emergency arise, such as psychotic decompensation or acute suicidal ideation, intervention can be provided at once in the Center and, if needed, in the holding unit of the hospital's psychiatric emergency room overnight (frequently under direct observation of the resident who dealt with the patient's emergency at the Center). Often this avoids the need for hospitalization, but if necessary the patient can be hospitalized in the intensive care unit of the psychiatry department. All professionals in the department of psychiatry interact in patient care; this leads to coordination of services and continuity of care. A patient from the rehabilitation unit if hospitalized in the intensive care unit will likely have contact with psychiatrists, nurses, and social workers whom he already knows. The environment is, thus, less threatening, and trust can be established more easily. Because the psychiatrists and other professionals in the HRC program are on the staff of the hospital's department of psychiatry, all facilities of the hospital are available with minimum liaison problems.

The intrapsychic, interpersonal, instrumental, educational, and vocational aspects of rehabilitation coexist and interact at HRC to enable the patient to achieve his optimal role in society. Defining when an individual has in fact reached his highest potential is difficult. Often it is done by trial and error. However, there seem to be two major tests that are universally accepted: is the individual engaged in work, and is his quality of life good, is he reasonably independent in a suitable community setting.

I was curious to learn how patients coped with life after having been treated in the rehabilitation program. In 1977, I reviewed 22 patients who had been systematically followed for five years after completing the program successfully. I found that 16 of them could be considered as having achieved and maintained satisfactory levels of functioning, with 13 gainfully employed and 3 capably taking care of the home. This represents approximately 70% success. That same year, I reviewed the status of 121 patients admitted during the previous calendar year. The patients from this group who had left the program fell into three categories: those who had completed successfully, those who had dropped out, and those who had been discharged because of behavior problems. These three categories of patients were compared with each other according to age, sex, education, diagnosis, and number of hospitalizations. They were found to be similar in all characteristics except for sex: males were more likely to be discharged because of behavior problems. Of the patients who had completed successfully, 86% were functioning well in their roles, with 43% competitively employed, 31% in training or in sheltered employment, and 12% taking care of the home.

These two studies, despite the difference in time factor, showed similar results—that completing the program is highly related to good outcome. This suggests strongly that patients improve in their ability to function because they gain from their treatment. My experience at HRC reinforces my belief that for many patients disability caused by the combination of mental illness and social handicaps is reversible.

The program and results described in this chapter are those of a component of a psychiatric unit of a general hospital. Psychiatric units were developed in general hospitals because of their easy accessibility in the community. It was hoped that by providing crisis intervention and short-term hospitalization close to the home, chronicity could be avoided. President Kennedy in 1963, when calling for the establishment of comprehensive community mental health centers, stated that "ideally, the center could be located at an appropriate community general hospital" (3). Psychiatric units in general hospitals responded to this and, in many instances, increased the number of inpatient beds and added other elements of service, such as emergency, outpatient, and consultation. However, rehabilitation, seen by the Joint Commission on Mental Illness and Health (4) in 1961 as an essential part of all services for the mentally ill, was not among the new services added.

As reported by Greenhill (5) in 1979, "by 1971 the largest proportion of psychiatric inpatients and outpatients—30%—were treated in general hospital services." Who are the patients who seek help at a general hospital? At Harlem, the psychiatric emergency room receives a large number of patients—40–60%—with a history of two or more hospitalizations, of whom 75% are estimated to be in need of improving their coping skills (6); over half of the patients at HRC also suffer from physical illnesses. It is clear from these statistics that at Harlem Hospital, and very likely at other general hospitals, patients coming to the psychiatry unit are in need of three types of service: general psychiatric, medical, and rehabilitative. On the other hand, a sizeable group of patients treated at a general hospital for medical-surgical illnesses that have a chronic course develop psychological, social, and vocational dysfunctions. For such patients the approach to reinstatement to satisfactory life is the same in principle and practice as it is for psychiatric patients. A department of psychiatry in a general hospital can and should assume leadership for pinpointing the presence of psychological components in medical-surgical chronicity and recommending rehabilitative intervention as developed and practiced in psychiatric rehabilitation facilities. Provision of rehabilitative services based on the biopsychosocial model seems to have the best chance for correcting all deficits in the patient. As a locus, the general hospital presents an advantage and a challenging opportunity. Provided it is a teaching hospital, it can also be the locus for an effective training program.

The crucial and fundamental need for appropriately trained professionals to care for the chronic psychiatrically ill is well documented, most recently by the President's Commission on Mental Health (7) when stating that "the chronically mentally disabled . . . need dedicated and specially trained personnel to care for them" and that "it must be understood that high quality services . . . can only be ensured when dedicated employees are recruited, properly trained, and equitably rewarded."

All professional service providers in the department of psychiatry are the ideal target population for such training. In addition, because HHC is a teaching hospital, medical students, residents, student nurses, and students in the related disciplines all are placed, for varying lengths of time, in the department of psychiatry. Role models for each of these students, so important in the development of career choice, are already in place. The students who are placed in the rehabilitation component of the department of psychiatry, except for medical students and residents, are extending their professional education in an area basic to the goals of that education but also are adding a psychiatric dimension. The psychiatric resident is for the first time viewing mental illness and health from a new vantage point. He is called on to apply his assessment and treatment skills to a broader perception of the patient by going beyond identification of pathology to consider assets and liabilities of the personality. As Kolb (8) has commented, "In our professional training as psychopathologists we more or less consistently occluded and overlooked other aspects of personality organization."

Traditional training of psychiatric residents based on separation of inpatient and outpatient assignments deprives the resident of the opportunity to observe patients over time and, thus, to recognize the importance of continuity of care. Because general hospitals have not usually stressed care of the chronically ill, and the resident's rotation to a state hospital affords him only a partial and skewed view of chronic illness, he fails to learn the importance of disability as part of chronic illness and, certainly, how to treat the disability. Because in most traditional programs there is little exposure to principles of socialization and rehabilitation, psychiatric training ignores an increasingly important aspect of professional competence: functioning as a psychiatrist in a rehabilitation program and assuming a role as a member of the treatment team in such a program. Rotation to the psychiatric rehabilitation component of the general hospital's department of psychiatry, as at Harlem, will fill this gap in professional preparation. Such exposure for residents will make psychiatrists better diagnosticians, therapists, and consultants, whatever they concentrate on eventually, but, most importantly, it may influence them to devote their careers to the chronically ill.

A strong belief in the need to provide such training led to its institution at Harlem Hospital Center Department of Psychiatry by its director, Dr. Elizabeth B. Davis, and the training has been taking place at Harlem Rehabilitation Center since 1975.

NOTES

1. Bennett DH: Principles underlying a new rehabilitation workshop. In Wing JK, Hailey AM (eds): Evaluating A Community Psychiatric Service: The Camberwell Register 1964–71. London, Oxford University Press, 1972

2. Christmas, JJ: Rehabilitation—General and specific considerations. Psychiat Ann 4:24–28, 1974

3. Kennedy JF: Message from the President of the United States Relative to Mental Illness and Mental Retardation, 88th Congress, 5 February 1963, H.R. Document #5

4. Joint Commission on Mental Illness and Health: Action for Mental Health, Final Report. New York, Basic Books, 1961

5. Greenhill MH: Psychiatric units in general hospitals: 1979. Hosp & Comm Psychiatry 30:169–182, 1979

6. Hetrick E: Personal communication from Emory Hetrick, M.D., Chief, Psychiatric Emergency Treatment and Crisis Intervention Service, Department of Psychiatry, Harlem Hospital Center, 1977

7. The President's Commission on Mental Health, Report of Task Force Panel on Deinstitutionalization, Rehabilitation, and Long Term Care, 15 February, 1979

8. Kolb LC: Ego Assets: An Overlooked Aspect of Personality Organization. Symposium of Manhattan Federation of Rehabilitation Agencies, New York, 1978

Chapter 13

A PRIVATE PRACTICE MODEL

Douglas R. Bey, Jr.
Robert E. Chapman
Robert A. Kooker
John J. Schetz
Paul L. Taylor

This chapter describes our private psychiatric group's work with chronic mental patients in our community. We will stress those aspects of our involvement which seem to us to be of particular value to this patient population as well as those areas which may be somewhat innovative. We have much room for improvement, and it is not our intention to present these techniques as an ideal model. Further, our professional background and our community will differ from those of other private practitioners, and therefore, our methods may have limited application to their work.

OUR PSYCHIATRIC GROUP

Our eight-year-old private psychiatric practice is located in Normal, Illinois. We are a group of three adult and one child board-certified psychiatrists and one Ph.D. clinical psychologist.* We provide primary psychiatric care for a medical population of approximately 200,000. We are active staff members of five general hospitals. The nearest of these is within two blocks of our offices, and

*Since this paper was written we have added an additional board-certified psychiatrist and two additional Ph.D. clinical psychologists to our group.

this hospital contains our psychiatric inpatient service. We began this service by admitting our psychiatric patients to a general medical floor. Although our inpatient population has grown, we have resisted attempts to make this area of the hospital into a solely psychiatric unit. On this service, we treat the entire gamut of psychiatric illness, utilizing a comprehensive range of recreational, occupational, social, somatic, and psychological services. However, we continue to have nonpsychiatric patients in with our patients. As a result the psychiatric nurses who work with our patients also perform medical nursing services for the nonpsychiatric patients. (We feel this dual capability benefits both types of patients.) Also, the integrated service arrangement has had an educational impact on our community. It is one thing to read a pamphlet or hear a lecture to the effect that "mental illness is an illness like any other" and quite another experience to have a hospital roommate who is being treated for a psychiatric illness. Psychiatric patients and their families find it easier to enter this typical hospital atmosphere, which holds less of a stigma for them. Finally, the atmosphere of a hospital medical ward seems to have the effect of encouraging appropriate behavior.

In our practice, we see acute and chronic psychiatric patients of all ages and socioeconomic classes. The sources of payment may be public or private, but the services provided for the chronic patients are essentially the same.

The four psychiatrists in our group rotate night call one week at a time and make rounds on Saturday and Sunday when on call. Office patients coming for medication visits will usually see the same psychiatrist but over a period of time will likely see several if not all of the group's psychiatrists. Thus, our call system and office coverage enables our chronic patients and their families to become acquainted with all of the psychiatrists in our group. They know that one of us is always available to them 24 hours a day, seven days a week, and that emergency consultation and hospitalization is always available if needed. Further, if any agency wishes to refer a client on an emergency basis, it may do so without an appointment. This relationship with our group and assurance of our availability serves to reduce the stress experienced by chronic patients when one or more psychiatrist is out of the office and has, we believe, enabled many patients to avoid hospitalization. The group approach to the treatment of our chronic patients tends to lessen the intensity of the attachment to the individual physician. Instead, the relationship becomes one of a more generalized attachment to the entire group (including our office staff and the office itself).

Our offices consist of three suites in the same medical building where we began our practice eight years ago. Two of our office workers have been with us for eight years, while the other six have subsequently joined us. There has been very little turnover among office personnel. Most of the staff have been local residents for many years. The majority have had experience in local agencies or hospitals prior to joining us, and thus were already acquainted with many of our chronic patients. Because of their familiarity with the patients, our staff are able to judge when to refer calls to us and when to tell a patient to come in to the office at once for a visit. Patients and their families often call the office to talk with staff members with whom they have developed a relationship over the years. The rotation of the psychiatrists and the more generalized transference to the group tends to lessen the emotional drain on the individual physician in his work with the chronic mental patients. In reading of Otto Wills and Frieda Fromm Reichmann's work with schizophrenic patients, Madame Sechehaye's description of her therapy of a schizophrenic girl (1), Des Laurier's movement therapy, Moreno's psychodrama, J. N. Rosen's direct interpretive approach, one cannot help but wonder how these individuals could achieve successful results with chronically ill patients with such a diversity of theoretical techniques.

Kurt Goldstein (2) attempted to explain the common elements of various therapists' work with schizophrenic patients. He noted that some of these were a face-to-face, physically close relationship between therapist and patient; an avoidance of abstract ideas (and, in fact, a neglect of content); and behavior by the therapist that makes the patient feel that there is not so much difference between his world and the therapist's world. Other common elements mentioned by Goldstein were endurance, courage, and deep devotion to one's work.

In our group's relationship with chronic patients, we respond to their physical complaints in a concrete manner and examine them physically. Our focus is on their physical status, medication, and their chronic mental illness (which we may also discuss in concrete terms with them). We concur with Dr. Goldstein's impressions and emphasize that the above therapists stayed with their chronic patients over a long period of time sustained by their desire to prove their techniques were effective. Not having this stamina and lacking the zeal for a particular theory, we have substituted the group approach to our patient's care to keep us going over the long haul. This approach also provides us with continual peer review and a fresh look at each case. Communication on a daily basis is a requirement imposed by this approach which also forces us to establish general principles of treatment upon which we all agree.

We attempted at one point to reduce treatment costs by establishing a lithium clinic (3) for chronic patients on this medication. The clinic was run by a registered nurse who met with patients as a group to review their lithium levels, instruct them regarding their medication, and answer their questions. The cost was $5.00 for an hour session. Patients, however, preferred to pay the additional $15.00 for an individual office visit with a psychiatrist. We also considered structurally combining our three office suites in the service of increased efficiency, reduced staff requirements, and smoother patient flow. This idea was also discarded when we found that our patients and their families preferred the relative privacy and more personal setting of individual suites and waiting rooms.

RELATIONSHIP TO THE COMMUNITY

When discussing our work with chronic mental patients, we cannot overemphasize the importance of our group's background and relationship to our community. What is often omitted in discussions of organizational and community consultation, is the background, training, and experience of the consultants, as well as the informal relationships they have with their consultees. In this chapter, we emphasize the medical model, the psychiatrist as a primary physician, our attention to general medical problems and to psychotropic medications. In order to provide an accurate description of our work, we must also acknowledge that we all trained in psychoanalytically oriented programs; we have all had considerable training and experience in individual, group, and family psychotherapy; and we have worked and published in the areas of organizational and community mental health consultation. This background and training is not left at the door when we see our chronic patients for a medication visit nor is it forgotten in our work with the community. Further, we feel that our deep involvement in our own community has enabled us (and has influenced us) to practice in our present manner. One psychiatrist in our group was reared in our community. Another was director of the local Mental Health Center for two years and initiated the inpatient services in the general hospital before beginning private practice eight years ago. Our group is on the active staffs of five general hospitals in the area. We have service contracts with 11 agencies and provide indirect (staff consultation) services to five of these agencies. We are all faculty members of a nearby medical school and lecture at two local schools of nursing whose students rotate through our psychiatric inpatient service. Our professional staff and their wives have served as officers or chairpersons of 17 community boards and organizations not directly related to mental health services and on 18 boards of organizations which are directly involved with mental health services in the community. Although 90% of this community service was performed by the two senior group members and their wives, we anticipate that a much greater involvement will ensue as the newer members of our group and their spouses become rooted in the community. As our practice continues, we find ourselves treating various members of the same families. In our setting, we seldom lose patients for any length of time and thus continue to see our failures as well as our successes. We work "in a fishbowl" in that our efforts and results are observable by the community. We are provided in this way with feedback as to the effectiveness of our methods. Businesses and medical practices in this small town atmosphere seek to satisfy customers and patients in a way that a lifelong positive relationship is established.

PAYMENT FOR TREATMENT

In a January 1979 brochure of the American Psychiatric Association, an article appeared entitled "Call to Action for Chronically Ill." This article quoted the "Call to Action" publication and urged psychiatrists and other physicians to take an active role in attending to this patient population. One important area which was not discussed in this brief article was: Who pays private practitioners for their involvement with the chronic patients? How can private psychiatrists be involved in a way that their unique talents may be most efficiently and economically utilized? We believe the system of care in which we are presently involved does provide answers to these questions in our community.

Illinois has gone from psychiatric treatment in large state hospitals to emphasis on the care and treatment of the mentally ill in community facilities. The local Mental Health Center was given primary responsibility for the sustaining follow-up care of chronic mental patients in our region. Many of these patients were transferred from the state hospitals to local nursing and sheltered care homes. Most of them were receiving psychotropic medications in combinations and dosages which the local nursing home physicians were not accustomed to prescribing. Initially, the Mental Health Center thought it necessary to hire their own psychiatrist. The cost to the agency was $30,000–40,000 a year, plus benefits for a psychiatrist to do outpatient work. Psychiatrists who applied for this position were unwilling and physically unable to do additional inpatient work or to be continually on call. Their work for the Center consisted of medication evaluations and follow-up visits, supervision of mental health workers, psychotherapy, administration, and program planning. Emergency (after-hours) consultation and inpatient treatment were provided by our group via a contractual arrangement with the Mental Health Center and with the State Department of Mental Health. Following the resignation and departure of four consecutive psychiatrists from the Mental Health Center, a contract was established between our group and that agency to see any patients they might refer for any service we had to offer. The services requested have primarily been emergency outpatient consultation, medication evaluation visits, medication follow-up visits for chronic mental patients, and some forensic cases. The patients are seen in our offices and are usually accompanied by a referral or progress note from the Center. A copy of our progress or consultation note goes to the Mental Health Center, which pays for the patient's visit. We are pleased with this arrangement, since we do not have to be concerned about payment and we are primarily asked questions as to the patient's medical-psychiatric status, which we feel qualified to answer. Further, we feel we are able to provide good care for these chronic patients, whom we may see whenever and for as long as we feel appropriate. The Mental Health Center is pleased with the arrangement, since they have found that they now have four psychiatrists available to them 24 hours a day, seven days a week, for less total money than they were paying for one in-house psychiatrist. Therapy supervision, program planning, sustaining care supervision, day treatment center supervision, and other nonmedical activities that are used by these patients are now conducted by the Center's clinical director, who is a Ph.D. psychologist. The clinical director shares with us his ideas and plans and welcomes our suggestions. The acceptance of this arrangement and the support of the State Department of Mental Health, have led to similar contracts with 11 agencies within a 30-mile radius. In addition, we provide indirect (staff consultation) services to five of these agencies. Some common elements (explicit and implicit) of these contracts are as follows:

1. We are paid on a fee for service basis at our usual and customary rate by the agency.
2. If the patient has resources for payment, the agency collects from the patient with a sliding fee scale.
3. Patients referred by agencies are regarded as the agencies clients. Our role is one of patient-centered consultant, who makes recommendations regarding medication, laboratory tests, other medical consultations, treatment, and follow-up visits, with the understanding that the agency may choose to disagree or ignore these recommendations. (In practice this seldom happens.)
4. We have the right to refuse a referral. (This rarely occurs.)
5. Implicit in the contract is the understanding that the agency and our group are free agents who have a peer relationship. The agencies buy specific services for the clients from us, and we may refer patients to them for specific services. In some instances, our patients become primarily their clients, while in others we may remain the primary providers to patients who purchase specific services from the agencies.
6. The contracts are renegotiated annually.
7. Payment arrangements are reviewed by the agencies' boards of directors. Committees from the boards meet with us to discuss the contracts and our services.
8. No member of our staff or their families serve as advisors or as board members of agencies with which we have contractual agreements. Constant vigilance is maintained to avoid a conflict of interest situation.
9. No concensus is necessary as to the appropriate theoretical approach to a client. Our communication with referring agencies is primarily in the area of the service we provide.

The community is pleased with this arrangement. There is one class of treatment for chronic mental patients (rather than a dual system of private and public), which is local and makes available a wide range of services.

THE MEDICAL MODEL

We regard the chronic mental patient as a medical patient with a chronic mental disease. Chronic mental disease like any chronic condition often requires little active medical treatment and greater rehabilitative, socialization, and educational efforts. The goal is to help the individual work around a residual handicap and to function as well as possible. Our approach to the newly diagnosed potentially chronic patient and the family is similar to that of any physician discussing with a patient the diagnosis of a serious chronic illness. After careful evaluation, and in some instances a trial of treatment, we present to the patient and the family our findings and encourage them to consider a referral to other psychiatrists for a second opinion. In our experience, failure to discuss the diagnosis and prognosis with the patient and family often leads to disappointment later when the patient is not "cured." This disappointment may lead them to seek "miracle cures" and practitioners who may instill false hope of an end to the chronic illness.

Occasionally, an agency (e.g., the jail or a developmentally disabled service) may refer patients with behavioral problems which are not secondary to a mental illness. In these cases, we indicate that medication, while often helpful in modification of behavioral symptoms secondary to mental disease, should not be used for the control of disruptive behavior. A patient may be referred for medication evaluation when the problem is actually one of countertransference or an organizational problem within the agency. In these cases, we may discuss our findings with the appropriate agency member and suggest some alternative approaches.

A not infrequent cause for referral is a sudden change in a patient's behavior which is the result of a covert nonpsychiatric medical condition (e.g., a patient who suddenly becomes psychotic is found to have a fecal impaction, a heart attack, an electrolyte imbalance, an organic brain syndrome secondary to medication, a stroke, or pneumonia). In this regard, we see ourselves as the chronic mental patient's primary physician. The patient and family often see us in this role and come to us with their medical problems. We assume this responsibility and examine, diagnose, and treat those routine medical problems within our capability or refer to appropriate medical colleagues when indicated. Chronic mental patients are weighed and their blood pressures are recorded by our office nurse before we see them. We routinely examine patients' fundi, check for neurological sequelae to their psychotropic medications, and listen to and examine patients pursuant to any physical complaints they might have. We believe it behooves the physician to exercise great care in examination and diagnosis of medical conditions in chronic mental patients who may not be capable of providing a coherent description of their symptoms. The chronic mental patient has many mental health helpers who can explain psychodynamically the alteration in the patient's behavior, while we are often the only professionals who can investigate the possible medical etiology of these changes. The nursing home staff and family physicians may tend to minimize or fail to appreciate the mental patient's complaints. They also see us as the primary physician in these cases. Therefore, we are particularly careful to investigate the medical and neurological aspects of our patients' symptoms and complaints in addition to the psychosocial aspects of their problems.

Frequently, chronically ill (and actively psychotic) mental patients have little or no insight into the fact that they are ill. As a result, they do not take important medication, or see the reason for appointments with a physician. Many of these patients benefit from long-acting injectable antipsychotic medication (fluphenazine decanoate). This medication provides us with a means to control these patients' psychotic symptoms. Through the use of this medication, many chronic patients are able to establish working relationships with us. In addition, they are able to make use of resocialization, vocational, educational, and rehabilitational programs aimed at reducing the limitations of function their illnesses have imposed on them (6). Visiting a physician's office on a regular basis for a shot is regarded by most patients as an acceptable medical procedure. Some patients have minimal therapeutic effect from high doses of oral medication but do well on long-acting injectable medication.

Our large patient population has enabled us to provide group therapy to patients with similar problems adjusting to their chronic mental illness. We foster the development of self-help groups among our patients and their families (e.g., families of chronic schizophrenic patients).

SUMMARY

We have attempted to describe a private psychiatric group's work with chronic mental patients. We have emphasized the importance of our community involvement and described a system of care and treatment of chronic mental patients whereby the private psychiatrist may be paid for services which make minimum demands on his time but which are very important to the total care of this group of patients. We emphasized the role of the psychiatrist as a primary physician in this system. Within this context, we feel the psychiatrist's adherence to the medical model is appropriate and psychotherapeutically advisable. Other community programs involved with the resocialization and rehabilitation of these patients find it cost effective to purchase medical-psychiatric services from the private sector for their clients. Consistency of professional and office staff and of location is helpful to our patients. The group practice approach to treatment and the availability of a familiar physician also are of value to these patients and their families.

DISCUSSION

Our program is not purported to be ideal. Psychotropic medications at best control the symptoms of our patients' illnesses. Hopefully, real "cures" will be forthcoming. While occupational centers, day programs, supervised apartments, and other programs are available in our community, many chronic patients reside in sheltered homes which remind the visitor of chronic wards in old state institutions. A new mental health code in our state protects the patient's rights but makes involuntary treatment of mental illness within the community nearly impossible. More should be done to educate patients' families as to what is known about these illnesses and what they may expect in the future.

While the understanding and acceptance of mental illness has increased in recent years, there remains some degree of confusion among professionals and lay citizens in these areas. Some professionals have in the past been outspoken in their criticism of medication and hospitalization of mental patients. Many of these nonmedical critics have mellowed over the years and currently accept the ancillary medical role in the care of their clients. The question appears to have changed from "Who knows best how to cure the patient?" to "What can we each do with what we've got?" As one consultant put it, "You talk as though you have an orchestra, when actually you have a cheap fiddle and you're doing a damn poor job of playing that!" At this point, it appears we are doing better with our fiddle, but we await the arrival of new instruments and more players.

NOTES

1. Sechehaye M: Symbolic Realization. New York, International University Press, 1951

2. Goldstein K: The organismic approach. In Arieti S (ed): American Handbook of Psychiatry (ed 2); Vol 1, The Foundations of Psychiatry. New York, Basic Books, 1974

3. Bey D, Chapman R, Tornquist K: A lithium clinic. American Journal Psychiatry 129(4):468–470, 1972

4. Bey D: Division psychiatry in Vietnam. American Journal of Psychiatry 127 (2):146–150, 1970

5. Bey D: Organizational consultation in a combat unit. American Journal Psychiatry 128(4):401–406, 1971

6. Marriott P: Personal Communication with Dr. Peter Marriott at the Melbourne Clinic, Melbourne, Australia, 1976

Chapter 14

A COMMUNITY MENTAL HEALTH CENTER MODEL

Paul R. Polak
Linda G. Mushkatel

Southwest Denver Community Mental Health Services, Inc. (SWDCMHS) is one practical working model for the provision of comprehensive, noninstitutional, community-based psychiatric services to the residents of its designated catchment area. The Center places highest priority on delivery of these services to the severely mentally disabled population of southwest Denver. In keeping with this philosophy, Southwest has developed a variety of treatment, support, and residential programs for the chronically disabled client. These programs will be the primary focus of the present chapter.

In the first section of the chapter, a brief overview of the Southwest Denver Mental Health Center system will be presented. The next two sections will provide a conceptual framework for tracing the development of the typical chronic schizophrenic client and describe the Southwest programs which currently are responding to the various needs of this population. The final section will consider future programming for the chronic client living in the community.

THE SOUTHWEST SYSTEM

The southwest Denver system originated as a cooperative endeavor between Southwest Denver Mental Health Center and a state hospital, Fort Logan Mental Health Center. In 1971, Fort Logan's geographically decentralized team was placed under the operational supervision of the mental health center director, and the intake process for both facilities was integrated into a single system. Crisis and social systems intervention became a routine part of intake for all clients, and a community-based inpatient alternative system was initiated. With the decrease in hospital admissions which resulted, Fort Logan staff serving southwest Denver clients were able to move into the community. In 1974, responsibility for adult psychiatric clients and the funding for their care were shifted officially from Fort Logan to Southwest Denver Community Mental Health Services, Inc.

With the support of its governing administrative board, SWDCMHS replaced traditional institutional care with a community-oriented system incorporating immediately responsive crisis services, home visitation and treatment, an inpatient family-sponsor system for the brief placement of acutely psychotic clients, appropriate social systems intervention, and long-term support and residential alternatives for the chronic client. These components of the total community care system have been described elsewere (1–4), and only the major features will be presented here.

Community Control through the Administrative Board

SWDCMHS has a citizen's administrative board, which is a governing rather than just an advisory board. The board is empowered to hire and fire the Center directors, set overall policy, and actively monitor ongoing programs. All board members reside in southwest Denver, and anyone who lives or works in southwest Denver, including Center clients, may vote in board elections. This structure ensures that the community care system is under the direct control of the community residents it serves.

Crisis Services

The majority of individuals or families who become clients at mental health facilities do so in a state of crisis. Therefore, the Center provides immediate crisis services for all clients at the point of entry into treatment. The crisis response system makes a home or family visit possible 24 hours a day, 7 days a week. The system is structured to ensure the availability at all times of an experienced clinician, a psychiatric nurse, and a psychiatrist.

Social Systems Intervention

Previous work indicated that social systems problems such as family upheavals were often more influential determinants of requests for mental health services than individual problems of the client *(5)*. Accordingly, all clinical services stress direct involvement with one or more of the social systems to which the client belongs if problems within these systems led to the request for mental health services. The initial crisis-oriented evaluation procedure generally occurs in the actual setting of the social systems involved (e.g., home, work). Attention to crisis resolution and social systems growth is routinely combined with work on the problems of the individual identified as the client.

Family-Sponsor System

A system of family-sponsor homes has been developed to replace hospitalization for the client in crisis *(1, 3, 6)*. When temporary or permanent separation from the client's natural living situation is indicated, the client can be placed with one of several carefully screened families living in southwest Denver, each of which provides a different type of family environment. Families accept up to two clients at one time as guests in their homes and contract with the Center to provide 24-hour care. Each family is assigned a staff coordinator responsible for supervision and support, and home sponsors meet regularly to learn from each other and from staff. The Center's psychiatric nurses are available to the families 24 hours a day by means of a bellboy paging system. Clients staying in these homes are seen in planning and treatment sessions by center staff every day until they are able to return to a more autonomous setting. Lasting personal relationships often develop between the family sponsors and clients, who frequently visit their sponsors long after formal treatment has been terminated.

Long-Term Support and Residential Alternatives

A variety of support and training activities have been combined with a broad range of noninstitutional living environments to meet the needs of the chronic client. These opportunities will be discussed in detail below.

As a result of the SWDCMHS system, the majority of southwest Denver adult clients, who otherwise might have been hospitalized, are routinely treated in the community. For the past five years, the community-based system has essentially replaced the psychiatric hospital for all adult clients from the catchment area who are treated by public mental health services. Table 14–1 illustrates the low rate of hospitalization for SWDCMHS: an average of one hospital bed per year for the entire catchment area of approximately 100,000 persons.

CHARACTERISTICS OF THE CHRONIC CLIENT

Two important issues must be taken into account when developing programs for the chronic client:

1. Clients identified as chronic schizophrenics generally have been prepared for careers in dependency, and treatment programs should be designed to promote autonomy to the fullest extent possible.
2. Chronic schizophrenics should not be stereotyped as a homogeneous population. In fact, there are several distinctive subpopulations requiring a variety of different kinds of services to meet their various patterns of need. Programs should be designed to provide as broad a range of alternatives as possible.

Chronic schizophrenia can be described best as a career in dependency. This career evolves in stages over time through an interaction between the individual and his immediate social environment. Because the social environment profoundly affects the behavior of the schizophrenic client, a logical conceptual framework for schizophrenia must address three areas:

The individual. This group of variables includes the psychological and physical characteristics of the individual, his genetic makeup, his personal history and adaptational style, and the characteristics of his illness if an illness is present.

Social systems. These include all of the small social systems in which the individual has membership and whose operations and upheavals have a direct impact on his life and illness. It also includes the broader social systems whose values about

Table 14–1.   Psychiatric Bed Usage for Southwest Denver Community Mental Health Center from FY 1973/1974 to FY 1977/1978

Rate	FY 1973/ 1974	FY 1974/ 1975	FY 1975/ 1976	FY 1976/ 1977	FY 1977/ 1978[a]
Total Bed Days Per 100,000 Population	836	385	129	126	467
Average Daily Hospital Bed Occupancy Per 100,000 Population	2.3	1.1	0.3	0.3	1.3

[a] In fiscal year 1977/1978 hospital bed days increased due to a change in policy at Fort Logan Mental Health Center, in which a lockable unit was established. This change resulted in some clients from Southwest Denver being treated in this unit who in previous years had been in locked units of nursing homes.

madness have impact on what happens to him. The upheavals of families, lovers, and the work place often are the key determinants of what is presented to us as schizophrenic behavior.

The environment. The environment refers to access to food, shelter, money, and work. Also included are the characteristics of the physical environment that make those key determinants of survival more or less accessible, as well as the characteristics of environmental change.

It has been our experience that the development of schizophrenic symptoms occurs under circumstances of social systems and environmental stress. If such transient psychotic symptoms occur in an immediate social environment in which they prove to have survival value, or if they are consistently positively reinforced, they are likely to persist and a diagnosis of schizophrenia is likely to be made. A genetic predisposition toward the development and persistence of schizophrenic symptoms interacts with these three groups of variables, and if dependency-enhancing training grounds are at hand, a full-fledged career in dependency may evolve among individuals identified as chronic schizophrenics.

Early training for such a specialized career often occurs when the individual develops schizophrenic symptoms within the specific social environment of a family that enhances dependency and undercuts autonomy. The young, unemancipated schizophrenic client, living at home with his parents under such conditions, receives an excellent lesson on how to manipulate dependency-enhancing organizations to his advantage.

The next step typically involves admission to a psychiatric hospital at the height of a family crisis. If at this point the client has the added misfortune of being admitted to a large, bureaucratic, dependency-enhancing psychiatric institution, he is at risk of having the basic pattern of a career in dependency set for life. Learned dependency skills can be practiced and refined in general hospital emergency rooms, with representatives of the social welfare system, in nursing homes, or in boarding homes.

Environmental factors also are strong determinants of a career in dependency. Most chronic schizophrenic clients are poor and have the same problems with the survival issues of food, shelter, income, and work that all poor people do. However, chronic psychiatric clients differ significantly from other poor people in two key areas:

1. Their backgrounds in families that treated them like invalids and their long stays in dependency-enhancing institutions often leave them with fewer skills in work and basic survival than most other poor people.
2. Their symptoms of illness may aggravate those deficiencies, but they offer the distinct advantage of providing eligibility for a variety of government subsidies, living settings, and service programs that continue to meet dependency needs.

The programs described below are geared to promoting client autonomy to the fullest extent possible in such survival areas as food, housing, self-care, and work. Not only are programs designed to enhance client autonomy, but also they are structured to provide a broad range of housing and training opportunities in order to meet the many different patterns of client needs. In a recent study which identified the needs of the chronically mentally disabled in southwest Denver, Kirby et al. (7) demonstrated that these clients do not constitute a homogeneous population. For example, significant variation exists in their demographic characteristics, work abilities, and community survival skills. Consequently, programming must be tailored to meet a heterogeneous set of requirements.

SOUTHWEST PROGRAMS FOR THE CHRONIC CLIENT

About one year ago, the specialized PINE (People in New Environments) team, composed of therapists, psychiatric nurses, and volunteers, was established at the mental health center to work exclusively with chronically disabled clients. The team and its services were expanded when SWDCMHS was designated the demonstration site for Colorado's National Institute of Mental Health–funded community support system. One team clinician is assigned to each chronic client upon admission to the Center, and this same clinician serves as case manager in coordinating all treatment and support activities throughout the client's treatment.

The team provides individual, marital, and family psychotherapy as well as a program designed to meet the specific community needs of the chronic client population. Program components include medication, social and recreational activities, community survival skill training, a variety of residential environments, and a graduated system of vocational opportunities.

Medication

A general trend in current psychiatric practice is to undermedicate acute schizophrenic clients while overmedicating chronic schizophrenic clients. SWDCMHS departs from this pattern by utilizing a system of rapid tranquilization (8) for clients experiencing acute crisis and of carefully monitored maintenance medication for clients who no longer exhibit extreme symptoms. This medication process significantly reduces the need for psychiatric hospitalization and promotes community-based care.

All clinicians are thoroughly trained in the therapeutic and side effects of psychotropic medication. The PINE team staff is responsible for monitoring the use of medication, and they meet regularly with the psychiatrist and client at a medication clinic to review and adjust medications. A special group for prolixin users meets every other week to educate the clients about medications and to provide an opportunity for clients to discuss physical concerns with a physician.

The PINE team expects the client to play a responsible role in taking medication as prescribed and in monitoring its effects. This goal often requires extensive persuasion and the support of significant others, especially for clients with histories of repeated hospitalizations.

Social-Recreational Activities

A number of ongoing groups meet regularly with the objectives of decreasing client isolation and improving social interaction skills.

Separate men's and women's groups, as well as mixed groups, participate in such activities as eating out; attending sporting events, con-
certs and movies; going on overnight hikes; and working on crafts.
Clients frequently plan and organize these activities.

Community Survival Skills

In order to maintain themselves in the community, chronically
disabled clients must be able to perform appropriately in six critical
areas: (1) work, school, volunteerism; (2) cooking; (3) self-care; (4)
housekeeping; (5) transportation; and (6) elimination of troublesome
behavior that often can lead to institutionalization. Clients vary in
the degrees of dependency and autonomy they display in each of
these categories. Table 14-2 displays the extremes of dependency
and autonomy observable in each of these areas.

The PINE team offers a number of time-limited courses to
individuals and groups, aimed at increasing their capacity to carry
out these community survival activities. Courses cover such topics
as grocery shopping, cooking, nutrition, grooming, budgeting
money, and getting along with roommates.

Student and community volunteers play major roles in the social-recreational and community survival training activities. Their
involvement substantially increases the number of staff hours available for these components and the degree of individualization possible. For example, a student volunteer teaching a client transportation
skills can follow the entire process from obtaining and learning to
read bus schedules, to mapping routes, to riding these routes along
with the client during the actual hours when the bus will be used.
Similar individually tailored training is made possible in other community survival areas as well.

Residential Settings

One primary objective of the residential component is to reduce
the number of chronic clients living in either institutional settings or
substandard housing and to place them instead in appropriate, high-
quality housing which is noninstitutional in character. The continuum of residential settings either in place or being developed for
chronically disabled clients in southwest Denver range from autonomous apartment living to intensively supervised settings. These living situations are designed to meet the specific capabilities and needs
of individual clients. Living arrangements and clients are matched

Table 14–2. Six Critical Areas of Client Performance

Area	Dependency ←——— 1	2	3	4	5 ———→ Autonomy
1. Work, School, Volunteerism	No income production		Sheltered work		Competitive employment
2. Cooking	All meals must be prepared and served				Provides all meals for self either by home cooking or eating out
3. Self-care	Poor grooming; erratic sleeping and eating; poor health maintenance				Well-groomed; good health maintenance; good judgment in sleeping, eating, etc.
4. Housekeeping	No concern or ability to carry out routine cleaning and housekeeping				Can keep up living environment without supervision
5. Transportation	Unwilling or unable to get to shopping, work, or recreation outside of home				Capable and motivated to transport self to work, shopping, recreation
6. Elimination of Troublesome Behavior	Frequent assaultiveness, suicidal behavior, inappropriate sexuality, substance abuse, or severe disabling withdrawal				No troublesome or provocative behavior

according to their abilities in each of the performance areas described above. Table 14-3 presents a matrix for matching clients and living situations, with each setting occupying a different position on the dependency/autonomy continuum.

In southwest Denver, the majority of chronic clients are either living with their natural families (6) or in one of the community apartment settings. Boarding and nursing homes are used for a small number of clients (about ten) who require the specialized services of such settings because of very specific combinations of organic and psychiatric disabilities. As residential options are expanded, the PINE team hopes to reduce even this small number.

Housing support provided by the Department of Housing and Urban Development (HUD) has enabled the mental health center to substantially increase the number of high-quality residential settings available. The Center was instrumental in broadening the eligibility requirements of HUD Section 8 Rent Subsidies for Existing Housing to include the chronically disabled psychiatric client. Under this program, the Center has placed 25 clients into apartments throughout the catchment area. The apartments now include autonomous settings and moderately supervised scatter and clustered housing; intensively supervised settings are being developed. The recent award of a HUD 202 demonstration grant for new construction to house the chronically disabled will provide support for intensively supervised apartment settings with a live-in supervisor.

Clients living in housing subsidized by HUD Section 8 pay approximately one-quarter of their total income for rent; the remaining rent cost is covered by the HUD subsidy. Rent subsidy levels are specified by HUD according to the fair-market value of housing in the geographical area in which the subsidy is used.

The PINE team requires that clients living in HUD-subsidized housing participate in some form of productive activity away from their residence each day and that they reponsibly maintain their apartments and pay their share of the rent. Therapeutic contracts are drawn up between clients and the team, delineating expected performance in such areas as rent payment, treatment fee payment, work or school-related activities, participation in PINE-sponsored programs, and independent activities. Compliance with the terms of their contracts is a prerequisite for continuing participation in the HUD residential program.

Living in a HUD-subsidized apartment has become a status symbol among clients, and proving that they are capable of living in their own apartments has become a strong motivator for them to improve their community survival skills.

Table 14-3. Degree of Autonomy/Dependency Associated with Residential Environments for the Chronically Disabled, Using Six Critical Variables

	Work	Cooking	Self-care	Housekeeping	Transportation	Elimination of Troublesome Behavior
Autonomy (5)						
1. Autonomous home or apartment living	5	5	5	5	5	5
2. Moderately supervised scattered housing	4–5	5	5	5	5	4
3. Moderately supervised apartment clusters	3–5	5	5	5	4	4
4. Intensively supervised family settings	2–3	2–3	3	2–3	3	2–3
5. Intensively supervised social distance apartment where no roommate is required.	2–3	2–3	3	2–3	3	2–3
6. Intensively supervised group home setting	2–3	2–3	3	2–3	3	2–3
7. Boarding home	1–3	1	2	2	3	2–3
8. Nursing home	1–3	1	1	1	1–2	2–3
9. Acute family-sponsor settings	1	1–5	1–5	1–5	1	1
10. Hospital	1	1	1–5	1	1	1
Dependency (1)						

Vocational Settings

A key determinant of a client's return to a psychiatric institution is the ability to get and keep a job either in competitive employment or a sheltered workshop setting. In cooperation with other local agencies, Southwest offers a number of different prevocational and vocational programs, which vary in the level of work capacity expected of the client. This graduated system allows clients to begin at a low level and move upward as their confidence and work skills increase. For some clients, their maximum potential is reached at a low- or moderate-level work setting; for others, vocational programming leads to competitive employment. Four work settings currently available include an activity program, an evaluation and training program, sheltered work, and a transitional employment program.

The lowest level setting is the activity program, which provides work training and socialization activities for severely disabled clients who cannot function in even a subcompetitive environment. This program is available through an agreement with Fort Logan Mental Health Center. Work tasks are simple, and clients are paid on a piece-rate basis for properly completed work. Consistent attendance is not required, and when clients do attend, they are not required to work. The objectives of the activity program are for clients to work around others, build confidence, and gain exposure to following tasks to their completion.

The next work setting on the continuum is the evaluation and training program, provided by the Industrial Therapy Workshop, also through agreement with Fort Logan. Clients participate for a limited time and are constantly supervised at jobs of varying complexity subcontracted from community businesses. Participants are evaluated and trained in such work skills as attendance, punctuality, and relationships with coworkers and supervisors.

The Center contracts with Bayaud Industries, a separate nonprofit corporation, for the provision of long-term sheltered employment lasting from several months to several years. Clients are expected to participate in this program on a regularly scheduled basis. The nature of their work is similar to the subcontracted tasks carried out in the evaluation and training program, and they are paid either on a piece-rate or hourly basis.

The Transitional Employment Program (TEP), arranged by Bayaud Industries, places clients in community businesses for a three-to-six-month temporary stay. Clients are paid the company's entry-level wage for such jobs as janitors, warehouse workers, kitchen aides, or factory workers. A program coordinator is assigned for each TEP position to help supervise and train TEP employees. Upon completion of the program, some clients with good work records are hired as permanent employees; others move to different competitive work settings.

FUTURE PROGRAMMING

Future efforts will be directed at filling gaps in the residential and vocational opportunities available to severely disabled clients in southwest Denver. Many different community residential settings are already in place. The application of HUD Section 8 rent subsidies will be expanded to include intensively supervised family settings. These environments will use healthy families recruited by a procedure derived from our experience with the family system described earlier for acutely psychotic clients. Families will provide long-term home settings for chronic clients who cannot function in more autonomous community settings and who require intensive supervision and support in such areas as housekeeping and meal preparation, and close monitoring of medication. These settings will reduce further the need to place chronic clients in boarding or nursing homes.

At the present time, a variety of graduated work settings already are available for Southwest clients. These vocational opportunities will be expanded with the establishment of a client-run business which will draw upon the talents inherent in any group of disabled persons. The therapeutic business will provide the closest thing possible to a small, self-sufficient competitive business. The objectives of a therapeutic business are not only to be a source of income but also to provide income in a manner that enhances client self-esteem and status while requiring productive social interaction among client workers.

A successful therapeutic business must make a profit or break even. Hence, the client-run business must be competitive with similar businesses in the community. In order to offset the differential in work performance between chronically disabled clients and the general work force, a business activity providing a high profit margin should be selected. For example, moderately priced single-family dwellings requiring upgrading could be purchased and the remodeling carried out by clients. This activity would require many different tasks that could be matched to client work skills. Although the cost of remodeling might well be excessive because of the disability of the workers, the increase in house value at resale could more than offset the cost of remodeling.

SUMMARY

Chronically mentally ill individuals constitute a hetereogeneous population, characterized by well-developed careers in dependency. This chapter has described a comprehensive system of community-based services for chronic clients, designed to meet their various needs and to promote autonomous behavior to the fullest extent possible. The services described include medical care, social-recreational activities, community survival skill training, a variety of residential environments, and a graduated system of vocational opportunities. Future efforts to expand residential and vocational programs were discussed.

NOTES

1. Brook B, Cortes M, March R, Sundberg-Stirling M: Community families: An alternative to psychiatric hospital intensive care. Hosp and Comm Psych 27:195–197, 1976

2. Polak P: Social systems intervention. Arch Gen Psychiatr 24:110–117, 1971

3. Polak P: A system of alternatives to psychiatric hospitalization. In Stein LI, Test MA (eds): Alternatives to Mental Hospital Treatment. New York, Plenum, 1978

4. Polak PR, Kirby MW: A model to replace psychiatric hospitals. J Nerv Ment Dis 162:13–22, 1976

5. Polak P: The crisis of admission. Soc Psychiatr 2(4):150–157, 1967

6. Polak PR, Kirby MW, Deitchman WS: Treating acutely psychotic patients in private homes. New Directions for Mental Health Services 1:49–64, 1979

7. Kirby M, French S, Polak PR: Identifying the needs of the chronically mentally disabled. Paper presented to the Annual Meeting of the American Psychological Association, Toronto, Canada, August 1978

8. Polak PR: Rapid tranquilization. Am J Psychiatr 128:640–643, 1971

Chapter 15

A COMMUNITY AGENCY MODEL

Jerry Dincin

Thresholds is an example of a psychiatric rehabilitation center with a strong emphasis on the chronic mentally ill. The agency has been in existence in Chicago since 1959 and has served this population exclusively since that time. The agency is a not-for-profit, free-standing facility with a city-wide board of directors. While catchment area clientele get intake preference, services are offered for the entire Chicago area, both city and suburbs, because of the many unique aspects of the program. Clientele is young—the average age being 26 —but, nonetheless, meets the criteria of chronicity in terms of age of onset and number of hospitalizations. The average "member" (as clientele are called) has had three prior hospitalizations and been unsuccessful in many of the tasks of adulthood, including finding and holding a job, social relationships, control of symptoms, and living independently. The agency serves about 300 members at any one time, with about a 100% turnover per year.

Thresholds was started as a project of the National Council of Jewish Women, who saw the agency as a clubhouse for former psychiatric patients. In its initial period, it was staffed by volunteers. The direction has changed since that time, and the agency now employs about 65 people in all aspects of its program, but it still recognizes its roots in that volunteer service remains a key program component.

Psychiatric rehabilitation programs exemplified by Thresholds are derived from an eclectic approach to the treatment of the chronic mentally ill. No single theoretical framework characterizes this form of treatment. Instead, its roots are to be found in several mainstreams of contemporary psychiatric theory, thought, and practice. These include the psychodynamic and humanistic approaches to treatment, as well as behavior modification and reality therapy.

GUIDING PRINCIPLES

At Thresholds strong emphasis is placed on changing members' behavior. It is clear that members must learn to function in the community at as high a level as possible. Insight, per se, is not a primary goal, and the notion that change must be preceded by insight is one that is rejected by Thresholds. The rehabilitation approach is extremely supportive and oriented toward members' behavioral improvement.

Experiential Approach

Closely related to the behavioral orientation is the belief that members learn through experience and that the agency has a responsibility for providing a wide variety of growth-inducing opportunities. How members relate to one another at a dance; how they relate to coworkers on job assignments; how they prepare for job interviews, all reflect the experiential nature of our approach. The pragmatic orientation to life's problems is one that is stressed.

Some professionals have regarded schizophrenia as a crisis in self-confidence. While Thresholds does not wholeheartedly agree with this, it is certainly true that self-confidence is a major issue with all of our members. Improving self-confidence is an arduous programmatic task. At Thresholds, we feel that creating opportunities for successful experiences—small successful experiences—is one of the best ways to build a more confident person. Since all of our members have been unsuccessful in one or more important life functions, they require experiences that slowly rebuild their level of confidence. Making successful, real life experiences happen is the most creative way we use our center. This means that to the greatest extent possible, programs are individualized to meet this end.

Since schizophrenia is such an insidious ailment, Thresholds is aware that progress may well be slow. We therefore emphasize a gradual movement through the program while a variety of opportunities for growth are provided. A sudden increase of stress frequently is seen as a precipitant to regression. We start members in our program at a point where they will surely succeed and then gradually add more complex experiences to build self-confidence and coping ability. The careful layers of increasingly stressful situations help our members to tolerate more realistic job and social situations.

Causes of Mental Illness

Thresholds is not sure about the "causes" of mental illness. Over the years, we have developed the following bases for discussion, subject to new evidence. Many of the illnesses now called schizophrenia have different etiologies despite the fact that the symptoms may be similar. In most cases, we suppose a genetic predisposition or genetic accident, which usually takes effect in young adulthood. The predisposition is chemical in nature, takes place within the brain, and can be precipitated by stress, including the stress of growing up with its hormonal changes, as well as interpersonal and family stress, such as moving away from home. A strict psychological interpretation is not held in the agency.

Use of Medication

Directly related to this interpretation of the causes of mental illness is the view that antipsychotic medications are useful. At Thresholds, these medications are extremely important in our treatment plans. A sufficient body of knowledge has been amassed that shows that the medications used have antipsychotic properties which arrest the psychotic symptoms. Too many of our members have required rehospitalization after stopping their medication and so many members improve dramatically upon taking it that the agency is convinced of its usefulness. Even though medication is important in our treatment plans, it by no means precludes the importance of the psychosocial aspect of our program. Medication generally makes people ready to accept further rehabilitation.

Dependency and Regression

We have wondered if Thresholds' program encourages too much dependency. Sometimes this may be true, but there are different kinds of dependencies. At Thresholds, we encourage dependency early in a member's relationship with the agency. This seems to us to be a positive experience and something that the member needs badly. Later on, the staff moves that dependency toward positive growth. So dependency itself is not necessarily bad. It is negative when it becomes the guiding principle of treatment on the part of either the client or staff. Regression, which to us means a return of symptoms, may be an inevitable part of the lives of our members. At Thresholds, we do not feel it is a positive experience. The hypothesis that patients come up stronger and better if their psychotic episode is allowed to run its course is not accepted in the agency. There is too much pain and disorganization in the psychotic episodes we observe. We therefore do not encourage or feel complacent about regression, and we work to stave off regressive tendencies and to keep people functioning.

Community Relatedness

Thresholds maintains a low profile in a residential area. We do not hide but do not raise a flag to identify ourselves. The separation of Thresholds from hospital settings or other easily identifiable institutions is helpful in our members' participation and in integrating our program into the community. The agency's community base is an important strength which enables us to link clients more effectively with non-mental health community activities, particularly those of a social nature. This is related to the strong emphasis on "community exits" for our members. Although we do not claim to assist every person in joining the normal stream of community activity, intensive effort is made to help the clients adjust socially to the larger world. Creating social exits into the community in the form of job placements and meaningful social relationships is a keystone of our center. To the maximum extent possible, we want to "mainstream" our clients; yet we recognize that many of them do not have the emotional stability to handle this and that programs of long-term continuous service also need to be provided.

Agency Milieu

A great deal has been written about the importance of the milieu in the treatment of psychiatric patients. The creation of a therapeutic atmosphere is one of the more elusive and yet important attributes of any rehabilitation center. Visitors can usually pick up the sense of hopefulness and future orientation that pervades the atmosphere of Thresholds.

Rehabilitative Relationship

Of crucial importance is the development of a rehabilitative relationship with our clientele. This carries with it several areas of special motivation and involvement. At Thresholds, we see this relationship as an active role. This includes a strong element of reaching out to clients, specifically through home visits and utilization of other professionals and family to encourage members to participate in the program. Since lack of motivation and a constructive routine is a major problem with schizophrenics, this outreach is particularly important. We look for staff who are energetic and who can be active. Ability in across-the-desk interviewing is not a crucial ingredient in staff selection. We also look for evidence of determination, persistence, initiative, empathy, and ability to set limits in a kind way. With our clientele, staff cannot give up easily. The ability to regenerate enthusiasm is crucial to prevent staff burn-out. Among other things that we see as important in developing a rehabilitative relationship are:

- a strong professional desire to influence the member;
- an ability to develop a feeling of "dynamic hopefulness" in the member;
- creativity that enables the worker to use the center for the member's involvement;
- professional tenacity in the face of symptoms, regression, hostility, and resistance;
- the genuine ability not to be fearful of the member's illness;
- great frequency of interpersonal contact; and
- a deep-seated investment in all areas of the member's current life situation.

GOALS OF THRESHOLDS

The goals of Thresholds are pragmatic and frequently discussed with the members. Thresholds claims to make some impact on these five goal areas:

1. Job readiness and job finding.
2. Ability to socialize.
3. Ability to live independently.
4. Improvement in the academic area.
5. Prevention of rehospitalization.

Vocational Rehabilitation

Thresholds uses a job-readiness program style. Our members work in various "crews" as volunteers assisting in the everday activities of the agency. Crew areas include food service, clerical, reception, building maintenance, and housekeeping. These are all led by professional staff who are specially trained to use the work opportunities that exist in the Thresholds building as an evaluation and training technique. Typically, members will join us before 9:00 A.M., punch in at our time clock, and report to their crews. They might work, for instance, in the clerical area, where they might type, take care of attendance records, do nonconfidential research, and perform clerical tasks. These jobs are carefully evaluated by staff who assist members in improving their work habits and skills. At Thresholds, training per se rarely seems to be the crucial problem. Rather, the other problems associated with work are the most important issues. To deal with these problems, Thresholds has, for example, a special job application skills program in which we utilize videotape feedback to assist members in mock job interviews. When members have shown they can work successfully in the agency, and this takes about three to six months at present, they are placed in part-time jobs that the agency finds. This model of transitional employment was developed by Fountain House in New York, and many agencies throughout the country now use it. Cooperating employers offer part-time job opportunities to the agency. Members are paid at an established wage rate, and the agency maintains contact with the employer. The agency also uses the model of group placements, in which one staff worker will work on a job with five or six members. Another opportunity for a paid job is employment in the agency thrift shop. This shop, unfortunately, is not yet a profit-making operation, but it does have major benefits for our members as a job placement and in addition provides much-needed furniture for our residence program. Members work as sales clerks, typists, bookkeepers, truck drivers, and helpers.

Social Rehabilitation

Since difficulties in forming satisfying relationships with others represent a central aspect of the disturbance experienced by Thresholds' members, social rehabilitation is an important part of the agency's program. Prior to their entrance into the Thresholds milieu, members have typically felt isolated from others; each new social encounter has become another failure in the attainment of mutual and intimate social relationships. The social rehabilitation program addresses members' social impairment in several complementary ways.

Problem-solving groups were established to provide a forum for discussion of concerns most frequently expressed by members. Frequently, these groups are oriented toward one specific topic. An example of this would be our medication program, in which a thorough explanation of psychotropic medication is offered to the members in a didactic model. A special group has been formed for those who have been hospitalized three or more times. Since research has shown that the number of prior hospitalizations predicts future hospitalization, we consider three hospital experiences a dangerous point in our members' lives (1). This particular group focuses on the antecedents and precipitants of each member's frequent rehospitalization. Other groups are offered of a more typical group therapy style. Members who can use the more advanced groups are sometimes those who can tolerate groups with a heavy interpersonal component, including groups related to sexual issues (2).

Activity groups have been formed in response to specific needs and interests not of a problem-solving nature. Groups on conversation skills, current events, athletics, pottery, cooking on a public-assistance budget, and utilizing community resources all promote socialization and provide practical instruction on skills which can be used to develop leisure-time interests and hobbies.

Holiday activities are particularly important in the agency, and there are planned activities on all important holidays. Staff are expected to work at least two major holidays a year. We find that without an agency alternative, out members slip back into negative family roles as they try to recreate the nostalgic fallacy of that wonderful old-time feeling of holidays in their childhood. A particular strain at holidays are the family gatherings, which we frequently see are not beneficial to our clients. Generally, they promote invidious comparison to more successful siblings' accomplishments. In short, holidays can be hell. The agency's strong program particularly in November and December does much to alleviate the pressure and give our members a social alternative. Weekend activities are also promoted in the agency, and usually we try to balance the desire for members' ability to function independently in the community against the frequent unwillingness of the members to venture out from protected surroundings on the weekends. The agency does not want to do it all for the members and wants to help them to develop their own strengths. Yet, some assistance is needed, and each weekend there are activities planned through which members can learn constructive uses of leisure time to help them become less dependent on the family of origin and learn how to have fun with other people.

Our camping activities are a special part of our social program. Periodically during the year, members and staff go camping together. There are a number of brief trips, ranging in duration from three days to two weeks. For example, we have sponsored ten-day canoe trips through the Canadian wilderness, a bicycling trip, a backpacking trip, and a base-camp trip. Once during the summer, the agency closes and all members and staff go away to a rented camp for five days.

The organizational status of the social program is important. This program is seen not as an afterthought but as a key program with significant staff energies devoted to it. At Thresholds, activities in this program take place three afternoons and two evenings a week, as well as on the weekends and holidays, as mentioned above. Changing members' social style is frequently a key goal but one in which it is extremely difficult to make an impact.

Residential Program

The philosophy of our residential program includes several controversial notions. We believe that in most cases members should learn to live separately from their parents. Both parents and children need to outgrow their dependent use of each other. Frequently, the greatest act of love that parents can offer their mentally ill children is to encourage them to live independently and, indeed, to insist upon it. In order to fulfill this general philosophical view, the agency has developed a wide spectrum of housing opportunities.

Most people coming out of the hospital need a sheltered environment that has some supervisory characteristics. Therefore, recently discharged members usually move into either Freedom House or Phoenix House. These are group homes with an average of eight to ten members and live-in house managers (not house parents). These managers are responsible for teaching the members how to cook, clean, live together, and enjoy their independence.

The next level of housing is Pinegrove, a group home for ten members *without* live-in house managers. The agency employs a cook-housekeeper, who works during the day and early evenings and assists the members with the same tasks mentioned above. The members stay without supervision at night.

At a still more independent level of functioning is Roscoe House, a building with ten separate apartments housing 18 people.

Each apartment has its own cooking facilities. Members are expected to maintain the apartment in reasonable order and cook for themselves. Staff is available for group meetings and is on duty at the house during specific hours.

The final and most independent level of housing comprises the 20 apartments the agency rents, furnishes, and subleases to members. These apartments are not in the same building, but generally they are located in clusters so that interdependence among members is possible. The Chicago Housing Authority rents apartments to the agency for this program. Members meet with a staff worker once a week for support and to discuss any issues of independent living that may come up. A staff member lives in a separate apartment close by the other members.

The demand for housing among members is enormous since the alternatives to Thresholds leave much to be desired in Chicago. All together, the agency houses about 60 members at a time, but since housing is the most pressing need, it is hoped that this number will increase in the future. Volunteers help members to furnish apartments, residences, as well as to negotiate with landlords and tradesmen.

There are specialized groups for members to increase their independent living skills. Work with the parents of our members focuses on the need for independence. Parents need to learn how to be supportive yet consistent in handling the issues of independence, and the weekly group with parents helps them do this *(3)*.

Academic Program

The agency is accredited as a special-function school by the North Central Association of Colleges and Schools. We focus on the basic skills needed for passing the high school equivalency examination. If a member has the capability of passing, strong encouragement is given to taking this exam. There is a group of members, however, who do not have the capacity for obtaining a high school degree. Educational efforts with this group focus on teaching basic reading, writing, arithmetic, and survival skills. For those members who have dropped out of college because of emotional problems, the agency offers college preparatory courses geared to a high-level of proficiency, to help members in both the development of better study habits and the preparation of homework. Additionally, this group of members may become involved in tutoring the less capable members. The academic program offers the agency the opportunity to take a more comprehensive approach to our members' lives. Frequently, members who have been unsuccessful in school must have a successful experience before they can believe in themselves again.

Prevention of Rehospitalization

Preventing rehospitalization is the fifth and overall goal for all our members. We view rehospitalization negatively—an experience that should be avoided if at all possible. The whole program of activities just described serves to prevent rehospitalization, However, Thresholds has added several other components which should be mentioned. As noted above, the agency believes strongly in the use of psychotropic medications for our members. While not every member needs or responds to such medication, the vast majority can make good use of it. Our research has shown that about 70% of the members who must be rehospitalized have not been taking their medication or taking it irregularly (4). With this in mind, we view medication compliance as critical to the prevention of rehospitalization. A full-time psychiatric nurse and three part-time psychiatric consultants monitor and prescribe medications. We have found strong evidence that when Thresholds' psychiatrists manage medication, members are hospitalized far less frequently. This is because the entire staff is quite sophisticated in the use of medication, being knowledgeable about both its beneficial effects and its side effects. There is close liaison between the staff and the psychiatric consultants. To put it succinctly, we know the members very well and are frequently able to pick up deviations from medication compliance. The special group mentioned previously for those who have been hospitalized frequently is part of the general medication monitoring activities. Likewise, the medication group, which is run by the psychiatric nurse and psychiatrists, teaches members how to speak to the doctors about symptoms and gives in general a physiological approach to schizophrenia.

The rehospitalization rate for members who are active in our program is about 10–15% a year. The agency stands ready to assist members evenings and weekends if needed to prevent a rehospitalization. Members are sometimes housed in our residential program if there is a particular emergency.

ORGANIZATION OF PROGRAM

The agency is organized along vertical lines, with three parallel teams of eight staff members each. These staff teams are responsible for their own work-readiness program, job placements, social activities, and residential program. They serve about 80 members each. This vertical programming avoids departmentalization and enhances the generalist concept of staff functioning. Several functions cut across teams and are "all-agency" activities. These are the academic program, medication management, and intake.

The agency is goverened by a board of directors of about 35 laypeople from the community. Their functions include fund raising, development of agency policy, program evaluation, and maintaining the agency's public image. They serve on a number of committees and are active in the growth of the agency. The executive director serves as staff for the board and various committees.

BUDGET AND FUNDING SOURCES

The total agency budget was $1.5 million in 1979. About 75% of this income came from various governmental sources, including grants-in-aid from the State Department of Mental Health, federal research projects, Division of Vocational Rehabilitation service contracts, and provision of subcontracted residential services to the Northwestern Community Mental Health Center. Some funds, which help to finance our academic program, are obtained from the Board of Education. Perhaps the most difficult part of the fund-raising effort is securing income from the community. Our board provides vital assistance through their own contributions, solicitations of their friends, and help in approaching foundations and corporations in the greater Chicago area. In addition, we are fortunate to have several fund-raising auxiliaries which assist in specific projects.

Although fees are charged for services, these represent a negligible portion of our budget—about one-tenth of 1%. This is because our members are usually on welfare and are unable to pay fees. The agency is not eligible for any third-party payments.

SPECIAL PROJECTS

No description of Thresholds would be complete without a description of several special projects that are operated by the agency.

Branch Operations

In addition to the main center at 2700 North Lakeview Avenue in Chicago, the agency operates two branches on the South Side of Chicago. Because residential patterns are frequently along racial lines, these two branches serve a predominantly black clientele. This is all to the good, since services for black clientele are woefully underfunded in Chicago. Both branches operate in a manner similar to the main agency, although they are not quite so well developed nor quite so extensive. With the new attention that is being paid in this state to supplying services to the South Side of Chicago, it is felt that this program will increase in depth in the next few years.

Children at Risk

The agency operates a research program funded by the National Institute of Mental Health (NIMH) which is concerned with the prevention of mental illness in children of mentally ill mothers. A complex research design enables us to have a comparison and control group of mothers. The objective of this program is to assess and remediate incipient emotional problems of preschool children of schizophrenic and psychotically depressed women. The agency has developed a nursery school for this purpose, and a staff of psychologists and nursery-school teachers work on these issues with the mothers themselves. In addition, the mothers are involved in the full rehabilitation program that has already been described. Several additional components include a course on child development, group therapy, special medical attention for mothers and their children, a camping program, and a special program of videotape intervention designed to work through special mother/child issues. Issues of child abuse are frequently dealt with.

Adolescent Program

Within the context of the regular rehabilitation programs mentioned above, the agency operates a special program for 16- to 18-year-old psychiatric patients. Special aspects include family therapy and an emphasis on peer group transactions. A special residence is operated for this group. We service about 30 people in our program at any one time.

Recidivist Project

There is a special group of psychiatric patients who have been rehospitalized very frequently for whom the structured program of Thresholds does not seem to be helpful. These are people who cannot get attached to any agency program or who are unable to make any commitment to the specific goals in the agency. A project funded in 1978 has identified 50 catchment area clients who have been hospitalized at least five times each and three times in the past year. This program is modeled after the Program for Assertive Community Treatment program in Madison, Wisconsin, described by Mary Ann Test in numerous articles (5). Staff make daily contact with the clients, usually by means of home visits, and attend to any and all problems as they arise but without the structure of a specific program. The objective is to reduce the recidivism in terms of both the frequency of hospitalization and the number of days hospitalized.

SUSTAINING CARE

A significant number of members have utilized the rehabilitation aspect of our program to the fullest extent to which they are currently capable. Such members need long-term support, and this is provided in our sustaining care program, which meets outside of the agency in rented church facilities three days a week. Regular Thresholds staff members are assigned to work with this group to provide a stable social network, community activity, and medication maintenance. When these clients are ready to take advantage of a higher level of rehabilitation, they may either come back to the Thresholds program for a more intensive work-readiness experience or find jobs themselves with the help of our staff.

OUTCOME STUDIES

Thresholds is dedicated to pragmatic research on the effectiveness of our program. In addition to the Children at Risk project mentioned above, NIMH has sponsored research on adolescent programs in cooperation with the state hospital. Two other research projects have recently been completed. The first, a three-year study using a control group, was designed to assess the effectiveness of two different programs (6). The results were unequivocal and strong: the full Thresholds program prevents rehospitalization to a significantly greater degree than the alternative program (small social groups). Social rehabilitation also proved significantly more successful for the group using the Thresholds program. The ability to live independently in the community increased significantly. The comparison of results of the two vocational components were not significant, and further research is contemplated in this area.

The second study sponsored by the Chicago Community Trust was designed to test the importance of attendance in the programs as it related to results. It was found that significantly better results in terms of the major goal parameters of the agency were related to both *quantity* and *intensity* of attendance. This tells our members and staff that participating in the Thresholds program has a significant payoff in positive results (7).

FUTURE PLANS

The board of directors feels that further agency development should concentrate on increasing the number and variety of housing alternatives, establishing additional branches, and promoting further research efforts on program effectiveness (8). It is hoped that expansion in these areas will be funded by governmental and/or private resources.

NOTES

1. Rosenblatt A, Mayer JE: The recidivism of mental patients: A review of past studies. Am J of Orthopsychiatry 44:697–706, 1974

2. Dincin J, Wise S: Sexual Attitude Reassessment for Psychiatric Patients. Paper presented at AASECT, Washington, D.C., April 1979

3. Dincin J, Selleck V: Restructuring parental attitudes—Working with parents of the adult mentally ill. Schizophrenia Bulletin 4(4):597–608, 1978

4. Streicker S: Rehospitalization Report for 1978 at Thresholds, Chicago, Illinois (unpublished)

5. Test MA: From Hospital to Community, Alternatives to Acute Hospitalization; No. 1. San Francisco, Jossey-Bass, 1979

Further information on any aspect of the program, including the possibility of visiting Thresholds, can be received by writing the author at Thresholds, 2700 North Lakeview Avenue, Chicago, Illinois 60614. (Phone: (312)-281-3800)

6. Witheridge T, Dincin J: Comparison of Two Programs of Psychiatric Rehabilitation. Chicago, Ill., Thresholds, 1978 (unpublished)

7. Kaberon D, Dincin J: Attendance as a Predictor of Success in Psycho-Social Rehabilitation. Chicago, Ill., Thresholds, 1979 (unpublished)

8. Dincin J: Long Range Planning Committee Report. Chicago, Ill. Thresholds, 1978 (unpublished)

Chapter 16

A PRIVATE MENTAL HOSPITAL MODEL

Jack Greenspan

In whatever way we look at them, these lunatics are a burden upon the Commonwealth. The curable during their limited period of disease, and the incurable during the remainder of their lives, not only cease to produce, but they must eat the bread that they do not earn, and consume the substance they do not create, receiving their sustenance from the treasury of the Commonwealth or of some of its towns, or from the income or capital of some of its members.

The cost of restoring a lunatic to health and enjoyment and power of self-sustenance, and of contributing to the support of his family, and also bearing his part of the burden of the state, is limited and easily paid in money; the gain is unmeasured. But the cost of lifelong lunacy, distressing and oppressive to the friends who have the patient in charge, is immeasurable, and not to be paid in money. *(1, 5)*

In the ensuing 100 plus years since this statement was made much that is positive has occurred in the treatment of the mentally ill. The advent of somatic therapy, psychoanalysis, and psychopharmacology have altered the plight of the mentally ill to varying degrees. Nevertheless there is still much to be desired in the overall treatment of persons who become patients. Specifically, symptom reduction or symptom improvement is one treatment goal. However, those therapists who are concerned with maximum productivity and creativity, and maximum potential of members of society have additional treatment goals. Resolving neurotic, psychotic, and character disorganization, thereby producing a climate for a reasonable degree of happiness, family intactness, and social improvement, is an ambitious but, we believe, realistic treatment goal. The Group for the Advancement of Psychiatry report "Psychotherapy and Its Financial Feasibility within the National Health Care System" (2) speaks to the feasibility of a holistic treatment approach which would include not only reducing symptoms but also altering the person's capacity to relate more effectively to self, others, and society.

Although psychiatrists have been successful in altering and controlling the symptoms familiar to us in the diagnosis and treatment of the mentally ill, our current treatment planning for the problem of relatedness to self and others frequently falls short. In fact, to various degrees some forms of continued mental illness may be iatrogenic in origin. Several articles have been written that confront us with our treatment failures and the complexity of attempting reasonable treatment for the mentally ill (3, 6, 8, 9, 10, 11, 14). Specifically, the failure to diagnose and/or to create well-defined treatment plans, which are not only cost effective and efficient but performance oriented, have left many patients in a state of withdrawal, isolation, and unproductivity. Treatment modalities which are frightening, debilitating, or stigmatizing cause potential patients to flee.

Reliance on somatic and psychopharmacological methods of approach with a deemphasis on psychotherapy can lead to fear of treatment on the part of potential patients. Failing to develop therapeutic rapport with associated support, understanding, and providing reasonable improvement leads to a pessimism, a sense of hopelessness and helplessness, which only increases the patient's sense of social isolation and poor self-esteem. There is an associated fear that any attempt to involve oneself in the three most important areas of living—work, play, and love relationships—will lead only to failure. The patient, therefore, comes to believe what he has already suspected: that the need for relatedness is fraught with the danger of rejection, failure, subjugation, humiliation, and a confirmation that he, a human being, is weak, ugly, unacceptable, and not of this world.

Other criticisms of our treatment of the chronic mental patients are legion. They include finding fault with the public mental hospital, community mental health centers, community mental health professionals, and politicians. Certainly the private sector has also frequently been accused of abandoning the psychotic and the chronically mentally ill. Gunderson et al. found that "only 35 percent of all schizophrenic patients who registered at an outpatient facility actually received any treatment. Over half of the remaining 65 percent received nothing more than intake services or a diagnostic evaluation; and another 13 percent received only psychological testing with no follow-up. About half of the 35 percent who began outpatient treatment abandoned it" *(4)*. Although the literature of the late 1970s is replete with positive descriptions of halfway houses, day hospital programs, day care centers, transitional care services, sheltered workshops, welfare hotels, and the like, each report ends with the statement that "evaluation of the program is in progress." However, one gets the impression that much experimental work is going on and that we possess a host of techniques for improving our present poor record and providing community care services if we have the will. Yet, the documentation that such services do perform well is far from satisfactory. The Group for the Advancement of Psychiatry report on "The Chronic Mental Patient in the Community" *(3)* draws some frightful parallels with the history of the treatment of the mentally ill. The ideological emphasis on the interpersonal and humanistic understanding of the mentally ill was previously replaced by an emphasis on cellular and brain pathology. More recently, we see a resurgence in the preoccupation with psychobiology and psychopharmacology, including a deemphasis of the humanistic approach to treatment. Paralleling the demise a century ago of the moral treatment of the mentally ill is the present segregation of the mentally ill, now not in a far-off state hospital but in the ghettos and residential care facilities of our blighted urban areas.

In the past, rising costs and financial distress at a national level have caused cutbacks in hospital services. At the start of the 1980s, the burdens of recession and inflation are again upon us. We can be assured that it will require quixotic efforts if the mental health professional will even be able to keep pace with our present understanding of the humane and scientific progress we have made in the recent decades in the approach to the mentally ill.

Langsley prophetically tells us, "Changes in human services are not accomplished simply by scientific fact. They also depend upon the economic and political scene" *(7)*. As never before, psychiatrists, organized in their professional societies and on an individual basis, must become political beings.

If mental health care is ever to reach the same fiscal support as the public's cry for dental care accomplished, much public education will be necessary. Most importantly, it must be carried out in a sophisticated manner. All of these economic and political realities impinge on the treatment of our patients in the private sector. We have responded by encouraging the formation of quality assurance programs where cost containment and quality concerns remain equally important emphases. Peer review has become an important part of our armamentarium in dealing with the problems of fiscal intermediaries' concern for getting "the most for their buck." Where in the past medical care was a privilege for those who could afford it, during the latter part of this century the public has demanded that medical care is a right of every individual. In an attempt to respond to this humanistic ideal, the private mental hospital has developed programs suitable for all those who are motivated for treatment. Needless to say, the current economic and political situations create a stress at the interface of ideals versus the practical reality of meeting staff salaries and other inflationary demands on the administration of any inpatient facility.

In describing how the private facility is unique in the health care delivery system of the chronic patient, it is important to recognize that there are overlapping facilities available to a patient, including the community mental health center, the psychiatric unit of a general hospital, and day hospital programs. One of the most important generalizations is that private facilities frequently have a mission which extends past symptom improvement. When successful, short-term therapy permits the patient to return quickly home or to an outpatient status. Frequently, the desire to improve the person's capacity to relate requires an elaborate treatment program, a longer stay, and an intensive psychotherapeutic approach in an effort to rehabilitate the patient prior to discharge. There have been model criteria developed for this form of treatment. We will outline and describe this approach:

I.   Admission Review for Intensive Inpatient Treatment.

    A.   There are no diagnoses which, in themselves, uniformly mandate or preclude hospitalization. Therefore, it is stressed that the need for inpatient treatment and length of stay are always to be determined by careful consideration of the symptoms present, the patient's environmental circumstances, the patient's immediate long-range needs, the dangers inherent in lieu of intensive in-hospital treatment, and the nature of past therapeutic efforts. This treatment decision is based on the history of the illness and the incapacity of the patient to establish adaptive, goal-directed behavior in work and relatedness to others.

Although the etiology of mental illness has not been clearly established, it is recognized that the complex of genetic, constitutional, and environmental factors are important causative agents in the ultimate failure of a person's capacity to maintain a reasonable level of emotional health. While theories of the cause of psychopathology and its treatment differ, there is increasing recognition that the final common pathway in the restoration of mental health comes with the capacity to adapt to the environment and to find a level of gratification in at least one of the three major areas of interpersonal involvement—work, avocational activity, and love relationships. Failure to address these goals during an acute phase of illness seems to lead to an assurance that chronicity and maladaptive behavior will be the outcome.

The observation of the past, as an example with the schizophrenic, that one third get better, one third stay the same, and one third will get worse no matter what the approach, has come under serious attack, most recently by Bleuler (1). There have been repeated observations that failure of continuity of care leads to a much higher percentage of chronicity, with all of the associated problems of any chronic debilitating disorder, and that continued therapeutic input reduces regression, including associated withdrawal behavior.

B. Reasons for *exclusion* of patients to long-term treatment. Long-term treatment requires a continuity of services including inpatient, partial hospitalization, and outpatient programs. Because of the numerous limitations on program development it is improbable that all facilities would be able to provide care. Therefore, we believe that crisis intervention is appropriate for many patients who are having an acute episode of illness. We recommend that failure to respond to such approaches should then be considered for transfer to an appropriate facility where all modalities of approach are available.

1.   First acute episodes of functional, toxic, or organic disorders which are preceded by a history of good life adjustment.
2.   Major affective disorders, bipolar or unipolar, with a history of adequate adjustment between episodes.
3.   Severe organic brain syndromes.
4.   Absence of an adequate trial of outpatient care prior to admission as an inpatient when clinically feasible.
5.   Long-term treatment requires the availability of services including a continuity of services including inpatient, partial hospitalization, and outpatient programs.
6.   Court-mandated referrals with special reference to criteria 1, 2, 5 above.

II.   Continued Stay Review.

   A.   The goals of extended, inpatient treatment should include not only symptom improvement but also improved intrapsychic and interpersonal functioning with increased capacity to tolerate ordinary stress, improved impulse control, and significant changes in the capacity to relate to others. The goal is to permit constructive functioning outside the hospital.

III.   Critical Diagnostic and Therapeutic Services.

   A.   Medical, psychiatric histories; neurological, physical, psychological, and psychiatric examinations with appropriate laboratory and radiographic studies in order to formulate the diagnosis.
   B.   The use of psychotropic drugs or Electric Shock Therapy (ECT), unless these modalities are contraindicated by the absence of a positive response in past treatment planning.
   C.   Intensive psychotherapy which involves the patient in the following functions. These *functions* are seen as the sine quo non of the therapeutic effort which addresses the issue of the problem of relatedness. We believe this to be the basic final common pathway of the psychopathology causing the person to become a patient.
      1.   *Continuity.* In recognition of the resistance to change and the associated inertia, fear, and gratifi-

cation associated with the lower level of mental functioning, we have reached awareness that continuity of care throughout the course of the therapeutic effort is most important. The existence of a primary therapist who provides the appropriate therapeutic involvement is crucial in treatment planning. The therapist has an in-depth understanding of the patient's remote and recent past as well as the current life situation, and is frequently an advocate for the patient. The need to make ego-alien certain characterological attitudes and behavior, as well as creating ego-syntonic modes of thinking, feeling, and behavior frequently, becomes a battleground for the patient and therapist. It is our experience that change within a patient, his family, and his environment requires emotional as well as intellectual involvement. Therefore, commitment to the therapeutic process is important. It is the care-giver's acknowledged continuity that must be present during the numerous storms and calms, and the regressions and progressions associated with the engagement and disengagement of all members of the team involved in the patient's care.

2. *Integration.* The function of the integrator who has demonstrated expertise in individual and group therapies, administrative expertise in inpatient treatment, knowledge of other modalities of treatment, including biological therapies (i.e., psychopharmacology, ECT) behavior modification approaches, is most important. Empirically, there are periods when an objective overview of the progress of therapy is most important. Maintaining a therapeutic milieu requires a recognition of the storminess of therapy and the need for timely intervention or, more importantly, nonintervention during the inevitable crises that arise in treatment. Recognition of potential negative therapeutic reactions on the part of the patient, primary therapist, and staff, and techniques to deal with same must be incorporated in treatment planning.

3. *Family boundary functions.* Expertise in family

dynamics and the appropriate use and treatment of the families of our patients has been a recent and recognized development in inpatient care. Frequently, our patients must return to the family. During the course of treatment, families can be advocates or saboteurs of a therapeutic approach. It is not infrequent that the primary patient is but one part of a network of psychopathology, and there is a disequilibrium within the family that must be addressed in treatment.

4. *Significant activities programming.* Such a program provides the patient with activities of daily living and promotes significant interaction, be it through occupational, recreational, or other rehabilitative services. Such programs are more than diversionary and can become a fruitful area of confrontation, interpretation, reinforcement of health versus the repetition of pathology which heretofore the patient has lived out in ways that are destructive to his interpersonal relationships. Sophisticated knowledge concerning psychopathology, character problems, symptom formation, and secondary and primary gain is, therefore, important if activities are to be meaningful in an individualized approach to the patient.

D.   Function of reentry into the community. From the time of admission, it is important that there be ongoing discharge planning. Consideration of cost containment, while emphasizing quality of care, requires a continued underlying philosophy by the treatment team and facility. When another level of care is truly appropriate, it is progressive to encourage movement in that direction. However, a premature discharge to a lesser level of care may undo much of the good that had been established early on in treatment. It is also to be recognized that within the protective environment of an inpatient facility, progress is to be tested by actual performance by reentry into the community. Much planning must be done. There are numerous modalities, such as halfway houses and transitional living, that may be important prior to complete independent living. Work adjustment programs and educational efforts which maximize the

patient's native capacities are part of the integration
and continuity of care that is the hallmark of our
efforts. Chronic failure in relating to others and failure
at work sets the stage for continuous illness. Improved
self-esteem is a complex phenomenon and goes beyond
merely a number of successful ventures in areas of work
and relatedness. Albeit very important that the patient
have some good, positive experiences, it is also recognized that fear of success and other self-defeating phenomena are very much a part of the psychopathology.
Rather than discouraging us in our endeavors, such
resistance to gain true improvement is to be expected
and becomes part of the therapeutic program.

E.   Peer review is an internal as well as external requirement in such extensive treatment. At the time of review, the original diagnosis and dynamic formulation
are reexamined.

Issues surrounding the appropriate use of psychopharmacological agents, including changes in medication
and appropriate dosages, are examined. The psychotherapeutic issues are addressed in depth. In an inpatient facility, which is providing reconstructive therapy
with the above-mentioned functions, it is recognized
that the disordered human relationships are the result
of patients viewing relatedness to others as dangerous.
This problem is manifested by reflex flight from others,
and, on an intrapsychic level, by problems with attachment (frequently described as pathological dependency), pseudoindependence, isolation, withdrawal
behavior, defects in the sense of self, and pathological
defenses via projection and denial which protect the
patient from relatedness. The whole thrust of hospitalization, therefore, becomes a corrective, therapeutic experience through qualitative and quantitative intensive
orientation addressing the self, the professional staff,
peers, and community. Through the continued confrontation, interpretation, introspection, and group
process, consensual validation and challenge of the patient's perceptions are possible. Since the threat of relatedness is experienced by such patients as having life
or death consequences, the climate of safety is imperative. The associated encouragement to experiment with

new methods of relatedness can only take place within a hospital setting which discourages or prevents flights from treatment. Such flights may be seen as "flights into health" as well as abstract or concrete efforts to sabotage continued treatment. Because there are powerful feelings associated with these problems, including the fear and the wish for merger with another important individual, time becomes an important factor in treatment. While recognizing that these complex issues are not quickly resolved, we also recognize that impasse may take place in a treatment. We know that there is a dilemma for the patient as he attempts to address experientially the problems of relatedness and that the patient will reenact past conflicts in his or her present life. The patient must be helped to delay action and to think of alternate ways of behaving at an adult level.

IV.   Addressing the Problems of Impasse.
    A.   Definition of impasse
        1.   There can be a real, or apparent, interruption in treatment where previously established treatment goals are stalemated or there can be a resurgence of illness as manifested by altered behavior, unexplained significant changes in symptomatology, lived-out destructive behavior to self or others, or continued missed psychotherapeutic sessions.
        2.   Impasse is not synonymous with termination of the treatment effort by patient or staff.
    B.   Elements to be evaluated in suspected impasses are.
        1.   The etiology
            a.   Is the therapeutic approach, as based on the original formulation of diagnosis, dynamics, and treatment plan appropriate?
            b.   Has there been improper placement of the patient in the hospital in relationship to other patients or staff, appropriate program and activities, and the physical environment (e.g., is there sufficient patient supervision, unit structure, constraints, or freedom)?
            c.   Has there been a "mismatch" between patient and therapist; is the therapist an improper choice for this patient (due to lack of experience

of the therapist, discomfort in treating the specific patient or the specific disorder)?

d. What are the transference, or countertransference, issues that might be the cause of the impasse?

e. Have the patient and the therapist recognized, or failed to recognize, the impasse; has there been confrontation of this?

f. Is the impasse resolvable or unresolvable?

g. Are there events occurring outside the immediate therapeutic situation which are causative in the impasse:

   1) Family interaction and/or interference?

   2) Fiscal intermediary, or are resources for continued care not available or restrictive (e.g., threats of retrospective denial of a claim)?

2. The degree of impasse

a. This must be assessed by the peer review process as to the absoluteness versus the reversibility of impasse—how it is perceived by the patient, the therapist, the team, or the family.

b. It is to be underscored that regression, that is, a return to more primitive cognitive, affectual, or behavioral states may be an important part of the therapeutic process. When acknowledged and within reasonable control, regression is adaptive in the analytic situation and is a source of experiential learning and future progress.

3. Is the impasse historical to the patient, in that it is a repetition of the patient's previous life story, that is, the impasse currently is an event between the patient and environment that has been causative of the difficulties which have led to the commitment to inpatient hospitalization? Again, has the patient frequently involved him or herself in a breakdown of previously agreed upon goal-directed collaboration and cooperation between him or herself and other significant others, be it family, friends, school, or work?

4. What are the documented recommendations concerning impasse?

a. Recommendation for a change in therapist?

b.   Change of unit within a hospital?

c.   Transfer of the patient to another facility appropriate to the patient's needs (this could be a partial hospitalization program, halfway house, custodial care facility, or termination of treatment) unless or until the patient demonstrates the motivation to return to treatment?

d.   Continuation of the present plan of treatment with reevaluation at the discretion of the peer review committee?

e.   Other recommendations in dealing with impasse?

V.   The operational needs of the faculty and staff that provide intensive, inpatient care.

As mentioned under functions of such treatment planning, continuity of care and, therefore, a high level of object constancy is a basic requirement for successful treatment. Therefore, the staff must be available and predictable, neither threatening nor threatened in the day-by-day interaction. Since there need be a continued engagement of the patient while maintaining an appropriate respect for his or her need for distance, a climate permitting these activities must be present. Integration of the various team members (such as the psychotherapist, social service personnel, activities therapist, psychiatric nurses), and where adolescents and young adults are in a program, various schooling and educational efforts requires the opportunity for conferencing and time to relate. This becomes quite important to those looking at cost containment, since other than one-to-one time with patients might be questioned as to efficacy. Yet this opportunity for conferencing supervision is very important.

There needs to be ongoing review and evaluation of the efficacy and efficiencies of any and all interventions. The team needs to confront its work, not only for purposes of accountability but also to combat the potential sense of helplessness which may occur in this work.

There must be availability of expertise in psychoanalytic, family, nursing, social service, and rehabilitation therapies.

VI.   What are the operational needs of the staff?

Their supervision must be underscored as a primary importance for staff sustenance and development. Since there must be an awareness and appreciation of the staff of its own primitive self and vulnerability, opportunity for supervision becomes very important. There also needs to be time and physical facilities for reflective work on the part of the staff. The goal of treatment is to permit the ongoing collaboration of self as an instrument of treatment, as well as an ongoing evaluation of where the patient is by means of utilizing the impact of the patient on the therapist. In no other medical modality of treatment does such personal emotional involvement become crucial as a therapeutic modality. In the battleground of emotion and conflict that is the nature of the etiology and psychopathology of seriously ill people, the emotional needs of the staff in doing its work becomes crucial, as pointed out by Stanton and Schwartz and others in *The Mental Hospital (13)*. Obviously, there needs to be an examination of the irrational events within and without the patient and staff interaction in an atmosphere where immediate suppression or fright to patient or staff does not take place.

SUMMARY

At a time in our history when automation is sought after in order to increase efficiency and decrease costs, the private mental hospital may appear as an enigma in the competing factors for the available medical dollar. Our work is about human conflict; to those professionals engaged on a daily basis, there is an exquisite sense of the humanism involved in this type of patient care. To those who call themselves realists and pragmatists, this costly, lengthy treatment approach remains questionable. The numerous variables involved in such care make adequate scientific methodology and study most difficult. At the time of this writing it is impossible to state categorically that such herculean efforts are statistically significant in improving patient performance. There are endless vignettes of how this treatment has succeeded where many other treatment modalities have failed dismally. There are also vignettes about endless efforts with hapless results. Even those who apply the golden rule to mental health care have difficulty in the appropriate interpretation of that rule. One example would be, "Do unto others as you would have them do unto you." Another interpretation is, "He who has the gold, rules!"

The philosophical, academic, or ideological stance of the therapist views reconstructive therapy on the spectrum of cynicism through optimism or idealism. Such major efforts of altering the human condition, even if scientifically proven to be effective, have created serious questions in the minds of all persons responsible for the health care dollar. As an effort to avoid or at least diminish the tragic effects of chronic mental illness on society, major commitments seem most reasonable when the outcome is positive therapeutically as well as in advancing our understanding of mental illness and health.

The private sector, through all of its resources, continues to provide the opportunity to learn, to earn, and to promote quality of care.

NOTES

1. Bleuler M: *The Schizophrenic Disorders: Long-term Patient and Family Studies,* New Haven and London: Yale University Press, 1978

2. Psychotherapy and its Financial Feasibility Within the National Health Care System, *The Chronic Mental Patient in the Community,* Vol. 10, No. 100, February 1978

3. The Chronic Mental Patient in the Community, *Group for the Advancement of Psychiatry,* Vol. 10, No. 102, May 1978

4. Gunderson JG, Autry JH III, and Mosher LR with Bushsbaum S: Special report "schizophrenia," *Schizophrenia Bull.* 9:16–54, 1974

5. Jarvis E: Report on Insanity and Idiocy in Massachusetts, by the Commission on Lunacy. Boston, William White, Printer to the State, 1855

6. Langsley DG and Kaplan DM: *The Treatment of Families in Crisis.* New York: Grune and Stratton, 1968

7. Langsley DG, Barter JT, Yarvis RM: Deinstitutionalization-The Sacramento story. Presented to the Annual Meeting of American Orthopsychiatric Association, Atlanta, Ga., 5 March 1976

8. The Discharged Chronic Mental Patient: A Medical Issue Becomes a Political One *Medical World News,* April 12, 1974, pp. 47–58

9. Pasamanick B, Scorpetti F, and Dinitz S: *Schizophrenics in the Community: An Experimental Study in the Prevention of Hospitalization,* New York: Appleton-Century-Crofts, 1967

10. Reich R. and Siegel L: Psychiatry Under Siege: The Chronically Mentally Ill Shuffle to Oblivion, *Psychiatric Annals,* November 1973, pp. 35–55

11. Santiestevan H: Deinstitutionalization: Out of Their Beds and Into the Streets, Washington, D.C., *American Federation of State, County and Municipal Employees,* February 1975

12. Solomon HC: The American Psychiatric Association in Relation to American Psychiatry, Presidential address, *Amer. J. of Psychiatry,* 1958, p. 115

13. Stanton AH and Schwartz MS: *The Mental Hospital,* New York: Basic Books, 1954

14. Zitrin A, Hardesty AS, Burdock EI and Drossman AK: Crime and Violence Among Mental Patients, *Amer. J. of Psychiatry,* Vol. 133, February 1976, pp. 142–148

Chapter 17

A VETERANS HOSPITAL MODEL
Ethan S. Rofman

HISTORY

The Edith Nourse Rogers Memorial Veterans Hospital in Bedford, Massachusetts, lies near the Great Road between Lexington and Concord, not far from the site where the Minutemen fired the "shot heard round the world." It came into being in 1928 as a hospital of the Veterans Bureau, the forerunner of the Veterans Administration. Its initial function was to provide protective and custodial care for psychiatrically ill veterans of World War I, the Spanish-American War, and the Civil War who were living in the area northwest of Boston. Like so many hospitals of this period, it was built on a large tract of land in a rural setting and consisted of ten buildings arranged in a large oval. Originally, each building contained four wards of approximately 45–80 patients.

During the 1930s, only a few psychiatrists at the hospital had been trained in the then newly discovered somatic and dynamic therapies. The prevailing opinion was that most psychiatric illnesses were untreatable. The patient population was increasing in age and chronicity, and a defeatist attitude was fairly widespread. During World War II, the situation changed considerably, because many personnel were lost to the service and because psychiatric casualties from the war swelled the census of the hospital to more than 200 patients over capacity. As the war ended, increased appropriations and extensive administrative reorganization improved the level of treatment. After the war, the number of personnel was doubled and ancillary therapies and services were improved. The hospital at that time had a large farm on the grounds, which provided meaningful work for many of the hospitalized patients. The farm's productivity enabled it to supply most of the food needs of the Bedford Hospital itself and some of the food needs of the other Veterans Administration hospitals in the area. The farm closed during the early 1950s as a result of a cost-effectiveness study which showed that it would be cheaper to purchase food on the open market than to grow food on the hospital farm (1).

In the early 1950s, as the result of participation in a Russell Sage Foundation project, changes on the chronic wards were made: patients were dressed in street clothes instead of hospital pajamas and attempts were made to get patients to eat and shower by themselves and to attend rehabilitative programs. The movement toward treatment in the community, which has reduced the hospital census from 1,800 in the 1950s to a 1979 figure of about 750, was at that time in its early stages. Care in the hospital was seen as the treatment of choice. In 1955 the Modified Community Employment Program /Community Employment Program (MCEP/CEP), which involved a gradual transition from a sheltered workshop within the hospital to a less sheltered working environment in the local community surrounding the hospital, was begun by staff of the Counseling Psychology Department. During the 1960s much progress was made in the pharmacological management of psychosis, consequently there was an increased ability to discharge patients into the community. Also during the 1960s, a network of family care homes was established by the Social Work Service. In 1968, a new director took charge of the hospital and another reorganization took place. There was again a wide split between the most chronic patients, who were cared for with minimal staff in a custodial environment, and the more acute patients, who were admitted to better staffed areas of the hospital.

During the early 1970s, some ward staffs attempted experiments of their own in which they subdivided their patients into more chronic and less chronic groups so that patients with the most potential could receive more in the way of intervention. This idea was abandoned in 1973 after about a year, in part because there was not adequate staff to cover two separate groups. At about the same time the hospital by necessity was once again increasing its commitment to acute services, and as usual, this commitment took place at the expense of chronic services. To implement this change, the seven chronic wards, each of which had been staffed by one full-time physician, were staffed by part-time physicians who also had responsibilities in other areas of the hospital. Administrative responsibility for the wards shifted from the physicians to the newly installed nurse unit administrators (NUAs), who assumed the task of coordinating all the activities of the chronic wards.

When these changes occurred there was almost no coordination of the many programs established to contribute to the care of the chronic patients. There were hospital-wide programs such as occupational therapy, recreational therapy, the Modified Community Employment Program/Community Employment Program workshops, as well as a network of community placement homes but little or no overall leadership in the area of chronic care. The three physicians assigned to all chronic wards made rounds independently of one another consuming large amounts of nursing time. Many of the patients were confined to their units and only left in groups for the various centralized activities. It was in the context of this setting that the current Psychosocial Rehabilitation Program at Bedford came into being.

DEVELOPMENT OF PSYCHOSOCIAL REHABILITATION PROGRAM

In September 1974 the Acting Chief of Social Work who was also in charge of community care proposed that the hospital increase physician participation in community visitation and undertook informal discussions with the three intermediate-care physicians to that end. This social worker felt it was difficult to get a doctor to see a patient in the community. No system of one doctor relating to one community care home existed, and community care workers were finding it very hard to readmit foster home care patients to their own hospital. The idea was well received by the Chief of Psychiatry, and he established a task force not only to study the assigning of physicians to the community care teams but to review rehabilitation programs in psychiatry. Its report stated:

> Since all patients have capacities not being used at optimal level, they all may be considered potential subjects for rehabilitation. The therapeutic focus with them shall be primarily the development of assets

rather than the treatment of pathology. The three major areas for rehabilitation shall be *interpersonal* (family, social and community), *productive* (work and performance skill including self care), and *recreational.* It is expected that the more focused emphasis on rehabilitation in this program will encourage all mental health professionals in the Veterans Administration Hospital to increase their concern and work with their patients' individual assets. *(2)*

This task force recommended that a special rehabilitation ward be established. An interdisciplinary evaluation team would screen all patients. Criteria for acceptance were suggested, for example, patients had to be ambulatory and not in need of intensive nursing care. Extensive treatment programs involving individual psychotherapy, group psychotherapy, family therapy, job training, recreational skills, and activities of daily living were outlined.

The emphasis of this unit was to be on meaningful discharge to the community. Discharge planning was to begin as soon as the patient came to the unit. It was initially thought best to have a 90-day limited stay for intensive work. It was stated that rehabilitation goals should be established at the time of admission and a record of the patient's progress in approaching these goals as well as periodic reviews of the goals be kept up to date. The treatment team was expected to set a specific date of discharge. Direct contacts with the people with whom the patient would be living after discharge would become part of the discharge process, and it was deemed essential that all members of the team who were needed be directly involved in supporting the move from hospital to community. As initially conceived, once the patient was in the community, the inpatient treatment team would gradually reduce its contact with the patient and pass responsibility to a community team, which would be responsible for the patient's overall care. Membership on both teams would be overlapping. Staffing for such a ward was thought to require a psychiatrist, a psychologist, nurses, nursing assistants, a ward social worker, a community care social worker, an occupational therapist, and a recreational therapist.

The task force report was positively received by the Chief of Psychiatry. He objected, however, to the concept of a single ward being devoted to the task of rehabilitation and was more interested in a comprehensive program which focused on most of the intermediate wards in the hospital as well as on the needs of those patients already in the community. He informed the committee that he wished to change the original plan to create a separate rehabilitation unit in favor of the hospital offering a rehabilitation program and organization which could apply its skills to all the intermediate units. The task force went back to work and formulated their ideas about providing a program for five of the seven intermediate wards, all the outpatients in community care homes, and selected outpatients who were living on their own.

In September 1975 the chief of psychiatry submitted a memorandum entitled "Proposal to Develop Comprehensive Rehabilitation and Support Services," through the chief of staff to the acting hospital director. This proposal received active support from the chief of staff. By November 1975, the task force submitted to the chief of psychiatry an 18-page report, which included detailed recommendations as to how to implement the program. Its major feature included the linking of five of the intermediate wards to five geographical areas with roughly equal numbers of family care homes and outpatients. Care for the patients on each intermediate unit was organized into multidisciplinary teams. Proposed staffing included 1 psychiatrist, 1 psychologist, 2 social workers, 1 occupational therapist, 5 nurses, 12 nursing assistants, 1 secretary, and part-time recreational and corrective therapists for 45 patients.

The important principle that team members functioning on the ward would also function in the community was clearly stated. No longer would the community care social worker function in isolation but could expect that he would be supported by an entire ward team and especially the team physician who would visit family care homes in the community at regular intervals. In turn, the community care worker would become an active member of the ward team. In this way he could contribute ideas about possible future placements as well as follow those patients he had sent into the hospital for readmission.

While care was organized according to geographic lines, the basic spirit was one of flexibility. Rigid geographic boundaries never prevented a patient from entering a program or interfered in his plan of care. The committee which had worked to establish this program proposed renaming itself the Psychosocial Rehabilitation Program Advisory Committee and continued to meet regularly to monitor the program's ongoing development and functioning. It was also determined that the whole program should be headed by a physician who would occupy a new position which would be called Assistant Chief of Psychiatry for Psychosocial Rehabilitation.

In December 1975, the final proposal was presented to the service chief members of the hospital's Mental Health Council. Several of the service chiefs felt that they had not had a chance to discuss the proposal adequately prior to its presentation and felt excluded from the planning. This difficulty was resolved by private consultations between the Chief of Psychiatry and service chiefs who had objected to the proposal as it was initially presented. In January 1976 the Psychosocial Rehabilitation Program formally came into being.

PROGRAM ELEMENTS

A report of the Psychosocial Rehabilitation Program's functioning after one year of operation recorded the following accomplishments:

1. Utilization and Establishment of Geographic Modules—The five intermediate inpatient units each function as the inpatient service of a system of comprehensive mental health services offered by the hospital to an assigned geographic area.
2. Movement of Patients—Patients are usually admitted directly to their geographically identified unit when they require rehospitalization. If the appropriate unit has no free beds, they are temporarily admitted to another unit. Only if their condition is such that it requires the staff and facilities of a very acute type of service are they admitted to the acute service. They are then returned to their geographically identified unit as soon as their condition permits.
3. Continuity of Care—Personnel are assigned to teams who care for an assigned patient group. The progress of patients is reviewed in one or two weekly interdisciplinary team meetings on the unit. The community care social worker participates in these interdisciplinary meetings. Members of the team, including physicians, nurses, occupational therapists, and psychologists, periodically accompany the community care social worker into the family care homes.
4. Program Administrative Identity and Location—The location of psychiatrists and community care social workers and program director in a building of their own has greatly facilitated collaboration and allowed for ongoing frequent formal and informal consultation among staff.
5. Functioning of the Advisory Committee—The committee

which established the Psychosocial Rehabilitation Program has continued to meet on a biweekly basis. It functions as an advisory body to the director on all ongoing issues and policy matters and has representatives from all five units. The Advisory Committee has been concerned with evaluation of staff education, patients, program needs, effectiveness, budget, and administrative and clinical matters.

6. In-Service Training, Administration, and Clinical Communication—Meetings of the Psychosocial Rehabilitation Program subserve all three functions. Two monthly case presentations are attended by all available staff. One monthly meeting of nurse unit administrators with psychiatrists and one monthly meeting of the psychiatrists also serve all three functions. Minutes of all meetings held (including those of the Advisory Committee) are distributed throughout the Psychosocial Rehabilitation Program to all levels of staff. Units keep logbooks of their own meetings. Notes on case presentations are systematically placed in patients' medical records. The director of the Psychosocial Rehabilitation Program attends regular weekly community care meetings with the director of community care and with each of the psychiatrists in the program.

In addition to the six service-wide accomplishments noted in the Program's first year report, several other innovative programs were established. For example, one unit began a program for patients called "the buddy system." They teamed patients leaving the hospital to "buddies" who were already residing in family care homes. The residents were encouraged to orient the new arrivals to the operation of the home and to help with social introductions.

Another unit began an outplacement group in which patients were taken on tours of several family care homes long before discharge was contemplated. This reduced patient anxiety about life in the community and stimulated discussion concerning family care homes based on impressions and experiences which took place as a result of the trip. This unit also acquired a pet dog, which belonged to one of the nurses but was taken care of by patients during the day. Several patients progressed from isolation to contact with the dog to contact with other people as a result of their caring for this ward mascot.

A system of yearly awards was developed by the Mental Health Council as a way of recognizing excellence in patient care. This award, an engraved plaque which could be displayed on the unit, was awarded first to a psychosocial rehabilitation ward. This ward through its excellent teamwork had successfully placed and maintained very difficult patients in family care homes.

A "day school" was begun under the auspices of the Psychology Service. This school for patients used student trainees and volunteers who employed didactic methods to teach such courses as "Your medication and how it works," "What to do when you're feeling low," and "Your room and how to take care of it." Patients from the wards as well as patients coming to the hospital from family care homes took classes together.

In addition to the programs begun in the hospital, a community program developed by a social worker and an occupational therapist in a small town 60 miles away from the hospital is worthy of note. When a day activity center run by the Commonwealth was closed for lack of funds, these two individuals lobbied the local town leaders and veterans groups to obtain a large room in the town hall and to establish a Comprehensive Employment and Training Act (CETA) position to run a day activity center which would serve the 100 or so veterans residing in family care homes in and around this town. This program has been so successful that the hospital has taken over funding of the CETA position.

As a result of these changes, it has been possible to place a larger number of patients in family care homes and to improve both patient and staff morale. Problems of patient flow, however, persist. Because of staff shortages, too many patients have to be admitted or transferred to acute inpatient psychiatric units when their behavioral disturbance exceeds the capability of the Psychosocial Rehabilitation Program unit. For the same reason, patients cannot always be expeditiously readied for discharge. A small number of long–term patients who are difficult to discharge absorb much of the staff's time with destructive behavior. Despite these problems, one ward increased its discharges from 17 in the year before the program to 79 in the first year of the program. An analysis of 29 consecutive discharges revealed that 23 patients (79.3%) remained in the community three or more months.

The establishment of an organized program in a systematic fashion, utilizing input from all those persons who would be most directly affected by such a program, is an important administrative strategy for motivating people to become interested in chronic care. Staff are attracted to and become identified with an organized program. When no organized program exists, positive identification with chronic care is not likely to occur. The very act of establishing a program, therefore, is a critical step.

NONSPECIFIC FACTORS WHICH HAVE IMPROVED PATIENT CARE

There have been broader influences within the Veterans Administration system as a whole, and at Bedford in particular, which interacted organizationally with the efforts of those wishing to establish a Psychosocial Rehabilitation Program and, in a variety of very important ways, provided additional and crucial support. By far, the two most important nonspecific factors motivating physicians to become interested in chronic care were the physicians bonus and emphasis on university affiliation. Both of these programs were system wide and the result of work done by the Veterans Administration Central Office in Washington.

The bonus bill and university affiliation enabled the recruitment of an outstanding group of young psychiatrists recently trained in an eclectic fashion (including experience in community psychiatry, psychopharmacology, neurology, family therapy as well as in the more traditional forms of individual therapy). At the present time, one of the psychosocial rehabilitation units is headed by a former assistant professor of psychopharmacology at Harvard Medical School and another by a former assistant professor of community psychiatry at Tufts New England Medical Center. Having individuals of this caliber run wards on the chronic care service not only attracts other good people to the service but also contributes directly to better patient care.

The introduction of a residency training program to our hospital has been significant to chronic care as well. By teaching and training residents, the personnel involved in chronic care are forced to formulate what they have been doing in a systematic way, and in turn they derive self-esteem and prestige by becoming the teachers of residents. Residents are gradually learning to differentiate between concepts of incurability and hopelessness. They are encouraged to study their work on the intermediate wards from the point of view of a social systems analyst.

Improvement in salary structure, university affiliation, and residency training programs alone, however, do not necessarily contribute to the improvement of chronic care. Without a clearly identifiable program, these factors might well lead to an erosion of chronic care in favor of seemingly more glamorous acute alternatives. A psychosocial rehabilitation program whose staff is vastly underpaid, deprived of intellectual stimulation, and unrecognized as a unique entity quickly can become demoralized, frustrated, and depressed. It has been the fortunate combination of improved salaries, academic stimulation, and an organized identifiable program that has enabled our staff to provide a high level of care to chronic patients, both in and out of the hospital.

NOTES

1. Greenblatt M, York RH, Brown EL: From Custodial to Therapeutic Care in Mental Hospitals. New York, Russell Sage Foundation, 1955

2. *Proposal for Rehabilitation Program in Psychiatry,* Bedford V.A. Hospital, Internal Memorandum, 1975

Part III

SPECIALIZED PROGRAMS FOR THE CHRONIC MENTAL PATIENT

Chapter 18

A RURAL PROGRAM
Bryce G. Hughett, M.D.
Mary J. Honaker

Rural areas vary greatly one from another. Mental health service delivery is in some respects easier, less complicated in a rural state such as Montana, where a population of 753,000 people occupies more than three times the area of Pennsylvania, than in the more urban areas of the nation. In some respects, more barriers and difficulties exist in rural areas.

This chapter will present a rural service delivery program—the South Central Montana Regional Mental Health Center—and address these barriers as well as the general characteristics and history of the catchment area, the special problems in service delivery for chronic mentally ill persons in rural areas, treatment care elements including our community support system, administration and coordination, staffing, training, and outcome data.

GENERAL DESCRIPTION AND HISTORY

Montana's mental health system includes five major regions, each with a federally funded community mental health center. Montana's only state hospital, Warm Springs, is in the western third of the state and more than 450 miles from the eastern most boundary.

The South Central Montana Regional Mental Health Center, Montana's Region III catchment area, covers 11 counties, 25,000 square miles, and 150,000 population. Included in the area is Yellowstone County, the most populous county in the state, with 99,000 people. The other ten counties vary from 700–13,000 in population. The largest city in the state and the county seat of Yellowstone County is Billings.

In December 1975, following enabling state legislation, a contract was signed between the state hospital and each of the centers to allow hospital funds to follow patients from the hospital to support community posthospital efforts and to expand prehospital screening. The contract between the centers and Warm Springs State Hospital ended in 1977, but state general funds to the centers were increased and a substantial Medicaid contract through the State Department of Social and Rehabilitation Services continued to support appropriate deinstitutionalization medical costs. Table 18–1 illustrates the progressive drop in state hospital patient census from 1,057 on 30 June 1974 to 369 in January 1979.

Region III had vigorously endorsed the concept of least restrictive appropriate placement of severely mentally ill persons even before a sweeping Montana reform of the commitment law mandated such in 1974. Table 18–2 indicates the effectiveness of this concept in progressively reducing patient admissions to Warm Springs from Region III, from 262 in 1974 to 58 in 1978.

In January 1978, Region III became the core agency for a rural state model demonstration of the federal Community Support Program (CSP) for chronic mentally ill patients.

SPECIAL PROBLEMS OF SERVICE DELIVERY IN RURAL AREAS

The range of comprehensive support services necessary to maintain the more disabled ex-state hospital patients is not available throughout a large isolated rural catchment area such as Montana's Region III. In our 11 counties, only in Billings are there any psychiatrists. The only colleges are in Billings. Transportation is a major barrier to mental health accessibility. The cost of traveling the distance between patient's home and service center is high. Our region's seven satellite offices have helped to minimize this barrier.

Most programs and reports of programs make no mention of rural populations. An example is *The Community Training Center,* which focuses on socially marginal, high-risk, and isolated groups considered different *(1).* Rural people include all of these character-

Table 18–1.

WARM SPRINGS STATE HOSPITAL POPULATION

June 1974	1,057
June 1975	904
June 1976	668
June 1977	490
June 1978	417
January 1979	369

Table 18–2.

REGION III
ADMISSIONS TO WARM SPRINGS

FY 1974	262
FY 1975	91
FY 1976	77
FY 1977	74
FY 1978	58

istics, and, in fact, generate a high incidence of chronic mental illness.

The President's Commission on Mental Health report states, "In rural America there are few facilities and few people trained to provide mental health care" (2). Part of the problem is the lack of meaningful data for specific mental health planning regarding the prevalence, origin, and resources for the chronic mental patient—or any other mental patient—in rural locales.

Rural people tend to be more independent, perhaps more skeptical, and to seek and accept help later than urban dwellers. For less serious conditions, rural people offer mutual support and acceptance of eccentric behaviors not tolerated in suburban and urban neighborhoods.

There are no medical schools, graduate schools of social work, or psychiatric residency programs within Montana. Cooperative arrangements with the Western Interstate Commission for Higher Education (WICHE) and with the University of Washington through the WAMI (Washington, Alaska, Montana, Idaho) medical education program have been to date of limited value. Personnel shortages continue.

A National Institute of Mental Health funded project contracted to the MITRE Corporation has the purpose of developing the means of improving mental health services in rural areas. Analysis and research directions pertinent to the subject of this chapter are included in the report published in the summer of 1979 (3).

A number of specific high-priority research directions for rural mental health have been identified in the report. These address one or more of the following five major service delivery problems in rural areas:

inadequate transportation,

inappropriate administrative and legal framework,

difficulties in recruitment and retention of professional staff,

lack of effective advocacy, and

lack of coordination (particularly among agencies) *(3)*.

TREATMENT AND CARE ELEMENTS

At South Central Montana Regional Mental Health Center, chronic patients are the responsibility mainly of the Alternative Services Division. Several programs have been added to this division as unmet needs have been identified. There are now six programs. Figure 18–1 shows the organization of the division.

Acute Day Treatment Program

Our initial day treatment program started in 1971 at the openning of the center. It ran 24 hours a week and was designed for acute and subacute verbal patients needing intensive therapy who would otherwise have required hospitalization. These patients need intensive crisis intervention, help in reentering the community after hospitalization, help maintaining themselves in the community, and more than once-a-week contact. The long-range goal was that the patient would ultimately no longer need psychiatric follow-up, other than perhaps maintenance on medications. After the program had been operating for several years, we became increasingly aware that for the chronic mentally ill patient, this long-range goal was inappropriate and based more on staff aspiration than on reality. This led to the creation of our second program component, which we refer to as neighborhood day treatment, for less verbal, more withdrawn and chronic patients. The emphasis is on daily coping skills.

With more patients enrolled in day treatment, staff time reallocation reduced the Acute Day Treatment Program from six hours to three-and-a-half hours, four days weekly. The two full-time staff members involved in the program now have time in the afternoons

Figure 18-1. Organization of Alternative Services Division South Central Montana Regional Mental Health Center.

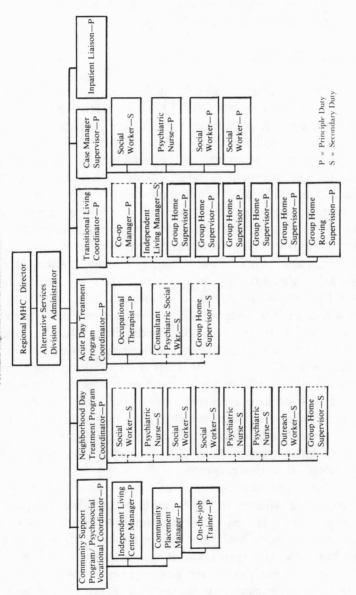

for case management and individual or family therapy. Patients were encouraged to spend afternoons involved with others in the program, in volunteer or part-time jobs, adult education, or on-the-job training. Although this was a temporary solution to a funding problem, we were pleased with the results in reducing patient dependency and have not returned to the six-hour program.

Chronic Day Treatment Program

The second program section then became our Neighborhood Day Treatment Program (NDTP), which began as a three-and-a-half hour program, four days per week for the long-term chronically ill patients who had received maximum benefit from the Acute Day Treatment Program or who had been many years in the state hospital and needed treatment designed to promote socialization, develop daily-living skills in the community, help them function more independently, and prevent rehospitalization. The program started using the local Boys' Club building in the mornings, next moved to a church, and is now housed in its own facility. Approximately 45 patients participate in the program, 32 maximum attendance on any given day. Patients range in age from 19 to 100 years. As deinstitutionalization and avoidance of institutionalizing has occurred, we have had an increasing number of younger patients. The NDTP is now staffed with a full-time program director. All case managers and group home supervisors spend some time staffing this program, which is an effective way to keep track of the patients' progress. Student psychologist and social worker interns, student nurses, and volunteers are used extensively in the program. Recreational, creative, musical, awareness, and relaxation therapies; daily-living skills development; self-evaluation of progress; social learning; work activities to earn money for trips; chemotherapy; and group psychotherapy are used in this program.

One of our early responsibilities in beginning this program was transporting patients to the program because we had poor public transportation. It was extremely time consuming and eventually "special transportation" took over, a service contracted for by various human service agencies needing transportation for their clients. The center switchboard operator is responsible for coordinating travel. Where transportation is not available or feasible, patients are picked up at home and from the inpatient local hospital unit to go to the Acute Day Treatment and Neighborhood Day Treatment Programs. Starting the patients in the programs before they leave the hospital greatly reduces their anxiety and prevents losing the patient between inpatient and outpatient services.

Transitional Living Program and State Hospital Liaison

The next addition to our services was our first group home and the beginning of our Transitional Living Program section. If we have confirmed any one maxim about meeting the needs of the chronically mentally ill, it is that the provision of a continuum of living arrangements, from closely supervised to independent, is mandatory.

The first group home was opened in December 1975, to serve the needs of four men and four women discharged from the state hospital. It was a duplex owned by the Billings Deaconess Hospital that was converted to serve our needs. The house was across from the hospital and four blocks from the center. This proximity allayed somewhat our anxiety, since none of the front-line staff involved had ever had experience with treating chronic psychotic patients in a community setting. The first eight patients had average stays of 15 years in the state hospital.

Two additional group homes, each with eight beds, were opened in middle-class neighborhoods in 1976. Our patients in those neighborhoods have not created any disturbance, although several neighbors had been apprehensive initially.

Group home supervisors were hired to live in three days one week and four days the next. This pattern has continued, with the requirement that every two months group home supervisors take off a shift using holiday time and a roving supervisor fill their shift. This still leaves ample extended vacation time and allows for a ten-day break every two months.

In the beginning of our group home program group home supervisors were not part of the center's treatment team and were seen in more of a caretaking role. It became quickly apparent that they needed to be full members of the treatment team in order to keep excellent staff, to prevent increased dependency by patients, and to insure patient progress to the least restrictive setting possible. It was also obvious that the group home supervisors were in an excellent position to observe pathologic behavior and to contribute to treatment planning. We have an ample supply of group home supervisor applicants because the professional community places a high value on the experience. The psychiatrist's contribution in giving feedback to the group home supervisors of their worth in behavior assessment cannot be overemphasized. Initially, we had a rather elaborate chain of command. Now the person most involved with the patient contacts the psychiatrist directly in emergency situations. The psychiatrists encourage this bypass of usual procedure because of the obvious merit of the direct feedback. Every contact is an opportunity for teaching and learning between various staff levels.

In 1976, money was not available for additional group homes and increasing numbers of patients needed housing. The only affordable accommodations available to our area were the flop house, a cockroach-ridden hotel, and a one-room substandard apartment. This led to the idea of a co-op living home for five or six persons sponsored by our mental health center and providing daily staff contact of about an hour. Because we do not have a boarding house in our region and foster homes are almost nonexistent in spite of the Department of Social and Rehabilitation Services' attempt to encourage them, the family-type support provided at a co-op seemed appealing. Patients able to graduate from group homes and those thought capable of living in a minimally supervised environment were the initial residents. A women's co-op was the initial venture, with a men's co-op added in 1977. Developing a cohesive working unit was found to be more difficult with the men, particularly in regard to housekeeping and socialization. Much has been learned in keeping the mix of patients such that there are at least two less withdrawn patients who provide support for each other and some leadership in decision making. We have found it best that the social worker managing the co-ops not carry any of the residents for case management because of the role confusion and competitiveness that can result.

Last to be added to our Transitional Living Program in 1978, thanks to the federal Community Support Program grant, is the Independent Living Center, a three-apartment cluster rented to center patients and having minimal supervision of one to two hours weekly. Monthly rates range from $85.00 for a person sharing a double room to $125.00 for a one-bedroom apartment with a mother and child. Residents in the co-op pay $65.00–70.00 for a double room and $85.00–90.00 monthly for single rooms. It is, therefore, possible to live on the $187.70 Supplementary Security Income (SSI) payments, which are the total means of support for some residents.

Case Management

Until 1976, there were no case manager supervisors other than the alternative services administrator. It became obvious that we needed to provide additional supervisory time for case management, and this was implemented with development of case management as one of the six key components of the Alternative Services Division.

Our use of the term *case management* is similar to that described in Principles for Accreditation of Community Mental Health Service Programs *(4)*. Case management is there defined as "activities aimed at linking the patient to the service system and coordinating the various services to achieve a successful outcome. The five case management activities are assessment, planning, linking, monitoring, and advocacy." A variation currently being tested in our program, funded by a federal action grant, is the use of carefully screened and trained volunteers as case managers. Using volunteers limits the assessment activity, but not the others.

Community Support Program—Psychosocial Vocational Program

In 1975, the beginning of our Psychosocial Vocational Program was initiated by creating the position of community placement manager, whose responsibilities were to evaluate a client's job potential, facilitate evaluation through sheltered workshop and vocational rehabilitation, and develop job placements. This service has grown, and in February 1979, the two Community Support Program staff began to devote increasing efforts in this area.

Since July 1978, we have had an on-the-job janitorial training program at the main center, and 14 chronically ill persons have been trained, receiving a certificate of achievement. We have been particularly fortunate that Billings Deaconess Hospital is willing to employ our patients in many areas of the hospital. In summers, we have a yard detailing crew, who contract to do such tasks as mowing and cleaning of yards.

Recently, we have arranged for vocational rehabilitation to have a counselor spend an afternoon a week at the center to evaluate patients, speeding the enrollment process and increasing agency communication.

We have found that to be able to work at some activity is extremely motivating and often is the final link in the treatment plan for most patients. Even for the elderly patients, putting packets of toiletries together for the hospital gives them a way to partly pay their way for day care trips.

Inpatient Liaison

The last addition to our Alternative Services Division is part-time inpatient liaison manager, who works between the local hospital inpatient unit and the center implementing treatment plans and linking with agencies and other center programs. This had been the responsibility of the alternative services administrator, who continues to meet with psychiatrists and inpatient staff four mornings per week. The inpatient liaison manager meets with the hospital staff five mornings a week and is responsible for implementation. The number of short-term crisis stabilization cases has increased in the inpatient unit, and prompt planning for discharge reduces inpatient days and avoids rehospitalization. Therefore, this staff position will become full-time when funding can be worked out.

Perhaps one of the most unique, gratifying, and vital parts of our service delivery is our relationship with the community's four private psychiatrists, who provide 70% of the center's inpatient admissions and follow-up for medication, and medical and psychiatric consultation for a large proportion of the center's chronic population. The employment of a full-time center staff psychiatrist in addition to the psychiatrist director has been invaluable in keeping up with the increasing number of patients remaining in the community.

Because we are committed to keeping our patients on the least amount of medication necessary for functioning in the community setting, careful monitoring of our patients by our psychiatrists is absolutely essential. Their willingness to teach our staff has been useful, but their willingness to listen has added a very special positive quality to our relationship. Perhaps this is because we are all painfully aware that, without each other, we cannot provide optimal care to those we have chosen to serve.

We are now convinced that the maintenance of the chronically ill is a lifelong process. It may utilize a variety of means. The minimum is a once-weekly social club run by volunteers, medication checks quarterly, and phone calls from the case manager. Far more often, there will be various degrees of assistance in one of three center group homes, one of the two co-ops or apartments, job placement, day care or treatment, daily case management, and frequent medication evaluation, always with the goal of providing less service as the patient progresses.

If patients are pushed too aggressively toward independence, they often regress. If not pushed hard enough, growth does not occur. The balance is delicate. Treatment plans and outcome goals must be flexible to allow significant alteration without the patient or staff feeling a failure. This is essential for this population especially.

ADMINISTRATION AND COORDINATION

The Region III center is a private, nonprofit mental health center, governed by a board composed of a county commissioner or commissioner designee from each of the counties within the catchment area.

Figure 18–1 gives the organizational scheme for the Alternative Services Division.

Internal coordination is provided by unequivocal policy from the board and director in support of chronic patient services. Specific elements include planned and regular interaction, that is, twice-monthly program managers coordinating meeting, twice-monthly staffing of patients identified for the Community Support Program, weekly meeting of urban services staff to coordinate high-risk and multiple service need patients, and weekly supervision of all Alternative Services staff.

External coordination is achieved by the assignment of a case manager for each patient and a planning-linking conference at regular intervals. A planning-linking conference is a case conference that always includes the patient, and, where possible, significant other family members, caseworkers, and supervisors in an agency setting to discuss problems and/or service plans regarding the patient. Efforts are made to keep the same case manager over the rather long period of time services are supported. Such efforts involve attention to staff as well as patient morale, reduction of staff (as well as patient) burnout, and greater weighting of personality and character rather than educational attainment in recruiting case managers.

STAFFING

Staffing of the Alternative Services Division at this center has evolved from a former public health nurse hired in 1973 to do outreach in a day treatment program, to a 17-member team divided by 1979 into the six programs already described. The team is composed of generalists who often have an area of primary specialization but are flexible enough to step into any other program as needed. All 17 members of the team carry case management responsibilities for assigned patients, the number depending on other assignments. Fourteen members of the team are beginning-level (BS) social workers, vocational rehabilitation counselors, or nurses who are experientially trained. In addition, an experienced psychiatric social worker, an occupational therapist, and a psychiatric nurse administrator complete the team. Seven members of the present staff were former student interns who worked in the program while in their undergraduate training. There is around-the-clock psychiatric coverage always available from one of six psychiatrists. The team is now seen by the other center clinical staff as having expertise with the chronically mentally ill rather than as caretakers for the poorly motivated, uncooperative chronic patient who could not use psychotherapy. The Alternative Services staff's growing feeling of being valued is seen as crucial to the excellent results of this program in maintaining only 13% recidivism to the state hospital and cutting admissions so that, although our region holds 20% of the state population, it accounts for only 10% of the population at the state hospital.

Another important factor in outcome is related to the value placed on combining "everything that works" regardless of model or discipline. Staff does not expend energy debating medical versus social, behavioral, or learning models. It is possible for any worker in the division to pick up on a patient with side effects from medication and arrange for psychiatric intervention. The psychiatrist may ask the group home supervisor to come in with the patient to give input about observations regarding medication compliance and behavior. One patient has been worked with at breakfast with behavior modification to increase the use of eating utensils rather than fingers at meals. This patient may be discussed at a supervisory conference in terms of her primary narcissism and the transference/countertransference problems being experienced by the staff. She may attend a day treatment program in the morning, using social learning models and process-oriented group therapy, and an on-the-job training program in the afternoon, using habilitation principles. In the evening, she will attend Hope Club, a social club run by the Mental Health Association volunteers. Her case manager may have helped her arrange a dental appointment the following day. The give and take between disciplines and levels of training is a constantly ongoing evolving exciting development.

The Alternative Services administration has found it extremely important to staff morale to give program managers decision-making responsibility for the programs they manage. For example, our day care manager, who is an extremely effective bachelor's-level prepared person, has the final decision regarding intakes to the program he manages. He is not questioned by more senior staff or a psychiatrist without meeting to thoroughly discuss the difference of opinion and coming to a mutual agreement. It is seldom that the alternative services administrator needs to be involved in everday program management, because it is clear the negotiations must start with the program manager. Because the alternative services administrator meets four mornings weekly at the local hospital inpatient unit with inpatient staff, center contract psychiatrists, and one full-time center staff psychiatrist, communication problems can be picked up on quickly and differences of opinion aired; in addition, appropriate staff can be asked to attend the staffings to give and receive input. Discharge planning begins the day of admission. Misunderstandings are more rapidly resolved in this way, and the patient is much less likely to "fall through the treatment cracks" between hospital and outpatient services. If a patient is to start day care or day treatment, this is begun from the hospital before dismissal. The Balanced Service System principles of least restrictive, most natural appropriate setting and emphasis of the case manager as assessor, advocate, monitor, planner, and linker are central to our operation.

Alternative Services staff handle the large majority of emergencies occurring with their patients, relieving general emergency service staff who may not know the patient's status. Crisis intervention in the home, at work, or in transitional living placement is attempted before hospitalization is considered. Occasionally, a patient who has become severely psychotic in the group home and who is not sleeping may be hospitalized briefly for stabilization. We have found that it is too exhausting for a group home supervisor to spend day and night with an overtly psychotic patient. For the infrequent times we have used brief hospitalization, we have not found it to be as harmful to the patient's subsequent progress as the literature sometimes suggests. The group home "family" visits the hospital as does any other family. Staff and other residents benefit from the "breather" and a good night's sleep. Thus, staff burnout is reduced. This is in contrast to the heroic, and at times inappropriate, measures we took initially to avoid hospitalization at all costs.

The use of the population center, Billings, to provide the many components necessary for successful community integration has proven more successful than duplication of day treatment and other services in small communities with only one or two satellite professionals. We have found the better-functioning patients are reintegrated into the small-town church and social activities if behavior is not too bizarre. The increased anonymity of a larger community and the many supports that in Region III only Billings offers, are the reasons most of the severe chronic patients gravitate to Billings.

TRAINING

All staff who are hired are given training on center and state policies and procedures; patient evaluation including mental status, role functioning, and recordkeeping; involuntary hospitalization criteria and procedures; depression, schizophrenia, medications, and emergency procedures.

Montana has partially solved the rural mental health personnel shortage by a statute under which certain nurses, social workers, psychologists, and other qualified persons may be certified as mental health professionals. In-service staff training is becoming geared toward helping uncredentialed staff become certified. New treatment staff are recruited from suitable applicants already certifiable when this is possible.

Training efforts for work with the chronically mentally ill involves role modeling; consistent, firm but sensitive supervision; and creation of incentive to learn more about a field where "the answer" is cloudy or nonexistent. Experienced and trained workers assist the inexperienced in home visits, family sessions, history taking, and other such responsibilities. During 1978, the alternative services staff, on their own, developed in-service training programs twice a month to help provide the knowledge or skills they identified as needed. They have held sessions on such topics as family therapy, death and dying, depression in children, homosexuality, transference and countertransference, group psychotherapy, listening, termination, and movement therapy.

Interest in these self-organized in-service programs has far surpassed that of in–service training developed without staff involvement. A planning committee rotates every three months to arrange programs.

Group home supervisors meet for an hour weekly for in-service training in interviewing, mental status exams, and other areas, as requested. Role playing and discussion of cases along with some didactic concepts are used.

A case manager training program is being developed by the Community Support Program for training new staff, outpatient staff who look beyond the traditional 50-minute hour, and volunteers who will be taking over case management for selected patients.

Staff burnout and its reduction is a training focus. Perhaps one of the things that most effects staff burnout is the every-other-year funding crises and the changing answer to the question, "What is important in meeting accountability this month?" Paperwork is sometimes a monumental task when several patients are in crisis and staff is working overtime. The very nature of the work with chronic patients who sometimes regress in spite of all diligent efforts is demoralizing. Building an acceptance that this sometimes happens is essential for beginning workers especially. This is where team support contributes so vitally, as long as someone on the team is able to maintain objectivity. Workers often feel as caught in the hopelessness of changing the system as their patients feel in changing their lives.

Vital also to the prevention of burnout is the ability to move staff to another position every few years to develop some new facet of the program and to do some other kind of service. Every Alternative Services worker has the option of working as cotherapist in an insight-oriented outpatient group, of doing family therapy, of working with a children's group, or, otherwise, of doing something very different than caring for the chronically ill. These options are helpful in maintaining and broadening one's perspective.

Group home supervisors and their spouses often get out together alternate Wednesday evenings for socializing. Originally, supervisors spent every Wednesday night with residents of the group homes. When resistance from residents arose over going out every Wednesday and it became obvious they were not nearly as anxious to go out as the supervisors, we compromised to every other week. Supervisors bowl, go out for pizza, play basketball, and engage in many other activities. They try not to talk "shop" and get to know each other as people. Obviously, if there is someone acutely psychotic or in difficulty, they do not leave the group home, but we have found the residents profit from knowing they can manage on their own and that help is just a phone call away.

OUTCOME DATA

Table 18–2 shows that the number of admissions to Montana's state hospital from the core agency, Region III decreased for each fiscal year from 1974 through 1978. From 1 July 1975 through 30 June 1978, 327 patients were discharged from Warm Springs State Hospital to Region III. Of these, only 35 had been readmitted to Warm Springs by the end of the period. National statistics indicate annual readmission rates to public mental hospitals have ranged from 30% to 60% (5). Region III figures show that 87% of discharged patients remain in the community over one year.

Job placement, successful for at least three months during the 12 months prior to March 1979, was achieved by 33 chronic patients (11% of the total). During the previous year, 60% of the patients placed in jobs were still working after six months.

The State Division of Mental Health and Residential Services Executive Summary, Annual Report, Montana Community Support Project (CSP), 3 March 1979 (6), includes the following: "An important part of evaluating the functioning of a new program is to assess the cost involved. Fiscal data was collected on a sample of 118 Community Support Program clients (in Region III) for the third quarter of 1978." Whereas the annual cost to the center per patient (all patients) was $383, the average annual cost for a chronic patient enrolled in the Community Support Program was $2,924. However, the CSP client in a supervised group home cost the center an average of $15,317 a year, whereas the chronic patient outside the group home cost $998 per year. It is important to keep in mind these are only center costs. The total annual patient costs are close to center costs for supervised group home residents, but far below the annual total costs for the other chronic patients. Total costs of the nonresidential clients for a year would still average less than $15,317. These residential supervised patients are costly to maintain in the community. Without such support, however, they would be back in the state hospital, which has an annual cost of $24,426. So it still appears economical to maintain chronic patients in the community. Since 1 January 1978, only one CSP client has been readmitted to the state hospital. A sample of 37 CSP clients revealed six who had been hospitalized an average of 16 days within the local general hospital (6).

Quality of life comparisons are difficult. With our project, comparisons of predata with postdata will not be available until later in 1979. Consumer satisfaction surveys conducted in 1978 indicated 96% were either "satisfied" or "very satisfied" with services received. This, of course, is not a measure of functioning. A global assessment of all patients on admission and those discharged or still enrolled three months later indicated average improvement in functioning of over 1 point on a 9-point scale. The change in functioning of chronic patients was less. We believe a minimum of six months must elapse between assessments of this population.

A striking result of focus and priority attention to the chronic mentally ill patient in this center is the marked increase in allocation of staff time and center resources in support of the chronic patient. During the ten-month test period, 26% of all clinical staff time went for the 35 group home patients. During the same ten months, 25% of all center expenditures were in support of the costs for these 35 patients. During the same time, 2,500 other patients shared the remaining staff time and costs. The intensity of services required per patient will continue to go up as long as our priorities remain high for this group.

Another factor of importance is the increase in number of chronic patients hospitalized locally in the general hospital with acute regressions and an increase in average length of stay. Without the active support of four private-practice psychiatrists in Billings, this center would not be able to respond as quickly and fully to this increased caseload pressure.

Although more time is required to test the long-range effectiveness of the rural program described in this chapter, the authors believe the model can be replicated any place the state, the state hospital, and the local community are committed to the approach described.

NOTES

1. Spiegler MD, Agigian H: The Community Training Center. New York, Brunner Mazel, 1977

2. Report to the President From the President's Commission on Mental Health, Vol. 1. Washington, D.C., U.S. Government Printing Press, 1978

3. Cedar T, Salasin J: Research Directions for Rural Mental Health. McLean, Va., The MITRE Corporation, Metrek Division, 1979

4. Principles for Accreditation of Community Mental Health Service Programs. Chicago, Joint Commission on Accreditation of Hospitals, 1976

5. Lamb HR, Allen P, Edelson MB, Goertzel V, Mackota C, Shadoan RA: Community Survival for Long-term Patients. San Francisco, Jossey-Bass, 1976

6. Montana Community Support Project: Executive Summary, Annual Report. Helena, Montana, Department of Institutions, 1979

Chapter 19

SPECIALIZED PROGRAMS FOR THE CHRONICALLY MENTALLY ILL CHILD

Sydney Koret

ASSESSMENT OF NEED

Delving into the provision of care for the young chronic mental patient leads across a multiplicity of settings, disciplines, and program formats. Even definitions become difficult. It is not realistically possible to categorize a child mental patient as "chronic" in the same specific terms that one can for an adult. For example, adults are frequently characterized as "chronic" in terms of the length of time spent in treatment or projection of time in need of treatment. With children, the term "chronic" may well mean the *anticipated* length of time for treatment, diagnostic category, or behavioral patterns. Even the questionable specificity of adult definition is lacking for children. One is constantly confronted with the danger of constructing classifications and diagnostic categories which in themselves become self-fulling prophesies.

An in-depth survey of programs serving the chronically mentally ill child reveals that these children are scattered in diverse programs. Until the twentieth century, they tended to be found in orphanages, correctional institutions, and agencies for dependent and neglected children. The responsibility for their care was far more frequently lodged in the hands of the social service rather than in the medical profession.

In the early part of the twentieth century, a shift occurred in the perception, detection, and care of the mentally ill child. The work of Sigmund Freud and his followers drew attention to childhood as the arena for personality formation and potential mental illness. The work and formulations of August Aichorn fired the imagination and moved those charged with the long-term care of children from a custodial to a treatment frame of reference. The concept of the "young village idiot" began slowly to fade. In the early 1920s, two processes occurred which profoundly affected the assessment and treatment of the mentally ill child and the provision of care for the chronically ill. The first of these was the emergence of the child guidance clinic concept, and second was the appearance of therapeutic residential programs and the residential treatment center. Since these were both interdisciplinary by nature, the course of planning and treatment was strongly influenced by social workers, educators, and child care workers, in addition to medical doctors and psychiatrists. Attention to children and unique treatment needs also became a major consideration for psychiatric hospitals. Separate wards and separate intensive training programs were created, primarily under medical direction and frequently concentrating on the organically impaired.

By 1970, there were over 310 institutions for emotionally disturbed children, primarily dealing with the "chronically" disturbed. Of this number, 286 were under private auspices and 24 were public, serving approximately 14,000 children. Of these, approximately 11,000 were in the private facilities and 3,000 in the public institutions. There were 145 psychiatric inpatient units for children; 65 of these privately administered and 80 in the public domain. Of the 8,000 children served in these units, 2,400 were under private care and 5,600 in public facilities (1). It becomes quite clear that private organizations provide by far the bulk of care for the chronically mentally ill child, offering services to three-fourths of this population. The figures tend to reverse for the psychiatric inpatient unit. In addition, there is a mushrooming number of private child care facilities which are filling their beds with the chronically mentally disturbed child patients. All of this presents a series of professional questions and challenges. Most children being so served are being treated and frequently, successfully so, by interdisciplinary teams, with psychiatrists having varying degrees of authority and supervisory input.

The precise number of emotionally disturbed and mentally ill children in this country is not known. Nevertheless, indications of the insufficiency of beds to service this population are clear from the waiting lists which are common in most treatment facilities. Admission criteria set to keep caseloads within reasonable limits must of necessity become discriminatory in terms of age, diagnostic classification, and so forth, and respond to the obvious difficulties in recruiting an adequate number of professional staff. A study done in Wisconsin in 1972–73 produced 280 cases of children diagnosed as autistic or schizophrenic. This indicates a verified rate of 3.1 such children per 10,000 children or one for every 3,220. The Joint Commission on Mental Health of Children conservatively estimated that ½ of 1%, or more than 450,000, were seriously disturbed *(2)*. The commission's projection was that if all of these children and youth were being given adequate treatment either in a residential center or in day treatment, with caseloads of 50 children per worker (obviously preposterously too great for effective care and treatment), there would be a need for six times the present number of child psychiatrists, more than twice the number of clinical psychologists, and an additional 18,000 social workers and 27,000 psychiatric nurses. The final statement of the joint commission was that .6% of young people are psychotic, with another 2–3% severely disturbed.

THE CHRONIC CHILD'S NEEDS

To understand, to devise, and to evaluate programs for the chronically disturbed child, one must be aware of the idiosyncratic needs of the mentally ill child. A basic difficulty in the past has been attempting to pattern children's mental health services in accordance with a format developed for adults. The movement in the mid-1960s led particularly by those devising community mental health centers, was based on the presumption that a stay in an inpatient unit would be extremely short, with a relatively fast transfer to day treatment or outpatient services. The total effort was devoted to returning the adult to his former optimum level of functioning and resumption of his position in the community. With such rapid turnover, a small number of beds could service a fairly large population. Longer stays were relegated to the state hospital and frequently slid into a custodial arrangement *(3)*.

When one deals with children, the situation is completely reversed. Most children have no former level of optimum functioning to which they can return. Almost in every case the situation has existed since early childhood, and it is its very chronicity rather than acuteness that leads to the referral to an inpatient or residential service. Agency after agency has demonstrated that there is really no such "beast" as short-term treatment for seriously disturbed children. When this has been attempted, it has either collapsed around the frustration of the staff or led to a gradual extension of treatment when plans for disposition became ultimately unresolvable. Pragmatically, except in very rare situations as in the case of some acute organic insult, almost every child referred for residential or inpatient service must be viewed as having a degree of chronicity. The condition which leads to the referral of the child has been an evolving process from infancy or very early childhood.

The basic component of personality functioning has never developed to a level approaching maturity. This is equally true no matter what theoretic framework is used for assessment. Basic relationships have never been adequately established. The concept of trust is extremely tenuous. Without a background of fulfillment and achievement, there is no reservoir of successful experiences for the child to fall back on. There is no frame of reference from which the child can operate. Primarily, that must be established at time of entrance into a program. In a very real sense, the chronic mentally ill child has been strangulated on his own psychological umbilical cord. He has not grown—only survived.

Because of this inability to develop the prerequisites for growth, this patient tends to have deficits in every area of personality and social functioning. The debilitating condition is pervasive, as though the child were trapped, since he cannot achieve step one, which leads to step two, which leads to step three, and so on. This then dictates a series of needs from which a well-thought-out program must flow.

A key, or perhaps *the* key, in working with child patients is the *familial relationships.* The development of relationships with this patient and his family has been disrupted. The normal communication, the interaction system between parents, siblings, and the child patient, has deteriorated or been severed. The dangerous and insidious corollary that parents are "uncaring," "unworthy," or "malevolent" in view of later studies and the appreciation of biological and neurological factors can by now be rejected out of hand. There are many potentially disruptive factors which belong more appropriately in a volume on child development, child pathology, or family systems. Unlike the adult, the child is completely dependent on an external support system. Unless he is in an advanced stage of adolescence by the time of discharge, he will still be dependent on such a system when he returns to the community.

Institutional living is designed to prepare the individual not for further institutionalization but for life in the world. A study of 42 children who had been treated during 1954–58 at the Convalescent Hospital for Children in Rochester, New York, indicated "the impact of the general environment on these children immediately after discharge" and the importance of a continued external support system for readmission to the community (10). This then points to the dramatic need for altering the misperceptions of the child and the family about each other and the establishment of usable relationships.

The second aspect of the child's life situation which requires drastic attention is *education*. For most children and youth, school is the area in which they spend the greatest amount of time and effort when away from home. It is also where, they can receive recognition for achievement, test their own abilities, pave the road for continuation into adulthood, and perceive their own limits and the credibility of their own aspirations. Unfortunately, for most of the children to whom we have addressed ourselves, it becomes the institution for failure, frustration, despair, and hatred. It has become fashionable to condemn the educational system for its inability to provide for these children. In actuality, these children frequently enter unprepared for the human relationships and freedom to learn, essentials in utilizing the educational experience. Of prime importance is the fact that it is not a happy situation. Children wind up denigrated, with a concept of themselves as failures and with a further reduced self-image. The teacher, the school, and the educational establishment become a source of embarrassment and exclusion, which frequently precipitates feelings of rage or withdrawal. Any program devised for the chronically disturbed child must make provision for a rehabilitative educational experience. This includes three basic factors: establishing a communicating relationship between the teacher and child, improving the child's perception of himself in relationship to the cognitive process, and establishing educational achievements which can phase him into the new noninstitutionalized academic setting.

The *social-recreational* phase is the final leg of the triangle in the treatment of chronically disturbed children. Because of the child's inability to function within his family and within the school setting, he most frequently has not developed skills and the feeling tone necessary to produce a social life with peers and the broader community. Behavior is frequently self-defeating, antagonistic, provocative, and destructive. Constant efforts to establish a peer base without preliminary training usually has the impact of producing its own isolation. This leads to a need to establish an extracurricular life which becomes bizarre or antisocial. Program design must enable the child to make adequate peer linkages, develop a social life, adjust it to his needs, and cope with the community which provides these opportunities.

The needs of the chronically ill child outlined above—familial, educational, social-recreational—require certain specific applications of skill. These are all designed to make possible the integration of the child into the community.

Program Components

The knowledge and application of *child-rearing* skills is a basic commodity of a treatment facility for children. Frequently, day-to-day teaching and training, assumed to be present in moving a child from infancy through the formative years, has been seriously inadequate. This includes the very basic aspects of self-care, accepted modes of surviving and flourishing, and acceptable standards for the society in which the child lives. These have frequently been conspicuously absent. Thus, the child does not know what to expect of himself and what the community expects of him in his presentation of himself as a human being. The lack may occur for a multitude of reasons. The parent may have been inadequate and ill-equipped to "bring up the child." The growing animosity between child and parent may have led to a complete rejection by the child of any standards introduced by the parent. Further, the rejection of parental norms may frequently be a method of securing affective attention and the only way the child knows. In extreme cases, parents may withhold their knowledge and let the child "hang himself" in a subconscious effort to have him complete emotional suicide without conceding parental responsibility.

Educational therapy or rehabilitative education is designed to enable the child to return to his world of work. For most children who are chronically disturbed, public schools have been a farcial nightmare fraught with catastrophic episodes. Their experiences with school failures, the inhibiting of their desire to learn or utilize the cognitive processes in educational fashion, and their perceptions of school authorities and teachers as perpetrators of diabolical tortures have to be dealt with within a facility which can deal with both the child's revulsion for the process and his fears, as well as the preparation for a forum in which he will spend most of his time after discharge.

Sociotherapy is the matrix through which all of the other services meet and impact upon each other. This is a discipline that utilizes paraprofessionals, variously termed sociotherapists, counselors, or child care workers. Since the children in treatment spend most of their hours with these clinicians, who are the most numerous and without prior professional training; their selection, training, and supervision are delicate and critical. For any effective program, they must become true clinicians, utilizing their ability to empathize, understand diagnostic implications, and implement treatment plans. Sociotherapy is the art of utilizing the milieu as a treatment medium. Sociotherapists must be prepared to serve as the eyes and ears of the professional staff. They enable the child to understand the inadequacies of his methods of coping with the environment and offer substitute techniques or defenses. They provide the identifiable role models. They deal with behavior, inner feelings, and turmoil in a special and uniquely prescribed fashion. They deal with the child's ego and its defenses in the daily clashes with the child's physical and human environment. Sociotherapists are with the child at play, at times of nurturance and during physical and psychological emergency and are frequently interwoven with the educational system.

Group work is an essential of the treatment modality for the chronically ill. It involves understanding the composition and formation of groups and the dynamics of small and large groups and their impact on any given child. For the child in long-term treatment, the group is the social community with which he must learn to cope. It is precisely in his peer relationships and his dealing with authority within the group that he has demonstrated his most flagrant and conspicuous symptom. Prior to treatment he probably was unacceptable to any group and had no real group loyalties, nor could he accept the intensities of the human relationships which flowed through the group structure. Some organizations have no formal group worker but must deal with the impact of the group and its structure. This may be relegated to a social worker, sociotherapist, or recreational worker. Recognition of the group process is pivotal in providing treatment for the seriously disturbed child.

Psychotherapy plays a major role in the treatment of the chronically ill child. Its role, however, differs quite markedly from that in other settings and with other types of individuals. The concept of complete confidentiality within the facility dedicated to treatment of the chronically mentally ill child is contraindicated. It is precisely the interaction between sociotherapists, educators, caseworkers, and psychotherapists that makes the program feasible and effective. Further, the psychotherapist may very well not be the most influential person in the child's life. The child has been offered a number of individual's to relate to, and at any given time, in accord with the problems of the moment, the sociotherapist, the social worker, the educator, or the psychiatrist rises to dominance in the child's hierarchy. The psychotherapist may not be the psychiatrist. This may not be financially or theoretically appropriate. The psychotherapist may well be a social worker or psychologist chosen to meet the needs of any given patient in terms of the therapist's own particular experience and training. The impact of the psychiatrist may be in terms of his diagnositc and assessment skills and his ability to understand and utilize the services of other disciplines.

Since the child is completely dependent upon the support of an external environment, work with parents is a sine qua non of treatment. It is the *social worker* who prepares the home for the eventual reintegration of the child. The social worker is charged with readapting the attitudes of the parents, causing the necessary shift that makes the child acceptable and supportable within the family. The social worker also maintains the essential liaison with the community during the total time of the child's treatment so that the final touch to remove the word chronicity becomes possible. The child must have a home to which to return, be it his own or another, since he is not able to establish an independent existence without the aid of collaterals *(6)*.

The very essence of a program for the care and treatment of the chronically mentally ill child patient demands the establishment of its own *cultural pattern* dependent very much on staff interrelationships, understandable communication, and instantaneous reaction to the needs of the child *(7)*. Within each facility, continuity of care establishes a mosaic which prohibits the utilization of staff from other facilities. Staff from another center or other clinics, hospitals, or private practice cannot normally continue with the child after he has been admitted to treatment for the chronically ill. The long-term nature of the commitment and the time involved, not only in providing services, but in conferencing and constant communication becomes prohibitive.

PROGRAM MODELS

There are several types of programs which can incorporate the clinical services discussed above. The type of program will dictate the intensity and any specific input, such as sociotherapy or education, which can be emphasized. The child's dynamics and his own particular deficits frequently determine the appropriate program.

Inpatient service for the chronically mentally ill child is usually provided in private psychiatric hospitals or in publically owned facilities, such as state hospitals. These services provide effective controls and programming for those children whose problems stem from an organic base. Medical supervision and monitoring is usually most intense. Inpatient services normally provide more in the way of maximum security than is available in other programs, and most approach the familiar medical setting.

The *residential treatment program* comes closest to providing long-term care for the chronically mentally ill child. It has the capacity for integrating all of the treatment modalities. It need not be hampered by many of the debilitating hospital constrictions which are inappropriate for long-term care. It can utilize nonmedical personnel without diluting medical authority and psychiatric responsibility. It can bring together sociotherapy, educational therapy, psychotherapy, pediatrics, group work, and social casework in a workable fashion designed to meet all the needs of the chronically ill. Unfortunately, its greatest strength has also proved to be its greatest weakness. Without the accreditation program and the discipline and supervisory system of hospital standards and the medical profession, until recently residential treatment programs were basically completely dependent upon self-monitoring by their own individual administrations. In the past few years, this has been primarily remediated as discussed below.

Many *day treatment programs* have sprung up in the past ten years which have the competence to deal with and treat the chronic mentally ill child. The prime function of a day treatment program for children is to provide them with a rehabilitative educational experience interwoven with psychotherapy and milieu therapy. Its goal is to return the child to the educational world from which he has been excluded, both socially and educationally, as well as to help the child adapt to a larger community. One *a priori* assumption is that the child can benefit from such treatment without removal from home and community. It therefore leans heavily on social work support to provide treatment and instruction to the family as a backdrop and as an essential for ongoing treatment. As in residential treatment, day treatment must incorporate and integrate the services of psychiatry, clinical psychology, educational therapy, sociotherapy, and social work. The past few years have demonstrated that many chronically ill children can be beneficially served in a day treatment program without the trauma to family and child of long-term complete separation. Day treatment must be conceived of as a relatively long-term process. Since the problem is so inextricably interwoven with school, one must conceive of working with school districts and school mental health people. Public Law 94-142 can be considered both an angel and a demon for day treatment. On the one hand, it provides necessary funding as an "aid for the handicapped child," but on the other, because of its sectarian myopia, it is focused only on the educational aspects and may in the long run deemphasize psychotherapeutic contributions toward the needs of the child.

Recently, other types of programs having a potential for the treatment of the chronically ill have emerged. For my purposes here, I combine two separate aspects: the *foster home* and the *group home.* Both of these programs maintain the chronically ill child in the community but not within his own home. They presuppose that the particular child involved can live within the community without outlandishly disrupting it and can utilize its resources. Children who have such a level of tolerance have been assessed as being unable to live in the intimacy of their own family and the kinds of emotional demands it places on them, or have no family of their own. Movement from foster homes to group homes is necessitated when the child cannot benefit from the intimacy of any family and needs more diluted relationships and closer supervision. The hurdle in the utilization of these programs has been the inability of the public schools, in many cases, to provide for children who are seriously disturbed. It is now possible with the utilization of day treatment programs and group home services to put together an individually prescribed program which can accommodate many children who formerly were institutionalized. Such children basically receive the services provided in other therapeutic programs, but a profound emphasis must be placed on the milieu and the sociotherapists who govern it. For the most part, the sociotherapists are self-functioning and supervision from professionals is not as immediate, as direct, and as close in geographical context as in the other programs, therefore, instantaneous communication systems and training of sociotherapy staff must be finely tuned if these are actually to serve as therapeutic programs. Nevertheless, the potential of foster and group homes has only begun to be explored. This is particularly true in the interaction between the group home and foster home and other therapeutic resources, such as day treatment.

STAFFING AND PERSONNEL NEEDS

Staffing for the chronically mentally ill child has presented the same series of problems as has haunted other psychiatric facilities. In general, there is a shortage of trained personnel an every level of care and treatment. Professionals assigned to work with the chronically mentally ill child must have more than a generic background and an assignment to a children's unit *(13)*. Understanding the problems of children and their families, and of developing the necessary tools and methodologies for treatment, demands specific training in such areas as child psychiatry and child psychology. Those trained in work with adults provide a different focus and inadequate tools. Further, because of the multidiscipline aspect of working with children, in-service training and staff development have an especially high priority. Psychiatrists, psychologists, social workers, educational therapists, and sociotherapists come from a diversity of backgrounds, training organizations, and theoretic contructs. Development of common language, a common meeting ground, a usable communication system, and an acceptable theoretic base must be arrived at if the chronically ill child is to be served rather than merely provided with a hodgepodge of discordant disciplines.

A psychiatrist enjoys a unique position within this operation. He is rarely providing direct service to the patient. He is most particularly involved with the diagnosis and assessment, training, supervision, and monitoring. It is only when medication is needed that he is the only one able to provide direct service. In order to guarantee medical involvement, there has sprung up in most glossaries, the remarkable euphemism "psychiatric input," rather than psychiatric treatment. The number of child psychiatrists is dangerously low. Since the millennium is not expected in the near future, the wise and judicious use of psychiatric time is an underlying principle in the organization of a facility to treat the chronically mentally ill child.

Clinical child psychology is another discipline that is in short supply. The clinical psychologist is directly responsible for diagnostic assessment, both in terms of intake and as an ongoing monitoring of a child's progress. The clinical psychologist is expected to provide psychotherapy, to engage in teaching, and in many cases to be involved in research. Indeed, it has been the clinical psychologist who in the last ten years developed most of the critical and experimental views of current practice.

Social workers with psychiatric training provide a major source of treatment. In most facilities for children, they are the most numerous professional group. Their entrance into the field from graduate school is usually marked by a lack of specialization, but their training makes adaptation to work with the chronically mentally ill child a natural consequence. They are responsible normally for working with families in casework, in family therapy, and in group therapy, as well as for providing psychotherapy. In most facilities, they provide the liaison between the external community and the treatment resource.

Educational therapists spend the bulk of the child's daytime hours with the chronically ill child. These therapists are teachers specially trained in working with the emotionally disturbed. As more and more schools have instituted specialized training in special education for the emotionally disturbed, the educator has moved from teacher to educational therapist. Their concept of education must be the integration of social and emotional as well as cognitive growth.

Sociotherapists have in the past required no specific background. They were judged on such personality characteristics as empathy, ability to relate, ability to tolerate deviant behavior, and ability to have made their own sexual and social identifications. In recent years, more and more sociotherapists have been college graduates with bachelor's degrees, with an emphasis on psychology, social work, and early childhood development. Community colleges have developed two-year programs leading to an associate in arts degree, specifically designed to produce workers in the human services. Further, some of the child care associations now provide certification for sociotherapists, and they are emerging as a group with their own body of knowledge and a new discipline.

ACCREDITATIONS

As was mentioned earlier one of the problems of psychiatric facilities until recently has been the complete dependence on self-monitoring. Except for the need to meet certain state provisions for licensing or certification, quality control was almost nonexistent from any external body. This applied equally, or even more so, to those facilities providing care for the chronically mentally ill child. Since most of the organizations providing care and treatment came from diverse backgrounds, there was no one body which took responsibility and indeed no common conception of what basic standards should be. The number of approaches and techniques were confounding and seemed to defy any one standard-setting body. Governance was in medicine, in social work, in education, and indeed, sometimes in completely lay groups. Only the American Association of Children's Residential Centers prescribed the concept of quality for its members, but even this organization failed to provide clear-cut measurable standards.

In 1970, the Joint Commission on Accreditation of Hospitals began to reconceive its standard-setting function. It became involved with the study and design of standards for health-related as well as strictly medical facilities. In 1971, a task force was appointed to draw up standards for psychiatric facilities for children. Following this, representatives of organizations involved with the mental health treatment of children became part of the Accreditation Council for Psychiatric Facilities, of the Joint Commission on Accreditation of Hospitals. Since 1974, such facilities have established standards to which they must comply if they desire accreditation by the joint commission. For the first time then, at least minimums of quality control are not only available but being implemented. It is of interest to note that many of the accredited organizations are free-standing, nonmedical facilities which provide most of the basic care of the chronically mentally disabled child.

Somewhat later, the Office of Civilian Health and Medical Program of the Uniformed Services (OCHAMPUS) of the Department of Defense became concerned about quality of service being offered the dependents of military personnel. They, too, established a set of standards and a process for implementing them. CHAMPUS standards have become heavily dependent upon the utilization of the Joint Commission on Accreditation of Hospitals within the last few years so that they are almost synonymous.

Membership in the American Association of Children's Residential Centers also connotes a degree of high quality for residential treatment centers providing psychiatric care.

There are now a number, though still an inadequate number, of facilities providing quality care for the chronic mentally disabled child. The diversity of models and the potential for a greater number of alternatives to institutionalization continues to increase. Accreditation mechanisms are now sufficiently developed to enable professionals to utilize services with a reasonable assurance of quality care.

NOTES

1. Pappenfort DM, Kilpatrick DM, Roberts RW: Child Caring. Chicago, Aldine, 1973

2. Joint Commission on Mental Health of Children: Crisis in Child Mental Health: Challenges for the 1970s. New York, Harper & Row, 1969

3. Glasscote RM, Fishman ME, Sonis M: Children and Mental Health Centers, Programs, Problems, Prospects. Washington, D.C., Joint Information Services, 1972

4. Glasscote RM, Fishman ME: Mental Health Programs for Preschool Children. Washington, D.C., Joint Information Services, 1974

5. Members of American Association of Children's Residential Centers: From Chaos to Order: A Collective View of Residential Treatment of Children. New York, Child Welfare League, 1972

6. Koret S: The children's community mental health center emerges. Child Psychiatry and Human Development 3(4):89–102, 1973

7. Koret S: A community mental health center for children, issues and problems. In Beigel A, Levenson AI: The Community Mental Health Center. New York, Basic Books, 1972

8. Cooper NA: Observations on a therapeutic residential setting for autistic children. Child Care Health Deve XII 437–441, 1977

9. Herstein N, Simon N: A group model for residential treatment. Child Welfare XII 601–611, 1977

10. Koret S, Wolfe A: Children Discharged from Residential Treatment of the Convalescent Hospital for Children (unpublished)

11. Davids A, Berenson JK: Integration of a behavior modification program into a traditionally oriented residential treatment center for children. J Autism Child Schizo XII 269–285, 1977

12. Zigler E, Balla DA: Impact of institutional experience on the behavior and development of retarded persons. Am J Mental Defic 1–11, 1977

13. Beigel A, Hollenbech H, Gurgevich S, Scanlon J, Geffen J: Practical issues in developing and operating a halfway house program. Hosp Community Psychiatry 601–607, 1977

14. Raynes NV, Pratt MW, Roses S: Aides' involvement in decision-making and the quality of care in institutional settings. Am J Ment Defic 570–577, 1977

15. Catterson A, Howell S: Mental health/Ottawa's group homes project. Can Mental Health 42–44, 1976

16. Charlton P, Fell R, Henshall A: Loreto House: A pattern of care. Child Care Health Dev 191–196, 1975

17. Leyland B: Alternate care, group homes. Psychiatric Nurs 9, 1976

18. Eyman RK, Boroskin A, Hostetter S: Use of alternative living plans for developmentally disabled children by minority parents. Mental Retardation 15(1):21–23, 1977

19. Baumann EH: A day treatment program for severely disturbed young children. Hospital & Community Psychiatry 27(3):174–179, 1976

20. Weintrob A: Long-Term treatment of the severely disturbed adolescent. Residential treatment versus hospitalization. J Am Academy Child Psychiatry 436–450, 1975.

21. Harris J: Working with parents of mentally handicapped children on a long-term basis. Child Care Health Dev 121–130, 1978

22. Clancy HG: Integrating the environment in therapy. Man-Environment Systems 6(5):305–312, 1976

23. Sugar M, Stuckey B, Salley P, Oppliger S, Stretch JJ: Use of college-student companions for psychotic children to avoid hospitalization. J Amer Acad Child Psychiatry 14(2):249–267, 1975

24. Holroyd J, Brown N, Wikler LY, Simmons JQ: Stress in families of institutionalized and noninstitutionalized autistic children. J Comm Psychology 3(1): 26–31, 1975

25. Brunstetter RW: Every day on an inpatient ward for psychotic children. Psychiatric Quarterly Supplement 42(2):203–217, 1968

26. Faux EJ, Dixon D: Children in the therapeutic community. Provo Papers 1–27, 1966

Chapter 20

A MENTAL HEALTH PROGRAM FOR GERIATRIC PATIENTS

Charles M. Gaitz, Nancy L. Wilson

This chapter discusses the problems and needs of the chronically ill aged and describes the evolution and status of one program model, the Geriatric Services Section of the Texas Research Institute of Mental Sciences in Houston, Texas.

The needs of the aged among all chronically mentally ill persons warrant discussion because persons over 65 represent the fastest growing segment of the population of the United States. As a group, aged U.S. residents have increased 700% during this century, compared to a 250% increase of the population under 65. In 1970, persons aged 65 and older constituted 10% of the population; their proportion is projected to be 25% in 2020 *(1)* .

Older people are at high risk for developing physical and mental illnesses. The aging process brings an increased tendency to develop chronic physical problems, and generally the recovery from an acute illness is slower for an elderly patient. Elderly persons represent the largest consumer group of outpatient and inpatient medical services nationwide, accounting for about 30% of all health care costs *(2)*. Perhaps the most dramatic health statistics is that the ill aged person is nine times more likely to be a long-term patient. Of the 1.2 million long-term care beds in the United States, about 90% are occupied by persons over 65 *(2)* .

Chronic health problems are part of a larger set of losses and stresses that place the elderly in a high-risk category for emotional problems and mental illness. Loss of spouse and other social relationships, loss of mobility, and loss of social roles and income because of illness or retirement create stress for individuals of any age. But as these accumulate in late life, they contribute to and compound the older person's inability to cope with emotional problems. It is not surprising that, according to available statistics, the incidence of psychopathology rises considerably with age. Studies undertaken in this country and elsewhere estimate the prevalence of moderate to severe psychopathology in the elderly to be somewhere in the range of 12–26% *(3)*. How has the mental health system served the aged population?

Before the community mental health movement of the 1960s, the aged were overrepresented in mental hospitals in proportion to their numbers in the population. Since then, however, the creation of outpatient services and residential facilities in the community has brought significant changes in the treatment of the mentally ill elderly. The creation of outpatient services and residential facilities in the community has promoted efficient use of available community resources and given responsibility for many mental health services to local authorities. These developments, coupled with the belief of many practitioners that older people were admitted to mental hospitals because they needed custodial care rather than psychiatric treatment, have influenced the policies for institutionalization of geriatric patients.

Across the country, efforts have been made to reduce the admission of older people to public mental hospitals and to seek care in the community for several of the long-term patients who had aged in state hospitals. The number of aged patients in state hospitals declined by 56% between 1969 and 1974 *(4)*. But, as the mental hospital admission rate for older people fell, the proportion of mentally ill aged found in nursing and personal care homes rose from 53% in 1963 to 75% in 1969 *(5)*. Nursing homes were most frequently substituted for psychiatric hospital care *(6, 7, 8)*. Unlike their younger counterparts who are treated in outpatient clinics, the elderly mentally ill who have remained in, or returned to, the community are placed in nursing and boarding homes and not referred to mental health facilities. "Rather than helping older persons, the great mental health revolution has only led to their dropping out of the psychiatric system" *(9)*. Utilization statistics show that people aged 65 and over make up only 4% of the community mental health center caseload and only 2% of all other persons receiving outpatient psychiatric services *(10)* .

Figures alone do not tell the whole story of developments in care for the chronic mentally ill aged. Although their number is limited, some specialized programs have been organized. State hospitals have developed residential resocialization and aftercare efforts to prepare older patients for living outside the hospital *(11, 12)* . Some community-based aftercare programs specialize in helping elderly patients discharged to single-room occupancy hotels or nursing homes *(13)*. Unfortunately, the "receiving" programs rarely play a role in discharge planning, thus missing an opportunity to facilitate continuity of care. More comprehensive programs that have bridged this gap include the Massachusetts Mental Health Center in Boston *(14)*, the Older Americans Resources and Services Clinic in Durham, North Carolina *(15)*, the Bellevue Hospital Geriatric Evaluation and Services Unit in New York City *(16)*, the West Philadelphia Mental Health Consortium *(17)*, and the mental health service program we established in 1973.

PROGRAM BACKGROUND AND HISTORY

The Texas Research Institute of Mental Sciences (TRIMS) is the primary research and training facility of the Texas Department of Mental Health and Mental Retardation (TDMHMR). Established by the state legislature in 1958, TRIMS provides a complete range of psychiatric services for patients of all ages in Houston and the surrounding metropolitan area of Harris County. Before the establishment of the TRIMS geriatric clinic in 1973, only 1% of all outpatients seen at TRIMS were 65 and older.

From 1966 to 1968, the TRIMS gerontology staff conducted a research and demonstration project titled "Comprehensive Care of the Suspected Mentally Ill Aged," funded by the National Institute of Mental Health. One hundred persons 65 years of age and older for whom a petition of commitment to a state hospital had been filed were offered comprehensive care by a multidisciplinary team *(18)* . This included diagnosis, planning, placement, and treatment, as well as coordination of services already available.

The conclusions and experiences of this project provided the impetus for developing a geriatric service unit. The project affirmed the principle that problems of psychiatrically impaired people are multiple and likely to fall into several interrelated areas. Therefore, effective psychiatric assessment and intervention must address the social, economic, physical, and psychological factors that affect an individual's ability to function *(19)*. The study showed that effective comprehensive care involves a multidisciplinary pattern of service delivery by specialists in psychiatry, medicine, nursing, and social work, coordinated by a case manager (a social worker or nurse) for each patient *(20)*.

When the study was completed, no agency accepted responsibility for provision of comprehensive care. Fragmentation of service delivery and unidisciplinary approaches continued for several years.

TRIMS initiated service delivery to older persons in 1972 through participation in the Houston Areawide Model Project (HAMP), which was funded by Section 305 of the Older Americans Act. The institute was given responsibility for developing a central intake, referral and information service to help isolated elderly persons obtain services provided by the other HAMP components, including in-home and ambulatory health care, social services, and transportation *(21)*.

When funding for the HAMP ended in 1973, TRIMS secured funds from Title III of the Older Americans Act to continue the information and referral (I & R) service. By adding older outreach workers in 1973, the I & R service was expanded to reach aged clients through nutrition-activity centers.

During that same year, TRIMS collaborated with the local mental health authority to create a clinical geriatric service. TRIMS provided space and financial support for a secretary and a psychiatrist, and the county agency offered the services of its geriatric team —a psychiatric nurse, psychiatric social worker, and mental health counselor. These staff members established the TRIMS geriatric clinic and soon thereafter added a small geriatric inpatient service in the existing TRIMS hospital unit. From the beginning, this clinical program served a broad spectrum of clients over 65, including those who were experiencing social problems arising from the stresses of late life and persons who had a long history of psychiatric illness *(22)*. In late 1974, TRIMS created another service component, an aftercare/alternate care program supported by Title IV-A and Title XIX funds from the Texas State Department of Public Welfare. Using mobile, community-based outreach workers, this program assisted physically and mentally impaired older clients who were moving up or down the institutional ladder—people going into or coming out of nursing homes, state mental hospitals, and local hospitals. Several factors influenced the evolution of the TRIMS program, including identified service gaps, the availability of funding, administrative support within TRIMS and TDMHMR, cooperation from other community agencies, and creative program leadership.

PHILOSOPHY AND ORGANIZATIONAL ISSUES

Two principles were reflected strongly in the organization and service delivery of the three out-patient components: that mental health is affected by interacting social, physical, and psychological factors, and that the majority of older people are able to make problem-solving decisions, given the necessary information and support and the opportunity to do so. The program provided several avenues into the mental health system, including access by telephone, community services, and inpatient and outpatient services. All components emphasized multidimensional assessment of each client regardless of his or her point of entry. Staff members were trained to communicate directly with older clients about their problems, consulting with family members or other agency personnel only to expand on their understanding of the situation. Workers were sensitive to the fact that older clients often choose to discuss their least threatening concern first and that careful follow-up is essential, therefore, to uncover other potential problems. Emphasis was placed on the early identification of an elder's problems before these became crises and on prompt intervention with the appropriate combination of services. Staff members of the three components cooperated to assure continuity of mental health care, avoid institutionalization if possible, and increase the accessibility of community resources and clinical services.

For good clinical and community experts to work as one team to assist a given client was often difficult to manage. The three components worked under differing funding guidelines and organizational policies; they used three different outpatient recordkeeping systems and a fourth for inpatient medical records. Scheduling team conferences and maintaining communication between team members proved time consuming and logistically difficult. The disparate intake systems required potential clients to confer with more than one "gatekeeper." This practice generated confusion and frustration for clients and care-givers.

The organizational structure also tended to damage staff members' personal development and morale. Program supervisors noted, for example, that fieldworkers in the aftercare program were developing stereotyped and limited viewpoints about aging, based on the experiences of their own clients. They began to view aging as an inevitable illness, and they adopted intervention patterns that emphasized the clients' dependencies rather than their remaining capabilities. The I & R members, who worked frequently with clients who were coping adequately with the demands of living and primarily needed help in obtaining services or discussing personal problems, tended to be less sensitive to a client's signs of emotional or psychiatric problems. The program's organization limited the exposure of some staff members to successful aging persons and restricted others from realizing the benefits of psychiatric services for older people.

The present organizational structure shown in Figure 20–1 was adopted in 1976. The Geriatric Services Section was coordinated under the leadership of a psychiatrist, and the outpatient services were reallocated to two components: senior information and outreach service (SIOS) and the geriatric clinic. The following discussion will focus on the way the TRIMS Geriatric Services Section serves older clients and its performance in meeting the special needs of the chronically mentally impaired aged.

TRIMS GERIATRIC SERVICES SECTION

The TRIMS Geriatric Services Section is a multidisciplinary unit which integrates the services of a community-based information and outreach program with psychiatric outpatient and inpatient services to assist older residents of Houston and Harris County. The section is funded entirely by state legislative appropriation. The two outpatient components share space in the TRIMS building located in the Texas Medical Center; the geriatric inpatient service is one part of the TRIMS inpatient facility in a nearby building. Although their work is interrrelated, the three components have distinct staffing patterns and perform particular functions to achieve the section's overall objectives.

Senior Information and Outreach Service

Directed by a professional social worker, the bilingual senior information and outreach service staff performs the functions of the former I & R and aftercare/alternate care programs (23). Two bilingual intake workers provide casework-oriented I & R counseling to elderly callers, and they receive all incoming requests and referrals for clinical services. Using their telephone interviewing skills and

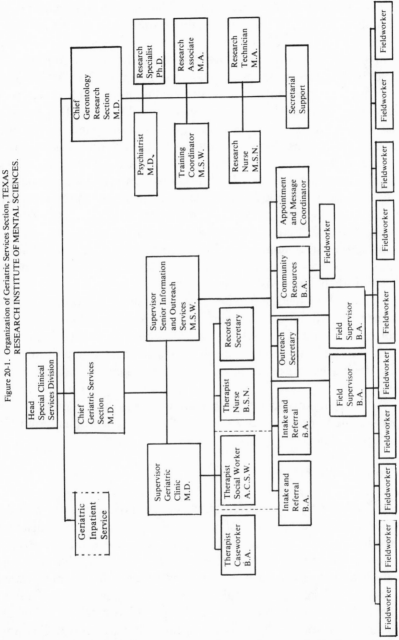

Figure 20-1. Organization of Geriatric Services Section, TEXAS RESEARCH INSTITUTE OF MENTAL SCIENCES.

knowledge of community resources, the workers explain the services available through TRIMS and other community agencies. At times, the workers may act as advocates to intercede with a service provider on behalf of an older client. Each client receives at least one follow-up call to see if the presenting problem has been solved or if others have arisen *(24)*.

A triethnic staff of part-time older paraprofessionals works throughout Harris County to provide resource counseling and supportive services to older clients and their significant others. Each outreach worker is trained as a specialist on the needs and resources of older persons in his or her assigned geographic area. Through interagency agreements, each worker maintains a mobile schedule of service delivery, assisting older persons in 29 Title VII nutrition-activity centers, three county public health clinics, and one congregate senior housing project. An outreach worker's duties also include aftercare, follow-along, or outreach services to elders referred by TRIMS or other agencies. Each SIOS worker maintains a community caseload averaging 20 –25 older clients who have disabling physical and/or mental conditions and who need assistance in coping with the social and economic problems of community residence. Through monthly home and nursing home visits and regular phone calls, the SIOS workers help clients to avoid social isolation and to keep up their clinic visits if necessary.

The SIOS field supervisors perform such program and case management functions as screening and staffing all referrals for the outreach community caseloads and taking responsibility for liaison with the staff and administration of SIOS sites. They visit all field sites regularly and accompany outreach workers on difficult home visits.

Both intake and outreach staff members help identify older persons who need clinical services and assist them with entering the geriatric clinic.

Geriatric Clinic

Directed by a geropsychiatrist, the geriatric clinic serves individuals who are 65 years of age and older and are experiencing emotional, social, or behavioral problems. Clinic referrals come from a variety of sources, including relatives and friends, public and private hospitals, social agencies, nursing homes, private physicians, and the judicial system. Only a small percentage (6%) of clinic clients initiate their own request for psychiatric services, but all clients must voluntarily consent to outpatient treatment. Comprehensive psychiatric services are provided on a sliding fee scale, and both inpatient and outpatient services are covered under Medicare.

Prospective patients and others involved with them are preinterviewed by telephone, followed by a face-to-face intake visit. An intake worker uses data from interviews and medical records to compile an intake summary of social history, personal background, medical and psychiatric history, and the worker's assessment of the client's presenting problems and available support system. Included in the intake interview is the administration of the Short Portable Mental Status Questionnaire.* A multiphasic physical examination, including extensive laboratory work, is completed under the supervision of a specialist in internal medicine. A psychiatrist evaluates each patient, and additional medical and psychological tests are obtained as needed. An individualized treatment plan is developed by a team consisting of the intake worker, the nurse or social worker, and the psychiatrist. On an outpatient basis, this treatment may include individual or group therapy, marital or family counseling, crisis-oriented counseling, medication monitoring, supportive social services, assistance in residential placement, and mental health aftercare.

At times, psychiatric hospitalization is the appropriate intervention for clinic patients who become disturbed or for new patients in crisis. A multidisciplinary geriatric inpatient team is available to provide intensive diagnosis and evaluation during brief hospitalization. Therapeutic and rehabilitative services are oriented to accomplishing the treatment goals for each aged patient and facilitating a speedy return to the community.

The hospital staff formulates discharge plans in conjunction with the clinic and SIOS to insure that the benefits of hospital care carry over to the patient's adjustment in the community. SIOS workers help to select new residences for patients, and they follow up patients after they are discharged. Each discharged older inpatient is routinely referred to the geriatric clinic to provide continuous care and prevent unnecessary rehospitalization.

Inservice Training

The integration of the three service components to meet older clients' needs requires a flexible staff willing to communicate regularly with team members and professionals from other disciplines.

*This questionnaire was designed and validated by Eric Pfeiffer, M.D. at the Duke University Center for the Study of Aging and Human Development, Durham, North Carolina. The instrument consists of 10 items which are used to aid a clinician in detecting the presence and degree of intellectual impairment in an elderly person. Further Reference: Pfeiffer, E: A Short Portable Mental Status Questionnaire for the Assessment of Organic Brain Deficit in Elderly Patients. J Am Geriatrics Society 23:433–441, 1975.

The TRIMS geriatric staff has weekly unit meetings, devoted partly to administrative and service-coordination issues and partly to in-service activities. These meetings include didactic material in gerontology and geropsychiatry as well as case conferences and client evaluations. The case conference format provides an opportunity for staff to practice their skills as multidisciplinary team members and an opportunity for students in various disciplines to observe the section's treatment approach. SIOS staff members also hold weekly in-service meetings to which guests from community agencies are invited to discuss their services.

TRIMS PERFORMANCE WITH THE AGED CHRONIC MENTAL PATIENT

During 1978, the Geriatric Services Section provided both clinical and supportive services to about 385 patients over age 65 and SIOS to another 2,900 older people and 950 agency workers and family members. The Geriatric Services Section accounts for 25% of all outpatient visits to TRIMS. The section's active and inactive caseload includes a large number of persons with long-standing psychiatric disabilities. Of all patients, 36% had a history of psychiatric disorder beginning before age 65. For those with onset late in life, about 33% had a history of illness for two years or longer before evaluation at TRIMS. Regarding primary diagnosis, 41% of all patients were considered to have an organic brain syndrome, 21% an affective disorder, and 16% schizophrenia. The remaining 22% were distributed among several diagnostic categories including paranoid states, neurotic personality disorders, alcohol and drug abuse, and late-life adjustment problems.

The group of chronic mentally ill aged receiving TRIMS services includes a large number of long-term patients discharged from the state mental hospital system. Many of these patients are returning to a community they left many years ago. Before the TRIMS clinic and aftercare services were established, all patients over 65 were commonly discharged to nursing homes or to family members, without referral to a psychiatric facility. Today TRIMS maintains close relationships with other state and private psychiatric hospitals, in addition to its own inpatient service, whose caseworkers consult with the patient and involved family before discharge. Every effort is made to help patients and family find an environment that allows each patient to function optimally, without overwhelming his or her capabilities. Since day care programs and supervised nonmedical housing situations are scarce in the Houston area, almost half of all aftercare patients served at TRIMS are discharged to nursing homes. The SIOS workers make monthly visits to nursing home residents and consult with nursing home staff about the patients' activity level. In turn, the patients visit the geriatric clinic monthly or biweekly for drug maintenance and monitoring. Clinic staff members are available for consultation with nursing home staff members about the patients' behavioral problems or mood changes.

Approximately one-half of all clinic patients reside with a family member—one-fourth with a spouse and one-fourth with children or other family members. Families provide invaluable expressive and instrumental support to their impaired older relatives. In doing so, however, family members themselves are subjected to considerable social, economic, and emotional stress. Care-givers must be aware of this probability and offer clinical and environmental support to the families. The TRIMS staff educates and works closely with the members of the patient's informal support network, remaining available to respond to the crises which may occur in the course of a patient's chronic illness.

In addition to providing direct geriatric mental health services, TRIMS is active within the local and state networks of agencies providing human services. TRIMS practitioners provide case and program-focused consultation to staff of other agencies developing and providing health and social services to the elderly. They participate on several advisory boards and are involved in training efforts for paraprofessionals and professionals. TRIMS sponsors a monthly gerontology conference for its own staff and others who work with the elderly in the community. These conferences have varied programs, including case presentations, lectures, and community resource discussions.

CONCLUSIONS

The multiple losses and stresses of late life result in a high incidence of physical and mental impairment among the aged. Traditionally, older people have received psychiatric care within institutional settings, although in recent years this has changed. Deinstitutionalization of chronic mental patients has resulted in impaired elderly patients returnig to or remaining in the community without receiving psychiatric treatment. A large percentage of these patients have entered nursing or boarding homes that provide custodial care but lack services to meet their mental health needs. Nationwide, aged mental patients have been underserved by community mental health systems. The provision of comprehensive geriatric mental health services requires attention to the social, psychological, and physical needs of older people. TRIMS Geriatric Services Section has developed a model for service delivery to the elderly. This model uses a multidisciplinary staff to provide community-based supportive and clinical services to a broad spectrum of elderly patients, including the chronically ill aged. Working closely with other health and social agencies, TRIMS helps older people resolve social and environmental problems through an information and outreach service and also treats the elderly with identified emotional and psychiatric problems with traditional inpatient and outpatient services.

NOTES

1. Butler R: Why Survive? Being Old in America. New York, Harper and Row, 1975

2. U.S. Senate Special Committee on Aging: Introductory Report of Subcommittee on Long-Term Care. Washington, D.C., Government Printing Office, 1974

3. Pfeiffer E: Psychopathology and social pathology. In Birren JE, Schaie KW (eds): Handbook of the Psychology of Aging. New York, Van Nostrand Reinhold, 1977

4. Santiestevan H: Deinstitutionalization: Out of Their Beds and into the Streets. Washington, D.C., American Federation of State, County, and Municipal Employees, February 1975

5. Redick RW: Patterns in Use of Nursing Homes by the Aged Mentally Ill. Statistical Note 107. Rockville, Md., Biometry Branch, NIMH, 1974

6. Stotsky BA: A controlled study of factors in the successful adjustment of mental patients to nursing homes. Am J Psychiatry 123:1234–1251, 1967

7. Gaitz CM, Baer PE: Placement of elderly psychiatric patients. J Am Geriatrics Society 19:601–613, 1971

8. Epstein LJ, Simon A: Alternatives to state hospitalization for the geriatric mentally ill. Am J Psychiatry 124:955–961, 1968

9. Kahn RL: The mental health system and the future aged. Gerontologist 15:24–31, 1975

10. Kramer M, Taube CA, Redick RW: Patterns of use of psychiatric facilities by the aged: Past, present and future. In Eisdorfer C, Lawton MP (eds): The Psychology of Adult Development and Aging. Washington, D.C., Am Psychological Assoc, 1973

11. Wiernasz MF: Quarterway house program for the hospitalized mentally ill. Social Work 17:72–77, 1972

12. Thompson J: I'm the most geriatric of them all: Community placement of geriatric patients. Mental Hygiene 55:375–380, 1969

13. Plutchik R, McCarthy M, Hall BH, Silverberg S: Evaluation of a comprehensive psychiatric and health care program for elderly welfare tenants in a single-room occupancy hotel. J Am Geriatrics Society 21:452– 459, 1973

14. Gurian, B, Scherl D: A community-focused model of mental health services for the elderly. J Geriatric Psychiatry 5:77, 1972

15. Blazer D, Maddox G: Developing geriatric services in a community mental health center: A case history of a university-based affiliate clinic. Durham, N.C., Center for Studies of the Mental Health of the Aging, NIMH, Duke University Center for the Study of Aging and Human Development, 1977

16. Sillen J, Feldshuh B, Frosch W, Metchik E, Parker B: A multidisciplinary geriatric unit for the psychiatrically impaired in Bellevue Hospital Center. Medical Care 12:766 –777, 1974

17. Santore AF, Diamond H: The role of a community mental health center in developing services to the aging: The older adult project. Gerontologist 14:201–206, 1974

18. Gaitz CM: Obstacles in coordinating services for the care of the psychiatrically ill aged. J Am Geriatrics Society 18:172–181, 1970

19. Gaitz CM, Baer PE: Diagnostic assessment of the elderly: A multifunctional model. Gerontologist 10:47–52, 1970

20. Gaitz CM: The coordinator: An essential member of a multidisciplinary team delivering health services to aged persons. Gerontologist 10:217–220, 1970

21. Calvert WR, McCaslin R: Central intake: Coordination or confusion. Gerontologist 12:73, 1972

22. Varner RV, Calvert WR: Psychiatric assessment of the aged: A differential model for diagnosis. J Am Geriatrics Society 22:273–277, 1974

23. Fields S: Texas TRIMS some red tape. Innovations 4:19–21, 1977

24. Gaitz CM, McCaslin R, Calvert WR: Information and referral: Components of comprehensive care. In Eisdorfer C, Friedel RO (eds): Cognitive and Emotional Disturbance in the Elderly. Chicago, Year Book Medical Publishers, 1977

Chapter 21

DISCUSSION
The Role of Model Programs in the Care of Chronic Mental Patients

Leona L. Bachrach

The preceding chapters contain descriptions of a number of successful and highly commendable programs for the care of chronic mental patients, both in and out of the community. Considered together, these programs are, when one thinks about it, extraordinary. It is unlikely that 20 years ago many of us could have foreseen that so much creativity and innovativeness—so much *caring*—could be applied in developing programs for chronic mental patients, particularly those who are removed from hospital settings.

The programs discussed in Parts II and III of this volume range from those, like the private mental hospital program, that are hospital-based to those, like the community agency and community mental health center programs, that strive for total independence from hospital affiliation. What is striking about today's hospital-based programs for chronic mental patients is their frank perception of themselves as belonging within a greater system of psychiatric and human services. They see themselves as integral parts of a comprehensive service network and assess their contributions on that basis. Hence, the private mental hospital program describes its mission as extending beyond symptom improvement toward an attempt to rehabilitate patients for outpatient care and community living. The nursing home model, which shares many of the characteristics of hospital-based programs, sees itself as "one part of the community continuum of psychiatric care." And the veterans hospital model places its primary emphasis on "meaningful discharge to the community," with discharge planning started as soon as a patient is admitted to the program. It appears that hospitals treating chronic mental patients are no longer isolated and independent in either a functional, geographic, or psychological sense.

As may be expected of contributions to a volume on treatment and programs for chronic mental patients as we approach the decade of the 1980s, most of the papers in this section describe services that are community-based. These are, in every sense, model programs for an era of deinstitutionalization. They are demonstration efforts that are seeking solutions for the many problems surrounding the care of chronic patients in nontraditional settings. As pilot efforts, they reflect the ideology and the assumptions that justify the philosophy of deinstitutionalization: that community care is a good thing and represents the treatment of choice for most, if not all, mental patients; that communities are able and willing to assume the initiative and responsibility in caring for chronic patients; and that communities are able and willing to provide, outside of hospital settings, effective alternatives for the various functions traditionally associated with in-hospital care (1).

This chapter will focus primarily on the community-based model programs that are presented in the preceding sections. By pointing out the similarities that characterize these efforts, the present discussion will attempt to define the limits of the role that model programs play in the spectrum of services for chronic mental patients.

SIMILARITIES IN MODEL PROGRAMS: EIGHT PRINCIPLES

One's initial reaction upon reading the descriptions of model programs in this volume is likely to be similar to a conclusion reached by Greenblatt and Budson (2) in 1976. In discussing five papers on community-based programs for chronic mental patients— one of them, incidentally, the state hospital-initiated Training in Community Living program described in this volume—Greenblatt and Budson state: "In general, the papers suggest a wide spectrum of effective community care. . . . Patients appear to have improved in self-esteem, in socialization, in ability to work, and in satisfaction with their lives. . . . These welcome results have been shown to apply generally . . . to a wide range of clinical conditions, some of them very severe."

Greenblatt and Budson's succinct and summary observations may be used as a point of departure for expanding on the similarities in the programs presented here. It is possible to extract from these models, diverse as they are, certain principles of planning and programming that appear to be common to them—common to them, and, incidentally, also to other model programs described in the literature (3). Despite differences in specific locus of care and in control—that is, whether the program is publicly or privately funded —these programs appear to be built upon a minimum of eight principles that together form a least common denominator for effective program design for chronic mental patients. The principles include: specific targeting of the chronically ill; linkage with other community resources; functional integrity; individually-tailored treatment; cultural relevance and specificity; specially trained staff; hospital liaison; and internal evaluation.

Chronic Patients Targeted

A first principle is that each of these programs assigns top priority to the care of the most severely impaired: it is targeted toward patients who are chronically and persistently ill. If this seems too elementary a principle to merit specific mention, I would only point out that the very failure to assign first priority to chronic patients in many community mental health programs has caused major problems for this population. Zusman and Lamb (4) contend that, although the "basic mission" of deinstitutionalization was originally community-based treatment of the chronic patient, "only limited aspects of the original conception have been implemented." The result is that community mental health has largely overlooked the chronic patient and has tended instead to focus on the "healthy but unhappy." Scherl and Macht (5) concur in writing that "the goal of improved care for the seriously disturbed, over time . . . [has become] the goal of community care for the acutely disturbed."

In a letter to the late Senator Hubert Humphrey, Polak (6). coauthor of the community mental health center program paper in this volume, expresses his concern over the failure of communities and community-based programs to assign high priority to the most seriously ill. It has become apparent that chronic mental patients, who are singularly impotent when it comes to advocating on their own behalf, have too often been underserved or unserved. Their very existence has frequently been denied *(7–10)*. When these patients, with their peculiar combination of service requirements, chronicity, and impotence, have had to compete for scarce resources with others who are less severely impaired and more socially acceptable, chronic patients have not fared well. The papers in this volume describe programs that unequivocally focus on chronic patients and thereby assert their right to treatment.

Linkage with Other Resources

A second principle is that each of these programs is realistically linked to other resources in the community. This is an affirmation of the range and diversity of treatment needs of chronic mental patients. In the words of the geriatric program, "effective psychiatric assessment and intervention" for chronic mental patients "must address the social, economic, physical, and psychological factors that affect an individual's ability to function." In a fragmented service system, linkages between the core program and the other agencies that serve the patient must be firmly established *(7, 11)*. In many ways, the planning of relevant deinstitutionalized programs for chronic mental patients is synonymous with planning for human services. In addition to psychotherapy, the chronically mentally ill "require additional special services. These include a range of living environments and resocialization, vocational rehabilitation, and appropriate work opportunities" *(12)*.

Planning effective community-based services for chronic mental patients, then, requires careful interagency planning and successful liaison efforts, and such strategies are discussed at length in the model programs reported here. While the reader is left with a particularly strong feeling of community integration in both the community agency and community mental health center models, the other programs described here also stress functional linkages with other resources. The geriatric program, for instance, is tied to other agencies through an area-wide referral and information service, while the general hospital model emphatically and proudly views itself as the core service in an intricately interwoven network of resources serving the needs of chronic patients. Since problems of linkage may be especially troublesome in nonurban communities *(13, 14)*, the rural model has had to use particularly imaginative planning in effecting this principle. However, against a backdrop of tremendous odds (transportation difficulties, an absence of trained personnel, counterproductive regulations imposed by outside agencies, and attitudinal and other barriers to care), the Montana rural effort strives to effect this principle through regular "planning-linking" conferences. In sum, it is no exaggeration to say that meaningful integration into the fabric of a community's human resources system is an essential condition for effective community-based care for chronic mental patients.

Special mention should also be made of the linking of some of these model programs with private practice psychiatry. The rural model refers to its relationship with the community's four psychiatrists as "gratifying and vital," while private psychiatry is, of course, the core service in the private practice model. That such linkage is practical goes without saying, but its significance goes beyond pragmatic considerations. In the past, community-based care of chronic mental patients has tended to stand apart from the more traditional forms of psychiatric care *(15)*, perhaps, in part, because there has been no articulated plan "regarding the interrelationships of the public and private sectors" in deinstitutionalization programming *(5)*. Deinstitutionalization has, indeed, been in some instances a divisive force and has been perceived as fostering a separate system of care in which private psychiatric facilities and psychiatrists in private practice play only a minor part. The model programs discussed in this volume give us grounds for optimism for improved linkages of this kind. Just as the more nearly traditional private hospital and veterans hospital models described here view themselves as part of a broader system of psychiatric and human services, so do private psychiatric practitioners and facilities appear, at least in some communities, to be actively seeking to provide care for chronic patients. It is too early to say how far this trend will go, but there are at least some signs that deinstitutionalization is "mainstreaming" not only the patients who are its target but also the concepts of care that are developing on behalf of these patients.

Functional Integrity

A third principle is that each of these programs, either by itself or in combination with the other resources to which it is linked, clearly attempts to provide for its patients the full range of functions that are associated with institutional care. The individual programs described here appear to be dynamically striving for functional integrity, a task made difficult by the very complex nature of institutional care. Sociological analyses of the literature reveal that traditionally mental hospitals have fulfilled a wide variety of functions *(16, 17)*.

These include, in addition to long-term comprehensive treatment for disabled individuals, a series of additional functions less readily perceived or acknowledged—like providing patients with a place of refuge or protecting them from exploitation. Many of the problems associated with deinstitutionalization efforts may be attributed to the tendency for service planners to overlook, or neglect to stress, the necessity for providing out-of-hospital alternatives for the full range of functions traditionally performed in institutional settings.

Unlike the numerous deinstitutionalization programs that fail to provide substitutes for even the better-acknowledged functions of treatment, asylum, and custody—not to mention the many peripheral functions associated with institutional care—the models described here are attempting to overcome the tendency for community-based programs to operate in a functional vacuum *(16)*. If anything, many of these models appear to wish to *extend* the range of their functions by performing special and previously unchartered services. Several of the programs, like the geriatric and community agency models, have, for example, explicitly adopted a liaison function in order to assure effective communication with other community agencies. Appropriation of newly designated functions is reflected throughout the papers, as, for example, in the Training in Community Living program's stated purpose of assuring the patient "freedom from pathological dependent relationships."

No matter what the central orientation of these programs, then, they show evidence that they care about the chronically mentally ill not only as patients but also as social individuals living in a complex society. By pursuing the principle of functional integrity, these models, in a very real sense, acknowledge that chronic mental patients comprise a dependent population for whom the fulfillment of certain basic conditions of human existence must be arranged—conditions that have traditionally, for better or worse, been met within large institutions. To this end, these programs are responsive not only to the psychiatric and medical needs of patients but also to their needs for asylum, respite, socialization, rehabilitation, and the like.

Individually-Tailored Treatment

A fourth principle is that each of these programs is tailored to individual patients. The models described all include personally-tailored treatment regimens, whether chemotherapy, psychotherapy, psychosocial rehabilitation, or some combination of these and other treatment modalities. Individual treatment is, in fact, the cornerstone of the state hospital-initiated Training in Community Living program, which describes itself as "prepared to 'go to' the patient to prevent dropout," if necessary. Similarly, the general hospital program assumes that "each patient's treatment requires an individual 'prescription' " for matching available services to "individual disabilities and abilities."

This principle of reaching out to patients on an individualized basis necessarily activates certain other elements of treatment that are widely understood as fundamental to the effective care of chronic mental patients. Such program elements as 24-hour crisis intervention and case management, specifically mentioned in many of the papers, are automatically assumed and assured when the principle of individualized programming is at work. Individualized programming renders these model programs the conceptual opposites of "dumping"—that is, the indiscriminate and wholesale placement of patients either in hospitals or in community settings without consideration for their specific needs.

Cultural Relevance and Specificity

A fifth principle is that, just as each of these programs is tailored to meet the needs of the individuals it serves, so is each tailored to conform to the local realities of the community in which it is found. Indeed, the very uniqueness of these programs stands out as one of their underlying similarities. The nursing home model has, for example, specifically evolved in response to California's political realities. The papers presented here all describe programs that are culture-specific and relate back to the cultures in which they are found.

This principle is explicitly emphasized in the chapter on private practice, which states, "We work in a 'fishbowl' in that our efforts and results are observable by the community. We are provided in this way with feedback as to the effectiveness of our methods." Similarly, the community mental health center model's citizens' administrative board represents an effort to "ensure that the community care system is under the direct control of the community residents it serves." The general hospital model located in Harlem is so intricately interwoven with its culture base that it is perceived as having a second purpose in addition to the care of chronic patients: the provision of employment opportunities for unemployed or underemployed community residents.

The chapters included here lead inevitably to the conclusion that each of the model programs is a very special event which can be studied and possibly adapted but which can never be precisely duplicated. As Abbott *(18)* points out, because the provision of community-based services to chronic mental patients "has major social components," any successful program for their care "must reflect the character of the community in which the patients are being served."

Specially Trained Staff

A sixth principle is that each of these programs emphasizes the need for staff who are attuned to the unique survival problems of chronic mental patients living in noninstitutional settings. This principle is of such central importance that Polak and Kirby *(19)* write elsewhere that any program lacking staff "who are trained and comfortable working with disturbed patients in community settings . . . is likely to have poorer outcome than psychiatric hospitalization." Thus, the general hospital model stresses the need to provide specialized training for professionals and paraprofessionals alike and utilizes its status as a program within a teaching hospital toward this end. And, while the reports of the nursing home, veterans hospital, and Training in Community Living programs reflect a current controversy *(20, 21)* by expressing different conclusions regarding the suitability of utilizing state hospital personnel in community programs, all three, in common with the other models described here, concur in stressing the necessity for specialized training of personnel for the job of caring for chronic mental patients outside of the hospital.

Several of the models mention staff burnout in working with chronic mental patients, a problem discussed in depth in an article by Lamb *(22)*, and have introduced positive measures to counteract this difficulty. For example, the rural model has made burnout and its reduction an integral part of the staff training effort, while the general hospital model provides regular opportunities for staff to be "heard, appreciated [and] supported" so as to "recharge the energies so constantly drained" by the demands of working with a chronic patient population. Burnout is only one of a variety of training issues for personnel involved in these programs. Each of the model programs described in this volume has found methods of dealing with training issues, and their combined efforts remind us of the basic need for great flexibility in deinstitutionalization program planning *(7)*.

Hospital Liaison

A seventh principle is that each of these programs is tied in some manner, however minimally, to a complement of hospital beds. (The beds utilized within the nursing home program are themselves, according to the author, equated with chronic care beds, since in California both are licensed in the skilled nursing facility category.) As stated succinctly in the description of the geriatric model, "At times psychiatric hospitalization is the appropriate intervention" for the target population.

Actually, the preceding chapters provide a range of views on the desirability of hospitalizing chronic mental patients. The community agency program perceives hospitalization "negatively" and as "an experience that should be avoided if at all possible." Similarly, the community mental health center model, which strives to eliminate hospitalization completely through its unique family-sponsor system —and appears to be relatively successful in this effort—nonetheless relies to some extent on backup hospital beds, as reported elsewhere in the literature (19). Thus, the various model programs discussed here all acknowledge—albeit some of them quite reluctantly—that hospitalization for these patients is sometimes necessary.

This principle is consistent with the growing view that there are certain patients for whom periods of hospital care continue to be a necessity. Irrespective of what specific reasons may be cited as appropriate ones for hospitalization—whether for protection of the patient or of society, or whether to provide the patient with diagnostic or intensive treatment services—these programs reflect the ever-increasing departure from the polarized antihospital stance that characterized the early years of the deinstitutionalization movement (16, 23, 24). There is, indeed, a pragmatic dimension to consider in utilizing hospital facilities. Communities vary in their readiness to implement total deinstitutionalization plans, and hospitalization for chronic mental patients should be perceived as being fully within the compass of the concept of continuity of care (7). As stated in the Training in Community Living chapter,

> First and foremost it must be understood that the role of inpatient care, for any community, must be seen in the context of what kinds of programming are available in the community for the chronically disabled psychiatric patient. Although hospitalization may have undesirable effects on patients, there may be greater patient harm and certainly greater burden to the community if use of the hospital is denied on

'principle' without providing adequate community programming in its place.

Internal Evaluation

An eighth and final principle is that each of these programs has built into it a kind of ongoing internal assessment mechanism. The nursing home model, for example, has given explicit attention to this principle by adopting the problem-oriented medical record and regularly scheduled evaluation procedures to assess patients' needs and progress. The Training in Community Living model has an experimental design that lends itself to constant reexamination of program procedures, while the community agency model describes itself as being "dedicated" to "pragmatic research" concerning its own effectiveness and has sponsored controlled studies to that end. This kind of continuous self-monitoring may be, and usually is, something quite apart from formal program evaluation. Computer-assisted program evaluation tends to be too complex, with too slow a "turnaround" time, to be of use in the kind of equilibrating function that this principle implies. The model programs described in this volume, by permitting care-givers to modify their programs in process, reflect in practice the frank acknowledgment expressed in the private practice paper that, "We have much room for improvement."

Indeed, these models, relatively small in size and uncomplicated in structure, avoid the disjunction between planning, management, and evaluation that tends to characterize evaluative efforts in larger and more complex programs (25). In addition, these programs afford unique opportunities for feedback of the kind identified by Suchman (26) as appropriate for demonstration programs, such as measuring the impact of specific programmatic efforts on the course of chronic mental illness; testing the acceptance of these efforts by the public; serving as a foundation for more intensive research; and contributing to the development of more complex and comprehensive programs.

CONCLUSIONS AND IMPLICATIONS

Together, the eight principles outlined here are basic to programs that effectively minister to the needs of chronic mental patients. By implementing these principles, the model programs described in this volume acknowledge that chronic mental patients have severe and recurrent problems; that they are frequently functionally impaired and in need of assistance in gaining access to the most basic of life's entitlements; and, most of all, that their individuality is of greater significance in effective treatment than is any categorical label, such as "schizophrenic," that might be applied to them.

All of these principles are concerned with the structural aspects of programming for chronic mental patients. They do not extend to program specifics like treatment modalities utilized or personnel patterns employed. They are simple enough to transcend differences in communities and in demographically distinctive target populations. Indeed, it is patently apparent that these principles are *so* simple that they may prove a disappointment to those who look to model programs to provide instant "solutions" for their own communities' problems. They tend to answer the basic question of "What should a successful program for the chronic patient look like?" but ignore the more complex question of "How should a successful program for the chronic patient operate?"

And there is a reason for this. Questions of how, although essential, must be determined by extraprogram considerations like timing, available resources, attitudes, and other local conditions. The answers to "how" questions are necessarily highly idiosyncratic. One need only look to the principle of cultural relevance and specificity to appreciate this fact. Polak and Kirby *(19)* write elsewhere of the community mental health center program described here that a "major question" is whether its methodology "can be generalized to other settings, such as rural communities, and to other treatment approaches." The same question must be asked of the other programs described in this volume.

Understanding the limited potential for generalizing model programs leads, of course, to the question: What is the use of these programs? The answer to this question depends on our conceptual approach. If we insist on looking at model programs as prototypes for diffusion, we are headed for disappointment. If, on the other hand, we alter our perspective and think of model programs as *hypotheses (26)*, not as answers, their value becomes more apparent. Each of the model programs described in this volume may be seen as an hypothesis—as a test for a series of assumptions regarding the effective care of chronic mental patients in a specific community. Each is an ongoing research effort with evaluative potential, as pointed out in the preceding discussion of the principle of internal evaluation.

The community mental health center model stands out among

the programs discussed here in that it exhibits a sophisticated working awareness of the steps that must be followed in effecting a communitywide mental health system that targets chronic mental patients. Nevertheless, the programs presented in this volume are not equipped to meet the aggregate needs for the care of all chronic patients living within a defined geographic area. They are, in short, not designed to provide answers for the global problems of mental health systems. Needs assessment techniques and resource allocation patterns differ substantially for model programs and for mental health systems. Whereas model programs are free to define their target populations and to limit care to those whom they choose to serve, total systems must concern themselves with a hierarchy of mental health needs and with the assignment of priorities.

Moreover, model programs and mental health systems are typically accountable to different "masters." The model programs discussed in this volume are primarily responsible for testing and evaluating innovative approaches for the care of those patients chosen as participants—a difficult and time-consuming task that is exemplified in their continuous struggle to achieve functional integrity. But mental health systems are typically accountable to governing bodies, like legislatures, for whom mental health services (and, even more so, specialized services targeted for the care of chronic patients) represent only a portion of their concerns. These bodies are not expected to be experimental in their orientation; they are more concerned with demonstrations of service comprehensiveness and cost-effectiveness than with the efficacy of treatment procedures or with the more abstract notion of quality of care. The basic function of internal evaluation, continuous assessment of programmatic relevance, is decidedly different from the goals of full-scale program evaluation as described in the systems literature *(27-31)*. In sum, the systems problems that characterize the delivery of mental health services are numerous and diverse, and model programs do not suffice either in number or in concept to provide solutions for them. Systems problems must be dealt with in other ways.

In no way, however, should the importance of the eight principles extracted here— or of the model programs that they characterize—be minimized. It is precisely the absence of these principles that makes for the horror stories of dumping and degradation that are now, unfortunately, so widely identified with the deinstitutionalization movement. Through an understanding of these principles, we become aware of some of the denial and the oversights that have been plaguing the provision of services for chronic mental patients in this era of deinstitutionalization. When a report to the President's Commission on Mental Health from its Task Panel on Deinstitutionalization, Rehabilitation and Long-Term Care states that deinstitutionalization has "fallen short of its goal" and has "often aggravated the problems" of chronic mental patients *(12)*, it is commenting upon the absence of these principles of programming in widespread deinstitutionalization efforts and expressing a need for their articulation. When a psychiatrist writes that "although the motivation originally underlying [the] tide of reform may have been noble," deinstitutionalization today is "more properly characterized as being maintained by pressures that are political and economic, or simply a policy fashion" *(32),* he is appealing for more widespread application of these principles in program planning. And when a daily newspaper reports that in the county hospitals of a major American city "some psychiatric wards are packed with patients forced to spend days sitting on wood benches waiting for a state hospital bed," and that some patients are "turned away after brief emergency treatment" *(33),* it is reminding the reading public that we must continue our search for ways to disseminate and effect these principles, whatever the local barriers to their implementation may be. These principles are basic and replicable and should govern the development of programs for chronic mental patients, wherever such programs are located.

In conclusion, it should be noted and appreciated that these eight principles are not necessarily limited to community-based care. In fact, they show great similarity to principles put forth by Talbott *(34)* as necessities for effective programming in state hospitals of the future. That is noteworthy. It reinforces the notion that the guiding principles of good planning for chronic mental patients transcend locational considerations. Principles of care for the chronically mentally ill have much more to do with good and humane medical and human service delivery practices than they have with geography. The model programs discussed here, by helping us to focus on these principles, provide us with a "minimum data set," as it were—a first step for the development of effective and humane programs for chronic mental patients in out-of-hospital settings. The next step in program development is even more complex and fragile. It involves the integration and expansion of programs so conceived into the larger mental health system in such a way that their viability is ensured, whatever the level of competition from other demands upon the system.

NOTES

1. Bachrach LL: A conceptual approach to deinstitutionalization. Hosp and Community Psychiatry 29:573–578, 1978

2. Greenblatt M, Budson RD: A symposium: Follow-up studies of community care. Am J Psychiatry 133:916–921, 1976

3. Stein LI, Test MA (eds): Alternatives to Mental Hospital Treatment. New York, Plenum, 1978

4. Zusman J, Lamb HR: In defense of community mental health. Am J Psychiatry 134:887–890, 1977

5. Scherl DJ, Macht LB: Deinstitutionalization in the Absence of Consensus. Presented at Annual Meeting of the American Psychiatric Association, Chicago, Ill., May 1979

6. Polak PR: Letter to Sen. H. H. Humphrey, 2 June 1977

7. Bachrach LL: Planning mental health services for chronic patients. Hosp and Community Psychiatry 30:387–393, 1979

8. Bassuk EL, Gerson S: Deinstitutionalization and mental health services. Scientific American 238:46–53, February 1978

9. Platman SR: Presentation to President's Commission on Mental Health, Washington, D.C., 17 January 1978

10. Stern R, Minkoff K: The effect of deinstitutionalization on a community clinic. Presented at Annual Meeting of the American Psychiatric Association, Chicago, Ill., May 1979

11. Bachrach LL: Developing objectives in community mental health planning. Am J Public Health 64:1162–1163, 1974

12. Report of the Task Panel on Deinstitutionalization, Rehabilitation and Long-Term Care. In Task Panel Reports Submitted to the President's Commission on Mental Health, Vol. 2. Washington, D.C., U.S. Government Printing Office, 1978

13. Bachrach LL: Deinstitutionalization of mental health services in rural areas. Hosp and Community Psychiatry 28:669–672, 1977

14. Berry B, Davis AE: Community mental health ideology: A problematic model for rural areas. Am J Orthopsychiat 48:673–679, 1978

15. Committee on Psychiatry and the Community: The Chronic Mental Patient in the Community. New York, Group for the Advancement of Psychiatry, 1978

16. Bachrach LL: Deinstitutionalization: An Analytical Review and Sociological Perspective. Rockville, Md., National Institute of Mental Health, 1976

17. Bachrach LL: A conceptual approach to deinstitutionalization of the mentally retarded: A perspective from the experience of the mentally ill. In Bruininks

RH, Best-Sigford B, Lakin KC (eds): Deinstitutionalization and Community Adjustment of Developmentally Disabled People. To be published by University of Minnesota Department of Psychoeducational Studies, Minneapolis

18. Abbott B: Tailoring the service system to the community. Hosp and Community Psychiatry 29:35–36, 1978

19. Polak PR, Kirby MW: A model to replace psychiatric hospitals. J Nerv and Ment Disease 162:13–22, 1976

20. Bennett FH: Using hospital staff to provide aftercare for discharged patients. Hosp and Community Psychiatry 28:138, 1977

21. Goldman H: Using hospital staff to provide aftercare: kudos and criticism. Hosp and Community Psychiatry 28:461– 462, 1977

22. Lamb HR: Staff burnout in work with long-term patients. Hosp and Community Psychiatry 30:396–398, 1979

23. Bennett D: Community psychiatry. Brit J Psychiatry 132:209–220, 1978

24. Community psychiatry depolarised. Lancet i:1079–1080, 20 May 1978

25. Bunker DR: Organizing evaluation to serve the needs of program planners and managers. Evaluation and Program Planning 1:129–134, 1978

26. Suchman EA: Evaluative Research. New York, Russell Sage Foundation, 1967

27. Ashbaugh JW, Bradley VJ: Linking deinstitutionalization of patients with hospital phase-down: The difference between success and failure. Hosp and Community Psychiatry 30:105–110, 1979

28. Boyd C, Henderson WE: Improving continuity of care through a state hospital-CMHC liaison program. Hosp and Community Psychiatry 29:384 –386, 1978

29. Gaver KD: Perspectives on accountability in mental health and retardation services. Hosp and Community Psychiatry 27:635–641, 1976

30. Holder HD: Accountability and Productivity in a System of Services for Chronic Patients. Presented at 29th Institute on Hospital and Community Psychiatry, San Francisco, Cal., October 1977

31. Stratas NE, Bernhardt DB, Elwell RN: The future of the state mental hospital: Developing a unified system of care. Hosp and Community Psychiatry 28:598–600, 1977

32. Rachlin S: When schizophrenia comes marching home. Psychiatric Quarterly 50:202–210, 1978

33. Cannon L, Kotkin J: Crisis grows in Calif. mental hospitals. Washington Post, 16 April 1979, A3

34. Talbott JA: The Death of the Asylum: A Critical Study of State Hospital Management, Services and Care. New York, Grune and Stratton, 1978

Part IV

MODEL SERVICE SYSTEMS

Chapter 22

THE ORANGE COUNTY MENTAL HEALTH DELIVERY SYSTEM*

Ernest W. Klatte
John E. Crowder

In 1969, Orange County, California, was given an opportunity that programs can have only once, that is to develop a totally new mental health delivery system. This chapter describes the birth, development, successes, and infirmities of the Orange County mental health program and delivery system.

LEGAL BACKGROUND

Until 1969, the state had the primary responsibility for the provision of mental health, alcohol, and drug abuse services in California. Starting in 1957, the state encouraged local communities to develop their own mental health services on a cost-sharing, elective basis. Under those provisions, counties often developed local services along the lines that met the concerns of particular community-inter-

*This chapter was written while the county program was in a state of rapid transition both fiscally and administratively. As of the spring of 1979 many of the top staff had resigned. Throughout California mental health staff were anxiously awaiting the vote on a new state tax limitation initiative which threatened to reduce up to 30 percent the amount of money available for local as well as state mental health services.

est groups or the interest of professionals involved in service. Often the local programs did not relate themselves to the seriously and chronically mentally ill patient who would otherwise have to be in a state hospital. The state hospital was seen largely as a separate system. In 1969, a new California Mental Health Act went into effect. The act transferred the basic responsibility for the provision of mental health services from the state to the county and mandated that every county with over 100,000 population had to develop a local mental health treatment program and outlined specific aspects of treatment that were to be provided. It declared an intent to establish a single mental health delivery system that included state hospital services as well as local services and to set up a funding mechanism whereby counties were required to put up 10% of the new cost of services at both the county and state hospital levels and the state would provide the other 90%.

The act also set strict limits on involuntary treatment, doing away with the previous indeterminate commitment and providing instead for a 72-hour hold for evaluation of patients on the basis of their being a danger to themselves or others or gravely disabled by reason of a mental disorder; a provision for a 14-day subsequent commitment on the same basis; and another 14-day commitment based solely on the provision that the patient is imminently suicidal. Although the law provided for a 90-day commitment based upon a patient's being dangerous to others, the restrictions for that portion of the law are so severe that the provision is seldom used.

The act also provided for establishing conservatorships for those people who because of mental illness are so gravely disabled they are unable to care for their basic needs. The conservatorship provisions allow for the appointment of a conservator for a one-year period, following which the conservatorship must be renewed if it is to remain in effect. The conservator has the authority to place the patient in any type of treatment or residential facility needed in the patient's best interest. In most counties, there is an elected position called the public administrator/public guardian. This office usually acts as the conservator. It is the conservator's responsibility to see that the patient receives whatever type of service the patient needs.

ORANGE COUNTY DEMOGRAPHY

Orange is a coastal county adjoining Los Angeles to the south and is the second largest county in the state with a population of approximately 1.8 million or about 9% of the total population of the State of California. It is one of the most rapidly growing counties in the country, and its population has doubled in the past 15 years. In the past, the county was primarily agricultural and recreational. As Los Angeles grew, the county developed more of a bedroom community aspect for upper- and middle-income commuters from Los Angeles county. In the 60's and 70's there was a very rapid growth of clean industry such as engineering firms, home offices of large companies, etc. employing a large percentage of college graduates. Geographically, the county is of moderate size and can be traversed in any direction within an hour.

The primary minority group is Chicano, which represents 13% of the county's population; blacks represent 1%. Orange County has been the recipient of a large number of Vietnamese refugees. It is estimated that approximately 23,000 Vietnamese are currently residing in Orange County. The county is relatively affluent, with a mean income considerably above the state average. In spite of its general affluence, the county does have a number of poverty communities with all of the concommitant social problems.

ORANGE COUNTY MENTAL HEALTH SERVICES PRIOR TO 1969

Prior to 1969, the county relied principally on the state hospital located in nearby Los Angeles county for its inpatient services to the indigent. In the years just prior to the enactment of the community mental health act, the county opened a 92-bed mental health facility adjoining the county hospital. The entire county complex was sold in 1976 to the University of California Irvine medical school and provides services to the county on a contract basis. In addition, there were two child guidance clinics in the county, which provided services on contract. There were a large number of private psychiatric beds in the community, and some of the facilities were able and willing to take Medicaid psychiatric cases. There has been no dearth of mental health professionals in the community for some years.

DEVELOPING THE STRUCTURE OF THE MENTAL HEALTH SYSTEM

Philosophically, the program was designed primarily to meet the needs of the most seriously mentally ill people in the community. Every effort would be made to treat the patient as early as possible and to prevent hospitalization. If hospitalization was required, it was to be kept at a minimum, and community support systems close to the patient's home were to be developed to provide the necessary aftercare services.

Structurally, the county was divided at first into six regions and subsequently reduced to four regions. A deputy director was appointed for each region. These deputies had the responsibility and authority to develop and coordinate all mental health and alcohol and drug abuse services within their catchment areas. At the same time, central responsibilities were established and deputy directors who had county-wide responsibilities were appointed for various specialized services. These included adult services, children's services, alcohol services, drug abuse services, training, and research and evaluation. The centralized deputies had various responsibilities, including establishing an overall treatment philosophy for their particular specialized services, determining program standards, establishing quality assurance systems, and deciding whether to contract for services or to provide them directly with county staff. The centralized deputies and the regional deputies related to each other on a matrix table of organization, wherein the centralized deputies had the responsibility to provide the necessary guidance, support, and resources for the provision of adequate services in each of the regions and the regional deputies had the responsibility for utilizing the resources in the most effective manner and within the criteria established by the special deputies. Administrative support services to the regions were centralized. Within this structure comprehensive mental health, alcohol, and drug abuse services in each of the four regions were developed. Overall, 43% of the services were operated on a contract basis.

Although the 1969 act was designed to reduce the need for the state hospital it was not intended to eliminate it. In 1973, the State Department of Health asked the county to design a comprehensive mental health system that would eliminate the need for utilization of state hospitals except for criminally ill offenders. The state director at that time offered to fund the project to demonstrate that a large metropolitan area could function independently of the state hospital system. After a great deal of effort on the part of state and county staff, as well as numerous public and private agencies and individuals, a plan was agreed upon and first-year funding was approved by the state. Although new money was appropriated for the start of the program, it was later to be funded by transferring money from the state hospital budget to the local program. (The counties do not have the authority to transfer funds between the state hospital and local program budgets.)

The plan was comprehensive and included a full array of outpatient, day treatment, activity programs, case management aftercare service, and gradations of residential programs from acute inpatient services to independent living programs.

The new program was being implemented when, after only one year's funding, the county was informed that the state had changed its policy regarding state hospital services and funding for much of the new program was withdrawn. Instead, the local program was again given an allocation of state hospital days and money to cover the cost of hospitalizing mentally ill county residents for that number of days. As a result, the county was unable to develop parts of the plan, and the staffing for those services already initiated had to be reduced. The specific services described are those remaining after the local program was forced to reduce the scope of its plans. The results of efforts to date would indicate the original plan was realistic and, if fully implemented, state hospital services for Orange County residents would not be needed at this time.

INPATIENT SERVICES

In order to prevent unnecessary hospitalization, to resolve crises when possible on a prompt basis, and, when necessary, to direct patients to the most appropriate inpatient services, the University of California Irvine Medical Center (UCIMC) developed an emergency admitting unit using one 15-bed ward. This unit became the primary portal of entry for involuntary patients into the various inpatient facilities. Patients were usually brought to this locked unit by the police or mental health staff on involuntary 72-hour observation commitments. Patients could remain on this unit up to 24 hours and were not officially admitted to the hospital. This procedure reduced both the costs of the required admitting procedures and the length of stay when hospitalization was required. In the 78–79 fiscal year approximately 600 patients were evaluated by the emergency admitting unit each month. Of those, approximately 36.3% were released directly, often with referrals to the regional nonresidential mental health services; 14.8% were admitted to the state hospital; 16.3% were referred to private psychiatric inpatient facilities; 17.9% were admitted to (UCIMC) University Inpt. Services; and the remaining 14.6% were sent to other institutions such as the therapeutic residential centers. No patient was admitted to the state hospital without having first gone through the local program and having been authorized for admission. Whenever possible, patients were referred to the two county-operated therapeutic residential centers in lieu of acute hospitalization.

The university established utilization review procedures, and the county set up strict limitations on length of stay in the various inpatient wards. Without prior specific authorization, the stay was limited to 17 days of hospitalization for most adult inpatients, 30 days for those with special problems, 60 days for adolescents, and 90 days for children.

In 1974, the county developed two therapeutic residential centers (TRCs). In each instance, the county contracted with a large skilled nursing facility for a discrete section of the facility which was completely separate from the rest of the facility. The nursing home provided all of the basic services usually provided by that type of facility. The county added county staff to a sufficient level to provide acute, inpatient treatment services for most acutely mentally ill patients who did not require a locked facility whether voluntary or involuntary. The two facilities provided a total of 94 beds. The treatment staffing patch provided in one 50-bed facility was as follows: 2 psychiatrists, 1 psychiatric social worker, 1 social work assistant, 3 psychiatric nurses (RNs), and 12 mental health workers.

The therapeutic residential centers proved to be very effective from both a clinical and a cost standpoint. The patients tended less to perceive of themselves as being in a hospital. The milieu was less formal than in a hospital. As of March 1979 the average length of stay was 26 days. The total cost per day was $88 as compared with $193 at the university inpatient facility and $134–155 at Metropolitan State Hospital. There was a free flow of patients between the therapeutic residential centers, the hospital program, and the aftercare programs in each of the regions.

THE ORANGE COUNTY MENTAL HEALTH ASSOCIATION

The county was fortunate to have an extremely active and progressive local mental health association at the start of the development of the local programs. The mental health association had recruited and trained volunteers to work in the county hospital and to visit periodically the state hospital which served the county. With the aid of the very capable executive director of the association, a relationship was established between the county program and the mental health association that may be unique.

As the local programs enlarged, the need for volunteer services exceeded the association's ability to recruit and train because of their limited budget. Rather than hire county volunteer coordinators, the county elected to contract with the mental health association so that the association could expand its volunteer activities. With this arrangement, the association placed hired volunteer coordinators in each of the service regions, took charge of all recruitment and training of volunteers, and worked with the county staff to define the specific roles in which the volunteers could be used most effectively.

The association then started developing activity programs on a part-time basis in donated space in various sites in the county. These programs proved to be extremely effective as a part of the support system for the chronically mentally ill residing in board and care facilities. As a need for such services expanded, a contract was signed with the mental health association to provide two full-time activity centers. The association used both volunteer and hired staff to operate the facilities. The programs were designed to meet the socialization activity needs of relatively regressed patients who were in need of less intense programs than provided in the day treatment services operated by county staff. The programs are less expensive than day treatment and, in 1979, cost $9.25 per patient visit as opposed to $62 per visit for county operated day treatment programs.

In addition, the county contracted with the mental health association for public information services. The association puts out a newsletter that was widely distributed and covered not only the county mental health programs but various private mental health services as well as other public interest items regarding mental health. It also included an insert regarding in-house news to be distributed to the county mental health employees.

Later, the mental health association developed, on contract, a drop-in support center for women alcoholics.

Although the question was raised from time to time as to the possible conflict of interest for the mental health association to play the role of both advocate for the mentally ill as well as direct provider, no conflict had arisen to date. Because of the large number of staff and volunteers that it had throughout the county programs, the association appeared better able than if it were not a provider to be aware of problems in the delivery system such as unmet needs of the mentally ill. The association aggressively spoke out on many issues in their advocacy role and showed no reluctance to criticize the county if need be. It was also extremely helpful from a political standpoint in working on such problems as reducing restrictions for the development of board and care facilities in the community.

AFTERCARE

There were many problems in developing appropriate support services for the chronically mentally ill in the community. After the change in the law in 1969, the state still retained a community services social work staff of state employees whose task was to provide follow-up care for people who had been hospitalized primarily in state hospitals. This organizational structure was extremely awkward, since the county also had an ongoing responsibility to care for the chronically mentally ill and it was difficult to coordinate the activities of the county staff and the state staff. Primarily, the state staff were concerned with developing board and care facilities, placing chronically mentally ill in these facilities, and providing some aftercare services. The situation was further complicated by the fact that the social services within the county had for years placed disabled people, including those disabled because of mental illness, in various board and care facilities throughout the county. Often patients on Supplemental Security Income (SSI) because of mental illness were not known to the county mental health staff. Lastly, the public administrator/public guardian had responsibility for many of the chronically mentally ill who were gravely disabled.

Early in the program development, a tripartite agreement was made between the county mental health program, the county social services department, and the public administrator/public guardian. In this agreement, the county mental health department agreed to be responsible for providing mental health services to conservatees and to those receiving SSI because of mental disabilities. This enabled the mental health department to identify large numbers of mentally ill previously unknown to the county mental health system. The social services department agreed to provide the necessary nonclinical social support system for the chronically mentally ill, which included recruitment and monitoring of board and care facilities, nonclinical follow-up of patients, and services to the public guardian. The mental health department provided funds for social services to hire staff to carry out their functions. These people worked in the regional offices conjointly with mental health staff. In addition, money was provided in the social service budget for the placement costs of certain mentally ill children in need of private institutional care who were not otherwise eligible for services through the welfare system. Finally, in 1977 the state allowed the local mental health program to take over the functions of the state social service staff and to absorb them as county staff so that the total aftercare system was integrated as a county function.

Centrally, an office under adult services was established to be responsible on a county-wide basis for the aftercare structure. In each of the regions, aftercare personnel were hired. Conceptually, the aftercare staff functioned primarily as case managers rather than as direct providers of services. The aftercare staff was responsible for identifying patients in need of aftercare services, opening of files, establishing the needs of the patients, and referring them to the appropriate clinical and nonclinical services.

Insofar as possible, the aftercare staff developed plans to meet the patient's aftercare needs before the patient left the hospital. The aftercare staff saw that the patient was placed in the most appropriate placement; arranged, when appropriate, for referral for vocational rehabilitation services through a contract relationship established with the State Department of Vocational Rehabilitation; and arranged for various aftercare treatment services as needed, including medication, clinics, outpatient treatment, day treatment, and activity programs.

Because the focus of this discussion is upon adult mentally ill, many aspects of the overall program will be mentioned either not at all or briefly in passing. There were children's outpatient staff in each of the regions, and there were contracts for child guidance services and day treatment services for children. The university operated a 12-bed children's inpatient service and a 13-bed adolescent unit. Contracts were established with several group homes which handled seriously disturbed children and had some clinical support staff. In addition, the county operated two shelter homes for status offender-type youth. Rarely was a child ever sent to a state hospital, and as of March 1979 the county had only four children in the state hospital system.

Because trained persons were needed to work with people with various specific types of life experiences, including certain cultural or ethnic backgrounds, or with past experiences as alcoholics or drug addicts, a mental health worker series was developed. Through the aid of a National Institute of Mental Health (NIMH) grant, a two-year training program was established for mental health workers. Later the mental health worker series was used also to recruit people with specifically needed educational qualifications for whom other job classifications did not exist. Through this series, for example, a rather large number of staff with master's degrees in marriage and family counseling were hired.

The training division of the program was integral to the development of all services. Many formalized training programs were developed to meet the particular needs of professionals as well as nonprofessionals. Most of the programs were open to individuals and various groups in the community having a need for the particular module. Of particular note for this discussion were training programs offered periodically to upgrade the clinical skills of board and care operators and other nonprofessionals providing services to the mentally ill.

A management information system was developed, which in addition to providing specific patient clinical and billing information was designed to provide a number of reports needed by the various levels of management on a monthly basis. A specific aspect built into the system was notification of incomplete referrals. Thus, if one facility referred a patient to another facility for service and the patient failed to arrive at the other facility, the referrer would be notified the following month. Unfortunately, the system never really functioned as designed, and reports continued to be prepared by hand.

PROGRAM RESULTS

How does one measure success of a large complex mental health program? It is difficult to measure whether, overall, patients are receiving better treatment in the community program than in a system primarily provided by the state hospitals. We did not carry out any large-scale outcome evaluations, and evaluative criteria were difficult to establish. Client satisfaction surveys were performed on much of the program and showed general overall satisfaction with services received. However, the results of such surveys are always subject to question. State and national statistics prepared in 1978 by Teknekron, Inc., for the California Assembly Permanent Subcommittee on Mental Health and Developmental Disabilities (1) allow some statistical comparisons between the Orange County system, the rest of the California mental health program, and, to a very limited extent, national averages.

Orange County demonstrated that if a local mental health program was designed specifically to address itself to the most seriously ill population, and if all elements were functioning properly, the utilization of state hospitals could be all but eliminated, except for the mentally disordered offenders which the local program does not principally address. In the 1978–79 fiscal year, Orange County was utilizing under 35,000 state hospital days per year, which translates into a rate of 5.28 beds per 100,000 population. This is a reduction from 44 per 100,000 population in 1967 and compares with 1975 data of 31.3 for California, 50.6 for Illinois, 129.1 for Indiana, 155.1 for Massachusetts, 186.9 for New York, and 127.6 for Pennsylvania. In 1978–79, one-third of this program's state hospital beds were utilized for patients in a drug abuse program, which was left in the state hospital for fiscal reasons having to do with funds being available for state hospital services but not local programs. In the fall of 1979 this service was transferred to a county facility. Correcting for this population, the current bed utilization per 100,000 for mentally ill patients was approximately 3.5. The mentally ill patients remaining in the state hospital broke down essentially into the following three categories: a very small number of chronic mentally ill who were so behaviorally disturbed that they required a locked facility on a continuing basis, acutely disturbed patients requiring a locked facility who were sent to the state hospital because of the shortage of locked facilities in Orange County, and a group of chronically mentally ill who periodically required hospitalization for purposes of continuity of care and were returned to the state hospital where they were well known.

The decrease in state hospital utilization did not seem to be reflected by an inordinate increase in more expensive community facilities. According to the Teknekron report, Orange County's budget per capita for 24-hour care in 1978 was $4.67, which placed it the lowest of the 29 largest counties in the state on a per capita basis (1). This cost figure was distorted somewhat by the availability of some private facilities which would take Medicaid patients that were not reflected in the budget of the public mental health program.

One might wonder if the above expenditure reflected a relatively small need for public inpatient services (which are largely involuntary) because of Orange County's relative affluence. This possibility seemed to be contested by the fact that the involuntary detention rate for 72-hour treatment and evaluation in 1967–1977 was 456 per 100,000 as compared with the statewide mean of 309, putting the county in the highest group for involuntary evaluations. By contrast, the county's detention rate for 14-day intensive treatment was half again lower than the statewide mean and for longer term conservatorship cases was less than one-sixth the statewide mean.

From the total cost standpoint, California's system of local care seems to be cost effective. Although figures published in the Teknekron report indicate that in 1976 California spent far more per capita for aid to local programs than six other major states, the additional costs seem more than offset in reduced hospital utilization. According to a report in August 1978 of the National Association of State Mental Health Program Directors (2), California ranks twenty-ninth in total expenditures for mental health programs. Within California, the statewide average expenditure per person for local programs was $20.23 in fiscal year 1977/1978. That year, Orange County's expenditures were $14.87 per capita.

From the subjective clinical bias of the authors, it appeared that the local mental health program as developed in Orange County was a much more humanitarian and clinically effective treatment system than the previous state hospital system. Certainly, the mentally ill were identified earlier in the community and many times more received treatment than previously. Although critics of California's mental health system at times tell horror stories of chronic mentally ill patients living drab lives in nursing homes and unpleasant board and care facilities, there is some evidence to indicate this was more apt to be true before the development of comprehensive local mental health services than after it. For example, in Orange County there were more people in the community living on SSI benefits because of a mental disability than there ever were in the state hospitals at any one time. A large percentage of these people were receiving no treatment whatsoever until they were identified by the mental health program. There seemed to be less social deterioration in the chronic patient who was residing in the community, and, insofar as one could tell, the quality of the chronic patient's life experiences is better when the patient is living in the community, travels to an activity center several times a week, and goes to the outpatient clinic for services than when that same type patient lived in the state hospital environment. By contrast, however, there were a number of seriously mentally ill people in the community who were receiving little or no treatment and were in need of a highly structured residential environment. A number of these people ultimately ended up in the correctional system. The neglect of this type of individual reflected problems in the law which seriously restricted the involuntary treatment of the mentally ill. This situation should not be confused, however, with results of community versus state hospital services.

PROBLEMS

Despite its earlier successes, Orange County's mental health program was operating under great stress by the spring of 1979. The local program was, and continued to be, involved in a major reorganization of county government at the time that Proposition 13 was enacted into law.

Orange County's mental health program was always marginally financed and held together in large measure by an aggressive and enthusiastic staff who strongly believed in the system they were developing. On 7 June 1978, California voters overwhelmingly approved the Jarvis-Gann Initiative (Proposition 13), a tax-limitation measure. Its major provision was to restrict the amount of money which could be collected from property taxes without prior approval from the voters. To the extent that public human services were financed locally, reductions in available funds would be expected to reduce available public services.

Funding for most local mental health programs in California was designated by the Short-Doyle Act to be provided 90% by the state and 10% by the local county government. Counties were free to pay 100% of the cost of unique programs which are locally desired but not a part of the state-approved program.

The impact of Proposition 13 was felt even before its passage. Perhaps for the first time in their lives, county mental health employees were told of the possibility of job losses. Approximately one week before the election, the County Personnel Office distributed a list of all employees in every department showing the seniority of each person. Layoff procedures were discussed at staff meetings, and employee organizations and unions were contacted by employees inquiring about their personnel rights.

Before the vote on Proposition 13, a hiring freeze was imposed by the Orange County Board of Supervisors to conserve funds in the event of passage. Including the vacancies unfilled before the hiring freeze and those which occurred after the freeze was imposed, there were 62 positions vacant on 7 June 1978 in alcoholism, drug abuse, and mental health services out of a total 638. One week after the passage of Proposition 13, the board of supervisors voted to abolish all vacant positions and to continue the hiring freeze. This abolition of positions affected some programs more than others. For example, due to recruiting problems and unavoidable delays in starting new projects, alcoholism services lost 10 of 62 positions and some contract programs as well.

Following the passage of Proposition 13, the California legislature was beseiged with demands from city and county governments to distribute the state's surplus, estimated to be $6 or 7 billion, to the hard-hit local governments. The legislature did consider these requests, and Governor Jerry Brown signed Senate Bill 154, a Proposition 13 "bail-out" plan, into law on 24 June 1978. This measure offered significant relief for some local programs, for example, school systems and social services, but provided no additional money for mental health. The measure did "forgive" for one year only the counties' 10% Short–Doyle match requirement for most mental health programs but also prohibited the granting of any cost-of-living wage increases to state and local government employees. Although the latter provision was subsequently found to be unconstitutional by the California Supreme Court, local programs were prohibited for most of the fiscal year from giving cost-of-living wage increases to employees and to contract agencies. As a result of this action, the salary of certain classifications of employees fell below the marketplace value and vacancies in some critical areas occurred. The situation was most critical in nursing services. The county had to close an inpatient treatment service at the Orange County jail for lack of nursing staff, and at times it appeared that there would be possible curtailment of services in the therapeutic residential centers. Some administrative positions were eliminated, elective services were curtailed, and a drug abuse prevention program was eliminated.

Although the state agreed to pay its usual 90% share, the Proposition 13 "bail-out" bill did not provide for the 10% portion previously paid by the counties. The state did allow some money unspent by the counties from the previous fiscal year to be rolled over to fiscal year 1978/1979. The final 1978/1979 fiscal year budget was $20,-537,998, down from $23,519,792 expended in the previous year.

Although no emergency or inpatient programs were curtailed as a result of Proposition 13, the budget cuts particularly affected the care of chronically mentally ill patients. The county's social service department, heavily dependent upon local property tax dollars, had traditionally provided social service supports and was forced to take major cuts as a result of Proposition 13. Prior to the cuts, the aftercare caseload had gradually increased without a concomitant increase in staffing. The situation was compounded by the loss of additional positions following the budget cuts. As a result, the continuing care staff informally started to restrict their caseloads by discharging patients from aftercare once they had been placed and an initial referral for treatment had been made. This action violated the basic concept of the case management system of aftercare, and the county then tried to redirect staff resources in the absence of any new funds to specifically service the chronic patients.

The legislature's Proposition 13 "bail out" bill provided for a waiver of the 10% match requirement by the county for the 1978/1979 fiscal year only. The waiver of the 10% county match was extended in the 1979/1980 fiscal year with the exception that the counties had to pay 10% of the cost of state hospitalization.

NOTES

1. Improving California's Mental Health System: Policy Making and Management in the Invisible System. Berkeley, Calif.: Teknekron, Inc., Health and Human Services Division, 1978

2. National Association of State Mental Health Program Directors Report, August 1978

Chapter 23

A SYSTEMS APPROACH IN NORTH CAROLINA

Nicholas E. Stratas
Clarence Boyd

A SYSTEMS PERSPECTIVE

Definition, design, and delivery of services for chronic patients is based upon how we think about and conceptualize the multiple issues involved. Our goals in this chapter are to describe some of the ways we find it useful to conceptualize a systems approach; to document an application of a systems approach to chronic patients that can be of immediate and practical use to practitioners, investigators, and managers; and to identify important issues to be examined by others developing programs for the chronic patient. To focus these goals, we will use parts of our experience in North Carolina.

An option in the development of any program activities is to leave the conceptual framework unstated. We believe that to do this creates unnecessary ambiguities leading to minimal program efficiency and questionable effectiveness. We prefer to explicate our frame of reference and believe that general systems theory offers a base from which to develop new strategies for the behavioral sciences which are particularly relevant to human service programs, providing design makers at all levels with different conceptual schemes for the analysis, direction, and improvement of formal organizations whose job is to administer and develop such human resource efforts as hospitals and local, regional, and state programs.

We make no assumption that existing programs or structures even though formally or legally organized are therefore "systems," as for example the "mental health system" and the "health system." In common practice, anything which seems extremely complex and difficult to define is frequently called a "system."

Basic system concepts have been more adequately expounded by other authors, and we will review only those basic segments relevant to our presentation (1, 2). Systems theory operates independently of any discipline or content area; it is a way of looking at the world. A system, as we define it, is a set of elements which have a definable organization or interrelationships functioning together over time. As a system moves from a relatively fixed mechanistic structure to a more adaptive monitoring structure, it becomes less a closed system and more an open system. A closed system is one which operates with fixed relationships requiring little or no outside intervention or energy and tends to lose its essential organization if disturbed.

An open system interacts with its environment as an essential part of survival. An open system has a monitoring component which provides it with feedback: information coming into the system from outside itself about the environment and about its impact on the environment and information from within its structure. Open systems are morphogenic, that is, they change their form or organization, as compared with morphostatic systems, which maintain a given form or organization. This characteristic is specific to our definition inasmuch as open systems are not necessarily morphogenic, for the ability to obtain information from the environment does not necessarily mean the system can change its form appropriately. A heating system controlled by a thermostat is an open but morphostatic system designed to maintain a given temperature level, something the system cannot alter. Feedback is used only to maintain a given structure or balance. An open morphogenic system, on the other hand, is able to evolve into new forms. Living organisms and groups of living organisms tend to have this characteristic, especially if they live over time.

Open morphogenic systems are goal oriented. The goals of the system are the work it seeks to accomplish and its purpose for existence. Ideally, the goals contain a specified, identifiable, measurable change and a time by which that change would take place or a time by which the work of the system would be complete. Goal clarification is the process of identifying these specifications. Purposefulness requires continuous interaction between the system and its environment. This includes, therefore, input, that which enters from outside the system, and output, that which goes from the system into its environment. It presupposes that in addition to the openness and the monitoring and information-gathering capability of the system there is an ability to analyze information. Information analysis changes raw, unstructured messages into meaningful and useful information. The process of interrelated, interacting elements moving toward goals, giving internal and external feedback, is called proactive. This is in contrast to the process by which actions are directed at stimuli coming from the environment, which is a reactive process. The thermostat, for example, comes closer to being a reactive system than a proactive system.

To define a patient as a living-person system and as part of a larger system in interaction with other person systems comprising the community, including such formal organizations as hospitals and local and state health programs, is to also be vitally concerned about system boundaries (3). A person, group, or community defines its own structure and identity by drawing and controlling its own boundaries. The exertion of boundary control is a requirement for an autonomous process, a process characteristic of living, open systems. Thus, an individual, whether patient or staff, would be stuck inside a program if he lost control of his boundaries and would lose autonomy as an individual person system. Patient and staff may be in collusion in reference to opening of the boundaries, which prevents change or production of goal-oriented work; the absence of change or goal-oriented work is a cardinal characteristic of a "chronic" situation. Inherent in viewing the patient as a person system and part of the system rather than only raw material to be acted upon by the system means that the system boundary is defined as the population to be served and the population who serve.

A Systems Approach

Activities necessary to move an existing social arrangement toward a purposeful self-managing system can be clustered as:

1. System Mapping—an empirical determination of the current operating nature of the system.
2. System Design—the determination of the arrangements which are desired.

3. System Engineering—the implementation of new arrangements and augmentation of existing arrangements.

Simply stated, we attempt to answer three questions. Where are we now? Where do we want to go? How do we get there?

System mapping includes a definition of boundary. At least four types of boundaries may exist for a service program.

1. The legal geographic boundary, defined by the mandate of the governing body.
2. The existing operational body, manifested by the types of activities or services in which the program staff engages.
3. The potential boundary in terms of the people we wish to serve.
4. The existing boundary in terms of the people currently being served.

Element identification is the process of definition of activity arrangements or units, whether within the formal setting of the hospital or outpatient mental health clinic or whether in other parts of the community. Element examination also includes what flows into it, input, and what moves out of it, output, including economically limited resources, such as materials, money, facilities, staff capabilities, human social status, and information.

A final activity in moving toward a purposeful self-managing system is the identification of the set of arrangements which constitute the human-relating social system of which the "chronic patient," and the program for the chronic patient, is a part and the ways in which each identified element is linked to other elements are determined.

This produces a working model of the existing human service system primary to the program and can best be described as the existing or natural system as opposed to a designed system.

Prior to 1963 in North Carolina, system mapping identified simply a hodgepodge of mental health and related activities not unlike those in any other of our states around the country at that time. There were four state hospitals, all of them receiving patients from essentially anywhere in the state. Similarly, there were three centers for the retarded and a fourth in planning and one alcoholic rehabilitation center, all equally vaguely defined. The only apparent boundary at that time was the legal boundary of the State of North Carolina. In addition, there were a few so-called mental health clinics dispersed throughout the state within local health departments and three or four child guidance clinics.

The 1963 legislature mandated more systematic planning and program development, which had begun to take place by the time the federal comprehensive health planning laws of the mid-1960s came into effect.

System design, the purposeful setting forth of goal statements and the systematic structuring of alternative strategies for the attainment of goals, created a number of shifts. Two of significance were the shift in viewing the action system as a passive reactive receptacle to viewing it as a system with a population orientation and a shift from traditionally formal institutional responses to a community support and development stance. These are two important boundary-defining statements which influenced the design of the action system in North Carolina. The state was divided into four large regions, each with a regional mental hospital and a regional center for the retarded, and three of the regions with an alcoholism rehabilitation institute. Each of the regions in turn was divided into single or multiple county areas, based on the population's self-definition of natural transportation, shopping, and political interrelatedness. These were established as flexible and evolving boundaries. Initially there were 29 service areas, but these had evolved to 41 by 1980 (4, 5, 6, 7).

Boundary flexibility was exercised in the region which did not have a preexisting alcoholism rehabilitation center, where a systems approach was introduced to the design process of the alcoholism programs. As of 1980, this region did not have a regional alcoholism institute, but rather the mental health and health programs in each area have their own individually tailored programs for problems of alcoholism.

Further evolution of the boundary has been exemplified by the state legislature's creation of a Department of Human Resources but more importantly by agreements and memoranda of understanding which have developed between the formal mental health, health, and vocational rehabilitation organizations; the departments of community colleges, hospitals, and corrections; and other relevant formal agencies at the state and local level, creating administrative arrangements which provide the greatest potential flexibility in the arrangement of resources (17). These relationships have been developed toward the implementation of a population-oriented boundary. Therefore, these relationships include in the definition of population not only the population of hospitals and community mental health centers but also the population in other formal agencies, such as corrections, and populations less clearly defined, such as migrant and seasonal farm workers, or dispersed unconnected populations.

By conservative estimate, the population in need would include 500,000 adults in North Carolina who experience a significant degree of mental illness. Perhaps 10% of this figure, or 50,000 people, have sufficiently severe mental illness to require a "moratorium" from stresses of daily life. If 10% of these individuals can be classified as being severely mentally disabled, this would be 5,000 or approximately 25% more than the average daily resident population in our four state hospitals. This crude estimation may in fact understate the situation.

For purposes of clearer exposition of our example, it is necessary to focus on one geographic subsystem of the total state system (8). Several community areas combined together to form a "region" served by specialized programs at the regional state hospital and the regional center for the retarded. We shall use one of these areas and one of these institutions. The area is Wake County, a primarily metropolitan area with a population of approximately 300,000 people. This is also the catchment area of the Trentman Mental Health Center Program, one of the earliest and more developed community mental health centers in the state. The regional hospital is Dorothea Dix, which is located in Wake County; this location has been a mixed blessing but has facilitated the use of the hospital as a convenient inpatient resource. Thus, we have a subsystem clearly defined by a boundary containing the 300,000 population in the Wake area. In this example, we will be looking closer at the activity elements within the formal institution of the hospital and the elements within the formal organization of the mental health center, both acting with the population of Wake County.

In the past, a variety of administrative and heroic individual efforts had been made to develop meaningful interconnections between the formal hospital agency and the formal mental health center (9). However, "chronic" institutional rigidities in both hospital and community continued. Stimulated by a proposal that would integrate fiscal responsibility for all patient care, both hospital and community, at the area level, a regional committee was assigned to study this possibility. The conclusion, in essence, was that the problems, cost, logistics, and personalities of such an integrated effort far outweighed the potential benefit that might be realized in patient care. This certainly raises a serious question in our minds as to the cost benefit of continuing agency reorganization at county, area, regional, state, national levels without a more systematic approach which would include a cost-benefit analysis. The recommendation was to continue current funding operations but maximize and improve upon coordinating mechanisms between the elements.

The recommendation was assigned to a team for development, and, in the consideration of the area's system, conceptualization included the identification of three important elements: the administrative, the technical, and the treatment or action element. Each element has appropriate tasks and appropriate information-processing activities. As a first step, the technical element of the Wake/Dix system undertook an examination of the existing services by studying 78 discharged hospital patients. General important observations were made (10). People learn to be chronic patients and receive reinforcement for the chronicity through the availability and reaction to them of formal institutional care, whether it be in a clinic or hospital. Much of the focus with chronic patients is on the failure of patients to take their medicine, to find a good job, to find a good place to live, to get into a day program. Little of the focus of current treatment and deinstitutionalization is on training and altering the responses and expectations of the chronic patient. There is little or no accountability for chronic patients and their reappearances for formal institutional care. Indeed, the chronic patient is a person who has minimal functional connections with other person systems. Professionals are trained to care for and to provide treatment for already enrolled patients, both inpatient and outpatient.

More specific observations were also made. There was no one portal of entry into the hospital. Half of the admissions came from sources within the county other than the mental health center; thus, the center never knew about many of the admissions to the hospital. There was no joint hospital/community goal planning about what was to happen during hospitalization. Wake County patients were placed within many different program activities and locations at the hospital, making tracking, coordination, and treatment planning even more difficult. Perhaps due to the proximity of hospital to community, very brief admissions were an inherent problem, with some patients signing in and out of the hospital in a matter of hours. Wake County patients left the hospital from many different programs within the hospital. There was no one portal of exit. This left little or no opportunity for any joint progress review or goal and treatment planning for continuing care by hospital and center staff. There was a four-to-six-week lag between time of discharge and patient's initial appointment at the center for aftercare or continuing services. Even after the patient was seen, information from the hospital was often not available. During one 16-week follow-up, one-third of the patients who were referred for continuing care failed to follow through at the clinic. It is important to recognize that these observations were made in organizations which had implemented a process of self-scrutiny and which are party to a general systems approach at the state level. The process of implementing a systems approach had occurred intermittently over a period of ten years. It was initially stimulated at the state level. However, here as well as in other examples, it was clear that the impact was primarily that of administrative rearrangement rather than patient benefit, with business continuing as usual.

In this instance, two middle managers representing both the hospital and the clinic (technical element) took the lead in the initial planning and development of a clinical liaison team, thus implementing an action or working element of the system. The liaison team was made up of a social worker from the hospital and a psychiatric nurse from the center. Each was sanctioned to spend 15 hours a week in liaison activities. They carried additional duties within their own agencies. They were charged with several responsibilities including identifying and contacting all patients admitted to the hospital; maintaining tracking data on these patients; participating in joint treatment planning with the admission staff; actively participating in discharge planning, including meaningful contacts with families and patients toward involvement in posthospital continuing services; facilitating the availability of appropriate program and policy information (e.g., "rules" of how each program conducted its business) to both hospital and center staff; facilitating the availability of hospitalization information for the patient's initial aftercare appointment; providing short-term transitional services for high-risk or less stabilized patients who need the continuing contact between the time of discharge and the initial aftercare appointment; and contacting discharged patients who failed to keep aftercare appointments.

Sanction was sought and received from top management, the administrative element, of both the hospital and the area mental health program, and each made a commitment of the recommended resources. Thus, initial administrative-level sanction and nourishment was identified as important and made available.

The middle-management level, the technical element of the system, provided a strong linkage between the day-to-day patient care activities of the liaison team, the action element, and the more system-wide concerns of the administrative element, top management.

This helped facilitate a more objective definition of problems and increased the efficiency of both the administrative and clinical tasks.

Initially, the boundaries and functions of the administrative and action elements were not clearly specified, resulting in confused connections, expectations, and actions. As a result, administrative issues and decisions were often inappropriately imposed and thrust upon the action component for problem solving, or for carrying out the decision. Oftentimes, patient-relevant decisions which continued to be bothersome were inappropriately imposed and thrust upon the administrative element. It became necessary to clarify ambiguities in the structure and to separate out, but appropriately link for problem solving, administrative issues from treatment system issues and, within the treatment system issues, differentiate between action issues and technical issues (16). For example, information sharing between two service agencies is an administrative issue and not a treatment system issue, but often the energy and affect that gets focused around information sharing is more appropriate to treatment issues. Policies on information sharing oftentimes act as lightning rods for an obscure discussion of the treatment issues. Therefore, to intervene in such a system, it becomes very necessary to clarify ambiguities in the structure and to separate out administrative and treatment system issues, so that thinking and emotions can be routed appropriately. Major problems are likely to occur if administrative elements try to problem solve around clinical elements issues. Political decisions, similarly, do not easily convert to clinical action. Chaos results when boundaries are blurred between political, administrative, and clinical elements. Maintaining such functional boundaries and the routing to the appropriate problem-solving element is a chief function of the technical element of the system. Such functioning is vital in the maintenance of the original trust and spirit of cooperation. Through experience, it was learned that if tension (usually in the form of suspicious, paranoid behavior) was increasing that the routing function needed to be focused upon.

As the administrative, technical, and action elements were clarified and made functional, patient information became even clearer, reinforced by the implementation of a plan for one portal of exit. Three subgroups of chronic patients can be conceptualized and identified: the stabilized, long-term hospital patient resettled into a community setting; the in-and-out patient with multiple admissions to a hospital; and the "treatment failures" who never leave inpatient care but who go in and out of psychosis while remaining in the hospital. Problem solving with each of these subgroups necessitates different strategies.

For the stabilized long-term hospital patient, administrative strategies linking up a support system—nursing homes, boarding homes, aftercare visits—with minimum treatment strategies, such as medication maintenance and consultation with the staff, are oftentimes sufficient. For the in-and-out patient, the strategies become more complex and implementation more difficult. The administrative strategies include closer collaboration between the hospital and the community around such issues as criteria for admission, readmission, and discharge, and the design of ways to implement joint treatment planning. For example, in the Wake/Dix project, a number of patients have been identified as "causing more problems" than others. For these patients, staff from the mental health center will come to the hospital for planning conferences, and a treatment plan will be jointly defined. Therefore, there is one plan for the patient rather than a community plan and a hospital plan. This one plan comprises the discharge planning for follow-up services, including whatever agency—mental health, social service, or rehabilitation—may have the relevant activities. Such a plan will often specify under what conditions the patient is to return to the hospital (13, 14).

For the "treatment failures," a more critical definition of administrative and treatment interventions is necessary. We are faced with a most difficult job with this group in clarifying goals and setting priorities. Staff experience fusion in their thinking and emotions. Administrative concerns and issues may serve as a readily accessible scapegoat or smoke screen for more painful core feelings. For example, the hospital may become involved in making accusations to the community about its lack of interest in developing alternatives in a community setting for these patients, or the hospital may blame the mental health center for not developing appropriate alternatives to "office" support and treatment. A community can become involved in similar projections, accusing the hospital of simply wanting to get patients out to the community and to keep them out. The question becomes one of how to improve the problem-solving ability, functioning, and work at this "treatment failure" level; that is, how to get staff to conceptualize a treatment plan for a treatment failure.

If a chronic patient is conceptualized as a person/system functioning and interacting within a context or environment, then the definition of the problem of chronicity is a breakdown in these interactions. The hospital and center have a major share of looking at this breakdown and in the development of a problem-solving action response calculated to increase interconnections between the patient and other persons. The appropriate place to start is not with the patient but rather with the patient/staff system. Assessments, need identification, and training in skill development must be stressed. For example, a characteristic of chronic patients is that they are cut off from their family system. The system boundaries are closed. Therefore, a first step is to reengage families or surrogate families as a support system in the problem-solving effort. A by-product of such an effort is to decrease the isolation of both the patient and the staff, with the family becoming an ally. Often, there is a lack of agreement over a treatment plan, but more realistically, there is a deficit in the staff on how to conceptualize an appropriate treatment plan for these very difficult patients. In such a situation, the staff feel the inadequacies and become nihilistic, which is reflected in their verbalization and attitudes toward these patients; this leads into a vicious circle, symbiotic, self-destructive set of relationships between staff and patients, often characterized by outbursts of violence. As well, there is often projection onto administrative elements and individuals, such as the hospital director or the secretary of the Department of Human Resources. Therefore, solutions have to start with the conceptualization for treatment planning rather than with the assumption of business as usual.

Teams and staff members must learn to conceptualize the dynamics of a support system in the community. For example, staff usually do not know how to involve family members and patients in a treatment plan. A treatment plan is something that is "done on" the patient; the family may or may not find out about it, but there certainly is no joint planning. The family must be seen as a resource *(15)*. Recently, within a particular program for chronic patients at Dorothea Dix Hospital, staff members decided to invite cutoff relatives of patients to the hospital. Fifteen invitations went out to families that had visited their relatives during the year. The staff was very much surprised when positive responses came from 100% of the inquiries. An important question is, why was the staff surprised? This group of relatives has continued to meet and has provided a strong, problem-solving resource to the staff during the times of crisis the program has experienced. This example can be generalized and used in other areas of the community support system. Dynamics of a support system, the relationships among the elements of the support system, can be specified, discussed, and made rational and operational.

A further example relevant to these difficult patients has to do with the violent and threatening behavior, or the fear of such behavior, which is frequently a part of the symptomatic picture and one which potentially involves family, police, and community, often escalating into the political system. Therefore, quite specific goals and the actions to be taken must be spelled out in advance. Examples of important considerations include the conditions under which the patient will return to the hospital, or be taken to jail, or perhaps to the mental health center, or even to the home, if the first contact is the police. When the plan is put into action, it must be monitored to prevent potential staff anxiety, whether at the clinical or administrative level, from circumventing the specified original plan.

Feedback regarding accountability issues in a design where an action component is working directly with clients around specific goals provides a number of pieces of information *(11, 12)*. A single and direct point of contact between case managers and patient provides an accountability relationship between the patient, the action manager, the administrator manager, and the system manager. The set of services required by each client is developed as an integrated set and provided within the existing administrative relationships or, if not possible, then the appropriate rearrangement of resources needed are brought to the attention of the administrators. As a plan of services for each client evolves, some generic steps or sequences are identified which can be called the patient pathway.

PROBLEMS TO BE ADDRESSED AND ISSUES TO THINK ABOUT

We have proposed in this chapter the use of systems theory in approaching the issue of chronic patients. We have shared portions of our observations and our own applications. Innumerable considerations have arisen which we would like to now identify and which must be deliberately considered. They will arise in the process of development of activities around chronic patients. The following is a sampling of these issues:

1. Conceptual framework and definitions of those involved in administering, advising, and providing such activities.
2. Application of general systems theory approach to chronic patients.
3. Current status of the target population.
4. Goals.
5. Strategies and steps to be taken.
6. Boundaries—how structured and how open?
7. Input and output.
8. Current formal activities and their relationships, if such exist.

9. Development of connections between agencies and staff.
10. Identification of the administrative element and its appropriate level of concerns and tasks.
11. Identification of the technical element and its appropriate level of concerns and tasks.
12. Identification of the action element and its appropriate level of concerns and tasks.
13. Training program for patients, families, and staff.
14. Accountability.
15. Single portal of entry and exit, and tracking system of patient movement.
16. Unified information system regarding admissions and discharges.
17. Unified goal and treatment planning.
18. Unified progress review and follow-up planning.
19. Monitoring and proactive follow-through.
20. Reorganization.
21. Interagency teams.
22. The place of the family in the process and in the system.
23. Administrative commitment of resources and assignment of priorities, and continuing nourishment.
24. Patient characteristics and patient pathways.
25. Scapegoating, escalating triangles.
26. Patient/family/staff interaction.
27. Staff training.
28. Patient interpersonal linkages.
29. The support system.
30. Monitoring of the whole system.

In conclusion, we believe people learn to be chronic patients and to establish chronic, nonproblem-solving relationships, whether in their family system or in the patient/staff system, and receive reinforcement for their chronicity through the availability and teaching of institutional care and the institution's response to them. Definition of what is meant by our various words, and particularly the word *chronic* as compared with the word *acute,* is significant in attempting to establish a meaningful goal-related system. It may be a mistake to assume that acute and chronic are opposite ends of the same continuum. For problem-solving purposes, it is perhaps more helpful to think of a chronic context or a chronic situation. Attention must be given to the process of labeling citizens, with its accompanying implications for community support access. Appropriate elements of a response system must be defined, along with their interconnections. Attention must also be given to the information and skill base of the staff, their training needs, and skill development; to the interaction of patient behavior and the actions and behaviors of others, whether in the community or by staff and program; and to development of the support system, including the family, neighborhood, alternate-living arrangements, and work arrangements, and including all the persons in the client's system which, although preexisting, may be alienated.

In summary, commitment of resources is essential to the consideration of the problems of chronic patients. However, merely obtaining more of the existing resources will not lead in itself to an improvement in problem solving. Quite the contrary, it may lead to more despair and more chronicity! An important starting place in approaching the chronic patient is the consideration of how we think in reference to the chronic patient. Clarifying our definitions and concepts is essential, and concepts of general systems theory and family systems theory can bring possible solutions to old problems. We have shared our conception of a systems approach; we have shared, in part, segments of our application of a systems approach to chronic patients; and we have identified important issues to be examined by others developing programs for the chronic patient.

NOTES

1. Bertalanffy L: General systems theory. New York, George Braziller, 1968

2. Miller JG: The nature of living systems. Behavioral Science 20(6):343–365, November 1975

3. Durkin J: Boundarying Processes in the Formation of Therapy Groups. Presented at 36th Annual Conference, American Group Psychotherapy Association, New York, 16–19 February 1979

4. Osberg JW, Stratas NE, Rollins RL: Area Programs—The North Carolina Model. Raleigh North Carolina Department of Mental Health, 1968

5. Stratas NE: Gaps in psychiatric linkages. Delivering Mental Health Services. American Psychiatric Association, 1975

6. Stratas NE: A systems approach to service delivery. Delivering Mental Health Services. American Psychiatric Association, 1975

7. Stratas NE: A model for a psychiatric service delivery system and discussion. Delivering Mental Health Services. A publication of the American Psychiatric Association, APA, Washington D.C., 1975

8. Rollins RL, Stratas NE: A geographic unit as a phase in merging hospital and community programs. Hospital and Community Psychiatry 25(6):378–380, 1974

9. Stratas NE: Gaps—What Don't We Do. Presented at 26th Institute on Hospital and Community Psychiatry, Denver, Colorado, October 1974

10. Stratas NE, Bernhardt DB, Elwell RN: The future of the state mental hospital: Developing a unified system of care. Hospital and Community Psychiatry 28:598–600, 1977

11. Holder HD: Building accountability into the service system. Hospital and Community Psychiatry 29:38–39, 1978

12. Holder HD: Accountability and Productivity in a System of Services for Chronic Patients. Presented at 29th Institute on Hospital and Community Psychiatry—American Psychiatric Association, San Francisco, California, October 1977

13. Boyd C, Henderson WE: Continuity of Care: A Shared Responsibility of the State Hospital and Local Mental Health Program. Presented at the 29th Institute on Hospital and Community Psychiatry—American Psychiatric Association, San Francisco, California, October 1977

14. Boyd C, Henderson WE: Improving continuity of care through a state hospital—Community mental health center liaison program. Hospital and Community Psychiatry 29:384–386, 1978

15. Spiegel J: The family: The channel of primary care. Hospital and Community Psychiatry 25(12):785–788, 1974

16. Bowen M: Toward the differentiation of self in administrative systems. In Bowen M: Family Therapy in Clinical Practice. New York, Jason Aronson, 1978

17. Statewide Community Support System, Strategy Development Project: Technical proposal by Division of Mental Health Services, State of North Carolina, 1978

Chapter 24

THE MASSACHUSETTS EXPERIENCE
Robert L. Okin

We as a nation continue to warehouse our mentally ill citizens. This state of affairs persists despite the community mental health movement, despite considerable national attention to this issue, and despite the recognition that we are hurting rather than helping many of the people we shut away in our institutions. We have spent the last few years grappling with how to transform this situation in Massachusetts. This chapter will describe some of the approaches we have taken to this problem in hope that some of our experience may have application elsewhere.

At the outset, we decided that we had to go far beyond the guarantees embodied in most right to treatment litigation and commit ourselves to the principle that mentally ill people at risk of institutionalization have a right not only to treatment but to treatment in the least restrictive, most normalizing setting suitable to their needs. We believed that guaranteeing the mentally ill a right to adequate treatment, as articulated by the court in *Wyatt* v. *Stickney,* for example, did not fundamentally alter the second-class status accorded to severely mentally ill people by this society, because it did not challenge the practice of institutionalizing people who could be treated in less restrictive, less isolated settings. Far from doing so, the courts have in a sense legitimized this practice by stating the preconditions which make unnecessary institutionalization permissible. They have said in effect that states can involuntarily commit people to state hospitals so long as the latter provide treatment to those so confined—even if those people could have been treated in less restrictive settings. In contrast, and notwithstanding the egregious manner in which deinstitutionalization has been implemented in many states, we have come to believe that, for most patients, the institution is deficient, not simply because it is understaffed or old, but because it is impersonal, isolated from society, distant from family and friends, and an excessively restrictive form of care. Doubling the staff, modernizing the facility, and upgrading its treatment capacity does not fundamentally rectify the situation, since most of the institutionalized population are capable of treatment in a setting less restrictive than a state hospital, if those settings were made available to them. The right to treatment principle espoused by the courts in most progressive mental health litigation allows that treatment is the only thing which justifies proper commitment. The principle embodying a right to treatment in the least restrictive alternative, however, implies that no amount of treatment can justify the institutionalization of people, involuntary or voluntary, unless they in fact require that degree of restrictiveness.

Having taken upon ourselves the affirmative obligation to develop a service system which provides people at risk of institutionalization opportunities for treatment in the least restrictive setting, we set about to translate this into operational terms. In 1972, we undertook an exhaustive clinical assessment of every single patient in each of our state hospitals. We carefully analyzed each patient's level of functioning, his behavior, his mental status, his medical and nursing needs, and so on. We assessed whether he needed help dressing himself, whether he tended to wander, whether he could communicate verbally, whether he was dangerous to himself or to others. It was a most extensive survey. We then determined from this assessment the residential and support services which almost every patient needed in order to live in the community. After we had developed an individualized community service plan for almost every patient, we determined the resources which would be necessary to implement this plan and thereby developed a blueprint of the services and resources necessary to treat all but a small group of dangerous patients in the community.

The results of this assessment process were really quite striking. Of all the people still living in the state hospitals in Massachusetts, the vast majority, almost 90% in fact, although quite disabled, were determined to be capable of living in the community *if* the community mental health system were expanded and organized to help them do so. To one who has not spent much time in a state hospital, this may not seem like a terribly remarkable conclusion. If one is familiar with the remaining patients in state hospitals, it will be quickly brought to mind just how disabled and dysmorphic many of these patients are. Many have been sitting in the corners of state hospitals for the last 30 years with only minimal rehabilitation and do not look as if they could walk across the ward, much less into the community. Now a handful could not, but most in fact could if a continuum of residential and supportive services were established in the community and tailored to their individual needs.

Another thing which the clinical assessment process pointed out vividly was just how many people were being admitted to the state hospitals simply because general hospitals were unwilling to accept involuntary patients. To rectify this situation, we established a forum consisting of the association of general hospitals in the state, the Massachusetts Association for Mental Health, and the Department of Public Health. In 1979, after a year of deliberation, these groups unanimously concluded that hereafter the hospitals in every catchment area requesting a Certificate of Need for psychiatric beds had to organize themselves so that all voluntary and *in*voluntary patients except for the most violent could be cared for in the community. This agreement has been embodied in the state's health plan and will be enforced through the Certificate of Need process.

Having completed the clinical assessment process, and having determined the services which would be necessary to implement the individual community service plans for most of the patients living in our state hospitals, we turned our attention to a problem which more than any other has discredited the deinstitutionalization process in many states: the tendency of many state hospitals to dump patients into communities without adequate services. As we looked at this issue, we came to feel that the very dichotymous structure of the mental health system in most states contributed to this problem and almost guaranteed a lack of continuity of care. The complete administrative separation between the institution and the community mental health system, the lack of a common governance responsible for both, meant that there existed no single point of accountability for the patient's treatment when he either entered or left the institution. Under these circumstances, continuity of care between the institution and the community, when it did take place, was often dependent on the vicissitudes of the personal relationship existing between individual professionals in each system. It was not something which occurred because of the administrative structure of the mental health system but in spite of it. Discontinuity of care then seemed to us to be the preordained result of the existence of divided authority between two isolated systems, one responsible for the patient's institutional care, the other for his ambulatory care. No one person had direct or indirect responsibility for both.

In a partial attempt to deal with this problem, we have begun to change the administrative structure of the mental health system in the following way: in place of the traditional administrative structure of most geographically unitized institutions, in which each unit director reports to a superintendent, we are putting in place a structure in which the superintendent becomes a hospital administrator responsible only for the hospital's central support services. Clinical care on the unit remains under the authority of the unit director, but now each unit director reports not to the superintendent but to a community mental health catchment area director who is ultimately responsible both for the treatment provided within his particular state hospital geographic unit and for all other Department of Mental Health supported services in his catchment area. Each unit director then reports to his respective community mental health catchment area director, who is based outside the hospital and has ultimate authority over all admissions and discharges to and from his particular state hospital unit, all treatment which takes place on his unit, and the hiring, firing, and supervision of all clinical personnel on his unit. In addition, the area director has responsibility for all Department of Mental Health supported services in his community mental health system, which he carries out either directly or through contractual arrangements with local service providers. We have thus broken down the state hospital into units, each of which is administratively integrated under the authority of a community mental health system.

While it is much too early to evaluate the effects of this new organizational structure, we are hopeful that it will reduce the tendency to discharge patients inappropriately from the institution before services are in place to care for them. Since one person, the community mental health catchment area director, is responsible for both community as well as state hospital services for his area, it should be possible to hold him accountable for the care he provides to people living in his catchment area no matter where they receive treatment —inside or outside the institution.

But dumping will not disappear simply as a result of reorganization alone. It will only disappear when there are sufficient resources to care for the people who are discharged. I would like to turn then to the ways we have tried to solve the most difficult problem in implementing the principle that people have a right to treatment in the least restrictive setting suitable to their needs: the financing problem.

When I first came to Massachusetts as commissioner in 1975, it was obvious that the financing problem was one of both quantity and distribution of resources. Not only was there an inadequate amount of money available to the mental health system as a whole, but the distribution of what money there did exist was completely inconsistent with the principle that the treatment of most patients would occur in community settings. Indeed, 80% of the mental health resources in most states have historically been allocated to institutions. Massachusetts was no exception.

Clearly, one of the ways that is available to change this distribution of resources is for the commissioner to reallocate resources from the state hospital to the community mental health system. In fact, if he is not able to do this, the latter system will remain as impoverished as its patients. In a world where Proposition 13 and all of its variants are increasingly coming to dominate public policy, the inability of the departments of mental health throughout the country to effect large-scale reallocation has had disastrous consequences for the treatment of society's sickest, most vulnerable, and most disenfranchised patients. Indeed, the inability of most state governments to reallocate resources has been among the most important reasons that many states have only been able to tinker with the mental health system instead of transforming it.

It must be asked why it has been so difficult to effect large-scale reallocation? Unless the answers to this question are understood, it is unlikely that the financing problems of state mental health systems will be solved or that their patients will be properly cared for in the community.

In this connection, it is worth remembering that early in the community mental health movement, it had been thought that massive reallocation of resources would inevitably accompany decreased state hospital utilization and thereby reduce state hospital budgets or at least permit them to be level funded. In certain cases, this was almost promised by mental health advocates in return for legislative and executive support of the deinstitutionalization process. There developed in consequence a strange alliance between mental health advocates and state budget directors, both advocating a reduction in state hospital utilization, though clearly for different reasons. This alliance gradually broke down when it became clear that vast amounts of money were not to be immediately saved through the deinstitutionalization process, at least the way it occurred in most states.

Ironically, it was the very dearth of new resources for community services for the institutionalized population which acted as the greatest obstacle to reallocating institutional resources. Most states in fact made the mistake of trickling monies into the community mental health system at so slow a rate that the decline in the state hospital census was simply not sufficient to free up institutional resources.

In fact, far from being able to reallocate resources from the hospitals, states were faced with rising hospital costs at the very time that their census was declining. Severe inflationary pressures on institution budgets, a shift in the composition of the state hospital toward a more disabled population, the wave of right to treatment suits, the increasingly rigorous standards imposed by accrediting and certifying authorities, and a change in the orientation of the hospital from custody to rehabilitation—all these factors increased the need for institutional resources, despite the declining census. The result was that most new resources which might have been directed to expand the community mental health system were directed toward the rising costs of state hospitals instead.

The commissioner then found himself in a vicious political, clinical, and economic cycle. Because he had to increase the state hospital budget, he had no resources left over to expand the community mental health system. Without the expansion of the community mental health system, however, patients could not be responsibly discharged from the institution. As a result, the state hospital census remained relatively high and made it impossible for the commissioner to allocate his scarce new mental health resources anywhere but to the state hospitals. And so the cycle continued. Reallocation of resources from the state hospital were clearly impossible under these circumstances.

Adding to the irony of this situation has been the fact that, even when new resources were appropriated to expand the community mental health system, the state hospital census was often not greatly reduced over the last five years. One of the reasons for this was that frequently these limited resources were not focused on developing community alternatives for the institutionalized population but spread instead among many population groups in an attempt to satisfy everyone. The result was that the severely mentally ill patient received very little of the resources which became available to the mental health system.

Financial considerations have not been the only obstacles to reallocation. There have been administrative and political obstacles as well. I mentioned earlier how the divided administrative structure of most mental health systems tended to promote discontinuity of care between the institution and the community mental health system. It has created other problems as well. For one, the very organizational structure of the mental health system has necessarily set up conflict between the state hospital and the community mental health program as attempts were made to move resources from the first to the second. The mere existence of a structure in which the superintendent of the institution was losing resources to the community mental health system was bound to create problems between the two in any resource transfer. The very real political power of a superintendent who had built up an important constituency among employees, families, patients, and legislators has often been sufficient to impede reallocation of state hospital resources even when the resources did become available.

Moreover, the budget structure of the traditional mental health system paralleling as it did the dichotomous organizational structure has made it impossible to transfer resources smoothly from the hospital into the community. The rigid compartmentalization of the budget into impenetrable hospital and community mental health components has meant that nothing short of an act of the legislature could move resources from one to the other. In order to even *propose* such a reallocation to the legislature, the commissioner has had to clearly identify excess state hospital resources and, in so doing, risk losing them altogether to the insatiable state treasury. Even if this did not occur, the very possibility of losing the funds made commissioners very reluctant to take the chance on identifying resources for reallocation. If the budget structure of the mental health system had not been so compartmentalized and if resources could therefore flow as needed between institutional and community services, a major obstacle to reallocation would have been overcome.

Finally, reallocation brought with it the spectre of a major disruption in the institutional employment situation. Employees, fearing the loss of jobs attendant on institutional phasedown, have repeatedly turned to their unions for protection and political action. This has often taken the form of strident attacks against the whole deinstitutionalization process, which they have identified as the source of their economic dislocation.

I would like to describe the strategies we have used to solve the reallocation problem in Massachusetts. While many problems persist, we have begun to have some very modest success in extricating ourselves from the vicious cycle I described earlier.

The first task that had to be confronted was how we were going to get additional monies into the community mental health system, for without this, reallocation of state hospital resources is impossible if it is to be done responsibly. Interestingly, the clinical assessment and planning process I described earlier was extremely helpful in this endeavor. Not only did this process yield a complete clinical profile and individual community service plan for the vast majority of our institutionalized patients, but for the first time we were able to predict the cost of implementing these plans. We were then able to predict the cost of developing a comprehensive community mental health system for all but a handful of institutionalized people. The executive and legislative branches of state government for the first time could see in concrete fiscal and programmatic terms what it would take to tear down what everyone agreed was a dehumanizing institutional system and replace it with a good community system. Although the new system would require somewhat greater resources in total than was currently being spent in the mental health system, the possibility of being able to radically transform the existing mental health system was exciting to both the administration and many legislators, especially when they could see just how much additional money would be necessary to simply maintain the existing institutional system. The result was that with the assistance of professionals and citizens we were able to obtain new resources, which were used to expand the community mental health system. It must be stressed that without these additional resources we never could have developed the community mental health system rapidly enough and agressively enough to set the stage for the reallocation of institutional dollars. This process cannot be accomplished in most places without additional resources if it is to be done responsibly. Anyone who promises that it can be done without additional resources is bound to repeat the serious mistakes of the past, mistakes which have given the whole deinstitutionalization process such a terrible reputation in many states.

But obtaining new resources, while necessary, is not sufficient. These resources must be sharply focused in order to make an impact on the very disabled patient. We found that we had to use almost all of our new resources for those community mental health services which would responsibly reduce the state hospital census: crisis intervention services, a spectrum of residential alternatives, day treatment programs, and case management services. Moreover, instead of spreading all of the resources equitably across the state, we allocated them to those areas which we knew could develop community alternatives rapidly and responsibly. Although we had to tolerate a certain amount of anger from those whose needs we were not able to satisfy, I believe that this focused approach is critical to achieving any kind of results. Between 1975 and 1979, with a relatively small amount of new resources, we have increased the number of supervised residential placements in small, well-staffed community residences by almost 300% and the number of day treatment programs by a similar percentage. The result of focusing the new community mental health resources on residential and day treatment services to the most disabled patients is that the state hospital population in Massachusetts declined from 5,000 to 2,700 during the four-year period, a decrease of 46%. The drop in some hospitals has been so substantial and so rapid that it has been possible to close many buildings and thereby release significant amounts of resources for community services.

But there is more to accomplishing significant reallocation than simply phasing down institutions. There must also be a way of moving the money from the institutional accounts to the community accounts. I referred earlier to the obstacles which the budget structure presents to this process. In order to deal with these obstacles, we have begun to amalgamate each catchment area's community mental health budget with that portion of the state hospital budget which funds its geographic inpatient unit. In this way, the community mental health catchment area director is given fiscal authority to complement and support his programmatic authority for all Department of Mental Health supported community and state hospital services provided to his area.

What are the implications of this new budget structure for reallocation? They are truly profound. In that part of the state where we have implemented the new structure, state hospital resources can be moved to the community mental health system smoothly as the needs of the patients dictate.

Through the foregoing process, we have begun to extricate ourselves from the impossible situation in which we had found ourselves —a situation in which a high state hospital census made reallocation impossible. During the fiscal year 1981/1982, we anticipate that we will be able to reallocate almost $9 million from the state hospital budget to the community mental health system. This will be reflected as a decrease in state hospital expenditures of almost 15% in contrast to the average increase in state hospital expenditures in other Atlantic states of 30% over the last few years. This means that every new dollar spent in the community mental health system will liberate one dollar from the state hospital, which can then be reallocated to the community mental health system for further expansion. In other words, the community mental health system will expand at a rate twice as fast as would occur with the addition of new resources alone. This in turn will permit an additional decrease in state hospital census through the provision of good community alternatives and liberate more resources for reallocation and so on. In fiscal year 1981, we will be spending approximately 60% of our total mental health resources for community mental health services. In 1975, we were spending approximately 30% of our resources for community mental health services. This in fiscal terms is a reflection of the beginnings of change in our mental health system.

In closing, I would like to emphasize that despite the considerable progress we have made over the last few years in Massachusetts there is an enormous amount left to be done. We still must actually develop those psychiatric units within general hospitals to which I referred earlier. We have only begun to make a dent in the need for a full-fledged community support system. We have not adequately started to touch the nursing home population with either our services or our philosophy. And finally, we have not been able to keep many very troubled clients connected to the service system after they have left the state hospital despite our attempts to do so. Given the many unfinished tasks facing us both in Massachusetts and elsewhere, it is important that we not allow the atmosphere of extreme fiscal austerity prevailing in the country to stifle our outrage at the way mentally ill people have been treated by this society. For indeed, they have always been treated as second-class citizens. They have been warehoused in overcrowded, understaffed, barren, and isolated institutions during some periods of our national history and summarily dumped out of these institutions without adequate services during other periods of our history. They have been kept impoverished and disenfranchised in the state hospital and out of the state hospital.

In my opinion, there is no way of responsibly addressing this situation unless we commit ourselves to a radical transformation of the current mental health system. This cannot be done without a significant infusion of resources into the community mental health system, so that people can receive treatment in the least restrictive alternative suitable to their needs. A large portion of these resources can come from the state hospital system, but this can only be responsibly done if there has been rapid and aggressive community mental health expansion as a result of new resources. Only in this way can reallocation take place without compromising the quality of care to the remaining state hospital clients even further. Only in this way can the mental health system be transformed as opposed to merely tinkered with.

Chapter 25

DISCUSSION
Systems for the Chronically Mentally Ill
Alan M. Kraft

The creation of a system of care for the chronically mentally ill is not simply a matter of applying effective treatment and rehabilitative measures, though surely it depends on doing this and more. As the previous descriptions amply demonstrate, such a system must also be politically viable, fiscally feasible, and capable of being administered.

The design and administration of such a system is a problem of orchestration. It requires the selection of the effective elements, putting them together so that they complement and supplement each other, setting the overall purposes and priorities, protecting and supporting them as they do their work, and, not the least important, assuring adequate financial and public support for their work.

Previous sections of this volume have dealt with the treatment and rehabilitation elements that constitute the parts of the system of services for the chronically ill. The need for skilled persons to provide psychopharmacologic therapy, psychotherapy, socialization, vocational rehabilitation, housing, and case management has been described. Each of these is essential, yet no one element constitutes a comprehensive treatment system. They must be woven together.

In another section, various program auspices have been described—private, state, county, federal, and voluntary. Each may contribute an important part to the system. However, when we consider such a system of care as the one in Orange County, California, described by Klatte and Crowder, it is clear that each of these auspices or sponsors plays only a part in the entire system of care for the chronically ill patient. No one sponsor is capable of doing this entire job. The larger system of care is required to delegate a part of the task to individual sponsoring agencies, such as a general hospital or a nursing home. The significant questions in the design of such a system are which parts, to whom, for what purposes.

The accounts of the systems in Orange County, North Carolina, and Massachusetts offer an opportunity to examine some of the issues to be considered when building a system of care. In this context, *system* should be taken to mean a comprehensive program with many varied interdependent elements which serves a large population such as a county or a state. It is made up of treatment and rehabilitation programs. It is managed by an individual who is responsible to the governmental executive and who therefore must be responsive to political initiatives, constraints, and directions.

What are some of the key issues which are highlighted by the descriptions of these three programs and, by implication, by all such systems?

COMPREHENSIVENESS

The needs of the chronically mentally ill patients are myriad. The system of care must provide a range of services that spans from inpatient through partial hospitalization through outpatient care. It must include the availability of therapy and rehabilitation services. It must enable integration with housing and social services. It must articulate with the social security agencies so that financial assistance may be provided. It must make it possible for patients to have vocational training and job placement available.

No single agency can do all this. A system which services a large and varied population must involve itself with many different agencies. One of the critical factors in successful programs is the ability to meet the essential needs of their patients without leaving gaps in services. It is essential that the system be designed in such a way that all the programs exist and that they are functionally articulated.

FUNDING

Funding is a key to establishing and maintaining programs. The optimism and public generosity of the 1960s has given way to the fiscal constraints and conservatism of the 1970s. As Klatte and Crowder so dramatically illustrate, Proposition 13 has had a profound and generally deleterious effect on Orange County mental health programs. The economic uncertainties in the United States are not limited to California.

The growing community health centers in the 1960s did not focus sharply on the needs of the chronically ill patient. Consequently, the thrust of interest on this underserved population is more recent and comes at a time when additional funding is not available. Funds for new programs for the chronically ill patient must compete with existing programs.

This sharply limits possible initiatives. In Massachusetts, the problem has been partially resolved by a reallocation of existing resources. It seems clear that federal participation in financing programs for the chronically mentally disabled is very limited, if not insignificant, except as a symbol. The total federal contribution for services for chronically ill patients is less than that budgeted by some states.

The cities and counties are heavily taxed and have resisted undertaking additional responsibilities for the care of the mentally ill. Therefore, for the most part, the funding of mental health programs falls to the states. Until now, most states have invested their mental health funds in the operation of large mental hospitals. During the years up to 1954, these hospitals grew rapidly. After 1954, they no longer grew in size, but they became more expensive because of increased dissatisfaction with their custodialism, which led to a large-scale mental hospital improvement program.

In the middle 1960s, the community mental health centers were established and grew in size and number, but few were programmatically integrated with the state hospitals and fewer still addressed the needs of the chronically mentally ill.

By the 1970s, there existed two separate public or quasi-public systems of care—the community mental health centers and the state hospitals. Each of these was competing with the other for scarce funds. In many areas of the country, the competition has been fierce. But fundamentally, the two kinds of programs have been overlapping and in many ways redundant and poorly integrated.

As Okin points out, it was not possible to improve programs for the chronically ill patients while saving money. Good programs cost money, and these costs have rapidly escalated due to inflation and factors which are increasing all health costs. It has not been possible to develop excellent programs without additional funds. And increased funds have not been forthcoming from the state governments.

In Massachusetts, a creative approach has been initiated in which a phasing in of community programs is funded by concomitant reductions in state hospital funding. This plan is worthy of study and should be watched carefully by planners.

The issue of finding funds for these programs is a serious dilemma. Programs for the chronically ill population are seriously underfunded, and there is little hope that the states, from which the funds must come, will have the resources to invest in these systems of care.

INTEGRATION OF STATE HOSPITALS AND LOCALLY OPERATED PROGRAMS

In every state, the integration of state hospitals and locally operated programs is a critical issue, handled in a variety of ways. Each of the model programs described in this volume addresses the problem, and each attempts to solve it in a different way.

So long as the state hospital and the local programs dealt with different populations, there was no clinical need to integrate the purposes. But when they serve the same patient, certain problems become apparent, such as continuity of care, entry and exit from each program, and the need for simultaneous services from several different treatment agencies. This is particularly significant for chronically ill patients for several reasons. Such patients are often multihandicapped and use many different kinds of services. Also, they tend to use different services episodically. For example, from time to time such a patient may need emergency services or hospitalization. Generally when such services are needed, they are needed quickly. Accessibility and availability are crucial.

No single agency is able to meet all the needs of a general population of chronically mentally ill patients. The problem has been to find mechanisms for integrating all the services for all the patients across agency lines.

One means is the case manager. Such a person acts as advocate for the patients, to help them find access to the programs they need when the services are needed.

Administratively, it has been difficult to break through agency boundaries to provide accessibility of services to patients in need of referral. This problem manifests itself in the difficulty in making referrals. What mental health clinician has not had the frustrating experience of referring a patient to a program only to learn the patient does not quite meet the admission requirements?

In Massachusetts, the problem has been met by administrative decision to place state and local programs under one clinical director. This places the responsibility on a single individual and eliminates the interagency conflicts by converting them to intra-agency conflicts. This has been found to be successful in a number of other programs, including the Capital District Psychiatric Center in Albany, New York.

Another mechanism, used in Orange County, is the utilization of specific contracts with private and quasi-public agencies which stipulate the services which are being purchased. The administrative agency, in this case the county, has the responsibility for monitoring the performance of the contract, which will assure accessibility and availability.

In Wake County, North Carolina, the local and state program set up a coordinating council which attempts to resolve problems as they arise. This is a "voluntary" coordinating effort and lacks the "clout" of a more formal arrangement, such as those described in Orange County and Massachusetts. It seems that, while everyone agrees that coordination is a good idea, few agencies want to be "coordinated."

EVALUATIONS OF EFFECTIVENESS

One of the developments of the 1970s has been an increased emphasis on accountability and responsibility for the expenditure of funds. This is not unexpected in a time of fiscal constraints. Nor is it unreasonable to require that programs which expend amounts of money demonstrate they are effective and that the public is getting a fair return on its investment.

It has been characteristic of mental health services that the measures of effectiveness are often not compelling. In the preceding three chapters, reference is made to various kinds of measures. Understandably, the measure which is chosen is often one which shows the particular program in good light. There are presently no widely accepted and widely applied standard measures of effectiveness. The methodology has not yet been developed and universally accepted.

As a result, there is often a bitter struggle between budget analysts and program directors. Budget people tend to wish results to be measured against dollar costs. They look for information which enables them to measure the outcome of services against costs, not an unreasonable wish. Program directors have great difficulty providing the information, because it is so difficult to measure outcomes in this field in these terms. As a result, program directors use other measures like:

1. *Effort*—numbers of patients admitted, treated, and discharged by the system. This is a measure of work performed, not a measure of outcome. Admissions and discharges may be accelerated or deaccelerated without necessarily affecting quality of care or outcome. Since it is so easily subject to clinical and administrative manipulation, it is distrusted as a measure by budget people.

2. *Client satisfaction*—a useful measure of output, but it is only a partial measure. The desired outcome is not necessarily to please but to rehabilitate the patient. Budget people distrust this measure because it may be manipulated by the treaters, who are able to influence the views of patients who are dependent upon them.

3. *Total dollar costs per capita*—this figure taken by itself only measures expenditure but does not measure it against the accomplishments of a program. This measure has the virtue of being simple. But it has the enormous danger of leading to the view that the least expensive is best. One could, for example, reduce costs to zero, eliminating all services. A low level of cost per capita may be viewed as a success by some and as a failure by others.

4. *Number of occupied beds*—since inpatient services are the most costly, the most confining, and the most infringing upon the patient's life, the number of beds used has been a widely accepted measure of effectiveness. The assumption has been made that a high number of beds per population is bad, a low number is good.

   Initially, there was virtue in such a measure. In 1950, at the height of the era of custodialism, there were unquestionably too many hospitalized patients. In 1954, this index began its inexorable decline. However, in the 1970s, there was widespread recognition that there are parts of the country in which patients have been discharged from the hospital to their personal disadvantages. All other things being equal, it may be better for a patient to live in the community. But often, all other things are not equal. Patients discharged from mental hospitals have found themselves in inadequate single-room occupancy dwellings, poorly managed propietary care homes, hotels, and, too often, jails. The quest for moving patients out of hospitals has led to poorly conceived and inadequate alternative arrangements. Every patient is *not* better off outside the hospital. The fervor to reduce hospital census, which is an administrative and political imperative, has sometimes been translated on the clinical level to a personal tragedy for the patient.

Furthermore, though the names of such patients do not appear on hospital roles, they do become wards of the state in other guises! Their names now appear on welfare roles, general hospital roles, and police blotters. Perhaps worse still, they live lonely, desolate lives without planned programs for socialization from which they might otherwise benefit were they in the hospital.

Thus, the number of beds utilized is useful as a partial measure but must be considered with caution, since to reduce beds below a certain level results in grave injustices to certain patients. There is not yet a defined and accepted minimum toward which programs might aim. This figure would depend greatly on the number and quality of alternate living situations, such as apartments, family care homes, and nursing facilities, which were available in an area.

5. *Peer review*—there are currently in use a variety of peer review mechanisms which measure the process of treatment rather than the outcome. They address the important question of whether the treatment is being performed skillfully. They are important to the treatment but are not as useful as measures of effectiveness when system directors negotiate with budget personnel.

A system of care must provide a range of treatment and rehabilitation services which meet the varied needs of its chronic mentally ill patients. These services must be skillfully performed. They must be available and accessible to the patient. Administrative boundaries between agencies must enhance rather than impede availability and accessibility. The management of the entire system must be able to monitor the system so as to determine roadblocks to and gaps in service. The failure or success of one element in the system will have effects on the entire system. For example, a superbly functioning crisis intervention unit which intercedes in the lives of patients to treat or prevent their impending psychotic exacerbations will reduce the number of hospital beds required but will increase the number of partial hospitalization places needed. As a result of this kind of phenomenon, the overall system management must be able to move quickly to stimulate and support specific kinds of services where they are needed.

There seems to be a tendency for clinicians and clinical systems to shift their interests to favor patients who are responsive to treatment. This works to the disadvantage of the chronically ill patient. The system management must attend to this. Problems of staff morale and staff "burnout" must be addressed.

The system director must also provide for personnel development and recruitment. There are inadequate numbers of well-trained professionals dedicated to work with the chronically mentally ill.

The managers must also be able to evaluate and measure effectiveness of the system, partially in order to administer the system on a day-to-day basis, but also in order to provide information in a persuasive way to the executive and legislative bodies which determine the funding of these systems.

What has been described is a herculean and imposing task.

INDEX